NATION-BUILDING AND COMMUNITY
IN ISRAEL

Nation-Building and Community in Israel

DOROTHY WILLNER

PRINCETON UNIVERSITY PRESS
PRINCETON, NEW JERSEY
1969

To the memory of my mother

CONTENTS

CONTENTS

PREFACE

This book describes and analyzes transformations in the social order of a new state. It does so by examining changes in a major national development program, rural land settlement, during Israel's first decade of independence, changes in the agencies charged with carrying it out, and changes in the organization of new villages and in the lives of their settlers.

The book has been long in the writing, for it represents a substantial departure from the community study tradition of anthropology in which I was trained. While still working in Israel, I found it impossible to describe the new villages or the land settlement program independent of each other and independent of changes in the larger society and in the social origins and traditions of the immigrants swelling its population and being brought into the villages as settlers. In writing this study, I had to develop new concepts or make use of concepts being developed in other fields as well as those introduced by other anthropologists. Nation-building is a concept which came into currency after I had completed an earlier version of the study, and I gladly substituted it for some of my own formulations. Modernization is another currently fashionable concept, but I have found it still too ambiguous to substitute for either "development" or "Westernization" as these terms are used in the book.

A previous draft of Chapters II through VI were the corresponding chapters of my doctoral dissertation, completed in 1961. Professors Sol Tax, Milton Singer, Lloyd A. Fallers, and Elihu Katz of the University of Chicago read the dissertation as I was writing it and offered helpful criticism and suggestions.

Professor Bert F. Hoselitz made it possible for me to spend a year as Research Associate of the Research Center in Economic Development and Cultural Change at the University of Chicago. Thanks to him, I was able to become familiar with interdisciplinary approaches to development while carrying out the library research for Chapter VII at one of the few American universities with the necessary resources. While I was writing Chapter VIII and an earlier draft of Chapter IX, Dr. Vera Rubin kindly put at my disposal the facilities of the Research Institute for the Study of Man.

In preparing the final draft of the manuscript, I profited from the creative comments of Professor Manfred Halpern of Princeton University. Professor Fallers also reviewed the manuscript and offered valuable suggestions for the final chapter. Discussions with Professors Marion J. Levy, Jr. of Princeton University and Murray Wax of the University of Kansas helped me formulate some of the ideas expressed, respectively, in Chapters I and IX. Dr. Raphael Patai put his extensive knowledge of Judaism, Zionism, and Israel at my service. He also made available to me material from the as yet unpublished *Encyclopedia of Zionism and Israel,* of which he is editor. Those who have delved into the literature of Zionism in attempts to verify elusive facts can appreciate how much this has meant. Professors Anna Cienciala of the University of Kansas and Robert S. Merrill of the University of Rochester read the completed manuscript and gave me the benefit of their judgment on various points still open to modification. Dr. Ann Ruth Willner allowed no faltering in my attempts to achieve clarity. Although I have fallen short of her standards, she has sustained my efforts and morale in innumerable ways.

I wish to thank the University of Kansas for granting me funds for research assistance and for having the final version of the manuscript typed. Ronald Rogowsky was my peerless research assistant and Mrs. June Traube has been a most helpful and accurate typist. Mrs. Linda Peterson of the Princeton University Press has been a conscientious and gracious editor.

The book is based on personal knowledge of Israel's land settlement system during the years 1955 to 1958. I gained this knowledge while initiating a program of applied an-

thropology in the Land Settlement Department of the Jewish
Agency. Until the usefulness of such a program and of social
science in general could be demonstrated to policy-makers
in the Jewish Agency, I worked for the Agency through the
Henrietta Szold Foundation for Child and Youth Welfare.

Serving as an applied anthropologist had advantages as
well as imposing constraints. On the one hand, it gave me a
participant's knowledge of the changing public organization
described in the book; and I played a part in the organization's activities in different geographic and administrative
areas of Israel and at various levels in the land settlement
hierarchy. On the other hand, it limited the intensiveness
with which I could carry out research in any one village,
while precluding the use of systematic research techniques
I wanted to employ in examining a sample of villages. I refer
to these limitations more specifically in some of the footnotes
to Chapters VII through IX.

Nonetheless, chance and the extraordinary sensitivity and
devotion of Miss Margot Kohls compensated for these limitations to some extent. Chance allowed me to observe the
several villages discussed in this study which were settled by
immigrants from the Atlas Mountains of Morocco. In carrying out relatively intensive research in one village under my
supervision, Miss Kohls was the most reliable and gallant of
colleagues, serving me as a surrogate self.

Dr. Moshe Smilansky, then director of the Szold Foundation, was my first guide in the labyrinth of organizations
carrying out activities in the villages. Dr. Ra'anan Weitz,
then director of the Land Settlement Department, unhesi-
tatingly granted the indispensable condition of my work: the
freedom to publish my findings. Arie Eliav, then director of
the Land Settlement Department region in which I first began
to work, set the standards by which I still evaluate administrators. It is impossible to acknowledge my debt to other
associates in the Land Settlement Department and to the
many village workers and hundreds of settler families who
accepted me as a friend and gave me hospitality in the
villages.

NATION-BUILDING AND COMMUNITY
IN ISRAEL

I

INTRODUCTION

SCOPE AND AIMS OF THE STUDY

This book deals with those processes of change currently termed nation-building and development, as they are illustrated by the case of Israel. One of the some fifty formerly colonial or otherwise dependent territories that have achieved statehood since World War II, Israel during the decade of the 1950s shared the following features with most of them: (1) governmental planning of development, with a socialist ideology as orientation; and (2) the presence of a substantial population to whom the institutions of a developed society were alien, as were claims of ideology which were not linked to traditional values. Sharing these features with other new states, Israel and its governing elite also shared such problems of development and nation-building as increasing the national productive capacities and per capita national income, establishing a rationalized system of public administration, and welding culturally diverse and fractionated masses into a modern national society and political community.

However, Israel has been unique among new states in its inversion of the order of basic transformations characterizing all others. They are new states, constituted from old societies [1] and struggling to develop what is currently termed a national identity,[2] i.e., common denominators of unity that can transcend their populations' traditional and parochial loyalties and legitimize the national authority. Israel, in contrast, is a new society as well as a new state. Indeed, a case can and will be made that it became a society only after it was established as a state. Furthermore, the creation of both

[1] Cf. Shils 1963.
[2] For a discussion of this concept in regard to the United States as a new nation, see Lipset (1963). Shils (1963) and Geertz (1963) also use the term in reviewing problems of post-World War II new states.

state and society was made possible and legitimated by the prior existence of an identity, rooted in ancient Jewish nationhood and maintained through religion as a primary commitment during millennia of its bearers' dispersion. Although this ancient traditional identity can be considered parochial by criteria of national modernity,[3] commitment to it and/or strains involved in being born to it inspired and legitimated the founding of the most modern of new states, the recruitment of its diverse population, and the loyalty [4] of this population to state and government, a loyalty on which modern nationhood is based.

This study suggests and seeks to demonstrate that the inversion in the order of transformations which distinguishes Israel from other new states offers, at a high level of abstraction, an explanation for Israel's success in dealing with problems of nation-building and development that it shared with these other states. Explanation at a less abstract level calls for delimiting specific factors encompassed in the formulation just given—factors which are attributes of the units and activities conceptualized as "state," "society," and "national identity" as well as of the processes termed "nation-building" and "development"—and for showing their crucial connections. The specific factors made possible by the sequence from "national identity" to "state" to "society," seem to include: (1) sufficient centralization of national authority; (2) sufficient resources for generating and maintaining both programs of action and the organizational units for putting into effect and sustaining these programs; and (3) sufficient solidarity among most of the population who joined in the formation of the new society to enable Israel, as a consequence, progressively to realize its basic national goals.

One aim of this study is to document these statements. However, they focus on the uniqueness of Israel among new

[3] For a discussion of criteria of national modernity, see Bendix (1964: 18–19) on the distinction between "association" and "order in a political community."

[4] "Loyalty" in this context refers to the Jews; the question of Arab loyalties is outside the scope of this study.

states. This uniqueness involves its pre-state as well as post-state history, and the former is discussed insofar as it bears on the points made here. But the main body of the study deals with post-independence Israel, and more specifically with a key sector of its national life, rural land settlement. This is a sector in which Israel's characteristics and problems, rather than being unique, were similar to those of other new states in ways already specified.

Therefore, a second aim of the study is to present and analyze on a case-history level transformations which took place in the social order of a new state, transformations comparable to those desired and initiated in other new states, in developing countries that are not new states, and even in modern nations concerned with the development of neglected or disadvantaged areas or of such segments of the national population.

Features of post-statehood rural land settlement in Israel, particularly during its first decade, which were similar to those of other such programs of purposeful social action include: (1) decisions by the national governing elite to institute or to extend and accelerate an area of development as part of its national goal; (2) the vesting of authority for planning and implementing this development in one or more central agencies; (3) their formulation of a program or programs assigning new activities and roles to a target population unprepared and less than willing to assume them, but whose mobilization into the program is essential for carrying it out and indeed may in itself be part of the development goal; (4) the emergence, expansion, and/or proliferation of administrative units in the agency or agencies responsible for the program; (5) the development, as part of this bureaucratic expansion, of a special field staff to serve as the day-to-day representatives of the program to the target population, holding the lowest posts in the administrative hierarchy, yet responsible for eliciting the population's compliance with the activities and roles assigned it by the program; (6) conflicts between bureaucracy and target population, the field staff bearing the brunt, as the population resists the demands made on them by the program, and even possibly the legitimacy of the authority claimed by the program.

Furthermore, an inevitable feature of the Israeli land settlement program and, it may be claimed, of all programs of purposeful social action, was the emergence in the course of its implementation of consequences not anticipated in the original planning. Subsequent modifications made in the program in response to these unexpected consequences continued to generate other such consequences. It may be hypothesized of all planned change that unanticipated consequences are inevitable when the number of variables, i.e., of uncontrollable and/or unpredictable factors, exceeds those that are constant or subject to prediction and/or control.[5]

In the case under review, ideological and political considerations placed constraints on the possibilities of response by planners and policy-makers to the unanticipated consequences of their actions. This, too, is not unique to land settlement in Israel, although the rigidity and pervasiveness of these constraints may be unusual in a democratic society where physical coercion was neither employed nor considered as a possible means of effecting the almost total transformation in the target population set by the program's goals.

A third aim of the study, therefore, is to describe the implementation of a program so suffused with the unanticipated consequences it generated that it can be seen and is here conceptualized as a paradox. For its basic goals were accomplished, despite continual and pervasive conflict between those in authority and the target population and among segments of each.

Within about a decade of Israel's independence, the major objective of the program, the establishment of hundreds of new farming villages, both agriculturally productive and strategically located for Israel's defense against enemy infiltration or attack, was largely attained. Furthermore, these

[5] Merton (1936:898ff.) makes the same point, although not in these words, citing a number of other theorists.

villages brought into a technologically advanced sector of the national economy, and provided the necessary vocational training for, tens of thousands of families previously unequipped for more than marginal participation in the occupational structure of a modern economy. An ideologically-based concomitant goal of the program was at least nominally achieved, for the villages' formal organization embodied the cooperative principles of labor ideology. Furthermore, total village economy was linked to the nationwide federations of cooperatives, labor unions, and industrial and financial holding companies which dominated Israel's economy and development during that period in accordance with the dictates of labor ideology.

Explanations for the overall success of the program, its attainment of national goals, have been suggested earlier, and their expansion and documentation have already been specified as an aim of the study. The aim separately noted here is that of describing and analyzing the program from the perspective of the villages it created.

The distinction drawn here is between the macrocosmic universe of the total program, a major national enterprise with goals of national development carried out by an interlocking series of public agencies, and the microcosmic worlds of the villages established by the program and their particular articulations with various segments of the national land settlement agencies. On the macrocosmic level, in relation to society and nation, the program was largely successful by the end of Israel's first post-independence decade. But on the microcosmic level, that of the villages in relation to the program, the goals set by the settlement agencies for village development were far from being attained with regard to the villages themselves.

For in the hundreds of new settlements peopled by immigrants from Asia and North Africa, the cooperative and self-governing provisions embodied in the villages' formal organization were only exceptionally maintained by their settlers. Practically all the villages were still under the jurisdiction of the settlement authorities and were managed and governed by their village field staffs. Settlers holding elective village offices that formally conferred decision-making power were either under the tutelage of the field staff, or could be overruled by them or displaced from office and new elections called. The majority of the villages, including many in existence for five to ten years, either still seethed with conflicts and crises, or else the overt expression of conflict in crises was averted by the strategic or temporary tacit acquiescence of the settlement authorities in the villagers' partial evasions of their demands.

Yet despite the pervasiveness of conflict in the universe of immigrant settlements and other characteristics these settlements shared, set by such constants of planning and implementation as village formal organization, the villages during the 1950s differed greatly among themselves. Such differences involved a range of variables which will be set forth in this study, some deriving from variable factors in village planning and establishment, some from variable factors in the heterogeneous population recruited and brought together as settlers, some from variables in the administration of the program and of the villages, some from variable settler acculturation in the course of a village's history. Each village can be seen as initially constituting a specific constellation of variables, in which it differed from other villages and which differed in the same village as conditions changed. It is suggested that these differing constellations can account for different village histories and differential village development within the range of village variability generated by the program.

A salient feature of the Israeli post-state land settlement program was its permeation by both coercion and democracy. On the one hand, all means of coercion possible in a democratic welfare state were utilized by members of the land settlement bureaucracy in their relations with the immigrants, although coercion was far from the only tactic utilized. On the other hand, the way in which the program was organized and carried out, related both to its origins and to its linkages with the politics of the larger society, made for diffusion of political power among all those in-volved in it, including the villagers. This diffusion of power offered the immigrants modes of countering coercion other than open dissidence. The ways in which a program both generated and responded to a juxtaposition of coercion and democracy may represent an aspect of Israeli land settle-ment relevant to problems of nation-building and develop-ment anywhere.

CONCEPTS AND UNITS OF ANALYSIS

Israel has been characterized as a new society as well as a new state. A state is here defined as a bounded territory or country whose inhabitants are under the rule, or claim to rule, of a central authority. This authority also claims a monopoly of the legitimate use of physical force within the territory. This definition of state is based on that of Weber, but departs from it in not also characterizing the state as a human community.[6] For it is the existence of a sense of com-munity among a state's population, at least in the political sphere, that makes for nationhood. Not until a state's in-habitants, whatever their more parochial loyalties and feelings of community, recognize as legitimate the claims of the state's central authority and yield it their loyalty can state be equated to nation. So much for the distinction between state and nation (or, more precisely, nation-state), which follows cur-rent usage,[7] informed by the study of the problems of nation-building in new states as well as of the historical development of the established nation-states.

This distinction between state and nation is less useful for the analysis of nation-building in regard to Israel than it is in regard to other new states. For almost since the state's establishment, only the Arab segment of its population has questioned the legitimacy of its central government's claim

[6] In "Politics as a Vocation" (Weber 1946:78). His more rigorous defi-nition in the "Basic Concepts of Sociology" section of *Wirtschaft und Gesellschaft* also dispenses with the "human community" phrase (Weber 1947:154).

[7] E.g., cf. Bendix 1964:15–29; Deutsch and Foltz (eds.) 1963. However, Akzin (1966:37) equates nation and nationality.

to rule and to the monopoly of the use of physical force.[8] Nation-building in Israel, while directed to the state's establishment, has involved, both before and after statehood, the creation of a unit fundamental for the existence of both state and nation. This unit is the society itself. I now turn to defining this unit in terms that can clarify the inversion earlier suggested of the order of transformations characterizing Israel as contrasted to other new states.

The comparative study of societies and their cultures is the traditional domain of anthropology, which is the disciplinary background of this study. But the societies studied by anthropologists have been there to be studied, and arguments within the discipline over definitions of society as a concept have taken as a given the fact that these societies exist. It may be "by no means easy to say precisely what a 'society' is," as a distinguished anthropologist has noted.[9] Nonetheless, he continues, "whatever we may wish to include in a sophisticated definition of society, certain things are clear and can be stated quite simply. To begin with, societies are made up of people; societies have boundaries, people either belonging to them or not; and people belong to a society in virtue of rules under which they stand and which impose on them regular, determinate ways of acting towards and in regard to one another."

This definition refers to a membership unit, without specifying a territorial base as its precondition or established rules as an attribute of its social order. Nonetheless, these characteristics are implied. And whatever the other uses of this definition of society, it has little bearing on the attributes of a new society, unless in highlighting its distinctiveness as compared to established societies.

For a new society is by definition composed of people recruited from other preexisting societies, at least until these

---

8 Two armed military units besides the Hagana, which became the Israel Defense Forces, existed until September 1948, three months after the state was founded. These were the Stern Gang (Fighters for the Freedom of Israel) and the armed forces of the Irgun Zvai Leumi. Cf. Halpern 1962.

9 Nadel 1957:8.

people give rise to a generation born and reared within the society. Whatever the conditions resulting in the creation of a new society, its members have to develop rules (or norms) of behavior that will provide for their physical survival, regulate their interaction, and—hopefully—insure the survival of the society as a unit.

This minimal characterization of any new society should indicate that people recruited to it do not have imposed on them regular, determinate ways of acting toward and in regard to one another, but rather have had to develop such ways. In other words, their behavior is innovative by definition, although the areas of life subject to innovation may vary from one new society to another, as may the heritage on which members of the society draw and the extent of their conscious experimentation. Finally, new societies may not have clear-cut boundaries, except by reference to the boundaries of their territory, since people's membership in them and their dissociation from their societies of origin may not always be unequivocal.[10]

The definition of a society that seems most useful for the analysis of new societies, specifically of Israel, also deals with a membership unit without explicit reference to its territorial basis. The starting point of this definition is the concept of social action, i.e., the actions of "a plurality of interacting individuals," [11] rather than the people themselves in the totality of their actions. Since actions take place in situations, people's orientations [12] to the situations in which

[10] This point can be generalized beyond new societies, since immigrants to established societies may not be unequivocally dissociated from their societies of origin for some time after migration, and some may return intermittently or conclusively. The Chinese in Southeast Asia represent a case in which dissociation from the society of origin did not occur despite generations of residence elsewhere.

[11] The concept of social action goes back at least to Weber: "Action is social in so far as, by virtue of the subjective meaning attached to it by the acting individual (or individuals), it takes account of the behavior of others and is thereby oriented in its course" (1947:88). The brief definition in the text is taken from Parsons (1949:6). Levy's initial formulation of the concept is more extended (1952:7-8).

[12] The various types of orientations discussed by Levy (1952:171-73, 195) represent conceptual differentiations more precise than seem necessary to this study.

· 11 ·

they act, including those with whom they interact, enter into the definition of society as a membership unit. A society is defined as "a system of action in operation that (1) involves a plurality of interacting individuals . . . whose actions are primarily oriented to the system concerned and who are recruited at least in part by the sexual reproduction of the plurality involved, (2) is at least in theory self-sufficient for the actions of this plurality, and (3) is capable of existing longer than the life span of an individual . . . ." [13]

This definition by Levy, as contrasted to that of Nadel cited previously, directs attention to the orientations which, among other factors, bring together the individuals who initiate a new society, which maintain their interaction, and which bring about the recruitment of other grown individuals into the "plurality." It further offers an approach to examining the development of rules or norms of action in situations where behavior is, at least initially, innovative, as in a new society.

Furthermore, this definition, particularly its stipulation of self-sufficiency, explains my earlier claim that Israel became a state before it became a society. For, as is generally known, over two-thirds of Israel's present adult population has been recruited from beyond its borders since its independence in 1948,[14] and this increment in its population since statehood may have been necessary for Israel's survival in the face of the enmity of its neighbors. Similarly, its economic survival for at least five years after its founding as a state demanded resources mobilized outside its borders. Indeed, it was through a system of action extending far beyond the frontiers of Palestine, but oriented to it as a Jewish homeland, that the population which founded the state was

[13] Levy 1952:112–13.
[14] In 1966, Israel's Jewish population aged twenty or over was 1,348,006. Of these, 1,076,902 had been born elsewhere. Israel's total Jewish population then numbered 2,344,877, including 254,059 in the 15–19 age bracket. In 1957 approximately two-thirds (66.1 percent) of Israel's total Jewish population had been born elsewhere. See Central Bureau of Statistics 1967:40–42.

originally recruited and the initial means for its survival secured.

In sum, two interrelated and interdependent "systems of action" were involved in Israel's creation as new state and new society, i.e., in nation-building and development as these terms apply to the Israeli case. One system included the interlocking and partly competitive Zionist organizations, which linked the Jews from many nations who supported Zionist goals, channeled the movement of people and resources from its membership to Palestine, and represented the interests of a Jewish national homeland in international negotiations prior to the establishment of the state. The other system was that created in Palestine by those who migrated and settled there, adding to their numbers by reproduction as well as by recruitment through the former system.

Until statehood, the leaders of the Zionist movement—whether or not they were also members of the system created by those who settled in Palestine—constituted the central authorities recognized as legitimate by most of the Jewish population of Palestine. Statehood effectively transferred the central governing authority to those whose primary orientation included personal commitment to Israel as their home. But the boundaries of the society as a membership unit could not be set by the system of action involving only those who were already members of the state. Their own estimate of requisites for the state's theoretical self-sufficiency and survival led its governing authorities to extend the system of Zionist activities to Jewish populations hitherto little, if at all, involved in it: the Jews of Asia and North Africa. As many of them as possible were actively recruited as migrants to Israel, largely, although not exclusively, on the basis of their traditional orientation to Judaism. Simultaneously, the mobilization of resources also drew on the long-established system of Zionist activities involving sympathizers with the new state, whose orientation to it was far from primary but who were committed to its survival and willing to help it achieve at least minimal self-sufficiency.

By the end of its first post-independence decade, Israel's development had progressed to the point where it could be considered a society in the terms of Levy's definition. The Zionist system of action has not been dismantled and continues to support the new society, adding to both its membership and its resources. But since at least 1958, Israel can be seen as in theory self-sufficient for the actions of the plurality of individuals constituting its inhabitants, whose numbers constitute a major basis for this theoretical self-sufficiency.

While Israel is exceptional among new states in that it became a state before it became a society—granting Levy's definition of society—it could not have achieved statehood without the prior existence in Palestine of a Jewish part-society.[15] Although Jews have continued to dwell in Palestine possibly since the Roman conquest, and certainly since the Middle Ages,[16] they constituted there, as throughout the Middle East,[17] a segment of a culturally heterogeneous population, living under the rule of successive conquerors of the country. The part-society oriented toward the creation of a modern Jewish state and society originated during the 1870s and 1880s with the founding of Jewish farming communities by immigrants from Eastern Europe.[18] Nation-building and

[15] For a discussion of the concept of "part-society," developed in reference to peasant communities and their relations to the larger society, see Redfield (1956) and Kroeber (1948:280–84). The term "part-society" is used to indicate the nonautonomy and non-self-sufficiency of a community within a complex differentiated society as compared to communities which are coterminous with societies; cf. Redfield (1955) and this chapter, pp. 15ff.

[16] Cf. Matras 1965:20, 22.

[17] Coon (1951) discusses the "mosaic" social system, into which the ethnically diversified peoples of the Middle East were organized for millennia. Each culturally distinctive ethnic group maintained its own identity and "part-culture" (Kroeber 1948:280–84) while living in juxtaposition and playing different roles in a long-established and differentiated complex society.

[18] In fact, the very first rural village founded, which could not be maintained, was initiated by a few members of the long-established traditional Jewish community of Jerusalem, augmented by a few individuals who had earlier immigrated from Hungary. Cf. below, p. 32.

development in Jewish Palestine and in Israel began with land settlement, and this continued to be a major focus of Zionist action. A society has been termed the unit fundamental for the existence of both state and nation, but communities are the units fundamental for the existence of a society. This was recognized by the initiators of modern Israel.

In its study and analysis of societies and their cultures, anthropology has traditionally been oriented to the study of communities.[19] For communities have been largely coterminous with societies throughout much of human history. This has remained the case, at least until recently, in the small societies, largely organized on the basis of kinship and residence, which have traditionally been studied by anthropologists.[20] The anthropological study of complex societies, of which the explicit beginnings are found at least as early as the 1930s,[21] has continued to focus on communities, or at any rate to be firmly anchored in the study of local groups which could be conceptualized as communities.[22]

The term "community" as used in this study follows the usage proposed by Arensberg,[23] involving an explicit differentiation between community and local group. Communities, defined as "basic units of organization and transmission within a society and its culture," [24] are based on territoriality, but so are other kinds of human groupings. In addition to the geographic and ecological factors associated with territoriality, the unit termed a community must have certain demographic and organizational features.

The necessary demographic characteristics include a personnel consisting of both sexes and a minimum of three gen-

[19] Cf. Redfield 1955.
[20] Some societies so organized have not been particularly small, either in size of population or size of territory occupied. The differentiation here made is between the classes of societies termed "tribal" by Gluckman (1965) and complex societies in which civilizations emerged.
[21] E.g., Warner and Lunt 1941, and subsequent volumes of the Yankee City series; Arensberg and Kimball 1940.
[22] E.g., Steward et al. 1956.
[23] Arensberg 1961.
[24] Arensberg 1961:248.

erations, comprising individuals at all stages of the life cycle. For this is the minimal population unit that can both maintain the species and carry and transmit a culture or way of life. Organizational features include either the presence of "the persons or roles and statuses, or the transmitted and learned awareness of them, for every kind and office of mankind that the culture knows." [25] Differing in each culture, these "roles and institutions . . . mark off the society of one human culture or civilization from another." [26]

In sum, communities are territorially based groups. However, the boundaries of the territorial and membership unit termed a community are delimited by reference to specific demographic and organizational criteria. These criteria specify that a community must have certain features which both (1) give it the character of a whole, including sufficient completeness and cohesiveness of personnel for its maintenance and continuity as a social unit and its transmission of a way of life; and (2) allow it to be regarded as minimally representative of the larger society's organization and minimally inclusive of the society's culture.[27]

[25] Arensberg 1961:254.
[26] Arensberg 1961:253.
[27] Arensberg (1961:247–55) specifies and discusses the four attributes of (1) representativeness, (2) completeness, (3) inclusiveness, and (4) cohesiveness as those both characterizing a community, defined according to the demographic and organizational features noted in the text, and rendering a community, so defined, a legitimate "sample" of the larger society and its culture. He does not, however, define the controversial and ambiguous term "culture," beyond substituting for it such terms as "way of life," the analogue in social science of the "biogram" in biology (Arensberg 1961:250), or "learned behavior," as differentiated from "that genetically determined" (Arensberg 1961:252).

While accepting this usage, which has been generic in American anthropology, I agree with those who find it too diffuse to have theoretical and operational rigor within social science. Yet, given the encompassing nature of the phenomena subsumed under the term "culture," whether in regard to all mankind, as contrasted to other genera, or in regard to the "way of life" of any society, it is not easy to define the term, as Kroeber has stated (1948:252–56). Indeed, difficulty in defining basic concepts has been noted not only in regard to culture by Kroeber, but by Nadel in regard to society (above, p. 10) and by March and Simon in regard to organizations (March and Simon 1958:1), the latter being another key concept and unit of analysis of this study; and neither Kroeber nor March and Simon present formal definitions. Nevertheless, some specification of the term "culture" seems called for in a study dealing with the formation of a new

Community is defined more concretely and empirically by Arensberg than is society by Levy, but the two definitions are not incompatible. Arensberg's definition of community appears to be equivalent to Levy's definition of society when they are applied to the small, relatively undifferentiated tribal societies traditionally studied by anthropologists. In the case of more complex societies, some of which are tribal,[28] a possible translation of Arensberg's definition of community into the language used by Levy might read as follows: a community is a system of action in operation (1) that involves a smaller plurality of interacting individuals than that comprising a society; and (2) in which the actions of this plurality are oriented not only to the system concerned but also to that of the larger society, of which it is not independent.

Whatever the legitimacy of this translation, Arensberg's definition of and criteria for community, both in their own right and in the perspective of Levy's definition of society, (1) differentiate the villages created in Jewish Palestine

---

society and the interaction in it of people who had learned different ways in their many and diverse societies of origin.

Although I have doubts about limiting the term to "whatever it is one has to know or believe in order to operate in a manner acceptable to . . . [a society's] members," more specifically "to the forms of things that people have in mind, their models for perceiving, relating and otherwise interpreting them . . ." (Goodenough 1957:167–68), my own field-work experiences support this definition as the heart of culture, i.e., that which maintains a "way of life" and/or transformations in it carried out by members of a society rather than by an external power. But while the data on values, interaction, and communication presented in this study support Goodenough's position and those analogous to it (e.g., among others, Parsons and Shils 1951:15, 105; Kluckhohn 1951; Barnett 1953), other classes of data illustrate its limitations in regard to the totality of phenomena encompassed in a way of life. For changes in "the constellation of features which are most closely related to subsistence activities and economic arrangements . . ." (Steward 1955:37), which Steward terms the "cultural core," act on people's perceptions, cognitions, and values, as well as vice versa. Nonanthropologists who have incorporated the term "culture" into their technical vocabularies may find it of interest that contrasting intellectual stances in regard to its definition, reminiscent of Weber's position as compared to Marx's, have emerged in the ethnography of tribal societies (cf. Wolf 1964 for an extended discussion of contemporary orientations to "culture" in anthropology, and their possible sociological and intellectual background).

[28] Cf. Gluckman 1965.

and in Israel from basic units of organization and transmission within an established society; and (2) relate them as successive systems of action to those involved in the formation of Israel as a society. The villages as units were local groups years before they became communities. However, two very different kinds of village local groups were founded.

One kind of local group consisted of the villages founded by the successive waves of self-selected pre-statehood immigrants; these were not communities but relatively cohesive communities in formation until late in the life span of their founders. For these committed village pioneers were generally young people when they went on the land. They were usually separated from their parental generation both in space and in their deliberate repudiation of the way or ways of life of their ancestors. They were seeking to create another way of life, including both new roles and new kinds of persons, to transmit to their offspring and to future generations.

The post-statehood villages, founded by the land settlement agencies and peopled by unprepared and uncommitted new immigrants at every stage of the human life cycle, were not initially communities at all. Established on the model of one of the types of village created by the prestatehood pioneers, their formal organization embodied a way of life developed by these pioneers and called for the kinds of people able to enact the roles involved. However, most of the immigrants from Asia and North Africa wished to maintain much of the way of life transmitted to them and/or to achieve a way of life to which they had aspired before immigration. Village staff and settlers, both initially in roles new to them, often had little or no understanding of each other's cultures and could be in conflict in much of their interaction. They also might clash in their separate interaction with, respectively, other members of the village staff and administrative supervisors, and with other, often alien, settlers. These villages—unlike the pre-state village communities in formation—were systems of action in which the plurality of interacting individuals were diversely oriented. The orientations of the field staff were to the villages and village development as part of the system of action of the larger society in formation. The settlers, on the other hand, were oriented to the systems they had known and now sought to maintain, insofar as possible, in their new situation, as well as to the situation itself.

The pre-statehood villages, despite their initial demographic incompleteness and the resulting innovation of new roles at all stages of the life cycle, had the characteristics of a whole. For these villages could be maintained by their first generation of settlers as units of organization and transmission. In contrast, the post-statehood immigrant villages considered here lacked the characteristics of a whole, despite the demographic completeness of the settler personnel. Given the discrepancy between the roles transmitted to the settlers in their communities of origin and of preimmigration settlement and the roles they had thrust upon them in the Israeli villages, these villages could be maintained as social units only because they were managed and under the authority of the land settlement agencies. And the agencies' authority over the settlers was often not accepted by the latter as legitimate, although the settlers generally accorded legitimacy to the central authority of the state.

However, for all their differences, both kinds of villages stood in a similar relationship, during the initial period of their historic emergence, to the larger society in formation. For the creation and development of both were made possible by the Zionist system of action, which also made possible the society's creation and development both before and after statehood. Furthermore, as subsequent chapters illustrate, both kinds of villages manifested organizational features salient in and representative of this society in formation, at the time they came into existence and during their subsequent development. The villages can be considered representative because of, rather than despite, their not constituting communities for years after their founding.

The final unit of analysis central to this study is commonly termed "organizations." The concrete units discussed in the study under the term organizations are those which developed as part of the Zionist system of action. Some of these became as basic as the villages they founded to nation-building and development in Jewish Palestine and Israel, and to the formation of the new society.

Organizations are here minimally defined, following current sociological usage, as social units devoted primarily to the attainment of specific goals on a more or less continuing basis.[29] Even this minimal definition implies basic features that organizations share, in contrast to the units here defined as society and community. These features include: (1) a personnel limited to a specialized segment of the personnel necessary for maintaining and transmitting a way of life; (2) recruitment of an organization's personnel from that of the units which do maintain and transmit a way of life, i.e., from community and society; (3) relative specificity rather than diffuseness of goals; (4) sufficient recognition by community and society of the legitimacy of an organization's purposes to make possible recruitment of its personnel and their sustained joint action in pursuit of its goals. Finally, organizations must have centers of power, or at least of co-ordination, whereas these do not seem to be essential for the maintenance of societies and communities.[30]

Social movements are generally excluded from the category of organizations. However, as is noted in a recent study of complex organizations, "most movements have an organizational core," [31] sharing the characteristics distinguished as typical of complex organizations, of which bureaucracies may be considered the prototype.[32] Zionism as a movement—

[29] This definition amplifies the minimal definition of organization given by Etzioni (1961:xi n.) following Parsons (1960:17), i.e., "social units devoted primarily to attainment of specific goals." The amplification draws on the definition presented by Scott (1964:487).

[30] On an abstract level, Weber differentiates between associations (*Verbände*) which must have an administrative staff (i.e., administrative centralization) and other kinds of social groupings (*offene soziale Beziehungen*) which need not have one (Weber 1947:145–46). On the level of ethnographic specificity, there are societies without administrative centers on a continuing basis; cf. Steward 1955:101–50, and Gluckman 1965:91–122.

[31] Etzioni 1961:53ff.

[32] Weber 1946:196–244.

in fact, as an aggregate of related movements—has had organizational cores and bureaucratic units almost from its inception, and certainly from the founding of the World Zionist Organization in 1897. Villages founded earlier than this were not without organizational ties to the Diaspora, and agencies of the World Zionist Organization increasingly aided and coordinated land settlement during the decades of its pre-statehood development. Moreover, the pre-statehood immigrants, whether they arrived in Palestine through their own efforts or aided by Zionist organizations, created or helped to create a variety of movements and organizations for coordinating their efforts, recruiting further immigrants, and defending their interests in regard to the Zionist system of action. An interlocking series of partly competitive voluntary organizations and bureaucracies developed to effect pre-statehood land settlement goals and different ideological variants of the Zionist goal. Moreover, these organizations were linked to ramifying systems of organizations, created as part of the development of the Jewish part-society in Palestine.

Statehood brought about transformations in the total social order, as described in this study in relation to transformations in the land settlement sector. Here it is sufficient to note that organizations can be seen as units basic to the formation of the new society. They provided the links through which personnel born into established societies could become the founding generations of communities in formation of a society in formation, and through which resources could be secured and allocated to sustain this personnel in their actions to achieve specific common goals: the creation of state and nation. For Palestine, unlike other countries developed by immigrants, was a largely devastated land before the beginnings of the new society. It offered no material inducements for immigration, no existing ecological base that could sustain the intrepid by their unaided efforts.

The inversion earlier suggested in the order of transformations of the Israeli case, as compared to other new states, can be enlarged to include the role of complex organizations as agencies of nation-building and development. In the case of Israel, their establishment preceded the establishment of the society and made possible state, rural communities, and society.

METHODS AND UNITS OF DESCRIPTION

The relationships so far suggested to explain Israel's relative success in nation-building and development, as compared to other new states, represent a form of explanation known as scientific. Relationships are posited between concepts, which have empirical referents, to explain a state of affairs which also is defined and delimited by reference to concepts. In short, theories have been proposed, which I seek to support by evidence presented in the body of the study.

This approach can exact a toll for the results it yields. The toll, for studies such as this, has to do with what may be excluded from consideration. For in cases where changes initiated decades earlier have resulted in an indisputable transformation of the previous social order, explanations of this transformation entail linking it to factors abstracted from discoverable earlier conditions and events. In brief, causal relations are proposed. Nonetheless, however demonstrable these relations may be, and whatever their implications for other situations in which this kind of transformation is taking place or may be desired, such explanations have the advantage of hindsight. Conditions, events, and their discernible consequences are detached from their historical matrix according to criteria of relevance set by the concepts employed, and are presented as evidence for the determinate pattern of relations offered to explain the transformation.

In the descriptive chapters which follow, I seek to minimize what I consider to be a toll exacted by the approach employed here. This toll involves the determinacy that may be implied by explanations of this kind. An objection to determinacy derives from the transitory nature of any given state of affairs which is presented as the outcome of a transformation. It may be found, with the passage of time, to represent a historical phase whose meaning, examined in the

light of subsequent developments, by no means is as unequivocal as when it was perceived as outcome. Indeed, circumstances and events considered irrelevant to the explanation of such an earlier phase when it is treated as outcome, may later be found very relevant to the play of
factors that most adequately explains previously unpredictable or erroneously predicted developments.

Moreover, the uncertainties of the future also existed in
the past.[33] People made decisions and embarked on courses
of action uncertain of the consequences, particularly under
conditions of instability or limited knowledge of, or limited
control over, factors they may have considered relevant to
the goals they sought. Neither they nor anyone else can more
than speculate on what might have resulted from the courses
of action they did not choose. However, the circumstances
surrounding the decisions they made and the actions they
took may have greater relevance for the conditions and
events culminating in a given outcome than either they or
anyone else may recognize if only the consequences of these
decisions and actions, and not the circumstances surrounding
them, are drawn on to explain this outcome.

Therefore, my criteria for determining what data are relevant and should be included in the descriptive chapters of
this study go beyond those implied in the concepts and
units of analysis already defined. Indeed, these concepts,
such as that of community, do not imply criteria for determining what data are relevant to the analysis of the
Israeli immigrant villages, beyond indicating why they
cannot be considered communities during the period under
review. Moreover, the future of most of these villages was
not predictable, beyond the fact that someday most of them
would become communities of some kind, given the external pressures and the resources devoted to maintaining
them. Their origin and observable course of development,
rather than an indeterminate outcome, provide the bases
for describing transformations then in process but far from
completed. And while, by 1958, the achievement of na-

33 Bendix (1964:13–14) makes the same point.

tional goals regarding the land settlement sector seemed to be an unequivocal outcome—an outcome which has been consolidated rather than reversed during the years since then —this achievement was not attained without transformations of the total land settlement sector. The consequences of these transformations for the new society were, and to some extent still are, far from determinate.

In the descriptive chapters of the study I therefore seek insofar as possible to present data that support the theories proposed but which are not so bounded by them and by the aims of the book that they cannot serve other theories and aims and illuminate unpredicted or unpredictable developments since 1958. In the tradition of anthropology, the method I have chosen for doing so is deliberately, although far from exclusively, ethnographic.

Within an analytic framework, whose debt to Max Weber may already be apparent, I begin with a review of the systems of belief and values and the specific historic circumstances underlying the origins of land settlement in Palestine and of the Zionist system of action. This leads to a review of land settlement in Palestine and the delineation, as a social system, of the patterns of action and relations which emerged among the people successively recruited into land settlement.

This system came to include many units, not simply many villages but various consciously constructed types of villages, most of them embodying principles of Labor-Zionist ideology. This ideology or, more accurately, class of ideologies, sharing certain principles and goals but differing in regard to others, became the cultural system to achieve predominance in the land settlement sector and in the larger part-society which founded the state. Its adherents dominated the land settlement sector. They also organized into political blocs, some of which included in their membership large numbers of adherents in other sectors of the part-society, to implement their specific policies and to extend their spheres of power and influence in the society in formation and in the Zionist system of action.

The description, in the chapter which follows, of the emergence of the pre-state land settlement system, in the context of the formation of the pre-state part-society, is historic rather than ethnographic, although ethnographic accounts of units in the system and of its baseline, the way of life of Eastern European Jewry, are cited in the account given of the development of the system. However, much of the subsequent description consists of ideal type accounts or partial ethnographies of units, relevant to the post-state transformation of the system.

One such account is that of the specific village type, the cooperative small-holders' settlement, or *moshav ovdim,* which constituted both model and goal in the planning of the immigrant villages. In the absence of a scholarly ethnographic account of a village embodying the type, an ideal type is presented here, constructed from available literature.

A major partial ethnography, comprising much of the data of the book, deals with the complex system of organization through which the land settlement program was carried out during the first post-statehood decade. There is little precedent in anthropological literature for the ethnography of a national bureaucracy,[34] and only a handful of studies of complex organizations qualify as ethnographies. Nonetheless, all the comparative evidence suggests, as should be expected, that bureaucracies are social units no less subject to cultural variation than are other kinds of cross-culturally recurrent corporate groups.[35]

Still another partial ethnography is a reconstruction of the traditional way of life followed by a community of Jews in the Atlas Mountains of Morocco prior to immigration to Israel and settlement in a series of immigrant villages. A description of one of these immigrant villages during its first

---

[34] Anthropological studies of political systems do include descriptions of some bureaucracies, both autochthonous ones and those effected by colonial powers, e.g., Fallers 1956 and Ray (ed.) 1958. Reining (1966) also delineates part of an administrative system which planned and implemented a land resettlement program in Africa.

[35] As is evident in a comparison of U.S. and French bureaucracies in relation to the larger society described respectively in Selznick 1949 and Crozier 1964.

year constitutes the final ethnography of the book. It is followed by brief reviews of contrasting village histories and an analysis of factors contributing to the differential history of the immigrant villages at different phases of their not always successful evolution into communities or, at least, into communities in formation.

The ethnographic reconstruction of the life of Jews in the Atlas Mountains has two purposes. One is to provide a counterpoint to both (1) the traditional way of life of small-town Eastern European Jewry, the background of most of the founders of the new society and its land settlement sector, and (2) the way of life embodied in the village type, the moshav ovdim, created by immigrants from Eastern Europe and used as the model for the post-statehood villages in which immigrants from Asia and North Africa were settled. Hopefully, this counterpoint will indicate the extent of acculturation demanded of these new immigrants.

The other purpose of this reconstruction is to serve as the baseline for analysis both of the Israeli immigrant village, described in detail, into which these people from the Atlas Mountains were brought, and of two other such villages, whose early histories are merely reviewed. In these three immigrant settlements an apparently similar initial constellation of village variables resulted in quite different outcomes before the end of the villages' second year. One village could be regarded as successful in terms of national development goals as well as by the criteria of a community in formation. Another failed and had to be resettled. The third remained in existence with its initial settler population, but could be termed neither success nor failure as of the end of the period under review, neither cohesive community in formation nor population in clear disorganization. As with many, perhaps the majority of, such villages, its future was indeterminate within the time span of observation.

The succession of partial ethnographies and ideal type descriptions through which most of the data in this study are presented is one method both of describing the different kinds of units in a complex and changing society—

units involving the national as well as local levels—and of tracing the links between them. This method is not without distinguished precedents in anthropology.[36] Whatever novelty it may have in this study can be attributed to the situation described: the formation of a new and changing complex society as illustrated in the development and transformation of a major national sector.

In this new and changing society, both the pervasiveness of goal-directed action throughout its history and the massive transformations which occurred during the decade following independence made for pervasiveness in the society of "the unanticipated consequences of purposive social action."[37] For the actions purposefully undertaken were directed toward the achievement of multiple goals, goals which could not be realized concomitantly.

Prior to statehood, adherents of Labor-Zionism sought to create a special type of new society, one embodying ramifying socialist principles. Yet even before the end of the mandate period, the social units deliberately constructed to realize this total goal, i.e., new types of communities and a new type of complex organization,[38] had already demonstrated that some of the principles they had been designed to implement were in practice irreconcilable. Their institutionalization as viable units had not occurred without the emergence of organizational arrangements[39] which their ideological charters had decried. After statehood, Israel's

[36] E.g., Leach 1954; Fallers 1956; Steward et al. 1956.
[37] See Merton 1936.
[38] The organization is the Histadrut, the General Federation of Labor in Palestine (now the General Federation of Labor in Israel). Cf. pp. 40, 61–68.
[39] The term "organizational arrangements," as used here, is equivalent to Firth's definition of "social organization" as "the working arrangements by which a society [or, I would add, any social unit] is kept in being" (Firth 1954:10). Social organization, so defined, is differentiated by Firth from "social structure," a concept which he discusses, citing many usages, but does not himself define. Given the theoretical issues this concept poses, I use it as little as possible in this study. When I do, it refers to abstract principles of order holding some correspondence to discernible patterns in social relations. I accept Lévi-Strauss' restriction of the term "social structure" to "models" (Lévi-Strauss 1953:525), but I do not attempt to develop models with the properties which give meaning to the word as a scientific expression.

governing and administrative elite, including the innovators of the now institutionalized, deliberately constructed social units, sought to perpetuate the ideologically based systems of action which had given rise to and maintained these units. However, they held as even more primary goals the survival and development of the state, and they encouraged the mass immigration both in the interest of these goals and as a basic Zionist value. In doing so, they brought into the nascent society a population to which all the pre-statehood ideologies not related to religion were alien, thereby eroding the voluntary basis of the systems of action established before statehood.

The term "paradox" is used in this study to refer to irreconcilable principles or goals underlying the purposive actions which seek to bring a new social order into being. The term is used to denote inconsistencies or latent inconsistencies so fundamental that attempts to translate into action the totality of principles and/or goals impose contradictory modes of action or internally contradictory roles on the people involved. In seeking to resolve these inconsistencies, they face dilemmas of choice which cannot be resolved without opting for one set of goals or principles and discarding others that, on the level of values, have not lost their claims. The actual decisions made under such circumstances indicate priorities of necessity or choice if purposive action is to be sustained. However, the social order established is not that originally envisaged.

THE PRE-STATEHOOD FOUNDATIONS
OF THE NEW SOCIETY
AND ITS LAND SETTLEMENT SECTOR

IDEOLOGY, IMMIGRATION, AND LAND SETTLEMENT

Three systems of beliefs and values underlie the actions that gave rise to Israel as new state and new society. These are Judaism as religion and tradition, Zionism, and socialism.

Traditional Judaism maintained throughout the millennia of dispersion the orientation of Jews to Palestine as their once and future homeland. Indeed, the power of Zionism to evoke the commitment of large numbers of people from quite diverse socio-economic backgrounds cannot be understood apart from the place of *Eretz Israel,* the Land of Israel, in Judaism. The Old Testament and the Talmud describe a way of life that was once lived, and set forth directions for preserving its essentials in anticipation of the coming of the Messiah and the return to the Holy Land. The religious Jew lives simultaneously in two worlds: the one of his immediate surroundings, which governs his mundane preoccupations; and in a timeless world centered upon the Holy Land, from which his identity derives in terms of the Covenant with God. The yearly cycle of prayers and ceremonies is studded with references to the awaited return to the Holy Land or to the Holy City of Jerusalem. The Talmud states that the duty of settling in the Land of Israel is as great as that of observing all the rest of the laws it ordains; throughout the centuries it was considered a holy duty for Jews to contribute to the support of those who had succeeded in remaining in or returning to Palestine. Small groups from all over the Diaspora had succeeded in returning; and most Jews sought to have buried with them a bit of earth from Palestine.

Traditional Judaism, with its orientation of return to Zion, was the force which had motivated the settlement in Palestine of the perhaps 24,000 Jews living there by 1882,[1] the eve of the emergence of modern Zionism as an organized movement. Supported largely by the contributions of Diaspora Jewry, they were concentrated in the four holy cities of Jerusalem, Safed, Tiberias, and Hebron, and were dedicated mainly to the study of religious law. They represented both the Ashkenazi and the Sephardi traditions of Judaism, i.e., respectively, the tradition which had emerged among the Jews of Central and Eastern Europe, and that which centered in Spain prior to the expulsion and dispersion of its Jews, largely to Moslem lands.

These two traditions differ in liturgy, custom, and ritual surrounding the prescribed forms of worship; to some extent in points of observance; and in the daily behavior surrounding the prescribed observances. They became identified with many other elements in culture; and Ladino, which bears a relationship to Castilian Spanish analogous to that of Yiddish to medieval German, remained the household language of the Sephardi Jews who settled in Greece, Bulgaria, Turkey, and, to a lesser extent, in the Near Eastern countries formerly part of the Ottoman Empire. These two traditions became an index of differentiation among Jews, including those in Palestine and in Israel. In Israel, for example, the Sephardim and the Ashkenazim have their own chief rabbi, as well as their own congregations.

However, while popular stereotypy in the new society tends to associate the distinction between "Ashkenazim" and "Sephardim" with the distinction between immigrants of respectively "European" and 'Oriental" provenience, the immigrants from the countries of Asia and North Africa include members of ancient non-Sephardi Jewish communities, some dating from the first dispersion from ancient Israel. They have maintained in Israel their own congregations and specific patterns of observance, including liturgy and customs associated with prescribed festivals and life-crisis ceremonies celebrated in synagogue and home.

[1] Cf. Matras 1965:22.

The power of Zionism to evoke the allegiance of large numbers of people of varied socio-economic backgrounds cannot be understood apart from the significance that the Land of Israel holds in Judaism as religion and tradition. Indeed, much of the post-state mass immigration has had, at least in part, a Messianic character, as will be discussed further. However, the emergence of modern Zionism as a social and political movement did not occur until the unity of the Jewish people, founded on the primacy of religious commitment as a basis of identity and solidarity, had begun to disintegrate from within. Until the Age of Enlightenment in Western Europe, religious orthodoxy and Jewish identity were inseparable, both within the dispersed Jewish communities of the Diaspora and in the eyes of the populations among whom they lived. Differences in socio-economic status, class, or regional subculture, or even adherence to one or another tradition of observance, did not challenge the primary commitment to Judaism. This commitment united all Jews in a geographically discontinuous culture-bearing socio-religious entity, all members of which felt in some way responsible to and for all others insofar as their existence was known to them.

The French Revolution effected the political emancipation of Jews in the countries of Western Europe, and the Age of Enlightenment introduced new currents of thought, aspirations, and possibilities into the Jewish communities of these countries. With relative secularization and assimilation of the Jews into the cultures of their countries of residence, a Jewish identification ceased to be primary, and even ceased to be internally maintained by increasingly large numbers of people. However, anti-Semitism continued, even while secularization and assimilation created the new problem of the meaning of a Jewish identity.

Even before the middle of the nineteenth century, the idea of the return of the Jewish people to Palestine had begun to be advanced by both rabbis and secularized Jewish intellectuals in Europe, stimulated by the nationalist movements around them and by political as well as traditional anti-

Semitism.[2] With a concomitant growth of the Jewish population of Palestine, philanthropy among wealthy Jews of Western Europe in support of this population increased, as did sentiments for the resettlement of oppressed Jewry in Palestine.

Of the various events and currents of thought during the nineteenth century that resulted in the emergence of both the Zionist system of action and the origins of the new society, those most significant to land settlement in Palestine and to the formation of the society involved Eastern European Jewry. Significant differences existed between the ways of life of Western and Central European Jews and that of the Jews of Eastern Europe, where the mass of European Jewry was concentrated. Of these differences, no more need be noted here than the absence among the latter of political emancipation, and their relatively minimal exposure to European culture of the Enlightenment until almost the middle of the nineteenth century.[3] By then a more liberal policy toward the Jews began to be adopted in the Austro-Hungarian Empire, and fundamental socio-economic changes began to take place there. For some Jews of these lands, these changes led to middle-class status; the economic position of others became increasingly precarious. For the next few decades, both assimilationism and socialism began to make inroads into the traditional Eastern European Jewish way of life until, in 1881, a wave of pogroms began in Russia. Vast numbers of Jews began to migrate to the United States, Argentina, and Western Europe; others joined revolutionary movements; another response was the initiation of organized Jewish immigration to Palestine.

Although the first modern Jewish attempt at founding a farming village in Palestine had been made in 1878 by the combined efforts of a few natives of Jerusalem and some young immigrants from Eastern Europe, conditions proved too harsh for the settlement to be maintained. However, between 1882 and 1903 some 25,000 immigrants, largely from

[2] Cf. Halpern 1961:10ff., 57ff.; Herzberg 1960:15–32.
[3] Cf. Halpern 1961:Chaps. I, III, IV; Herzberg 1960:32–60.

Russia, arrived in Palestine to double its Jewish population. They have been categorized by one of the major authors among them as of three types: traditional scholars who differed from other learned orthodox Jews in refusing to defer return to the Holy Land until the advent of the Messiah; simple people unable to explain the urge that prompted them to turn to Palestine; and Western-educated men and women who arrived at Zionism as the result of rational thought.[4]

A pamphlet entitled *Auto-Emancipation* was a major example of such thought. Written by Leo Pinsker, a Russian Jewish physician who had earlier sympathized with Enlightenment and assimilationist ideas, it appeared in 1882. It rejected political emancipation as a possible solution to anti-Semitism in Europe and called for an immediate resolution of the latter through immigration of Jews to Palestine and their establishment there as a nation. Published in Russia, it reached an audience which earlier Western and Central European advocates of the Zionist idea had not. Although various Zionist-oriented societies were already in existence in Russia, they became united in 1884 into the Hovevei Zion (Lovers of Zion) movement, of which Pinsker was elected president, and which spread beyond Russia.

Immigrants to Palestine, including a group of Jewish university students in Southern Russia who organized specifically for the purpose of land settlement,[5] founded over twenty rural settlements between 1882 and the early 1900s. Their initial efforts were only partially successful. They bought land and undertook its cultivation, but most of them had neither the means nor the experience to make a success of farming under the difficult local conditions, and had to turn to outside sources for financial aid. This was then extended to them on a philanthropic basis by Baron Edmond de Rothschild. With it he sent technical assistance in the form of French experts, who became administrators, dispensing means and making decisions for the settlers. By the turn

[4] Smilansky, as paraphrased in Frank 1955:31.
[5] This was the much publicized BILU group, the name of which is made up of the first four words of a verse from Isaiah: "House of Jacob, come, and let us walk" (Isa. 2:15).

of the century, many of those who had remained in Palestine had become a subsidized "gentry" supervising estates largely based on viniculture, with the actual work done by Arab labor. Immigration to Palestine from Yemen also began in 1881.[6] Although it originated spontaneously, on the basis of a rumor that Rothschild had bought land in Jerusalem which he was donating to Yemenite Jews, it was encouraged, starting in 1911, by Zionist emissaries, who wanted to provide workers able to compete with Arabs in their capacity for physical labor in the Palestinian climate.

Political Zionism as an organized movement did not come into being until 1897. Its founder, Theodor Herzl, was an assimilated Central European journalist and playwright who reacted to the Dreyfus Affair in France by conceiving the idea of an independent Jewish State as a solution to anti-Semitism. Unaware of the previous publications on the subject or of the Zionist activities that had already taken place, he wrote his own booklet, *The Jewish State,* originally intending it for the great Jewish philanthropists of Western Europe, whose aid he hoped to enlist in the creation of the sovereign Jewish State he envisaged.

Published in 1896, after months of Herzl's unsuccessful negotiations with the great Western European Jewish patrons of persecuted Jewry, *The Jewish State* elicited a response incomparably exceeding that aroused by anything published or undertaken earlier. Following this up with extensive organizational activities, Herzl convened in 1897 the First Zionist Congress, which brought together orthodox, reform, and secular Jews representing most of the European countries and much of European Jewry, as well as representatives of the Jews living in the Ottoman Empire. The Congress founded the World Zionist Organization, which sought—and claimed—to represent the entire Jewish people and their sovereign will as a nation.

This claim was opposed by different segments of Jewry. Despite the early rabbinical proponents of the Zionist idea

[6] Cf. Patai 1953:185ff.

and the presence of representatives of religious orthodoxy in the World Zionist Organization, Zionist political aims and participation in the Organization were repudiated by a movement of extremely pious Jews, originally settled both in Eastern Europe and in Palestine. In opposition to Zionism, they established in 1912 their own worldwide organization, Agudat Israel, advocating the ultra-orthodox traditional position that the destiny of Jewry was in the hands of God, and calling for absolute observance of religious law and submission to the jurisdiction of the rabbinate. The adherents of this organization settled in Palestine constituted themselves, after statehood, into one of the political parties of Israel.

Opposition to Zionism also developed, for different reasons, among the assimilated Jews of the West, since the new Jewish national movement challenged the tenets of the emancipation and the claim of segments of Western Jewry that Judaism was a religion rather than a basis of national identity. Finally, Eastern European Jewish revolutionaries, whether adherents of Marxism or of other radical positions, regarded Zionism as reactionary, and rejected it in favor of the class struggle. Indeed, in 1897, the very year that the First Zionist Congress was convened, a socialist and trade union organization of Jewish workers in Russia and Russian Poland called the Bund was founded, many of whose members were anti-Zionist. The Bund, further, espoused the cause of Yiddish and Eastern European Jewish culture as part of its ideology.[7]

Factions also rapidly developed within the World Zionist Organization. They manifested the spectrum of commitments, orientations, and interests of European Jewry. During Herzl's brief lifetime, a fissure developed between those holding that a basis for statehood, i.e., a grant of territory for Jewish settlement and sovereignty, was the primary condition for effective Jewish migration to and development of Palestine, and those advocating settlement on the land as

[7] For a discussion of the ideology and history of the Bund, see Scherer 1954.

a condition for the attainment of sovereignty.[8] Herzl supported the former position; and until his death in 1904 he negotiated with the monarchs and great personages of the time in an unsuccessful attempt to persuade the Sultan of Turkey to issue a charter permitting large-scale Jewish immigration into Palestine. While these negotiations were in progress, the encouragement of immediate immigration was postponed, not without the opposition of delegates from Eastern Europe, who were committed—as Herzl was not— to a spectrum of views regarding the new national culture to be developed. Indeed, at the Fifth Zionist Congress in 1902, a secular faction of Eastern European background, committed to the development of a secular Jewish culture through the revival of Hebrew as the national language, succeeded in having approved a program for a national but secular school system in Palestine. The religious Zionists within the organization then formed their own faction, Mizrahi. This faction successfully established the right of the orthodox Jews both to maintain their own organized activities in accordance with religious law in the society being created and to seek to extend the jurisdiction and influence of traditional religion in the Zionist movement and in the prospective state. Some members of Mizrahi later left the Zionist Organization to join Agudat Israel. A labor bloc, with a socialist orientation, had also developed within the World Zionist Organization by the early 1900s.

Western supporters of the idea of resettlement as a solution for those exposed to virulent anti-Semitism were not committed to Palestine as the site for the Jewish national home. Herzl himself, like Pinsker before him, also initially lacked this commitment, differing in this respect from Eastern European Zionists, who were closer to Jewish tradition and could look back upon a history of Zionist ideology and settlement in Palestine. When negotiations with the Sultan of Turkey still remained stalemated in 1903, the British government offered territory in Uganda for Jewish settle-

[8] For a discussion of this issue and its consequences, see Halpern 1961: 27ff.

ment. Almost at the same time a new wave of pogroms broke out in Russia. Herzl was willing to consider Uganda as a temporary refuge, although conceding that acceptance of this offer would be a defeat of the basic Zionist goal. He was dead by 1905, when the Seventh Zionist Congress, led by representatives of Eastern European Zionism, successfully opposed the possibility of accepting the territory in Uganda. Adherents of the Uganda offer, largely well-to-do Jews from Western Europe, then broke away from the World Zionist Organization to form the independent non-Zionist Jewish Territorial Organization.[9] While the activities of this movement, like those of the anti-Zionist socialist Bund, are outside the scope of this study, repercussions of the Uganda issue and of the spectrum of orientations prevailing among European Jewry during the initial decades of Zionism are anything but irrelevant to nation-building, as regards both the Zionist system of action and that which developed concomitantly in Palestine in the founding of the new society.

Beginning in 1904, a second wave of immigration to Palestine began. Consisting of some 35,000 to 40,000 immigrants during the decade preceding World War I,[10] this was the wave of immigration crucial for the development of the new society and for its socialist orientation when statehood was achieved. For it included thousands of young people from the Russian Empire, most of them from the *shtetl*, the recurrent type of small-town Jewish community of Eastern Europe, [11] and also primarily from orthodox families, apparently of neither the poorest nor richest strata.[12] Most of these young immigrants had been students in the traditional religious academies and also had learned Russian. Stirred by all the currents of change around them, they had

[9] The author, Israel Zangwill, founded the Jewish Territorialist Organization (ITO). A review of its history and goals is given by Steinberg 1954.
[10] Cf. Matras 1965:24.
[11] Zborowski and Herzog (1952) constitutes a detailed anthropological reconstruction of the life of the shtetl. Briefer presentations which add to the picture are Joffe (1949) and Rosenthal (1953, 1954); Diamond (1957) offers a conceptualization of shtetl social structure and its relation to kibbutz ideology.
[12] Cf. Diamond 1957:78; Zemach 1945.

secretly read and discussed the literature of Zionism and socialism, and it captured their imaginations. By their own testimony,[13] they found the literature of the Enlightenment empty.

Because of the new outbreak of pogroms, because they were imbued with a sense of Jewish identity and with Jewish traditions, because of the appeal of Zionism or something in their own personalities, or probably due to a combination of these reasons, they rejected further secular education, which some of them had begun. In doing so they rejected a profession and assimilation into Western European culture as personal solutions and as solutions to the problem of the Jewish people. They also rejected immigration elsewhere than to Palestine, as well as the way of life of the shtetl. The latter they considered restricted and empty of hope, and they were no longer satisfied by orthodox Judaism as a guide to life. One group had already formed itself into a self-defense organization which defended a Belorussian ghetto town against a pogrom—the first time this had occurred in almost two millennia of Jewish history, since to shed blood or resist the will of God were considered contrary to traditional religion.

Revolutionary socialism, which provided a solution and goal for many of their fellows, they considered only a partial solution. It offered a satisfactory analysis of the basis of anti-Semitism, linking it to the inherent injustice of a class society and to the Jewish occupational structure in the Diaspora, where Jews hardly engaged in the fundamental "productive" occupations. However, its blueprint of a new kind of society, to be achieved through class struggle in the Diaspora, did not offer them an immediate resolution to the problems of personal and cultural identity, as did Zionism.

Inspired by a fusion of socialist and Zionist values and goals, these young people began to immigrate to Palestine in groups of twos and threes, even without the sponsorship of the World Zionist Organization or aid from its urban branches. The concept of redemption of self and homeland

13 Zemach 1945. Selections in Frank (ed.) 1955.

through manual labor in Palestine was their synthesis of elements of Judaism, socialism, and Zionism into a new ideology.

On arriving in Palestine, they found that the settlers of some, although not all, of the established villages, known as *moshavot* (singular, *moshava*), were not only living as subsidized "gentry," employing Arab labor, but were also pro-Uganda in political outlook, and influenced by and oriented to French language and culture rather than to Hebrew and to the development of a new national culture. In the value universe of the newcomers, this constituted a triple betrayal of the ideal of national and cultural redemption. It strengthened their commitment to their own ideology, its socialist and redemptory ethos, and their sense of mission. Separating themselves from other segments of Palestine Jewry, their own numbers constantly increasing through the immigration of like-minded young people, they spent the years until World War I turning themselves first into agricultural laborers and skilled workmen in construction and other manual trades. Some of them formed an organization for guarding the established settlements against Arab marauders. By 1909, they began establishing their own rural settlements.

However, the adherents of Labor-Zionism by no means constituted an ideologically or politically united body. Two factions, based on different ideological syntheses of socialism and Zionism, were already in existence by 1906. One faction was Marxist, whereas the other was relatively unconcerned with class conflict. Under the leadership of an older fellow-member, A. D. Gordon, the adherents of the latter developed a quasi-religious devotion to manual labor as a means of developing the homeland. Seeking employment in the established villages in competition with Arab labor, often without success, each of these factions, motivated by ideology and necessity, began to pool resources and develop cooperative associations and organizations. These included cooperative kitchens and laundries in the moshavot where the young immigrants worked as day-laborers, employment offices through which to negotiate with the estate owners, mutual aid funds, committees to receive similarly committed new immigrants and tide them over until they could find work, consumers' cooperatives, sick funds. These organizations were the nucleus of the Histadrut, the General Federation of Jewish Labor in Palestine, founded in 1920.

Among the Diaspora-based organizations involved in the Zionist enterprise and in the purchase of land in Palestine for Jewish settlement, two were in existence prior to the initiation of this Second Wave, or Second *Aliya,* of Jewish immigration to Palestine. The earliest was the Jewish Colonization Association (ICA), founded by Baron Moritz de Hirsch primarily for the resettlement of Jews in Argentina, to which Baron Edmond de Rothschild turned over in 1899 the management of the Palestinian Jewish villages he had aided. Even earlier than 1899 this association had established a model farm, Sejera, in Lower Galilee, where Jewish immigrants were trained in anticipation of their prospective settlement in new villages; the ICA founded over five such villages in the early 1900s, many of whose settlers had been trained in Sejera. However, Baron Rothschild continued to purchase large tracts of land for future Jewish settlement and, after World War I, organized the Palestine Jewish Colonization Association (PICA), which took over the management of his holdings from ICA.

Although PICA in turn founded several villages and engaged in draining swamps and in industrial enterprises, the significance of these organizations to the immigrants of the Second Aliya was mostly confined to Sejera. There, groups of them engaged in farming and mingled with immigrants from Kurdistan and Yemen, with native-born young people —both Ashkenazim and Sephardim—who had left the religious schools, and others.[14] It was at Sejera that the use of Jewish rather than Arab or Circassian young men as village guards began.

Although PICA continued in existence until almost a decade after Israel's independence (when the Rothschild family donated its holdings to the state), far more important

[14] Ben-Gurion 1954:12–13.

to the pre-statehood development of the new society was the Jewish National Fund (Keren Kayemet L'Israel). Established in 1901 as an agency of the World Zionist Organization, the Jewish National Fund was created to purchase land in Palestine, drawing on the contributions of sympathizers everywhere. It was to retain title to the land in perpetuity in the name of the Jewish people, and lease it for agricultural settlement and for the building of homes, industries, and public buildings on a renewable forty-nine-year contract. This period harked back to the Biblical law of the Jubilee Year (set forth in Leviticus 25:8–13), in which all lands reverted to their original owners. In 1908, the World Zionist Organization authorized activities in Palestine, despite the absence of a political charter for Jewish settlement, and opened a Palestine office.

The head of this office, Dr. Arthur Ruppin,[15] immediately extended his sympathies to the young Labor-Zionists, and established training farms for them on Jewish National Fund land. Members of the Second Aliya, drawing on his aid, began to experiment with various forms of social organization by means of which new agricultural villages could be established under very difficult conditions.

The *kvutza* (commune), the collective settlement, was the first new community type to emerge as viable. The first such village, Degania, was founded in 1911 by adherents of the non-Marxist Labor-Zionist faction, and practical considerations, no less than ideology, led to development of its communal form of organization.[16] The kvutza (plural *kvutzot*) was the earlier of two alternative types of collective settlements in Jewish Palestine and Israel, now famous under the generic name of *kibbutz,* and the most extensively studied and documented of the innovations that developed during the formation of the new society.[17]

[15] Ruppin, a sociologist, has written on his work and its goals. Cf. Ruppin 1936.

[16] See Baratz 1954.

[17] The substantial literature on the kibbutz can be divided into several categories for the purposes of this study. One category consists of accounts of kibbutz life by members of such villages, e.g., Baratz (1954) and Weingarten (1955). Studies of kibbutz life by social scientists constitute a

The kvutza was originally envisaged as a family-type collective society that would not have more than about twenty-five adult members, and the first such villages were founded on this plan. This number was soon found inadequate for carrying out all the necessary work, and the size of the adult primary group was allowed to expand, arriving after World War I at between one hundred and two hundred members. Common ownership of property and means of production, the pooling of labor, and equal services to all members of the community are basic principles of kvutza organization. Food preparation and consumption in a communal kitchen and dining hall, and the rearing and education of children on a communal basis, originated as practical solutions to the conditions of village establishment before they became crystallized as ideological principles of collective living.[18]

Other viable types of cooperative communities embodying principles of Labor-Zionist ideology, including both the kibbutz (plural *kibbutzim*), or large-scale collective, and the *moshav ovdim* (plural *moshvei ovdim*), the small-holders'

---

second category, which is not homogeneous. Anthropologists, e.g., Diamond (1957a, 1957b, 1957c) and Spiro (1956 and 1958), have approached kibbutz life through the intensive study of specific villages, whereas sociologists, e.g., Rosenfeld (1951 and 1957) and Talmon-Gerber (or Talmon) (1956, 1957, 1959, 1961) have carried out studies across a sample of communal settlements.

However, this division, according to disciplinary background of author, does not do justice to the different foci and conclusions of the studies cited. For example, Rosenfeld (1951) and Talmon-Gerber (1956) disagree on the extent and nature of social differentiation that actually has developed within the communal villages; and Rosenfeld joins Diamond and Spiro in discussing and analyzing the "crisis" in kibbutz life which has emerged as kibbutz members have sought to reconcile the principles of the community type and the ideologies on which it is based with the realities of community living under changing conditions. The debate between Diamond (1957a, 1957b) and Halpern (1957) illustrates some of the controversy surrounding the analysis of the "crisis" in kibbutz life, which, in the terms of this study, can be seen as a series of paradoxes. Because of the interest the kibbutz as a social experiment has held for social scientists, these paradoxes have been the subject of study and discussion far more extensive than that accorded the crises or paradoxes of the other deliberately constructed social units based on Labor-Zionist ideology. However, the crises of the kibbutz are largely irrelevant to this study, unlike the paradoxes of the moshav ovdim, reviewed in Chap. III, particularly in their consequences for the moshav olim.

18 Cf. Baratz 1954:20, 41, 49, 67–69.

cooperative settlement, were not founded until after World War I. However, the idea of a cooperative type of settlement had been discussed almost from the beginning of the Second Aliya, and its organizational principles were advanced in a pamphlet entitled *The Fundamentals of the Moshav Ovdim,* published in 1919.[19]

Organizationally, the moshav ovdim was to be a cooperative association of from seventy to one hundred landholding families settled on Jewish National Fund Land, each working its own farm, dwelling in its own home, and maintaining itself as an economic and social unit. However, buying and selling were to be engaged in cooperatively, as is described in the next chapter, and the village as a unit was to maintain basic services. Like the kvutza and the kibbutz, the moshav ovdim is governed by a general assembly of all adult members, which elects executive and administrative committees.

Underlying the blueprint of the moshav ovdim as a community type, as well as that of the kvutza, kibbutz, and an intermediate community type that developed during the 1930s, the *moshav shitufi* or semicommunal settlement, are four principles of Labor-Zionist ideology. The Labor-Zionist factions had reached agreement on these principles by 1913, and they were observed in the Labor-Zionist settlements during most of the decades preceding statehood. These principles were (1) cultivation of national land, i.e., land owned by the Jewish National Fund rather than privately; (2) "self-labor," a term meaning that all work in the village was to be done by the members themselves, without recourse to hired labor; (3) mutual aid; and (4) cooperative buying and selling. These principles had gained an almost sacred quality during the years of opposition to what the First Wave or First Aliya of Zionist settlers of moshavot had come to symbolize to the Labor-Zionist members of the Second Aliya.

However, founders of the first moshav ovdim (the first two were created in 1921) previously had been members of

[19] Its author, Eliezer Joffe, participated in a number of innovations before he developed the idea of the moshav ovdim and joined the first such settlement founded. Cf. Dayan 1947:62–64.

kvutzot. The idea of the cooperative small-holders' settlement not only represented an alternative to the communal settlement, but was a community type formulated in opposition to it as well as to the moshava, to which all Labor-Zionist rural settlers were opposed. Objections to the kvutza included the following points: it makes normal home life impossible; it stifles individual initiative; and it provides a framework within which less enterprising workers are supported by the greater efforts of more diligent members. Since the founding of the first moshvei ovdim, these objections have been raised by disgruntled settlers in some of the hundreds of collectively organized villages founded since the first kvutza. They illustrate some of the points of tension in the collective settlement as a community type. The post-statehood problems of the kibbutz have received considerable attention, but are largely irrelevant to this study.

Another class of villages, the *moshav* (plural *moshavim*) or small-holders' settlement, also was among the innovations of the pre-World War I decade, prior to the formulation of the plan for the moshav ovdim. Unlike the moshavot, the moshavim are established on land owned by the Jewish National Fund and engage in cooperative enterprises and mutual aid, although the degree of cooperation differs from village to village, according to the decisions of the settlers. However, unlike the moshvei ovdim, the moshavim did not prohibit the hiring of labor or seek to carry out an ideologically based system of socio-economic organization. Three villages of this kind were in existence before World War I; more were founded during the 1920s and particularly during the 1930s, primarily by immigrants with some capital, and they came to be known as "middle-class" settlements.

This review of the pre-World War I origins of modern Israel and of its land settlement sector has focused on facts, some widely publicized, others less well known, which indicate the context of: (1) the orientations and systems of action which gave rise to the new society and new state; and (2) the groupings, systems of relations, and cleavages which developed among the actors involved. Factionalism, expressing differences in the backgrounds and orientations of European Jewry, permeated and surrounded the Zionist movement from its inception. The number of factions within Zionism increased after World War I, as additional ideologies developed, or as new issues evoked a range of responses, some of which became crystallized into ideologies whose adherents created their own organizations and movements. These factions became basic elements in the organization of the society in formation, as this study seeks to illustrate. Constituting political parties within the Zionist movement, they channeled much of the nation-building activity carried out by their adherents in Jewish Palestine. They persisted into statehood not only as major political parties of Israel but also as social systems, shaping, while being transformed by, Israel's development during its first post-statehood decade.

The constellation of factors involved in the origins and early history of Zionism may also be relevant to the comparative study of nation-building and of purposeful innovative action directed at effecting a new social order. Viewed retrospectively, the development of Zionism and its goals in late-nineteenth-century Europe seems inevitable, given the contemporary ferment of European nationalism, continued anti-Semitism on both traditional religious grounds and reformulated nationalist ones,[20] and the maintenance of the ancient Jewish identity, linked to Palestine as homeland, which in earlier centuries was expressed in sporadic Messianic movements. The combination of these factors seems sufficient to explain the repeated emergence of the Zionist idea from at least the middle of the century, culminating in Herzl's conception of a Jewish state. However, whether or not the emergence of Zionism was inevitable, factors which seem sufficient to account for its emergence seem insufficient to explain its success in founding a new society and new state.

On the one hand, not all groups with traditional identities who were subject to persecution or political repression and

[20] Cf. Halpern 1961:10ff.

who developed nationalist sentiments during the nineteenth and twentieth centuries achieved statehood or a mandate for it, or seem likely to do so. On the other hand, a range of movements and possibilities arose or were acted on in response to the same factors which seem to explain Zionism and the Zionist-inspired migrations to Palestine. Both the Bund and revolutionary socialism, movements directed at effecting a new social order, claimed many more adherents among Eastern European Jewry than did Zionism. Among Western European Jewry, Zionism was relatively ineffective in combating the trend toward assimilation, with or without retention of Jewish identity as religion or tradition, under conditions of political emancipation. And immigration to places other than Palestine was accepted both by masses of persecuted Jewry and by Jewish philanthropists in the West as a solution to virulent anti-Semitism. The traditional orthodox position of resignation to the will of God and strict observance of Jewish law also crystallized as a movement opposed to Zionism.

However, the fact of organized movements other than Zionism, the recurrent organization of partisan factions within or in opposition to the World Zionist Organization, the Lovers of Zion movement preceding it and Zionism's tenacity under adversity—all these suggest that the tradition and experience of pre-Zionist Jewish voluntary organization contributed in no small way to achievement of the Zionist goal. From the perspective of history and of the comparative study of nation-building and development, organizational effectiveness seems a condition for the successful creation or transformation of a complex social order.[21]

In the case of Israel, voluntary organizations for community self-government and maintenance in a hostile preindustrial society long antedated both the founding of the World Zionist Organization and Zionist-oriented migration to Palestine. Traditions of voluntary organization already developed and maintained in Eastern Europe, including factional strife, were extended to the Zionist system of action.

21 E.g., Pye 1962:51; LaPalombara (ed.) 1963. On the history of Jewish organization in Eastern Europe, see Dubnow (1916).

The nineteenth-century revolutionary movements in Russia provided additional models of goal-directed systems of organization which were drawn on by proponents of Labor-Zionism.

At the same time, the practice of extending aid to the needy, ordained by Jewish law, the sense of responsibility toward oppressed Jewry, and political intercession by the powerful on their behalf continued among Jews in the countries of political emancipation despite pervasive loss of the primacy of a Jewish identity. The aid extended to the settlers of the first moshavot was continued and augmented after the founding of the World Zionist Organization by Zionist sympathizers throughout the Diaspora.

A consideration of the pre-World War I background and origins of Zionism not only indicates the conditions of the movement's emergence, but also suggests factors which may help to explain its success. These factors, significant for nation-building and development anywhere, include (1) organizational traditions and resourcefulness among those whose orientation to the goals of Zionism was primary, and (2) the availability of resources from a larger population to aid them.

A primary orientation to Zionism generally included, by the decade preceding World War I, a commitment to one or another of the partisan ideologies and factions already in existence among those most involved in purposive nation-building and development in Palestine. The role of the *halutz,* the pioneer, given focus by the young Labor-Zionists of the Second Aliya, continued to be directed to rural land settlement and to any kind of work considered productive and nonexploitative, i.e., to manual occupations that would further Palestine's development by Jews and which would not entail investment for private profit.

Between 1918 and 1923 immigrants from Eastern Europe (primarily from Russia), Labor-Zionist in orientation, augmented the Jewish population of Palestine by about 35,000.[22]

[22] Sicron (1957:16–17) gives the number of immigrants as 35, 183, of whom 16,751 are cited by Ben-David (1964:48) as members of the labor force. Of these, 4,952 registered as agricultural workers.

Known as the Third Aliya, they were a potent Labor-Zionist reinforcement to this population, reduced by the end of World War I to some 56,000 through deportations and depredations by the Turkish government. Better prepared than their predecessors of the Second Aliya for the role of pioneer, they both participated in and added to the former's society-building innovations.

In the sphere of land settlement and rural community formation, some of them developed the goal of combining industrial development with agricultural pioneering. They established a group known as the Labor Brigade, which attempted to found collectives that would have units both on the land and in towns.[23] However, the urban units did not take hold and, by 1929, the Labor Brigade was disbanded, one of a number of experiments in social organization among the Labor-Zionist segment of the new part-society which proved unsuccessful.[24]

The rural communal settlements founded by members of the Labor Brigade included industrial enterprises. These settlements, to which the term kibbutz originally was limited, were considerably larger than the kvutzot, and acceptance of anyone who wished to join them was part of their ideology and program.[25] In later decades, however, the kvutzot also instituted small industrial enterprises, not without soul-searching and ideological debate. The two categories of collective settlements subsequently manifested essentially the same organization, although some are still distinguishable by their size and consequences of size for informal organization and assignment of personnel to tasks. Those communal villages founded as kvutzot do not include more than several hundred members, whereas some of those founded as kibbutzim may have a membership of well over a thousand.[26]

Although the existing kvutzot and kibbutzim joined in

23 Cf. Halperin 1963:31–41.
24 Cf. Bein 1952:211–22; Dayan 1947:10–16.
25 The kvutzot were highly selective in admitting members.
26 Ben-David (1964:52) notes that most collective settlements now have an average population of 326 to 381, apart from three collectives of about 1,500 members each.

founding an association in 1926, this did not survive differences in ideology, some going back to the initial Labor-Zionist factions, others based on such issues as size and internal organization of the communal village. By 1927 the kibbutzim had formed their own association, while an association of kvutzot was organized in 1929.

A third federation of secular Labor-Zionist communal settlements was founded in 1927 by young immigrants who were members of a militantly Marxist Labor-Zionist pioneer youth movement created in Russian Poland in 1917. While the villages founded by adherents of this movement have followed kvutza principles in regard to size, the distinguishing features of its ideology and practice have included: a revolutionary Marxist political orientation, a stress on "ideological collectivism," i.e., a common outlook on all issues and problems of life and politics, to be achieved by majority through debate and then maintained by all members, and a rigorous application of collective principles throughout village life. The most detailed anthropological study of a kibbutz published thus far [27] deals with a village belonging to this federation, and neither its author nor other students of the kibbutzim consider its findings uniformly applicable to the entire class of communal settlements.

Of the three secular Labor-Zionist federations of communal settlements, the largest and strongest by the end of the mandate period was that founded in 1927 by proponents of the kibbutz community type, i.e., of large communal settlements which would engage in small industry as well as agriculture. Named Hakibbutz Hameuhad (United Communal Settlement Movement) it included by 1947 53 villages with an aggregate population of about 23,000. Next in size was the Marxist kibbutz federation, Kibbutz Artzi-Hashomer Hatzair (National Federation of Communal Settlements of Hashomer Hatzair), with a membership of 45 villages whose aggregate population was about 13,000. Smallest in size was the reconstituted federation of kvutzot, Hever Hakvutzot (Association of Communal Settlements),

[27] Spiro 1956, 1958.

comprising 34 villages with a population totaling about 8,500 in 1947.[28]

Immigrants of the Second and Third Aliyot were the founders of the variously oriented communal types of settlements, the three federations just described, the moshav, the moshav ovdim or cooperative small-holders' community type, its federation (also organized in 1927), and the Histadrut (General Federation of Jewish Labor in Palestine), to which all the secular Labor-Zionist villages were and are affiliated. However, the Third Wave of immigration had ended by 1923 with the official closing off of Jewish emigration by the U.S.S.R. It was followed, beginning in 1924 and continuing until 1931, by what is known as the Fourth Aliya or wave of immigration, numbering some 82,000. The majority of the immigrants were from Poland, and they included a substantial middle-class element. Most of the latter settled in urban centers, engaging in small-scale commerce, industry, and crafts. Some, however, entered the rural land settlement sector and established additional moshavot and a number of moshavim. Immigrants oriented to Labor-Zionism and committed to the role of rural pioneer either joined or founded communal villages or cooperative small-holders' settlements.

Members of the Third Aliya had also been attracted to the moshav ovdim community type, and had joined or founded such settlements from their inception in 1921. The first constitution of the federation or movement of moshvei ovdim stressed as a fundamental principle the freedom of the individual member in matters of politics and religion. This principle also obtained among the non-Marxist communal settlement federations. However, it did not preclude the founding of religious land settlement movements and village federations.

Although a religious orientation and religious observance were general among settlers of the early moshavot, agricultural pioneering as a deliberate, organized activity by the orthodox began during the 1920s. The ideal of restoring the

[28] Statistics from Kurland 1947:79, 82.

homeland to fertility affected even those in disagreement with Zionism, as is illustrated by the migration of a community of Hassidim [29] from Poland in 1924, and their founding of a moshava. Although most of them were mature people with large families, unprepared for the task they had undertaken, they were aided by the Zionist organizations and created a viable farming village. Of the orthodox within the Zionist movement, those with a labor orientation founded a religious Zionist labor movement, which underwent its own history of fission and reconstitution between 1921 and 1928. The first religious Labor-Zionist settlements were moshvei ovdim. Young people trained in a religious pioneer youth movement created in Germany before the advent of Hitler initiated the first religious kibbutz in 1930. The religiously committed settlers of these new villages began to revive, under modern conditions, that portion of Jewish law concerning agricultural practices in the Land of Israel.

The Fourth Aliya also included over 9,000 immigrants from Middle Eastern lands, mostly Yemen and Aden, Iraq, Persia, and Turkey.[30] The pre-World War I encouragement of immigration from Yemen had brought some 1,500 Yemenite Jews to Palestine, most of whom worked as agricultural laborers in the moshavot and settled there in their own quarters. The first independent agricultural village settled by Yemenite immigrants was founded in 1912, with the aid of Zionist funds. Three more such villages were created between 1931 and 1933, all of them moshavim.[31]

The Fifth Aliya or wave of immigration, from 1932 to 1938, brought over 217,000 immigrants to Jewish Palestine; in the meantime, 23,000 had emigrated during the Palestine

[29] For an authoritative account of the Hassid Movement, a religious sect founded in the eighteenth century with a large following in Eastern Europe, see Landmann (ed.) 1941:V, 237–41.

[30] Matras (1965:25) gives the figure of 9,200.

[31] On pre-statehood immigration from Yemen, a review of these villages, and a brief comparison of their development with the much more organized and flourishing moshavim founded by German immigrants, see Patai 1953:182–203. Dayan (1947:60) also lists another pre-statehood moshav founded by Yemenites in 1943, Irgun Yerushalaim, to which I have found no other reference.

depression years of the late 1920s. The immigration of the 1930s was composed of 91,000 from Poland, 40,000 from Germany and Austria, some 16,000 who succeeded in arriving from the U.S.S.R., 11,000 from Rumania, 7,000 from Yemen and Aden, and significant numbers from Greece, Czechoslovakia, Hungary, and North and South America. The latter added to a population of some 2,000 immigrants from the Americas, mostly the United States, who had been part of the previous wave of immigration.[32]

This Fifth Wave of immigration was significant to nation-building not only numerically, but also in developing and strengthening sectors of the new part-society which were vital to its survival and potential for modern nationhood. The restriction placed on Jewish immigration by the British mandate government from 1929 onwards made an exception of those bringing capital to Palestine, and provided other special categories. With Hitler's rise to power, immigrants from Europe included highly trained professionals such as physicians, lawyers, engineers, scholars, and scientists, i.e., representatives of the most developed sectors of contemporary Western society. Until then there had been a relatively limited number of such people among the Jewish population of Palestine. They promoted the development of industry and commerce on a much wider scale, contributed to the arts, sciences, and humanities, and added to the reservoir of skills necessary for the development of a modern society. Thus, between 1933 and 1939, 2,700 industrial firms were created by new immigrants with capital, giving employment to some 22,500, as compared to the 1,625 establishments with a total employment of less than 14,000 that were in existence at the end of 1932.[33] A Philharmonic Orchestra was founded in 1936, and the Hebrew University and the Haifa Institute of Technology were strengthened.

As regards land settlement, the number of moshavot in the process of being urbanized increased substantially,[34] and

32 Matras 1965:26–28, 25.
33 Zweig 1959:88.
34 Halperin 1957:73ff.

the final pre-statehood innovations in village and land settlement organization were developed. Of these, the most innovative was the semicommunal village (moshav shitufi), first created, within the framework of Labor-Zionist ideology, by three groups of pioneers from different backgrounds: a group from Bulgaria, one from Central Europe, and a third composed mostly of middle-class immigrants from a small village in southern Germany. The moshav shitufi took shape as a community type incorporating features of both the kibbutz and the moshav ovdim. It is communally organized in all economic activities, but each family has its own dwelling and constitutes an independent social and consumption unit. The family receives a living allowance from village communal funds, according to the number of its members; and married women devote a limited number of hours to a community labor pool, according to a sliding scale based on the size of their families, with the rest of their time reserved for their own households. The idea of such a village type had been suggested as early as 1913 by Arthur Ruppin; but it was not put into practice until it was rediscovered, probably independently, in the latter 1930s.

The number of moshavim was much augmented by the crystallization of a village type known as the *kfar shitufi,* the semicooperative middle-class settlement. These villages differed from other moshavim in being organized as cooperative societies, like the Labor-Zionist villages, and in practicing intensive farming, mainly poultry breeding and secondarily truck farming, on very small holdings of land.[35] Most of the villages of this type were founded by mature immigrants from Germany with some capital and a background in the liberal professions. Special units were established within the major Zionist governmental and development bureaucracies in Palestine to aid them and to encourage middle-class settlement.

[35] The kibbutzim and moshvei ovdim practiced extensive mixed farming prior to statehood, whereas the early moshavot specialized in viniculture and then citriculture, and raised some grain in the north. Cf. Rokach 1964:21–25.

Types of Communities Through Which Land Settlement Was Effected in Jewish Palestine
(Increasing Order of Institutionalization of Cooperation)

Type	Date of Founding of First Village	Aliya	General Description	Salient Historical Facts
Moshava (pl. moshavot)	1878	First and following.	Agricultural villages founded on privately owned land.	Early Jewish immigration to Palestine, deliberate choice of farming as vocation.
Moshav (pl. moshavim)	1908, 1933	Second and fifth.	Several categories, principally small-holders' villages on J. N. F. land. Varying degrees of cooperation and reliance on public farming.	First type founded on J. N. F. land near moshavot by members of Second Aliya. Second main type are middle-class settlements developed mainly by Fifth Aliya members from Germany.
Moshav ovdim (pl. moshvei ovdim)	1921	Second and following.	Cooperative small-holders' settlement. Family basic production and consumption unit, cooperative village economics.	Initiated by former kvutza members dissatisfied with communal living.
Moshav shitufi (pl. moshavim shitufiyim)	1936	Fifth and following.	Semicommunal settlement. Family basic consumption and child-rearing unit, communal production, buying and selling.	Organizational feature of both kibbutz or kvutza and moshav ovdim, instituted largely by young people of Fifth Aliya.
Kvutza (pl. kvutzot)	1911	Second and following.	Communal production, consumption, and child rearing. Usually restricted membership.	First viable and most revolutionary of the community types for Jewish land settlement inspired by Labor-Zionist ideology. Originally, restricted membership and focus exclusively on agriculture, since modified in practice.
Kibbutz (pl. kibbutzim)	1921	Third and following.	Same as kvutza, but no limit on number of members.	Initially founded by members of Labor Brigade.

Common Elements

Communal consumption and child rearing.

Communal production, buying and selling.

Labor-Zionist principles (national land, no hired labor, cooperative buying and selling, mutual aid); reliance on public financing.

J. N. F. land.

The middle-class cooperative villages established their own organization, the Agricultural Union (Mo'etza Haklait), whereas the semicommunal villages joined the federation or movement of the moshvei ovdim, the Tnuat Hamoshavim. Moreover, between 1938 and the end of the pre-statehood period, both kibbutz and moshav ovdim federations were set up by the religious Labor-Zionist oriented immigrants who engaged in land settlement and by those whose orientation was to a liberal rather than socialist ideology. Of the semicommunal villages created prior to statehood, a few were founded by immigrants sharing these orientations, and these villages have been affiliated to the moshav federations representing them.

The successive emergence of these village federations, starting in the 1920s, can be seen as part of the factional system of action through which both new communities in formation and the larger part-society were developed before statehood. For these federations were linked to an increasing number of pioneer youth movements in the Diaspora, which recruited and trained young people for immigration and land settlement. They were linked also to more inclusive organizations that had developed simultaneously in Palestine, such as the Histadrut, and to the political factions whose splits and mergers underlie the shifting spectrum of political parties in the emerging society both before and after statehood.

The pattern and sequence of the emergence of these federations illustrate a recurrent process in the development of the nascent society, a process which may be characteristic both of most revolutionary social movements in complex societies and of the politics of many new states and other developing countries which are not under dictatorial rule. This process entails the institutionalization of ideologically based goal-directed systems of action into organizations and blocs. These then multiply through imitation by adherents of competing orientations or through fission of the initial movement over divisive issues or in support of competing leaders or interest groups, or in any combination of these ways.

Antedating the formation of new communities, new society, and, of course, the village federations, was the emergence of Zionist-oriented youth organizations in Europe. One such movement of students in Russia participated, as already noted, in the First Aliya and in the founding of the early Jewish rural villages in Palestine. Prior to World War I, Zionist-oriented clubs and organizations of young people increased in number and membership with the development of the World Zionist Organization. During the war, emissaries of the Second Aliya, in conjunction with the Labor-Zionist factions within the Zionist movement, initiated in Eastern Europe the first pioneering youth movements and agricultural training farms, and these movements developed branches throughout Europe and in the Americas.

The formation of other pioneering youth movements continued during the 1920s and 1930s. Some were founded by existing Zionist political factions to meet Labor-Zionism's appeal to their young people. The emergence of the religious Labor-Zionist faction, Hapoel Hamizrahi, and of its youth movement and kibbutz federation, can be seen in this light, as can both the development of the pioneer land-settlement movement and kibbutzim of the nonlabor liberal wing within Zionism and the later formation of a labor faction and land settlement movement by even the anti-Zionist Agudat Israel. Other pioneering youth movements developed in Europe, founded their own villages and village federations in Palestine, and either created new political factions within Zionism or allied with and reinforced existing ones. The Marxist-Zionist kibbutz federation originated as a pioneer youth movement, Hashomer Hatzair (The Young Guard), and remained integrally united with it to form an independent Zionist faction that later served as the nucleus of a political party. Two other Diaspora pioneer youth movements—one which developed in Poland during the 1920s and another formed in Western Europe, initially as a scouting movement—became linked during the 1930s to the federation of kvutzot.

The pre-World War I and pre-World War II development of revolutionary movements in both Eastern and Western Europe, particularly in the former, and the appearance of student and romantic scouting organizations in search of new values and socio-political programs, provided a climate conducive to the expansion in number and membership of the European Zionist youth movements. The role of organizations of young people—seeking to implement revolutionary ideologies or in quest of them—in the transformations of the societies of Europe lies outside the scope of this study, as does the fostering and utilization of such organizations in European totalitarian states. Within the Zionist system of action the pioneer youth movements were agents of nation-building and development in Palestine, and such movements extended to young people in Palestine itself. These movements were the basis and precondition for a pattern of action in the creation of new rural villages, specifically of Labor-Zionist settlements. This pattern of action was institutionalized during the mandate period and by the decade preceding statehood it had become classic.

The key elements underlying this pattern were the ideology and role of the pioneer, as first formulated by members of the Second Aliya and transmitted to successive generations of young people through recruitment into the youth movements and role-socialization over a period of years. Many young people who joined these movements dropped out, and those who remained arrived in Palestine as a self-selected elite, committed to the role of pioneer and already organized as the nuclei of future villages. Since the youth movements in the Diaspora were primarily affiliated to the kibbutz federations and were oriented toward communal life, the settlement nuclei trained by them generally practiced a communal way of life both before and after arrival in Palestine, in preparation for communal village life. Years might elapse before their turn came to be assigned a village site from the limited resources of land that could be purchased by the Jewish National Fund. During this period their members generally worked as laborers, often in a moshava, while maintaining themselves as a collectively organized unit.

Unlike the kibbutz federations, those of the moshvei ovdim generally did not recruit future settlers abroad. Instead, they organized nuclei for their settlements from among Labor-Zionist-oriented young people, and some no longer in their youth, already in Palestine. Of these recruits, some had been members of youth movements but chose to organize their villages as moshvei ovdim rather than as kibbutzim while awaiting land for settlement. Others had been born in Palestine or brought there as children or adolescents, or had migrated without any youth movement affiliation. Indeed, Youth Aliya (Aliyat Hanoar), the organization founded in 1934 to rescue children and youth from Nazi persecution, oriented its wards toward generic Labor-Zionist ideology and land settlement. The majority of them were given a home and education within special groups organized in communal settlements of every ideological persuasion. On reaching the age of eighteen, these groups left Youth Aliya to reinforce existing villages and to provide nuclei for both new kibbutzim and new moshvei ovdim affiliated to all the federations.

Pre-statehood differences in settler recruitment as well as in village organization entered into the decision after statehood (reviewed in Chapter IV) to settle new immigrants, lacking a pioneer orientation and with different demographic and cultural attributes than their pioneer predecessors and contemporaries, in villages modeled on the moshav ovdim type rather than on the kibbutz. However, the pre-statehood classic pattern of Labor-Zionist land settlement—whether the new villages were organized as kibbutzim, moshvei ovdim, or moshavim shitufiyim—was based on the recruitment of young people prepared for and committed to rural life, to agriculture as both vocation and nation-building mission, to communal or cooperative principles of village organization, and to the pioneer ethos of pride in manual labor and in overcoming the hardships and dangers involved in founding new villages and establishing them as viable economic and social units. The hardships and dangers were not inconsiderable, since, as has been widely publicized, much of the land available for Jewish rural settlement would have been considered submarginal elsewhere. Moreover, the villages usually were located in areas strategic for the defense of Jewish Palestine, and were subject to Arab attack, particularly during and after the riots of 1936.

The classic pattern of land settlement also involved partisan ideological indoctrination and intense factional commitment, aspects of the pioneer role less publicized than its routinization of heroism. The moshvei ovdim as well as the kibbutzim were based on orientations and systems of relations in which the role of partisan pioneer was crucial. Indeed, its acceptance may be considered a condition for successful land settlement and rural community formation according to the classic Zionist pattern. Yet this was a role alien to the majority of the post-statehood immigrants recruited for land settlement.

Practical interests as well as differing ideological commitments were involved in pre-statehood Zionist factionalism, since groups had to compete for limited resources. The organization of village federations can be seen as a means whereby similarly oriented pioneer immigrants strengthened their bargaining power in negotiations with the officially nonpartisan Zionist agencies that allocated land and initial investment capital. However, these federations originated as part of the factional systems of action which permeated and structured the part-society of Jewish Palestine and implemented its development. After statehood they remained basic components of the political parties of Israel, which competed for the votes of the new immigrants. Post-statehood transformations in the new society, more specifically in its land settlement sector, altered but maintained as social systems the competitive networks of villages, village federations, settlement movements, labor federations, and political parties established within or in response to the Zionist movement under pre-statehood conditions of nation-building and development.

LAND SETTLEMENT IN RELATION TO THE FORMATION OF THE NEW SOCIETY

The element of commitment can be considered a driving force and pervasive theme in the formation of the new society as well as of its land settlement sector. As Jewish Palestine developed, the commitments of its members were given expression in the groupings, systems of relations, and cleavages manifest in its organization.

The pre-Zionist Ashkenazi and Sephardi populations mostly remained committed to orthodox Judaism and traditional ways. They generally kept aloof from the transformations taking place around them, except insofar as they might belong to Agudat Israel and make use of the health and welfare services established and supported by Zionist voluntary organizations in the Diaspora. Still concentrated in the holy cities of Jerusalem, Hebron, Safed, and Tiberias, they retained their traditional community organization, usually defined on the basis of ancestral provenience from some town, city, or region of Eastern Europe or in the Sephardi and Oriental Diaspora.[36] The community or *kolel* organization of the Ashkenazi and Sephardi orthodox included traditional, institutionalized channels for receiving aid from the devout abroad, as well as rabbinical academies, schools, and synagogues. The absence, among immigrants from the ancient Oriental communities, of the traditional kolel organization supported by donations from abroad both (1) indicates their relatively limited traditional experience of organizations and associations beyond the community level; and (2) suggests that this was a factor in their disadvantaged position in the Jewish part-society of Palestine even prior to statehood and the mass immigration.

In the new villages, in the new city of Tel Aviv, founded in 1909, and in Haifa and those earlier moshavot which had

36 Cf. Patai 1953:56–57.

become urbanized [37] lived the Zionist-motivated immigrants and their native-born descendants, all committed to building up Palestine as a Jewish national home. Within this population, the group dominant both politically and in the strength and solidarity of its organizations was committed to Labor-Zionism. The adherents of Labor-Zionism were committed to one of the varying interpretations of this ideology and to the organizations these had generated. Village settlers combined commitment to a particular community type (e.g., kibbutz or moshav) with a crosscutting commitment to a religious or secular world-view and to a socialist or liberal ideology.

Thus, all the secular Labor-Zionist villages, regardless of community type and village federation, belonged to the Histadrut, the General Federation of Labor. First organized in 1920, the Histadrut during the mandate period created a comprehensive economy and service network of interdependent cooperative enterprises. Its founders were Second Aliya members of the initial Labor-Zionist factions, augmented by an extreme left-wing splinter group and by the members of the Third Aliya already in Palestine.[38] In forming the Histadrut, they united in a single organization the various cooperative endeavors, trade union and collective bargaining agreements, and mutual aid services already established or being initiated by the major Labor-Zionist factions. The Histadrut's immediate practical objectives were to facilitate the reception of the post-World War I immigrants oriented toward Labor-Zionism and to provide them with new sources of employment. Given its founders' common

[37] Cf. Halperin (1957:73ff.) for a discussion of urbanization in eight of the forty-six moshavot in existence by 1942.

[38] Kurland (1947:339) reviews the intense factionalism overcome in the founding of the Histadrut. The lush rhetoric of his volume and its exclusion of any reference to non-Histadrut nation-building activities are characteristic of pre-state Zionist partisan publications and public discourse, although his volume lacks the acrimony of many publications of the partisan Labor-Zionist and other factions. High-flown rhetoric, permeated by ideology, is despised by the native-born offspring of the immigrant generation and had become outmoded by the statehood period. However, the acrimony of factional debate has continued to characterize the politics of Israel.

commitment to generic Labor-Zionist ideology, these immediate objectives were subsumed under the all-encompassing goals of developing the homeland and creating a socialist society.

Immediate objectives, ideological and nation-building goals, and the conditions existing in mandate Palestine during the 1920s and 1930s all contributed to the ramification and diversity of the Histadrut's activities and development. Included in its scope from its inception were (1) the pioneer Labor-Zionist villages and youth movements; (2) trade unions, such as the unions of agricultural workers already created by the Labor-Zionist factions in different regions of Palestine, which had achieved a partial consolidation the previous year; and the Union of Railway, Post, and Telegraph Workers, founded in 1919 by early members of the Third Aliya together with former members of Jewish military units active during World War I who had entered the communications sector during the immediate postwar military administration of Palestine; (3) health and welfare organizations, such as the sick funds already created by the Labor-Zionist factions which merged in the Histadrut into a single organization, the Sick Fund (Kupat Holim), and became the largest health insurance program in Palestine and Israel, offering total medical coverage; (4) cooperative economic enterprises, such as Hamashbir Hamerkazi, a consumers' cooperative founded in 1916 to supply goods to the agricultural settlements; and (5) educational provisions, initially for the dissemination of Hebrew. In each of these areas, activities expanded and organizations proliferated with the growth of the Histadrut's initial membership of under 4,500 young Labor-Zionist immigrants, of their activities and needs, and of development opportunities in Palestine.

An example of these opportunities, seized on and expanded by the Histadrut, was road construction by the mandatory power. It offered employment to immigrants of the Third Aliya, who were determined to become laborers but were in competition with cheap Arab labor. The newly formed Histadrut set up an Office of Public Works to serve as a contracting agency for such construction, thereby replacing the contracting agencies earlier created by its constituent factions and increasing the employment possibilities of its members. In 1923, with the reorganization of the infant Histadrut, the Office of Public Works was replaced by Solel Boneh, a cooperative society for public works, building, and industry.

The 1923 reorganization of the Histadrut, led by David Ben-Gurion, established a general holding company to found and manage the economic activities of the Histadrut's cooperative societies, separate from its trade union activities. However, membership in this general holding company, Hevrat Ovdim (Society of Workers), was to be identical with that in the Histadrut as a whole. Solel Boneh, the cooperative society focused on construction, thereby became the employer of the immigrants it recruited, trained, and put to work. But these workers also became organized in a Histadrut trade union, and the Histadrut, as it developed, met the difference between the wages allocated by the mandatory administration and those of its workers employed on projects contracted by the administration. As Jewish-sponsored construction increased, the Histadrut exerted its growing influence to have such construction allotted to Solel Boneh, whose Histadrut-organized workers received trade union wages. All construction in the growing number of Labor-Zionist settlements was, of course, carried out by Solel Boneh and used Histadrut workers exclusively. By the early 1930s, the Histadrut began sponsoring housing projects in the towns for its members. Solel Boneh, which had been dissolved, reorganized, and reconstituted between the late 1920s and early 1930s, entered the field of housing construction, and the Histadrut had also created by 1935 a separate housing company, with shares owned by Hevrat Ovdim.

In the course of its development, Solel Boneh established industrial plants for processing building materials. It also purchased existing enterprises which were threatened by bankruptcy, partly to preserve them as sources of employment for Jewish labor. When, in the 1940s, the Histadrut turned its attention to industrial development (previously not a major focus of its activities), a successor to Solel Boneh in the field of industry was organized as a separate Hevrat Ovdim corporation. Its purchase or founding of factories—jointly with private capital and/or the Jewish Agency, the body responsible during the later mandate period for the development of Jewish Palestine—set the pattern for much of the industrial development of Israel, in which Hevrat Ovdim, the Jewish Agency, and the government have been shareholders in most of the heavy industry created.

Another range of Histadrut enterprises initially was created by individuals or small groups as small-scale cooperatives. Of these, the most important have been the transport cooperatives, which practically came to monopolize the public motor transportation system in Palestine and, since statehood, in Israel.

Agriculture and construction were the major spheres of economic activity on which the Histadrut at first concentrated. The expansion of agriculture also resulted in the spawning of enterprises founded as cooperatives to link the economy of the Labor-Zionist villages with the other Histadrut organizations. Thus Hamashbir, the original supplier of the first Labor-Zionist settlements, was reorganized in 1921 as a cooperative wholesale society which established branches in each of the settlements and in the towns. It also served initially as the outlet for the produce of the settlements. However, as agricultural production increased, competing with the products of Arab agriculturalists for markets, a special agricultural marketing cooperative, Tnuva, was established to purchase and sell all the produce of the Labor-Zionist villages. Both Hamashbir and Tnuva in turn developed their own industrial enterprises and subsidiaries.[39]

The Histadrut also established Nir Shitufi, a special cen-

[39] By 1947, enterprises and subsidiaries of the holding company of Hamashbir included plants for the manufacture of edible oils, soap, shoes, and rubber goods, as well as for the processing of wool, weaving, textile manufacture, refining of sugar, and the production of agricultural machinery. Cf. Kurland 1947:200.

tral organization of all the Labor-Zionist villages whose original purpose was to represent them in negotiating land leases and capital loans with the central Zionist organizations, i.e., the Jewish National Fund; the Foundation Fund (Keren Hayesod), established in 1921 to channel contributions toward the economic development of Palestine;[40] and the Jewish Agency. Not accepted in this capacity by these organizations, which negotiate directly with the villages, Nir Shitufi became a holding company affiliated to Hevrat Ovdim and paralleling it in the Labor-Zionist agricultural sector. It also founded its own companies for agricultural contracting, initially in such fields as citriculture. It was also given the task of arbitrating between member villages in the case of disputes.

Another organization of the Histadrut in the agricultural sector, one with more varied functions, is the Agricultural Center. This is the executive body of the Histadrut's Agricultural Workers' Union, to which all members of Histadrut-affiliated villages belong. Representing their interests within the Histadrut as a whole, the Agricultural Center has also dispensed information and advice on agriculture and organization, and on problems of any nature, including social and factional problems within the villages, to settlers and settlement nuclei of all community types and to village federations.

It seems clear that the Histadrut's[41] development and ramification involved the same process previously distinguished in the development of the land settlement sector of the nascent society, a process which also can be elicited for the Zionist movement as a whole. This process begins with the evolution of experiments and innovations initiated by relatively small groups into a complex network of inter-

[40] Basic issues of Zionist policy and the allocation of public funds were involved in the establishment of Keren Hayesod. For a review of these issues and the disputes accompanying them, cf. Halpern 1961:180–90.

[41] A brief but objective review of the Histadrut and particularly of its post-statehood "problems" or paradoxes is provided by Safran (1963:127–46). Rubner (1960) indicates the association of national economy and Histadrut interests during the first post-statehood decade, whereas Muenzner (1947) and Kurland (1947) emphasize the nation-building role of the Histadrut during the mandate period.

related systems of action and organization. Once institutionalized, these organizational units develop vested interests, based on or rationalized in terms of ideology, and persist, engaging in new functions or having new activities thrust on them as conditions have changed.

The inclusion of a comprehensive educational system among the Histadrut's activities indicates its emulative as well as innovative role in the factional system of Zionist action. Since the Turkish government did not support public educational facilities in Palestine, and the mandate government did so only to a very limited extent, these were organized for the Jewish population by a range of voluntary organizations, mostly Diaspora-based and some of them non-Zionist. Prior to World War I, Hebrew was not generally accepted as the medium of instruction, and clashes over language occurred both in Palestine and among the Diaspora contributors to the schools established.[42] In 1918 the World Zionist Organization began supporting a Jewish national school system in Palestine. Of the existing schools and those which developed, a portion were specifically religious, and in 1920 two educational "trends" were recognized: the religious Mizrahi Trend, affiliated to the religious Mizrahi political faction within the Zionist movement; and a second, designated the General Trend, which was not oriented to religious orthodoxy. Soon after its founding, the Histadrut established a network of Labor-Zionist-oriented schools both in the Labor-Zionist villages and in towns, and this was given recognition as a third "trend" by the World Zionist Organization in 1926. A completely separate school system, outside the World Zionist Organization, was maintained by Agudat Israel.

The Histadrut also developed and supported vocational and evening schools; a youth movement within Palestine with its own educational program, lecture courses, and recreational activities; a theater company; and sports clubs and a sports organization. In 1925 it began publishing a daily

42 Cf. Halpern 1961:118–19.

paper, as well as books and periodicals, and established a central publishing house in 1942. The Hagana, the underground defense army that had its origins in a pre-World War I association of armed watchmen formed by immigrants of the Second Aliya, was also under the Histadrut's authority until 1936. Control then passed to a council in which non-Labor-Zionist-oriented groups as well as those in the Histadrut were represented.

The Histadrut's funds—for the initial development of its enterprises; for the expansion of its social and welfare services, which prior to statehood, included not only the Sick Fund but the full range of social insurance provisions of a modern welfare state; and for the financing of its educational system—were drawn from World Zionist Organization funds, channeled through various public agencies, and from direct contributions by sympathizers abroad. As the Histadrut's membership and range of activities grew, the development of each of its sectors fed on and contributed to developments in other sectors, and it piled up assets far exceeding those of any other organization in Palestine. It also created a range of financial and credit agencies. By the close of the mandate period, its network of affiliated organizations linked together perhaps 40 percent of the Jewish population of Palestine, some 145,000 members plus unemployed dependents.[43] Already accused by opponents of being a monopoly, the Histadrut constituted a total although diffuse organization.

However, the development of the Histadrut had not overcome Labor-Zionist factionalism. The three major secular Labor-Zionist factions, whose origins have been reviewed, each faction linked to one or more land settlement movements, constituted the major political parties within the organization. They were supplemented by much smaller parties. Of these the two largest, each representing some 3 percent of the Histadrut membership as of 1945, were the liberal

[43] Kurland (1947:50) suggests 260,000 as the total number of Histadrut members plus children and other dependents. He cites 175,442 as the number of actual members on August 1, 1947.

nonlabor faction, Ha'oved Hatziyoni, to which the liberal land settlement federation was affiliated; and a second faction, rather similar in orientation, representing immigrants from Germany and Central Europe. These two factions within the Histadrut were part of a larger liberal faction in the part-society. This liberal faction was affiliated to one of two wings of the General Zionists, the party with a middle-class orientation within the Zionist movement. Election of the Histadrut leadership, both on the local level of labor councils and for its central governing bodies, has been conducted through voting on a party basis according to a system of proportional representation, as with all the Zionist self-governing bodies.

As the Histadrut expanded, adherents of ideologies other than secular Labor-Zionism set up their own labor federations, as well as their own settlement and youth movements and service and interest associations. The religious labor faction within Zionism, Hapoel Hamizrahi, and that outside it, Poalei Agudat Israel, each created a labor federation. However, these organizations have been affiliated with the Histadrut's Sick Fund; their villages have been linked to its marketing and supply cooperatives, Tnuva and Hamashbir; and their members have been represented in its Trade Union Section. Conversely, while the middle-class factions did not create a labor federation, both the moshavim organized in the Agricultural Union and villages of the liberal land settlement movement used agricultural purchasing and marketing cooperatives founded by the Agricultural Union, other of its services, and an independent Sick Fund. The private farmers also had their own interest association, The Farmers' Federation.

Still another labor federation, Histadrut Ha'ovdim Haleumit (National Labor Federation), was founded in 1934 by the Revisionist Movement, the party which came to embody the most profound cleavage within Zionism. The Revisionist Movement, organized in the 1920s, maintained that Zionism had to be a militant political movement committed to the rapid creation of a sovereign Jewish state on both sides of the Jordan River.[44] The Revisionists also favored planned mass immigration, largely middle-class in orientation and economic deployment, and the large-scale investment of private capital to finance the basis for such a state. After the Nazi rise to power, the Revisionist Movement rejected the official Zionist policy of self-restraint in dealing with Arab attacks and in opposing the restrictive policy of the mandate government regarding Zionist goals and Jewish immigration. Between 1935 and World War II, it seceded from the World Zionist Organization to form its own organization. A Revisionist faction, Irgun Zvai Leumi, also organized an underground military organization independent of the Hagana, the illegal defense army. Subordinating the goal of land settlement under mandate conditions to that of pressing for statehood, the Revisionists hardly engaged in land settlement during the mandate period. However, their labor federation established its own sick fund and welfare services; and great emphasis was put on youth movements, which recruited in the towns and provided partisans for the Irgun. The young survivors of Nazism constituted another source of Irgun recruits.

From this review of the major orientations and groupings that gave rise to the pre-statehood Jewish part-society of Palestine, it should be apparent that the society took shape as like-minded individuals banded into groups, formed organizations and coalitions, and established alliances which added to their numbers, resources, and influence through recruitment of new members and allies among potential immigrants, supporters abroad, and newcomers. Differences in background and orientation among the successive waves of immigrants and their supporters gave rise to partisan systems of action which both effected the formation and development of the nascent society and structured its organization.

By the end of the 1930s the part-society had a population of over 400,000 and had achieved a relatively stable

---

[44] For a discussion of the history and goals of the Revisionist Movement, see Schechtman 1954.

social organization, within which groupings, cleavages, and systems of relations largely expressed the factional orientations and politics of Zionism. Labor-Zionism by then had given the part-society its dominant organizational character, expressed in the Histadrut-affiliated networks of villages, urban groupings, enterprises, and associations. Adherents of other ideologies, to the extent that their numbers and resources permitted or their interests seemed to demand, tried to replicate these networks and to engage in parallel nation-building activities, attempting to offer their supporters equivalent services, and to maintain their influence in the country and draw support from Diaspora Jewry.

Political integration of the part-society, despite factionalism, was achieved largely through two self-governing bodies recognized by the mandate government. Of these, the less important by far was the Jewish Community Government, elected by the Jewish population already in Palestine to administer its internal affairs. While the mandate power controlled the lawmaking and law-enforcement agencies of Palestine and administered the country as a whole, the Jewish Community Government was granted in 1927 the power to levy taxes. From 1931–32 onwards, it developed a social welfare program and took over from the Jewish Agency responsibility for administering the three Zionist-supported school systems and a health program. The second of the two bodies was the Jewish Agency, the official organization for handling Jewish immigration and for developing Palestine as a Jewish homeland, although mandate support for these goals was progressively diminished and then foreclosed by changes in British policy. The Jewish Agency was constituted by the World Zionist Organization, associated Diaspora Zionists, and the Zionist settlers of Palestine, and, as reconstituted in 1929, was designed also to give equal representation to non-Zionist philanthropists and philanthropic organizations contributing to the services and development of the nascent society. Following World War I, these non-Zionist sources of aid were centered in the United States rather than in Western Europe. The goal of equal representation was not achieved, and the Jewish Agency became in effect the agency of the World Zionist Organization responsible for the development of Jewish Palestine. By 1935, Palestinian Jews outnumbered members from other countries in the Executives of the World Zionist Organization and the Jewish Agency.

In addition to its Political Department (which was in effect a Ministry of Foreign Affairs, and became this when the state was established), the Jewish Agency had Departments of Labor and of Trade and Industry (which also became ministries after statehood), and of Immigration, Absorption, Land Settlement, Youth and Pioneering, Education and Culture, and Middle-Class Settlement, as well as departments concerned with finance and administration.

Elections to the legislative bodies of both the Jewish Community Government and the World Zionist Organization were carried out on the basis of proportional representation. For the first Community Government election in 1920, 20 political parties presented lists of candidates, appealing to an electorate of under 30,000 registered voters in a population of Palestinian Jews then totaling perhaps 75,000. The number of parties in the World Zionist Organization was considerably smaller, during the mandate period mostly consisting of those already reviewed.

Moreover, the Revisionists seceded from the World Zionist Organization in 1935, rejoining it with the outbreak of World War II. The underground military force organized by Irgun Zvai Leumi did not accept the authority of the World Zionist Organization Executive; it retained its independent existence, carrying out an independent policy until several months after Israel achieved statehood.

With the mandate restrictions on legal Jewish immigration to Palestine, the various Zionist political parties and their affiliated Diaspora youth movements competed for the immigration certificates issued through the Immigration Department of the Jewish Agency. Another set of voluntary organizations, associations of immigrants from the same countries of origin, joined in this competition. These associations operated politically on their members' behalf, and some of them achieved recognition as political parties in their own right. The Aliya Hadasha (New Immigrants' Association), which was composed mainly of immigrants from Germany who had arrived during the 1930s, and the Organization of Yemenite Jews, created in 1923, achieved recognition as parties within the Histadrut and were among the twelve national parties (out of the some twenty-five by then in existence) given representation in the Provisional Council of State created on the day of Israel's independence as part of its first government. Also represented was the Sephardi party, whose leadership and constituency included descendants of the pre-Zionist Palestinian Jewish population.

Of the several officially nonpartisan bodies with quasi-governmental functions in regard to land settlement, the Land Settlement Department of the Jewish Agency was the primary coordinating unit, channeling the allocation of land and settlement capital to the organized nuclei of prospective settlers, which were affiliated with partisan village federations and awaiting their turn for a village site. The land itself was provided by the Jewish National Fund, and initial capital was extended by the Foundation Fund in the form of long-term loans. The Land Settlement Department of the Jewish Agency instituted an agricultural extension service in 1925, and the Jewish National Fund, as well as the Agricultural Center of the Histadrut, provided guidance to the settlers of the new farming villages. However, the Executives of both the Jewish Agency, to which the Foundation Fund had been transferred, and the World Zionist Organization, which had retained jurisdiction over the Jewish National Fund, were politically constituted bodies, giving representation to the Zionist political factions according to their strength in the Zionist movement. Their policy deliberations and decisions were not insulated from political pressures and claims of partisanship. The Land Settlement Department, long directed by Arthur Ruppin, was one of the Jewish Agency departments consistently headed by an advocate of Labor Zionism and, after its founding, of **Mapai, the Labor Party** of Palestine.

The order in which the various settler nuclei—committed to the spectrum of factions engaged in land settlement and awaiting their turn to go on the land—were assigned village sites and development capital was settled through political negotiation at the leadership levels of the Jewish Agency, the Zionist movement, village federations, and Histadrut. Decisions in favor of a particular federation were not immune to accusations of partisanship. Community type as well as political affiliation was implicated in such accusations, for those committed to the moshav ovdim felt that preference was being given to the founding of communal settlements.

During the last decade of the mandate, the land settlement sector exhibited most of the range of organized partisan factions within Zionism which have been of significance since statehood. For of the Labor-Zionist parties within the Histadrut, Hashomer Hatzair drew most of its strength from the Marxist kibbutz federation, Kibbutz Artzi-Hashomer Hatzair. The kvutza federation, Hever Hakvutzot, propounded an ideology continuous with that of the original Labor-Zionist faction, Hapoel Hatzair (The Young Worker), oriented to the "religion of labor" and least concerned with class struggle, although kvutza members could vote as they wished. Hakibbutz Hameuhad, while also allowing the freedom of vote to its members, was ideologically closer to Poalei Zion (Workers of Zion), the more left-wing of the two original factions. Having joined forces in 1920 to found the Histadrut, Hapoel Hatzair and Poalei Zion merged in 1929–30 to create Mapai, while their village federations and youth movements retained their separate existence.

Mapai's program emphasized nation-building and development within a pragmatic labor ideology continuous with that of Hapoel Hatzair. Mapai immediately became the strongest party in the Histadrut, despite the existence of older labor factions among the Histadrut's other parties. However, on the level of the politics of the Zionist movement, the various secular Labor-Zionist factions and village federations (including Hashomer Hatzair) supported Mapai, as did Labor-Zionists in the Diaspora. During the decade of the 1930s, Mapai gained control of the Jewish Agency, of which Ben-Gurion became chairman; of the Community Government; and finally of the World Zionist Organization. It remained in power after statehood, and has governed Israel since then in shifting coalitions with other parties. Almost three-fourths of its leadership up through the first post-statehood decade was made up of members of the Second Aliya originally from Russia or Poland.

Labor-Zionist factionalism was reasserted on the level of the part-society and the Zionist movement in the early 1940s, with the federations of communal settlements playing a major role. For Hakibbutz Hameuhad then began to organize a left wing within Mapai named Ahdut Ha'avoda (Unity of Labor).[45] In 1944, prior to new Histadrut and Community Government elections, Ahdut Ha'avoda separated from Mapai and presented an independent party list. At the beginning of 1948, a few months before Israel's independence, it united with Hashomer Hatzair and another left-wing party, composed mostly of urban workers, to found Mapam (United Workers Party), a Marxist-socialist party with a pro-Soviet orientation; Ahdut Ha'avoda was the right wing of this new party. However, a number of kibbutzim affiliated to Hakibbutz Hameuhad remained loyal to Mapai, and five others were divided almost evenly and split into separate villages. These Mapai adherents left Hakibbutz Hameuhad and formed their own federation, amalgamating in 1951 with Hever Hakvutzot in a federation renamed Ihud Hakvutzot v'Hakibbutzim (Union of Kvutzot and Kibbutzim). Ideological dissension within Mapam, involving its pro-Soviet policy in the face of Russia's anti-Zionism and resurgent anti-Semitism, led in 1954 to the secession of the

---

[45] This name goes back to a merger of all the then-existing Labor-Zionist factions, except for Hapoel Hatzair, in 1919, prior to the founding of the Histadrut.

Ahdut Ha'avoda faction and its establishment as an independent political party.

During the remainder of Israel's first decade the main strength of Mapam was the Marxist kibbutz federation, while the mainstay of Ahdut Ha'avoda, despite constituents among urban workers, was Hakibbutz Hameuhad. However, while Ihud Hakvutzot v'Hakibbutzim remained affiliated with Mapai (as has Tnuat Hamoshavim, the original and strongest of the moshav federations), Mapai did not have to depend on land settlement federations for its organized constituency and for organizational support for the party. Instead, this was provided by the Histadrut itself, in which Mapai kept its majority, and there was much overlapping in the leadership of the two.[46]

Although the total population of the communal settlements never reached even 8 percent of the population of Jewish Palestine, and the percentage has been far lower since statehood,[47] the influence of the kibbutz movements on the political life of Israel reflects their importance in pre-state nation-building and in the development and defense of Palestine as the modern Jewish homeland. For both the fervor of kibbutzim members and village communal organization made for effectiveness in the transformation of wasteland into agriculturally productive farms. The compactness of the kibbutzim as settlement units facilitated their defense against attack during the pre-statehood period, and they guarded Jewish claims to isolated tracts after purchase. The security advantages of the kibbutz as a settlement form did not decline with statehood, and kibbutzim founded after Israel's independence have stood watch at some of the most critical points along its extended frontiers.

Moreover, the kibbutzim have served as way station and

[46] Splits within Mapai and within the Histadrut have taken place during Israel's second post-statehood decade, culminating in the founding of a new party by Ben-Gurion prior to the 1965 elections. Some of the background of these splits, in which the "Lavon Affair" has played no small role, is presented for the general reader by Safran (1963) and Friedmann (1967).

[47] The 7.9 percent (1948) had dropped by 1961 to 4 percent. Cf. Matras 1965:45.

Linked Systems of Action in the Land Settlement Sector and Larger Part-
Society and Society of Jewish Palestine and Israel

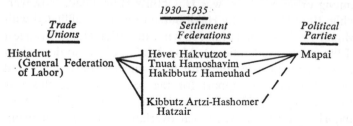

1930–1935

Trade Unions	*Settlement Federations*	*Political Parties*
Histadrut (General Federation of Labor)	Hever Hakvutzot Tnuat Hamoshavim Hakibbutz Hameuhad	Mapai
	Kibbutz Artzi-Hashomer Hatzair	

Beginning of religious
and liberal land set-
tlement movements.

Histadrut Ha'ovdim Ha-leumit (National La-bor Federation, found-ed 1934)	Revisionist Movement

Linked Systems of Action in the Land Settlement Sector and Larger Part-
Society and Society of Jewish Palestine and Israel

1948–1952

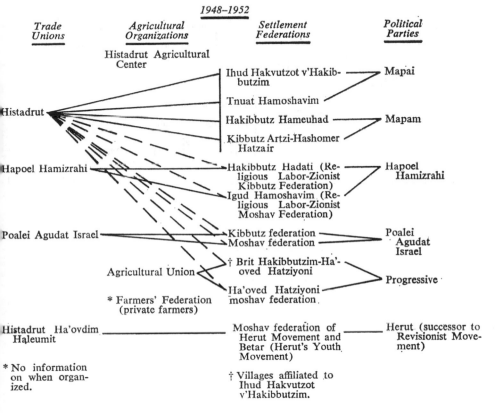

Trade Unions	*Agricultural Organizations*	*Settlement Federations*	*Political Parties*

Histadrut Agricultural Center

Histadrut

Hapoel Hamizrahi

Poalei Agudat Israel

Agricultural Union

* Farmers' Federation (private farmers)

Histadrut Ha'ovdim Haleumit

Ihud Hakvutzot v'Hakib-butzim

Tnuat Hamoshavim

Hakibbutz Hameuhad

Kibbutz Artzi-Hashomer Hatzair

Hakibbutz Hadati (Re-ligious Labor-Zionist Kibbutz Federation)

Igud Hamoshavim (Re-ligious Labor-Zionist Moshav Federation)

Kibbutz federation

Moshav federation

† Brit Hakibbutzim-Ha'-oved Hatziyoni

Ha'oved Hatziyoni moshav federation

Moshav federation of Herut Movement and Betar (Herut's Youth Movement)

Mapai

Mapam

Hapoel Hamizrahi

Poalei Agudat Israel

Progressive

Herut (successor to Revisionist Move-ment)

* No information on when organ-ized.

† Villages affiliated to Ihud Hakvutzot v'Hakibbutzim.

· 77 ·

Linked Systems of Action in the Land Settlement Sector and Larger Part-
Society and Society of Jewish Palestine and Israel

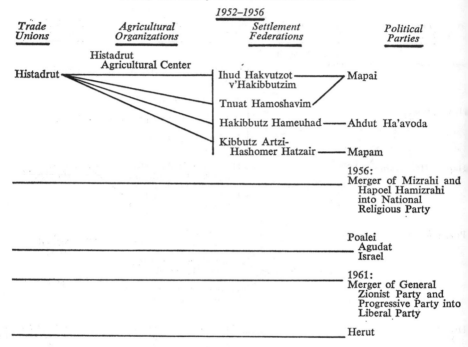

introduction into the nascent society for many times the number of people who have remained in them as permanent settlers. Among immigrants recruited and trained by the Diaspora youth movements, those who became disaffected with communal life generally found a place in other types of communities or in other sectors of the developing society, usually retaining allegiance to Labor-Zionist values and goals. From the inception of Youth Aliya, the communal settlements provided the major source of homes for youngsters rescued from Nazism, and kibbutz organization facilitated their absorption into Youth Aliya units created within the villages. Similarly, immigrants who entered Palestine illegally could find immediate refuge in the kibbutzim, undetectable from their members by outsiders.

The kibbutzim and other Labor-Zionist villages also provided the ever-ready nucleus for the Hagana, and served as depositories for secret defense stores. During the final mandate years, an elite corps of shock troops, Palmah, was established within the Hagana,[48] and much of its membership was drawn from kibbutzim of Hakibbutz Hameuhad. The prestige of its exploits in Israel's war of independence contributed to the national prestige of Ahdut Ha'avoda.

The suitability of the communal settlement and its appeal to young people as a means for effecting land settlement in remote areas under constant danger of attack are illustrated by the increase in number of kibbutzim from 43 in 1936, just before the outbreak of widespread Arab rioting, to 147 in 1947. During this same period, when villages were located at outlying sites strategic for Jewish claims to Palestine as homeland, the number of moshvei ovdim increased from 38 to perhaps 55 of the 72 villages generically classified as moshavim.[40]

---

[48] Cf. Halpern 1962:336, 342–43.

[49] The figures 38 and 72 are given by Halperin (1957:209, 94). Ben-David (1964:50), citing Gertz (ed.), *Statistical Handbook of Jewish Palestine, 1947* (Jerusalem, 1947), p. 38, gives 63 as the number of moshvei ovdim in existence in 1945; but Talmon-Garbier (1952:339) notes that 50 moshvei ovdim were in existence in 1946, when she concluded a study of them. Moreover, Halperin himself lists 18 moshavim as the number founded between 1936 and 1947 in the same table (1957:209) in

Another context in which to examine these figures is that of Labor-Zionist factionalism, for the communal settlements in 1935 were affiliated to three kibbutz federations, whereas the not much fewer moshvei ovdim belonged to Tnuat Hamoshavim. The number of moshav federations did not increase until 1940, when the villages associated with Hapoel Hamizrahi formed the labor-religious moshav federation, two years after the Poel Mizrahi kibbutz federation had been organized. The labor wings of other Zionist factions followed suit during subsequent years, two of them also becoming independent political parties.[50] Thus, the politics of the larger part-society and of the Zionist movement, rather than ideological dispute over organization of the moshav ovdim as a community type, led to the multiplication of moshav federations. In contrast, the greater number of kibbutz federations by the end of the mandate period also involved the ideologies and commitments differentiating the three original communal settlement movements, even after the obsolescence of such initially divisive issues as village size and presence or absence of small industries.

This contrast suggests that there is a correlation between the scope of the issues subsumed within the ideology of a movement and a tendency towards factionalism and fission, a correlation supported by the evidence of many social movements [51] besides Labor-Zionism and the submovements developed during its history, particularly in relation to land settlement. The kibbutz approximates a total organization more closely than does any other modern community type maintained through voluntary commitment rather than coer-

which he gives 38 as the number founded prior to 1935. Given these discrepancies, and the problem of finding accurate statistics for the number of villages of any community type in existence in a given year (a problem I discuss more fully in Chap. IV in relation to the moshvei olim), I have settled on "perhaps 55" as a compromise figure for the number of moshvei ovdim in existence in 1947.

[50] The labor wing of the General Zionist Party seceded to form the Progressive Party in 1948. The other labor wing was that of Agudat Israel; and it was pro-Zionist, in opposition to the parent body. Poalei Agudat Israel became an independent party in 1946.

[51] E.g., the history of the Protestant sects, and of the revolutionary movements of the nineteenth and twentieth centuries in Europe.

cion.[52] The ideologies underlying kibbutz organization and legitimizing it to its pioneer members and potential recruits have involved pervasive revolutionary principles regarding the social order.[53] These offered ample scope for disagreement among those committed to these principles and to purposefully initiating communities designed to put them into practice. Historically, such basic aspects of kibbutz organization as communal dining halls and communal child rearing in a succession of age-graded infants' and children's houses were initiated pragmatically to meet the need, under early conditions of land settlement, for maximum utilization of resources, including woman power.[54] But the generically revolutionary orientation of Labor-Zionism made possible their institutionalization as basic principles of collective living, which was the most revolutionary crystallization of this orientation. These principles then gave rise to new issues for ideological dissension regarding actual practices to be followed in the communal villages,[55] supplemented by disagreements over political issues of the part-society and the Zionist movement.

An intense commitment to a pervasive ideology may be necessary for the maintenance of voluntary movements which demand of their adherents a revolutionary transformation of their way of life. Such intensity of commitment among kibbutz partisans seems to have accentuated the differences

[52] The term "total organization" is used by Etzioni (1961:161), following Goffman, to refer to "organizations which include most or all of participants' activities." Goffman's own discusssion of the characteristics of "total institutions" includes a reference to the kibbutz as a "marginal case" (Goffman 1961:11n.).

[53] The most revolutionary of the Labor-Zionist ideologies was formulated by Ber Borochov (1937) and was taken over by Hashomer Hatzair. However, the generic revolutionary principles of even non-Marxist socialism pervaded Labor-Zionism, as Tartakower (1954) seeks to document, and as a review of almost any collection of Labor-Zionist documents makes clear.

[54] Cf. Baratz 1954:65.

[55] These could range from issues involving the degree of collectivization to be followed in child rearing to whether or not to permit private teakettles. On the issue of childrearing, some kibbutzim, such as Degania, the first kvutza, allow the children to sleep in the dwellings of their parents. Baratz (1954), Schwartz (1954), and Spiro (1956) discuss the decision-making process in different communal villages.

among them, as expressed in the kibbutz movements' pervasive ideologies, and to have strengthened factional loyalties.

The cooperative principles of the moshav ovdim remove family life and internal management of the family farm from the jurisdiction of village and federation. The moshav ovdim as a community type was far from revolutionary when initiated, and it demanded of its adherents a less than revolutionary transformation as regards the social order in which most of them had been raised. Moshav ovdim organization does make ramifying claims on village members and has some aspects of a total organization, but these go no further than is implied in the principles and goals of generic pioneer Labor-Zionism. While the initiation of communities embodying moshav principles involved issues of village organization over which there was dissension, as the following chapter describes, these were resolved in such a way as to apply to the whole class of moshvei ovdim and did not generate differentiated moshav subideologies and separate movements.

An intense commitment to the special cooperative principles of the community type was hardly lacking among moshav adherents. However, the principles involved were less pervasive than those of collective living and/or were not assimilated to a pervasive ideology which involved divisive political stands regarding issues facing the part-society and the Zionist movement. In any case, the intensity of their commitment seems to have contributed to the solidarity of moshav adherents in defense of common interests, particularly against the claims of the kibbutzim. The moshav movement could accept the affiliation, initiated during the 1930s, of the semicommunal villages, the moshavim shitufiyim, and welcome the increase in number of settlements and competitive strength they provided.

While intensity of commitment and pervasiveness of ideology within Zionism may have found their most total expression in the kibbutz movements, these qualities also characterized generic Labor-Zionism, differently oriented movements within or antagonistic to Zionism, and the socio-cultural climate in which they emerged. For the majority of the

Zionist immigrants to Palestine and of their supporters in the Diaspora were drawn from Eastern Europe, at least until the advent of Nazism. As is described elsewhere,[56] the traditional Jewish communities of Eastern Europe constituted a beleaguered part-society, within which intensity of emotion was both generated and sanctioned in many areas of life. Conspicuous among these was the life of the intellect; and passion was legitimately associated with differences of opinion and values, their crystallization into movements,[57] and their embodiment in factions.

Both orthodox Judaism and the revolutionary movements of Eastern Europe also represent, in very different ways, total systems. Judaism provides regulations for practically every detail of life, and a dialectic which brings these regulations within the sphere of systematic debate and analysis. The revolutionary movements left no area of behavior immune from discussion, reformulation, and incorporation within the scope of ideology. The ethos of Labor-Zionism originated in opposition to what its innovators considered to be the negative aspects of Jewish life in the Diaspora, and this included the orthodoxy in which most of them had been raised. The contemporary revolutionary movements provided them with a point of reference in their synthesis of new ideologies, despite their rejection of class struggle in the Diaspora as a solution to their search for a new Jewish identity.

In migrating to Palestine to create a new way of life and new society, the Labor-Zionist pioneers took on new vocations and developed new norms of behavior and new community types and forms of organization. However, the culture of Eastern European Jewry, and to varying extents that of the larger Eastern European societies, were the cultures in which they had been socialized and the only ones they really knew. Their basic modes of perception, symbolization, reaction, and interaction persisted, as did other components

[56] See above, note 11. Diamond (1957) goes so far as to conceptualize Labor-Zionist pioneer values and kibbutz organization and ideology as an over-reaction to shtetl values and organization.

[57] Hassidism was but one of the movements within Judaism that emerged in the centuries preceding the origins of modern Zionism.

of behavior that did not enter the system of conscious values open to deliberate revision. Both the Labor-Zionist ideologies and the organizations created to put them into practice had the ramifying character of total systems, within which ideological debate and dispute could be constant but to which primacy of commitment was expected. Adherence to partisan ideology and the drive to translate it into reality were maintained with an intensity fed by the conditions of land settlement and employment in manual occupations during the early decades of this century.

Cultural continuity with Eastern Europe and/or an adherence to religious orthodoxy, as well as defense of their own interests in competition with the growing strength of Labor-Zionism, contributed to the development of ramifying systems of action by the partisans of religious and Revisionist values and goals. For the intensity of commitment to religion which had maintained Jewish identity and orientation to Palestine for millennia prior to Zionism did not slacken among the orthodox, whatever the fissures in their ranks effected by concomitant adherence to Zionism, Labor-Zionism, or anti-Zionism. Pervasiveness of belief systems, of the ideologically oriented partisan networks of organizations and villages created by their adherents in Palestine; intensity of partisan commitment; factionalism, fission, and the acrimony of factional dissent—all these can be related to the Eastern European antecedents of the majority of the pre-statehood immigrants to Palestine and members of the Zionist movement.

During the crucial mandate years, the special ethos of Labor-Zionism and of the other strongly partisan Zionist or ultra-orthodox factions could be transmitted to successive waves of immigrants from much the same background, who had much the same motivations for immigration to Palestine as their predecessors. The pioneer youth movements in the Diaspora were agencies of ideological indoctrination, as well as organizations fostering immigration to and settlement in Palestine.

With the extinction or closing off from immigration of

most of Eastern European Jewry, the Diaspora-derived basis of cultural continuity was lost. Immigrants from other backgrounds have had different modes of perception, symbolization, and action, and these contributed, during the mandate period, to cleavages and associations which partly cut across and partly supplemented the ideologically based partisan networks. Cultural as well as economic and occupational differences were involved in the liberal political orientation of many of the immigrants from Germany and Central Europe. These differences were expressed in the organizations they created or helped to strengthen, such as their special immigrants' association, and the middle-class moshav community type and the Agricultural Union in the rural sector. All of these contributed to the constituency of the liberal Progressive Party, founded in 1948.

The Yemenite and Sephardi associations and parties also acted politically. For unless the immigrants of non-European provenience joined one of the nation-building partisan factions or could be politically effective through their own organizations, they had no share in the Diaspora-based financial support channeled through the Zionist movement, except insofar as it was distributed through the limited social welfare program of the Jewish Community Government.[58]

The relative lack of involvement of immigrants from the non-Western countries in the Zionist systems of action became a paramount national concern only with the post-statehood mass immigration,[59] and the body of this study deals with the mobilization of such immigrants into Israel's land settlement program and their politicization by virtue of its organization. However, it is not these immigrants alone

[58] Even those immigrants of non-European provenience who joined the Zionist system of action might remain in an economically disadvantaged position in comparison with immigrants from Europe. For example, the moshvei ovdim founded by immigrants from Yemen were among a number of villages that did not receive capital loans from the Foundation Fund. Cf. Bein 1952:464–66.

[59] By the end of the mandate period, immigrants of non-European provenience and the descendants of the pre-Zionist Jewish population numbered less than 20 percent of the Jewish population of Palestine.

who have been responsible for the decline in the intensity of partisan commitment progressively evident in Israel and its embattled politics since statehood.

For the native-born children of the pioneer Zionist immigrants were deliberately and successfully raised to be different from their parents. The society that its innovators fought for and achieved, in part by virtue of intense partisan action, is accepted as a fact by their grown descendants. For most of them, commitment to partisan ideology has long been secularized into history and politics, and Israel as nation-state claims their primary loyalties. While politically affiliated and active, they hardly manifest the beleaguered intensity of partisan adherence, still evident during the first post-statehood decade among many of their elders.

Even the post-statehood immigrants from Eastern Europe, intermittently and increasingly allowed to come to Israel from the Communist countries, had undergone protracted experiences which eroded continuity with the pre-World War II cultural universe. Moreover, it was the cultural climate of the shtetl, the small Eastern European Jewish town or enclave, that contributed to pervasive ideologies and fed intensity of commitment. These were less characteristic of the urban middle-class sectors of Eastern European Jewry. Zionist adherents from this middle-class sector had tended to support General Zionism since before World War I, deprecating the "hyphenated Zionism" of the religious and labor factions. While supporters of General Zionism constituted the majority of the Diaspora members of the Zionist movement, they were not strongly based in Palestine even with the middle-class immigration of the Fourth and Fifth Aliyot. Having already lost members to the Revisionist movement, they did not organize as a party until after the founding of Mapai and soon split into two factions, one of which supported the Histadrut. Members of the latter faction in Palestine were instrumental in founding the Progressive Party. Moreover, the General Zionists' lack of a pervasive ideology eliciting intense commitment further weakened their competitive position during the mandate period.

Since Israel's independence, its General Zionist Party has represented the interests of private industry, and has undergone a fluctuating history of increase and loss of strength in the national elections.[60] A long-discussed merger with the electorally weak Progressive Party was finally achieved in their founding of the Liberal Party before the 1961 elections. There is some evidence that post-statehood immigrants from Eastern Europe, whose numbers have increased considerably since 1956, contributed to the strong showing of the Liberal Party in this election. [61]

The politics of the new state express some of the transformations effected with autonomous political nationhood and the establishment of Israel as society as well as nation-state. The land settlement sector was actively involved in these transformations, both on the village level and in relation to nation and larger society.

In this sector after statehood, the moshav as a village type soon outstripped the kibbutz in the number of new settlements founded and in the relative proportion of moshavim to other rural villages.[62] However, during the first post-statehood decade, the great majority of new moshavim were not moshvei ovdim or middle-class moshavim, but *moshvei olim,* immigrants' settlements, the special type of managed villages founded by the land settlement authorities for the mobilization of new immigrants into land settlement. The moshvei olim were modeled on the moshav ovdim and were regarded as a traditional settlement type which would cease to be managed villages and become moshvei ovdim as soon as the new immigrants developed the requisite farming and management skills. The official view, even by 1958, was that

[60] It was second to Mapai in the 1951 national elections, polling 16 percent of the total vote and winning 20 seats in the Israeli Parliament (Knesset), which has a fixed membership of 120. In the previous elections of 1949, the first held in Israel, the General Zionist Party polled only 5 percent of the vote and held 7 seats. In the third national elections of 1955, it polled 10 percent of the vote and held 13 seats.

[61] I.e., 13.6 percent of the vote; cf. Matras 1965:88, 115–16.

[62] Halperin (1957:208) gives 216 as the total number of kibbutzim in existence in 1953 as compared to 250 moshavim, of which 108 were moshvei olim.

this would take four to six years, although it had been recognized several years earlier that this was an unrealistic estimate.

For moshav ovdim organization has demanded of the majority of immigrants from the Oriental lands pervasive and revolutionary transformations in their values and ways of life. Moshav cooperative principles of organization, based on the family unit, were neither revolutionary nor pervasive, given an initial orientation to Labor-Zionism or even to generic non-Marxist socialism. However, these principles, regarding both village organization and village ties to the ramifying partisan networks of the larger society, expressed the pervasive ideology of generic Labor-Zionism and its factional politics. A specific way of life and specific allegiances were embodied in the moshav as a community type, as described in the following chapter.

THE MOSHAV OVDIM AS MODEL
FOR THE MOSHAV OLIM

A discussion of the moshav ovdim, as of any class of social units, calls for distinguishing the recurrent features which characterize the class from the variable features which make for differences between the concrete units. The recurrent features of the moshav ovdim are those which are common to all villages in Israel expressing the Labor-Zionist principles and self-governing provisions of this community type as it has been concretely realized, and which distinguish it from the other types of communities initiated and institutionalized as part of the new society's development.

Of the eighty plus villages [1] embodying the type by the end of Israel's first decade of independence, variations from village to village involved many factors. Some have been ecological, such as climate, topography, soil type, water resources, etc., and their consequences for the size of the family farm and the kind of farming carried out. In principle, all moshvei ovdim founded until 1952 were based on mixed farming, but some leaned more heavily to dairy farming, others to field crops, while conditions in some regions favored citriculture. [2]

Other variable factors may be considered temporal, such as the age of the village and its bearing on the level of agricultural and economic development and on the demography of the village population. In this regard, it should be emphasized that moshvei ovdim have continued to come into

[1] Halperin (1957:208) gives eighty as the total number of moshavim (as distinct from moshvei olim) in existence in 1953/54, i.e., by September 26, 1954, the end of the Hebrew year. Since other statistical sources for the number of settlements founded during the first post-statehood decade do not differentiate new moshvei ovdim from moshvei olim, and since villages founded by a special army branch, Nahal, could be in existence for several years before their community type was decided, I have no figures for the number of moshvei ovdim founded between 1954 and 1958.

[2] Cf. Rokach (1964:21–25).

being since Israel's independence. They differ from the moshvei olim in that their settlers—whether native-born, residents of long standing, or recent immigrants—chose agriculture as a vocation and the moshav ovdim as their community type with full awareness and acceptance of the commitments involved. Correspondingly, the settlers have been self-governing, as in the pre-statehood moshvei ovdim, from the villages' inception, and these settlements have not been assigned instructors, with the possible exception of an agricultural instructor. Young people have tended to be the founding settlers of such villages, as in the classic Labor-Zionist tradition.

Organizational factors also make for variation among existing moshvei ovdim. Varying degrees of cooperation, beyond those prescribed by the village constitution binding on all such villages, have been practiced. And after 1953, increasingly rationalized national planning reduced the scope of village and family autonomy in decisions regulating agricultural production, while providing a more rapid and stable flow of capital for initial development than the older villages enjoyed at a corresponding period in their history. Differences in ideology and corresponding moshav federation and labor federation affiliation also constitute another source of moshav variation.

Possibly of most interest in relation to the moshvei olim would be the extent to which differences in village informal organization have existed in the moshvei ovdim at different periods in their histories. For variations in the patterning of internal village relations, particularly at the level of village politics and internal factionalism, were certainly indicated by moshvei ovdim histories generally known among members of Israel's rural sector and among veteran personnel involved in land settlement. However, the extent to which factionalism provoked major village crises, or may even have led to a temporary depletion in the membership of a moshav, were not subjects on which people willingly gave information or on which reliable accounts and statistics are available.

Differences in cultural climate—i.e., in style of interaction, values, and daily practices of the villages' members in the many areas of life outside formal ideology and formal organization—also contributed to moshav variation. According to statements of informants and to unelicited gossip, these variations in cultural climate, particularly during the first decades of the villages, were associated with differences in the provenience and background of the majority of a village's settlers of the first generation. However, these statements were not unequivocal, except in differentiating immigrants from Germany from those of Eastern European origin, a differentiation made throughout the part-society after the influx from Germany during the 1930s. Moreover, such statements hardly constitute reliable evidence, despite their hypothetical probability, particularly given the long tradition of mockery and stereotypy among European Jewry regarding differences in character associated with regional origin. It seems probable that there is some correlation between differences in cultural climate and the cultural backgrounds of the villages' settlers, but that this correlation could be crosscut by variations in the ways in which particular groups of settlers worked out their relations.

Given the paucity of scholarly studies of the moshvei ovdim,[3] it is not possible to indicate socio-cultural norms and variations generated within the universe of such villages. Moreover, interesting as it would be to compare such norms and variations with those of the moshvei olim, they had no bearing on the settlement authorities' choice of the moshav ovdim community type for rural settlement of members of the post-statehood mass immigration. Nor did they influence decisions concerning the administration of the moshvei olim, except insofar as individuals in positions of authority acted on their particular knowledge of life in one or more of the veteran villages.

In my experience, the model of the moshav ovdim used

---

[3] The only study of the moshvei ovdim by a social scientist that I know of is the article by Talmon-Garbier (1952). Schwartz (1955) discusses both a kibbutz (kvutza) and a moshav. Assaf's study (1953) is a detailed historical review of the development of the moshav ovdim by a moshav movement spokesman.

during Israel's first decade as generic baseline and official goal for the development of the moshvei olim was a stereotypic abstraction of features of perhaps six to ten of the older settlements. The members of these settlements, generally of Eastern European origin, had endeavored to be faithful to the ideological blueprint in working out the problems they faced in translating it into the reality of village life. Actual decisions of the settlement authorities regarding the moshvei olim were largely pragmatic, oriented to conditions current during the first ten years after statehood. Nonetheless, the classic moshav ovdim stereotype remained a point of reference, particularly to representatives of the moshav federations, whenever basic policy concerning issues of village development or of pervasive conflict in the moshvei olim came under review.[4] It is this abstraction, presented as an ideal type, which is discussed in this chapter. The present tense refers to conditions obtaining through the latter 1950s.

ORGANIZATION OF THE CLASSIC MOSHAV OVDIM

The characteristic feature of the moshav ovdim, as compared to other settlement types founded on Labor-Zionist principles, is the attempt to preserve the advantages of family initiative and enterprise while providing those of cooperative endeavor in an organizational system stressing equality. The extent of cooperation varies from moshav to moshav, but in all of them (1) marketing and purchasing are carried out through village marketing and purchasing cooperatives; (2) mutual aid provisions supply the individual family with a fairly complete system of insurance; and (3) village credit facilities are available for the individual farmer. Depending on the state of development of a particular village and the kind of farming practiced, common village assets may include water-supply and irrigation equipment, a dairy with a refrigerating plant, an incubator, a small plant for processing

4 Members of the Land Settlement Department of the Jewish Agency had no ideological commitment to any of the Labor-Zionist inspired community types over any of the others, and they were more ready than the moshav federation representatives to look to the nonclassic moshvei ovdim as points of reference.

foods supplementary to farm-grown fodder needed by the dairy herds, and facilities for storing, processing, packaging, and shipping produce. Common village services generally include a kindergarten, a school, perhaps a secondary school serving several surrounding villages, a dispensary, a postal station, a culture center with a library and an auditorium, a clubhouse for youth, and a guesthouse (which may be part of a private home) for visitors. A bakery and a butchery usually exist in addition to the village cooperative store, but a restaurant or a cafe is excluded by moshav ideology.

To a considerable extent, moshav economic organization functions in terms of credit. This is the case both in the development of a particular moshav into a viable farming village, and in the financing of its current expenditures. A newly established moshav ovdim receives a long-term loan [5] from the Foundation Fund. From this loan each family receives an equal amount of credit to invest in the development of its farm, while some of the funds are used for financing the minimum common village assets and services needed in the initial years. This loan, channeled through the Land Settlement Department of the Jewish Agency, provides each family with 70 percent of the total investment needed to make a farm economically viable. The remainder is to be supplied by the settlers from their own resources once the farms begin to produce.

Since the amount of money collected by the Foundation Fund has varied, the period over which the loans have been given to individual settlements also has varied. Settlements constantly have suffered from lack of funds for systematic agricultural development. Additional credit has then been sought from the credit institutions of the General Federation of Labor, from those of the moshav federations as they have been established, and from banks. Since all the newly established settlements apart from the moshavot (private villages) have been dependent on public funds for their initial development capital, the pre-state settlements were

[5] For provisions regarding repayment of loans at different periods in the history of land settlement, see below, pp. 181–83 (cf. Rokach 1964:38).

essentially competing for these funds until their economic consolidation was achieved. Similarly, the Labor-
Zionist settlements were in a competitive position regarding
the credit resources of the General Federation of Labor;
while the settlements of a particular federation competed
for the latter's resources. Thus, the federations served as
pressure groups in regard to the General Labor Federation's
credit resources for agricultural development; the Agricultural Center of the General Federation of Labor served the
same function for its affiliated settlements in regard to the
national institutions and their funds; and all the organized
movements sought to convince the Zionist Organization of
the importance of their own particular activities, while also
seeking funds abroad. It can be assumed that the necessity of
competing for available funds reinforced ideological differences in sharpening factional and organizational differences
and the beleaguered partisanship of the pre-statehood
factions.

To supplement these sources of credit, as well as for subsistence during the initial years, the settlers of a newly established moshav ovdim have generally sought outside work
until the moshav could become economically viable. Such
work might include rehabilitating their own or neighboring
lands, terracing, or reforestation, activities which are under
the jurisdiction of and financed by the Jewish National Fund.
They also might work as laborers in nearby moshavot or on
public works, do the preliminary work in middle-class settlements where the settlers as well as the national institutions
contribute to the initial investment, perform locally needed
services, etc. In pre-state days, this outside employment was
generally organized and allocated by the moshav itself
through its committees. Also, in some moshavim settlers
who had permanent positions paid a special tax to the mutual
aid funds to finance community enterprises carried out by the
unemployed or partially unemployed settlers.[6]

Within the moshav, once it becomes agriculturally produc-

[6] Cf. Dayan 1947:25.

tive, the settler families also live largely in a credit economy, in which their relations to the outside world are mediated through the village cooperative organizations. The farmer delivers his produce to the village marketing or producers' cooperative, where it is weighed or otherwise measured, processed, and packed, and from which it is sent with the shipments of the other farmers to the nearest branch of Tnuva or the equivalent non-Histadrut marketing organization. Each month he receives a slip on which are listed his shipments for the previous month and his total receipts. Also listed are that month's expenditures for seeds, chemical fertilizer and other supplies, which he has also obtained on credit, and his balance, credit or debt, for the month. Deductions for village taxes also may be made monthly, and among these taxes are those for the services provided by the cooperatives.

According to one list from a publication of the 1940s,[7] these services then included: (1) receiving produce from the farms and delivering it to Tnuva after grading and packing; (2) supplying water for household and irrigation requirements; (3) purchasing seed, manure, packing materials, etc. for the members; (4) maintaining a stud bull; (5) maintaining and operating agricultural machinery for plowing, harvesting, threshing, etc.; (6) engaging experts to advise members on various aspects of agriculture; (7) undertaking pest-control measures; (8) maintaining facilities for the transportation of passengers and freight to the nearest market town; (9) negotiating agricultural loans on behalf of individual members and for public projects.

Thus, the producers' cooperative is the organization through which much of the moshav's economic life is channeled. It and the consumers' cooperative are generally supervised by a village's economic committee together with the executive committee. The purchasing or consumers' cooperative tries to provide everything that the moshav families may need, including food not supplied from the farm. It pur-

7 Dayan 1947:28.

chases from Hamashbir or an equivalent organization and, following the Rochdale principles, sells only for cash.[8]

In some moshavim all the common village economic transactions are centralized in one organization. Such an organization in one veteran village was able during the late 1950s to allow an individual farmer to accumulate a debt of IL 20,000 ($1.00 = IL 1.80), a truly large sum in Israel at that time. Credit is also advanced for improvements in individual farmsteads, such as the purchase of additional machinery or livestock, the construction of additional facilities, etc. Such loans have to be approved by the economic committee, usually together with the executive and agricultural committees.

In addition to loans for agricultural development, families are entitled to have their basic needs provided for on credit at any time, regardless of their financial situation. The necessary funds may be advanced through the mutual aid funds, as one aspect of mutual aid provisions. In the early days of the pre-statehood villages' development, families sometimes combined resources during difficult periods, and each received an allowance according to the number of its members. Those who exceeded this allowance repaid the difference at a later date; those not drawing upon all the money available to them had the remainder refunded to them.[9]

However, this has not been the main function of the mutual aid provisions, either in terms of the formal moshav provisions or in the history of the moshvei ovdim. Mutual aid is supposed to cover a range of family misfortunes such as illness, accident, or death. It has largely been directed to providing assistance when, for one of these reasons, usually illness, the husband or wife could not work. Originally, other settlers took turns carrying out his or her work, given the

---

[8] The Rochdale principles are those formulated in 1844 in Rochdale, England by the founders of the Rochdale Society of Equitable Pioneers. The creation of this organization usually is considered to mark the beginning of the modern cooperative movement. The principle of selling only for cash was designed to prevent such trading practices, then common among tradesmen who extended consumer credit, as the adulteration of consumer goods. Cf. Cole 1944:8–9, 39–96.

[9] Cf. Talmon-Garbier 1952:343.

prohibition on hiring labor; and the mutual aid committee was principally concerned with organizing replacements. This arrangement was soon found to be impractical, and it became acceptable for the community to hire workers to replace an incapacitated member. Also, when members of the moshav might be called upon to engage in federation affairs or other public matters which required their absence from the farm, a substitute farmer would be hired. In the case of permanent incapacity or death, the remainder of the family would be aided in this way, if it were felt that they could continue to work the farm. Otherwise, they would be helped to find work and reestablish themselves, and the farm would be transferred to the moshav under the same conditions as when a family desired to leave. Also, in case of disasters to the farm through fire, etc., a system of community insurance operates. A spokesman for one veteran moshav ovdim reported that in his village the losses suffered in this way are calculated each year, and a tax sufficient to replace the loss is levied on the entire membership.

As can be seen, the moshav cooperative economic provisions are designed to maximize economic equality within the limits of cooperative endeavor set by the moshav form of organization. The nuclear family is defined as the basic unit of socio-economic organization, and all families begin with equivalent holdings and equal amounts of credit. No compensation is made for differences between families—in the number of growing children who can contribute to the family labor force, in physical strength, initiative, etc.—nor would it be possible to make any, given moshav principles. However, there have been attempts in various moshvei ovdim, as the farms developed, to give as much support as possible to the families with least success. In addition to the credit facilities indicated above, progressive taxation was introduced in certain villages, in place of equal taxes for the support of the moshav common assets and services. Either yearly income or value of the farm might be used as a basis for assessment.[10] As children grew to adulthood, the question

10 Cf. Assaf 1953:95.

was raised of whether the number of adult workers in a family should not also be taken into consideration in levying taxes. These are questions decided upon by each village for itself, and much internal disagreement and experimentation have occurred in instituting systems of taxation.

The working out of such issues proceeds according to the moshav self-governing provisions. The general assembly of all adult members is the basic governing body of the moshav. It is supposed to establish policy, delegate authority for the management of village affairs, and have the final say on all village matters. It meets at least once a month. Every year its members propose about twenty names for the village council (moetza), from which twelve or thirteen are chosen by ballot. This council meets about once a month to decide on implementation of policy on matters of common village concern such as investments and loans, the village cooperative organizations and municipal institutions, and shared agricultural interests. It also appoints committees to deal with moshav affairs, is responsible for coordinating and supervising their activities, and may itself implement policy concerning the village cooperatives in lieu of an economic committee.

The exact number and scope of these committees varies from village to village and may vary in the same village over a period of time. In addition to the executive committee (va'ad or hanhala) and an economic committee, an agricultural committee, and a committee on mutual aid, all mentioned earlier, there may also be committees for the mediation of disputes, for the organization of cultural activities, on education, on health, on security matters—in short, committees concerned with every aspect of public life. One list gives sixteen such committees.[11] Membership on these committees is voluntary, and members, with the one exception of the head of the executive committee, carry out their duties in their spare time.

As each committee consists of about four members, well

[11] Assaf 1953:80–81.

over fifty offices may exist for the management of village affairs in communities with a population of about 70 to 150 families. This division of managerial responsibility among as many committees as possible was deliberately planned. It was intended both to involve the largest number of members possible in public affairs and responsibilities and, concomitantly, to avoid the formation of a managerial group.[12] Other provisions with the same purposes originally included short terms of office and rotation in office, with no member to hold the same position for more than two years.

The most important committee in the moshav is the executive committee, which deals with current financial and organizational matters and represents the moshav in its dealings with outside organizations such as credit and financial organizations, national institutions, and various country-wide administrative networks. With the village council, it also coordinates the activities of the other committees and supervises all village institutions. Matters of policy or special village crises are referred to the village council and/or the general assembly. The head of the executive committee usually devotes all his time to village affairs, and may have to make many trips on village business. He usually receives a salary to compensate him for the loss of his labor on the farm; and his family usually maintains the agricultural branches requiring constant care, such as the dairy herds and chicken runs, limiting field crops to proportions they can manage. Or two members of the executive committee may divide between them both the full-time load of managerial duties and the salary that goes with it.

Despite the many links between the moshav ovdim and organizations of the larger society, members of a village can lead relatively self-contained lives within it, with relations to the outside world mediated through the village cooperative organizations and the executive committee. Moreover, even before the establishment of the state, planning tended to be taken over by the committees; and it is they who pass on

---

[12] Cf. Talmon-Garbier 1952:349–50.

the allocation of credit to the village members. Despite provisions to the contrary, the formation of a managerial group has tended to occur with the increased economic development of the villages, as will be discussed subsequently.

The agricultural committee deals with such matters as crop rotation, irrigation, and other agricultural concerns affecting the entire village. It, rather than the producers' cooperative, may supervise the tractor station and the common village assets and services directly concerned with agriculture. Like the economic committee, it works closely with the executive committee; and, according to an informant from a veteran moshav, this is the committee on which the young people of the second generation most desire to serve and to have a chance to demonstrate their knowledge, initiative, and ability.

Women are entitled to membership on all the committees, but tend to concentrate on those concerned with education, cultural activities, health, etc. However, a few women are generally members of the village council, and occasionally of the executive committee as well.

The position of secretary of the moshav ovdim (unlike the kibbutz or the moshav shitufi) is not an elective office conferring decision-making prerogatives, but rather a salaried post. The secretary is one of many public employees and artisans who, in an economically established moshav ovdim, may constitute 30 to 40 percent of the village population.[13]

The need for so high a percentage of nonfarmers, unforeseen in the original ideological blueprint, nonetheless stems from the basic tenets of moshav ideology and organization. Given the ban on hired labor, the farmer himself and his whole family are fully occupied by farm work, once the economic basis of the farm has been established. In the early moshvei ovdim the cultivation of cereal crops was envisaged, and relatively large areas, up to eighty dunams or even more (four dunams = one acre), were allocated to the individual farmer. In some villages these were subdivided in later years

13 Cf. Assaf 1953:83.

to accommodate more families, a practice which became economically feasible with the introduction of irrigation. Farmsteads in subsequently established moshvei ovdim may be less than half that size, depending on topography, types of soil, extent of irrigation, branches of agricultural specialization, and similar factors, with size calculated in terms of potential productivity. A typical farm in a veteran moshav may include a dairy herd with six to ten milk cows and several calves, a chicken run with from several hundred to two thousand laying hens, and possibly six to ten dunams of citrus or other kinds of fruit trees, with the remainder of the holding given over to field crops.

In a relatively young moshav ovdim the man is likely to work in the fields and orchards and to help with the milking. The principal responsibility for the livestock and kitchen garden, as well as for the home and child rearing, falls on the woman. It is proverbial that the success of the moshav farm depends heavily upon the wife's diligence and industry. As the children grow up, they help in the fields and with the livestock, and this contributes to the farm's productivity. A well-established farmstead easily supports two nuclear families, e.g., a two-generation family consisting of parents and one grown and married child with growing offspring; and there is work enough to keep all occupied.

Therefore, the labor involved in the maintenance and administration of the common village institutions and services is carried out by salaried employees. With the economic development of the moshav, necessary occupational specialists range from bookkeepers to mechanics and include the staffs of the village cooperatives. There also are the teachers and the medical personnel staffing the dispensary, who are not paid by the moshav itself but, in pre-state days, were paid by the Histadrut. The place of such personnel in the community was a controversial issue for decades. Since this issue indicates one of the paradoxes I consider inherent in the basic principles and goals of the moshav ovdim as a community type, a review of the dilemmas it generated follows.

Before the establishment of Nahalal, the first moshav ovdim, its nucleus of founding settlers worked out a plan for incorporating into the moshav's organization the non-farming personnel. According to this plan,[14] they were to be salaried public employees and also full members of the moshav. Like all prospective new members, they were to undergo a trial period prior to acceptance by a two-thirds majority. Once accepted as members, they could be dismissed only for violations of moshav principles or because of serious misconduct or neglect of duties. Their salaries were to be adjusted to the average income of the farming families, varying yearly with the economic prosperity of the moshav as a whole. Those receiving salaries from outside agencies were expected to turn them over to the moshav, receiving back from it the equivalent of the average income of the other members. Also, the salaried workers were each to be given a small plot of land as well as a house, this land to be cultivated by the employee's wife and children with his part-time aid.

Cultivation of this plot was to serve a dual purpose: (1) it was to provide most of the food for the nonfarming families, with this factor to be taken into account in the adjustment of their salaries to the average income of the farming families; and (2) it was to involve the nonfarming families in the same concerns as the farming families, and to demand of the nonfarming family as a whole the same pursuits and workday as those imposed on the farming family by the nature of intensive small-farming. As can be seen, the principle of equality underlay this plan, and it both presupposed and was designed to effect common identification with the moshav on the part of all its members.

An initial attempt was made to put this plan into practice. The founding members of Nahalal recruited the then small number of necessary professionals before the village was founded, in order to integrate them as fully as possible into the settler group. However, with the recruitment of addi-

[14] Cf. Assaf 1953:83ff.

tional employees, this plan could not be extended. In subsequently established moshvei ovdim, it was not even possible to introduce it.

At one level, the failure of the plan described above can be ascribed to the inability of ideology to effect the necessary common identification with the moshav among the majority of the employees hired. For the salaries of the employees, as fixed by the trade union regulations of the Histadrut, were generally higher than the incomes of the farming families for twenty years or so following the establishment of the first moshav ovdim.[15] The salaried employees in the moshvei ovdim, therefore, were being asked to accept voluntarily an income lower than union standards. Also, to have taken on the cultivation of a garden plot would have demanded of them additional expenditure from this income as well as their labor, since such subsidiary small holdings did not have priority in receiving shares from the scanty credit available to the moshav as a whole.[16]

Moreover, if their salaries were to be dependent on the average income of the farming families, the employees should have been given some voice in the way the farming families managed their farms, according to the moshav principles of equality. However, such an arrangement would oppose the fundamental principle of family autonomy in the running of the farm and would give nonagriculturalists a voice in agricultural affairs. It was unacceptable to the farming families.[17]

In order for the initial plan to have succeeded, the recruitment of the public employees would have had to have been even more selective than that of the farmers, for the employees were being asked to identify with the interests of the farmers even while remaining marginal to agriculture both as a way of life and as a source of income. Such selective recruitment did not and possibly could not take place. On the one hand, the moshav movement concen-

15 Talmon-Garbier 1952:447–48.
16 Cf. Talmon-Garbier 1952:346.
17 Assaf 1953:85.

trated on the recruitment of potential farmers for additional settlements. On the other hand, there seems to have been a scarcity of professionals prepared to see themselves as moshav members rather than as sympathizers with moshav ideals who would also consider employment elsewhere.[18]

By 1927, when the first constitution of the first moshav federation was promulgated, some village employees seem to have been full members of their moshavim with corresponding rights and obligations, except that they were not taxed for agricultural development. However, the majority of employees in most of the moshvei ovdim were not members. They were consulted in their respective spheres of competence by the village committees, but they did not serve on the committees or have a voice in village affairs.

Apparently, the salaried employees began to demand the right to participate in decision-making on common municipal issues not connected with agricultural matters. Concomitantly, some of the farming families felt that these employees served as bad examples in the villages and particularly for its younger generation, possibly disruptive of moshav ideology and community spirit.[19] For the employees enjoyed higher incomes, shorter working days, greater leisure, and greater savings; and their family members were not obliged to work. In 1945 the issue of the status of these employees was brought by the principal moshav federation to the Central Executive Committee of the Histadrut. The moshav federation demanded that the public employees renounce their memberships in the various professional trade unions which regulated their salaries and work conditions and become members of the moshav and moshav federation, according to a somewhat revised version of the original plan. The Central Executive Committee, which reached a decision only by 1948, granted most of the demands of the moshav federation except those concerning the salaries of the public employees. These were to be determined according to the

18 Talmon-Garbier 1952:346.
19 Cf. Assaf 1953:86ff.

income level of workers in corresponding professions in the cities.

Both the farmers and the employees were dissatisfied with the decision. After various attempts at revision, a tacit compromise was reached. The salaried employees were to become moshav members, and their affiliation to the nationwide professional unions was to be replaced by membership in a union within the moshav federation.[20] However, their salaries were to remain those prevailing in their professions in the country as a whole, and the provisions concerning cultivation of a garden plot were not, in fact, enforced.

In any case, the problem of a difference in the incomes of farming and nonfarming families within the villages has been largely reversed since then in the established moshvei ovdim. Agriculture as a vocation began to be profitable by the 1940s, and became extremely remunerative during the years of scarcity following the establishment of the state. The majority of the farming members of the veteran mosh-vei ovdim now enjoy an income and a standard of living that can be considered privileged in relation to those of salaried workers in the country as a whole.

PARADOXES OF THE MOSHAV OVDIM

From this review of the place of salaried employees in the moshav ovdim, there emerges one set of inconsistencies in the moshav ideological blueprint as apparent in its consequences for village organization: the ban on hired labor cannot be reconciled with the existence of centralized cooperative institutions. For the latter, as they developed, required the services of specialists in both mechanical and commercial fields, as well as a variety of less skilled workers. To staff these posts the moshav itself either had to hire

---

[20] Since both trade unions and members of the principal moshav movements were affiliated to the Histadrut, the creation of trade unions within the moshav federation had to be a Histadrut policy decision. The need for such a decision illustrates one of the many clashes of interest between different segments of the Histadrut's membership, clashes irreconcilable on the level of principle, i.e., a "paradox" of the Histadrut.

such workers, thereby permitting the corporate unit to engage in a practice forbidden to its members as exploitative, or else had to impose on its employees the arrangements envisaged for them in the original plan or a modification of it. But in the situation prevailing during the thirty years following the establishment of the first moshvei ovdim, these arrangements would have been truly exploitative, depriving the specialists of trade union conditions of employment.

To have assumed that this implicit economic exploitation would have been more than compensated for by the equal position as moshav members that the plan offered the specialists was, in my opinion, indicative of the naïveté of the pioneer planners and ideologists regarding the differences of interest inherent in the division of labor in the moshav ovdim community type. For the specialists could not have been given the initiative and autonomy in the management of their affairs which was prescribed for the agricultural members.

First of all, they could exercise no control over their income level without infringing on the autonomy of the farmers in the management of their individual holdings, as previously indicated. Secondly, and equally invidious in the light of the moshav self-governing provisions, they could not make decisions regarding the management of the enterprises they maintained or administered, as a farmer was free to do in managing his farm. The farmers were given some entrepreneurial freedom in regard to production, if not marketing. However, modern technical and commercial specialists, by the nature of their occupations, have no scope for entrepreneurship unless they are self-employed. The role assigned them, both in the original moshav plan and in the revised plan put through by the moshav federation, could not be equivalent to the role of the farmers, since there was no way in which they could work for themselves as well as for the community. As salaried employees with fixed working hours, they were in a position equivalent to that of fellow specialists employed in any enterprise observing trade union regulations. However, both the original plan and the revised proposal of the moshav federation would have deprived them of this position without being able to provide them with a position within the community equivalent to that of the farming members. Given the nature of their occupations and of moshav principles, such a position could not exist.

The compromise reached concerning the role of the salaried employees in the moshav may be regarded as a tacit recognition of a structural impasse which neither ideology nor idealism could break through. According to informants, the salaried workers who are moshav members do not participate in common agricultural decisions and tend to play a relatively passive role in public affairs, as might be expected.

However, the managerial autonomy of the farmers also began to be infringed upon with the agricultural and economic development of the moshvei ovdim. The increased scope and complexity of village affairs called for increasingly expert knowledge in agricultural and economic planning and in policy implementation. By the 1940s the committees had tended to take on planning functions, and the general assembly voted on, rather than initiated, policy. Decision-making also became increasingly concentrated in the committees, especially since their responsibility for channeling credit gave them a supervisory role over the operations of the less successful farmers. The need for expert knowledge and continuity in the maintenance and development of the moshav as an enterprise cut across the principle of rotation in office; and the same group of proven leaders tended to remain on the crucial committees or to be frequently returned to them.[21]

This seems to have been acceptable to the general membership, possibly because of the strenuous and time-consuming nature of the duties involved in holding office, and the recognition of the need for efficient leadership in economic affairs. Apparently many moshav members were content to concentrate their energies on farming, especially as they could thereby improve their economic position. According to sociological research carried out during 1945 and 1946

21 Talmon-Garbier 1952:350–51.

on the moshvei ovdim,[22] few of the most successful farmers were influential in public affairs. The leading office-holders were generally from the middle and upper-middle economic range.

Although this development of a managerial group, in op-position to moshav principles does not seem to have led to the resentment that the same phenomenon is reported to have occasioned in the kibbutzim,[23] possibly because far fewer areas of common life are involved, the fact of its occurrence constitutes one paradox or inconsistency in the moshav form of organization and points to still another. The latter incon-sistency has to do with the intrinsic limitations of the au-tonomous small holding for commercial agriculture. Small-scale mixed farming on a family holding is not an efficient form of agricultural production. Unit costs are high when the wage equivalent of labor in a developed economy is in-cluded, while productivity is low in comparison to that of modern large-scale, mechanized, commercial agricultural practices. These limitations are in part compensated for in the moshav ovdim through common agricultural and eco-nomic planning and development, common assets, and the centralization of economic affairs in the cooperative or-ganizations. However, the consequences of this centralization have been to reduce the area of the individual farmer's man-agerial autonomy.

In terms of agricultural economics, the moshav-type family farm originally envisaged can be considered more suited to the development of a peasant population, whose production is intended primarily for its own subsistence, with only the surplus being directed to the market, than for commercial agriculture. This is not inconsistent with original moshav ideology, but rather the contrary. One of the proclaimed aims of early Labor-Zionist land settlement, maintained for years in kibbutz as well as moshav ideology, was the development of an independent Jewish peasantry. Agriculture carried out in the homeland as a business enterprise was identified with

22 Talmon-Garbier 1952:353.
23 Cf. Schwartz 1957; Rosenfeld 1951; and Weinryb 1957.

estate owning and with exploitation. The alternative model for the pioneer settlers from Eastern Europe was the peasant. However, they did not wish to become like the peasants they had known. Rather, they associated the peasant with the values of rootedness in the soil and physical labor. Their image of themselves as peasants also included the high value on literacy and intellectual interests characteristic of their own background, the practice of modern agricultural methods, and the socialist-derived tenets of cooperative endeavor.

A standard of living that can support the desired educational and health facilities and the investment and upkeep necessary for modern agricultural facilities is not provided by subsistence farming and peasant economics, whatever the degree of cooperation practiced within a community. Nor were peasant economics ever practiced in the Labor-Zionist settlements. The kinds of economic and social relations that can be said to characterize peasants as a type [24] do not include either (1) the land and credit arrangements on which the Labor-Zionist villages have been based; or (2) their centralized marketing and purchasing, linked to the marketing and purchasing cooperative societies of an organization which is part of the larger society, and of which the villagers are high-ranking members who may influence policy.

Furthermore, given the large, authentic Arab peasantry in Palestine and the surrounding countries, the market price for such basic foodstuffs as grains, which the Labor-Zionist settlements originally produced for the market, could not provide sufficient returns for economic independence. The pioneer settlers accepted deprivation and a low standard of living as consistent with their ideology of austerity and self-denial in order to build up the national homeland. However, these conditions were envisaged as temporary. And for decades the development of their villages and their educational and health services were subsidized through the Zionist organizations.

[24] Cf. Redfield 1956; Belshaw 1965; Wolf 1966.

With increased immigration and the growth of the cities and of industry in the 1930s, agriculture was directed toward the production of such direct consumer products as eggs and poultry, dairy products, vegetables, and fruits; and the villages began to be economically viable.[25] World War II brought about a rise in agricultural prices which continued into the postwar period. After independence, the scarcity of food made commercial mixed farming an extremely profitable undertaking. However, agricultural planning on a national scale then began, as will be discussed in the next chapter. As long as the increased production of direct consumer products remained both necessary and profitable because of the mass immigration and the scarcity of food, the new moshvei ovdim and moshvei olim continued to be planned and organized to produce the various combinations of vegetables, dairy and poultry products, and citrus and deciduous fruits that had proven so successful in the established moshvei ovdim.

By 1953, the supply of these labor-intensive products was beginning to approach the needs of the country at the existing price and income levels. The agricultural planning of new villages focused on the production of sugar beets, peanuts, and industrial crops. For the cultivation of such crops on a low-cost basis, comparable to the prices prevailing in the world market, the autonomous family small holding is ill-suited.[26] In fact, the autonomous farming community, as a semiclosed economic unit, does not lend itself to agricultural and economic planning on a regional and national basis. Because of the influence of Labor-Zionist ideology and interest groups on national planning and policy-making, the existing Labor-Zionist-inspired community types remained the primary (although not the only) kinds of units through which the continued program of land settlement was implemented.

However, in the new development regions, planning and decision-making in regard to both the moshav family farm

25 Cf. Weinryb 1957:27.
26 Cf. Black 1958.

and the agricultural-economic development of the village as a whole have been carried out almost entirely by the settlement authorities, according to regional and national economic and agricultural considerations. Since many of the new immigrants, especially those from the rural and semi-rural regions of the North African and Asian countries, arrived in Israel understanding only peasant economics, the inconsistencies I have suggested in regard to the structure [27] of the moshav ovdim reached full circle in the moshvei olim. In the tradition of an ideology which included a glorification of the peasant way of life, these immigrants were asked to take on the role of scientific small-farmers in a quasi-socialist economy where individual initiative could operate only in the interstices of planned production and of marketing linked by fiat to the marketing societies of the Histadrut or to a competing network.

But by now settlers of veteran moshvei ovdim may permit themselves certain deviations from the principles of moshav ovdim ideology. In one classic moshav ovdim, a pillar of the principal moshav movement, chickens now may be sold to private merchants as well as marketed through the producers' cooperative to Tnuva. The hiring of seasonal labor by individual farmers also has begun. The paradoxes implicit in the moshav ovdim as a planned community type have begun to work themselves out through changes in the practices actually followed in the established villages.

A further inconsistency in moshav ovdim structure involves its consequences for future generations. Whereas a two-generation extended family has begun to supplant the nuclear family in the veteran moshvei ovdim, the individual farmstead cannot support more than two nuclear families. Therefore, only one, or at most two, offspring from each generation can expect to take possession of the farmstead. Nonetheless, in the process of moshav development, several growing children are an asset once the farm begins to be productive, given the ban on hired labor.

[27] Cf. Chap. I, note 38.

So far, the future of those offspring who cannot expect to inherit the farms has not presented a problem. The settlers of the veteran moshvei ovdim rarely had more than three children; and marriages within and between villages are reported to be common. The War of Independence and other hostilities also made inroads into the younger generations. Furthermore, the continued program of land colonization has made it possible for members of the second generation to hive off and form their own moshvei ovdim. In fact, a special voluntary unit within the Army establishes new settlements at strategic border points; and on demobilization following their period of conscription, members of this unit often remain as permanent settlers in these villages. Daughters of the moshvei ovdim often enter such service professions as teaching, nursing, and social work. Since there is a shortage of trained people in these fields, they are easily absorbed into the country's labor force, often working in their own or neighboring villages. With the expansion of the administrative networks dealing with land colonization and immigrant absorption, numerous posts have come into existence, from the level of village worker in the moshvei olim on up. Young people born into the moshvei ovdim are prized for these posts, although those who become village workers generally do so only for a limited period.

But in this, as in the other areas of moshav life indicated above, a temporary solution compensates for a paradox inherent in the community type, while its structural implications for future generations remain unresolved. The problem of farm inheritance is, of course, common to rural areas in many parts of the world. However, the usual resolution through urban migration would involve the moshav offspring in a repudiation of the orientations with which they are theoretically imbued. And in fact, the percentage of members of the second generation who remain moshav farmers is very high, reportedly over 90 percent.

And here, too, as in other areas of moshav life, structural dilemmas and inconsistencies of the moshav ovdim as a community type become acute in the moshvei olim. For immigrants from the countries of Asia and North Africa generally arrive with numerous children, and continue to bear more. Providing for these children may be extremely difficult during a village's initial years before the farms can sustain the families, when outside work is necessary.

But once the farms begin to develop, adolescent sons may be pulled out of school to work on the family holding, although they thereby lose the possibility of acquiring even a minimal Israeli formal education. Many adolescent and pre-adolescent daughters may never be allowed this possibility, both because their services are needed to help their mothers and because of culturally-rooted parental reluctance to allow them outside the household orbit once puberty begins. The daughters will be married off, usually through traditional arrangements within the ethnic group, as soon as Israeli law permits. Then, as adults, they face the prospect of a culturally marginal status within the new society. The full impact of limited education and of marginal status will fall on the sons, except insofar as this can be countered through the special educational programs of the Army. For as adults the majority of them will have to seek vocations outside the moshav, unless additional farmsteads can be found or made for them.

However, this problem is no greater in the moshvei olim than among immigrants settled in the cities, whose children also must contribute to the family's support. As such, it is one of many national problems brought about by the mass immigration, which moshav ovdim organization was not designed to absorb.

ORGANIZATION OF LAND SETTLEMENT AFTER
THE ESTABLISHMENT OF THE NEW STATE

The pre-statehood system of action through which Jewish land colonization was effected was based on consensus, for all its factionalism, and was highly egalitarian. Both the settlers of the Labor-Zionist villages and the officeholders in the quasi-governmental "national institutions" were committed to rebuilding the homeland and reclaiming the land. Also, the Eastern European provenience and socialization common to most of them made for shared understandings and sensibilities beyond and despite ideological agreement or disagreement. The national institutions channeled and coordinated resources, as already indicated, allocating them to the settlement groups according to a system of priorities influenced by Zionist politics. However, despite their initial dependence on the national institutions for land and funds, the pioneer settlers constituted the elite of the Zionist community. They were the equals of the officeholders in status and outranked most of them in prestige. In the making of policy their representatives participated as partners with the officeholders, negotiating and interacting on equal terms in a system whose rules were known and assented to by all.

After the establishment of the state, a new alignment of relations developed. The machinery of government had to be created even while the immigrants were pouring into the country. A gulf developed between those able to participate actively in the organization of the new state and/or to carry out tasks basic to the nation's survival and those unable to do so without direction. The latter included the overwhelming majority of the new immigrants, except for those survivors from Europe who previously had been members of Zionist organizations. In the case of most non-European immigrants, this gulf was maximized by their cultural distance from the values and goals of the pre-statehood Zionist population of Israel, and by their lack of shared understandings with the majority of this population, even apart from ideology.

With the recruitment of these new immigrants into the land settlement program and the resulting establishment of the moshvei olim, the relations between the land settlement authorities and the settlers of the new villages changed fundamentally. Except in the case of young Israelis and a continuing trickle of young immigrants in the classic tradition, these relations were no longer based on partnership and the assumption of equality. In the absence of shared goals, values, and understandings, the officeholders made the decisions and tried to impose their implementation. Authority replaced consensus in the maintenance of the system.

A concomitant and related change was the bureaucratization of the system, a process that was neither planned nor systematic. Rather, it emerged with the approximately tenfold expansion of the land colonization program between 1948 and 1955, its gradual coordination with the activities of the governmental agencies, and the necessary addition of new personnel to deal with the new and expanded tasks. The other public agencies followed a similar course of development. For the development of the machinery of public administration took place under conditions of emergency and improvisation and was highly politicized. The respective jurisdictions of the new governmental ministries—created from various departments and combinations of departments of the Community Government, of the far-from-dismantled Jewish Agency and the other national institutions, and of the many voluntary organizations that had participated in the development of Jewish Palestine—were worked out only gradually, in piecemeal fashion, during the 1950s. For about five years following the independence of Israel, administration throughout its public agencies was carried out by means of beleaguered improvisation.[1]

[1] Arien (1956), Bernstein (1957), and Samuel (1956) document such improvisation in the spheres of government and public administration, as does Rubner (1960) in regard to economic policy.

The bureaucratization of the land settlement program and the substitution of authority for consensus developed simultaneously. The former can be seen as a partial consequence of the establishment of the moshvei olim, since the incorporation of the new immigrants into the system brought about changes in its organization intended to compensate for their unpreparedness and/or demographic disqualifications for the classic role of pioneer. However, an equivalent expansion of land colonization and the need for its coordination with overall national development probably would have bureaucratized the system whatever the background of the settlers. Such a process of bureaucratization probably would have resulted, in any case, in centralization of authority in the administrative staff. Indeed, this has happened in regard to the kibbutzim, moshvei ovdim, and moshavim shitufiyim and middle-class settlements founded since the establishment of the state. The Land Settlement Department assumed much greater authority and responsibility in their planning and agricultural and economic development than had been the case with equivalent settlements during the pre-state decades. While decisions have been made with the settlers' participation, and the appearance and sentiments of equality have been preserved in the relations between Department and settlers, the Department has controlled policy as well as resources.

Thus, the changes just indicated in the land colonization system cannot be ascribed only to the introduction of unprepared and uncommitted new immigrants into it. Nonetheless, their recruitment accelerated the process of bureaucratization. And the substitution of administration by authority for administration by consensus has been explicit in the organization of the moshvei olim and the relations of the settlement authorities with the settlers. Although this substitution was neither envisaged nor desired when the moshvei olim were first created, the circumstances under which they were founded made it inevitable, as is discussed below.

NATIONAL POLICY CONSIDERATIONS
IN THE ORIGIN OF MOSHVEI OLIM

The expanded program of land colonization following the establishment of the state was embarked upon to meet three simultaneous and pressing national needs: immigrant absorption, food, and security. Of these exigencies, it was the rapid tempo of immigration, added to the background and provenience of the settlers, that gave rise to the moshvei olim.

In the period between the establishment of the state in May 1948 and August 1951, a total of 647,351 people entered the country,[2] doubling its Jewish population. During the first months of statehood, the Israeli-Arab war was still in progress, and immigrants consisted largely of young people able to take part in the state's defense. By September 1948 the mass immigration began, at first from the displaced persons' camps in Germany, Austria, and Italy. To immigrants from these sources were added, by the winter of 1948–49, others who had been captured and interned in Cyprus by the British during the last months of the mandate. During the same period there began the wholesale transfer of the Jewish community of Bulgaria, together with large segments of Yugoslavian Jewry and immigrants from Turkey. In 1949 the governments of Poland, Rumania, and Hungary placed restrictions on emigration, which the former two rescinded until early 1951 and 1952 respectively. By the time these restrictions were reimposed, 100,000 immigrants from Poland and 120,000 from Rumania already were in Israel.

In the summer of 1949 the "Magic Carpet" airlift of most of the Yemenite Jewish community began,[3] bringing more than 40,000 immigrants to Israel over the period of a year. From May 1950 through about September 1951, a mass transfer of Jews from Iraq took place, bringing 124,000 immigrants and in addition another 27,000 from Iran, includ-

2 Drabkin-Darin 1957:37.
3 Cf. Barer 1952.

ing the Kurdistan regions of these countries. In 1949 and in 1950 the major part of the Jewish population of Libya was brought to Israel. The period of mass immigration ended in October 1951, but the flow of immigrants from Morocco, and to a lesser extent from Tunisia and Algeria, which had begun with Israel's independence, continued and swelled as these countries approached independence.

Practically all this immigration has been organized and financed by the Jewish Agency, with the help of other Jewish organizations such as the American Joint Distribution Committee. Israel's policy toward immigration, set forth first in its Declaration of Independence and later in a parliamentary Law of Return, is to allow and encourage the immigration of all Jews. Until the end of 1951 a policy of unrestricted immigration was followed, whereby the Jewish Agency financed the immigrants' transportation to Israel and provided at least minimally for their needs during the first stage of absorption. However, by 1952 certain principles of selection were introduced, limiting the immigration of the aged and infirm unless their upkeep in Israel could be assured. These limitations do not apply to "rescue" immigration of Jews from areas where their lives and/or livelihoods are threatened, or to the immigration of those able to pay their own fare and be responsible for their maintenance in the country.

Provisions for receiving the mass influx passed through several phases. During 1948, temporary quarters for the newcomers were arranged, first in immigrant reception homes and then in former British Army camps. As these facilities became swamped, additional reception camps were hastily constructed. In these camps the newcomers received food, usually prepared in communal kitchens and served in communal dining rooms, and some kind of shelter, usually tents. Temporary kindergartens and schools were also set up, as were medical examination centers and dispensaries. During 1948 three-fourths of the immigrants remained no longer than six weeks in such camps. Employment opportunities existed, and the newcomers could be relocated in abandoned

Arab housing in the cities and towns. However, by the end of 1948 a population of 28,000 was to be found in immigrant reception camps; by the end of February 1949 there were 40,000 immigrants in these camps, and their number increased to 54,000 by May. With the construction of additional camps for the immigrants from Yemen, the population in reception camps reached 85,000 by September 1949, and 92,500 by October.[4]

By the end of 1949 another type of interim arrangement was instituted to eliminate the expense of feeding the immigrants and, it was hoped, to counter the demoralizing effects of enforced idleness and dependence on the absorption authorities. From January 1950 on, immigrant transit camps (*ma'abarot*) were built, replacing the immigrant reception camps except in the preliminary processing of newcomers. Food was not provided in the transit camps; instead funds (including those that would have gone for food) were allocated to public works, which would then provide employment for the newcomers while developing the country.

Such transit camps were constructed throughout Israel, generally near long-established smaller cities or urbanized moshavot and in designated development areas. Huts of canvas, tin, or wood were erected as rapidly and cheaply as possible; and the newcomers were transferred to these transit camps from the reception camps. They paid a nominal rent but no taxes; and they received health, education, and welfare services insofar as these could be made available. Labor Exchanges, then still under the Histadrut, were set up to channel work opportunities. By December 1951, after the peak of the mass immigration, a total of 179,140 new immigrants were to be found in such transit camps, out of the 256,606 in all kinds of temporary quarters.[5]

Food resources were also stretched very thin. During the mandate period, the food supply of the Jewish population had included Arab-grown produce as well as imports from neighboring countries. After independence and the war, food

---

4 Drabkin-Darin 1957:44.
5 Drabkin-Darin 1957:48.

stocks in the country were very low, and practically all the essential foodstuffs had to be imported to some degree. In 1949 the government instituted price control and the rationing of almost all foods except bread, subsidizing essential foods. The "period of austerity," austere even in Israeli terms, lasted until 1952. Then, with a change in government policy [6] and the rise in the local production of foodstuffs, rationing was gradually removed.

Not only housing and food but practically every resource of the country, including its supply of trained manpower and the existing organizational system, was vastly insufficient to cope with the demands created by the influx of immigrants. These demands loomed all the larger given the backgrounds of the immigrants and the aspirations and standards of the absorbing community. Many of the immigrants from Europe needed special care after their experiences in concentration camps, etc., and the aged, ill, and orphaned constituted special social aid categories. And except for those from Iraq, immigrants from the non-European countries included few people with the education, training, or skills needed in Israel. Indeed, the immigrants from such lands as Turkey and the countries of French North Africa were largely drawn from the poorest and least-Westernized segments of the population; and until the policy of selective immigration, they tended to include many of the social cases from the Jewish communities of these countries.

One may therefore wonder why mass immigration was not only permitted but even actively encouraged through continual recruitment abroad. In addition to ideological reasons for this policy, there were considerations of security and of politics. For the circumstances leading to the Arab invasion of Israel when statehood was declared, the flight during the war of most of the Arab population of the territory that became Israel, and the resulting problem of the Arab refugees had put Israel in a precarious position as far as its

---

[6] Rubner (1960:53–66) discusses governmental rationing and price control policies in relation to the politics of Israel and the interests of pressure groups, particularly those affiliated to Mapai.

security was concerned, as well as leaving it politically vulnerable to reversals of policy by the United Nations. Its neighbors refused to make peace and vowed its destruction. Arab refugee camps, from which infiltrators could be recruited and trained in commando tactics, were established around its borders. A rapid increase in its own population was necessary for its survival as well as for development and for countering the possibility of an imposed return of hostile Arab refugees.[7] Whereas earlier Zionist policy had stressed recruitment of the elite of the Jewish communities abroad, now everyone who wanted to come was to be accepted.

Domestic politics and the politics of the Israeli government's relations with the Zionist system of action, specifically with American Jewry, have also been considered factors in the immediate promulgation, on independence, of the policy of unlimited mass immigration.[8] For the ultra-nationalist dissident armed groups within Israel, the Irgun Zvai Leumi associated with the Revisionist Movement, and the Stern Gang or Fighters for Freedom of Israel, might otherwise have continued to bring in immigrants illegally, as they did during the mandate period. Such a possibility could have shaken the authority of the new government, whatever its response. Indeed, Ben-Gurion's decision to fire on the Altalena, the ship bringing arms to the Irgun in defiance of the government's orders, provoked much dismay in Israel and in Zionist circles;[9] and the government did not conclusively disband the dissident armed forces until after the assassination of Count Bernadotte, some three months after the showdown over the Altalena.

As for the state's relations with the Zionist system of action, the policy of unlimited mass immigration contributed

[7] Approximately 45,000 Arab refugees had been readmitted to Israel by 1961 to make possible the reuniting of families.

[8] Samuel 1956:20–21.

[9] Hecht (1954:597–625) discusses the Altalena and the Irgun from the perspective of an American Revisionist, while Ben Gurion's justification of his action to the Israeli Parliament stresses the danger to the state of an armed movement defying the authority of its government (cf. Ben-Gurion 1954:251–60).

to Israel's decision-making sovereignty despite economic dependence on contributions of American Jewry. In the words of Samuel:

If immigration were to be limited by the immediate economic capacity of Israel to absorb them [i.e., the new immigrants] (as under the Mandate between 1922 and 1938), the Americans could tell Mr. Ben-Gurion how much capital was available and how many Jews he could admit. For the economic absorptive capacity of Israel depends ultimately on the capital available for the development of Israel. By freeing immigration from all dependence on Israel's economic absorptive capacity, Mr. Ben-Gurion was in a position to tell American Jewry how many Jews had in fact arrived and to present America with the bill.[10]

The politics of the Eastern European and Arab countries, as these affected their Jewish populations, also entered into the continued encouragement of mass immigration and the unpredictability of the flow of immigrants. For permission given Jews to emigrate could be rescinded at any time, and both the prospective immigrants and the Jewish Agency have had to take advantage of opportunities when they have arisen. While it was recognized that much hardship might result from the mass immigration, this did not weigh heavily as a consideration with the Israeli policy-makers. The matter-of-fact acceptance and transcendence of hardship were part of their ideology and history. The lessons of the European extermination had been well learned, perhaps over-learned, if this be possible; material hardship in Israel was deemed preferable to the possibility of persecution abroad.

Thus, the mass immigration from Iraq was inspired, at least in part, by the promulgation of a terminal date beyond which Jews could not leave the country. The immigration from French North Africa occurred partly in anticipation of the independence of these countries and the prohibition of Jewish emigration to Israel. Even after the period of mass immigration, the rational pacing of immigration in accord

10 Samuel 1956:22.

with the country's current capacity to offer newcomers employment opportunities, housing, and so on, would not have been possible. Such events as the Hungarian Uprising, Poland's decision in 1957 to let Jews again emigrate, and a similar decision by Rumania (later rescinded) have made for continued unpredictability in flow of immigrants.

Also unpredictable in terms of long-term planning has been the flow of funds for Israel's sustenance and development. For while contributions of world, and especially United States, Jewry have been maintained over the years, a severe economic recession could have curtailed them at any time.

Furthermore, developments on the international scene and in the Cold War could at any time affect Israel. The Soviet Union's wooing of the Arab states, in addition to its historical anti-Zionism, has sharpened the threat to Israel's survival presented by the enmity of its neighbors. At what point Soviet "volunteers" might be found manning the Soviet armaments vouchsafed the Arab countries, and how the Western nations might then respond, remained open questions in the Israeli public consciousness well after the Sinai campaign.

An awareness of the many factors affecting Israeli survival and development which were beyond their control fed the attitude of determined improvisation that Israeli policy-makers and administrators brought to the areas in which they could take action. This was expressed in their encouragement and reception of the mass immigration, and characterized the post-statehood expansion of land settlement.

In this expansion, kibbutzim peopled by young Israelis and young immigrants in the classic tradition were located at the most crucial frontier sites, to the extent that this was possible. By 1951, settlements at such key security points also began to be founded by Nahal, the special army unit established for this purpose, and its recruits could choose to remain as permanent village settlers after they were demobilized. Ideally, the moshvei olim have been situated around and somewhat behind the villages positioned to stand guard on Israel's borders. In fact, many of the immigrant settlements were also placed very close to the frontiers, and considerations of national security have been no small factor in the choice of village sites, particularly during 1949 and 1950.

The first moshvei olim were situated on or near the sites of abandoned Arab villages. Indeed, the inception of the moshav olim as a settlement type is supposed to have occurred a few months after Israel's statehood, when the head of the Jewish Agency's Land Settlement Department (who, as of 1952, simultaneously served as minister of finance) [11] and the Agency's director were driving by such sites and were struck by the possibility of resettling them by drawing on the new immigrants then flooding the reception camps. They brought the proposal to the Agricultural Center of the Histadrut for consideration by the various settlement movements.

According to a spokesman of the leading moshav movement,[12] the proposal was received unfavorably by the kibbutz federations, whose leaders maintained that the immigrants lacked the ideological background and training for rural life and physical labor.[13] They argued for retaining the classic pattern of land settlement: recruitment among young people and the establishment of youth groups which, after proper training, would be able to found settlements in the customary fashion. However, the principal moshav federation, Tnuat Hamoshavim, supported the proposal and began to implement it. Representatives of Tnuat Hamoshavim and those of the other moshav federations began to organize nuclei of potential settlers from among the Polish, Rumanian, Bulgarian, and Hungarian immigrants then in the reception camps.

A somewhat different perspective on how the first moshvei olim came into being was provided in 1957 by various members of the Land Settlement Department staff. In the words

[11] He became Israel's second minister of finance in 1952, and has become the third person to hold the office of prime minister of Israel.

[12] Now deceased, he was a veteran moshav settler, served as deputy minister of education, and, at one time, was considered to be in line for the post of minister of agriculture.

[13] Cf. Assaf 1953:172–74.

of one middle-level official: "The kibbutz needs real idealists. We knew that the immigrants weren't such idealists. Which is the least idealistic village type? The moshav." Indicative of the ideological climate of the immediate post-statehood years was the automatic exclusion of community types other than those inspired by Labor-Zionism as possible bases for land settlement on national land and through public financing.

During the most intensive years of land settlement, the central coastal plain, stretching from Hadera in the north to Rehovot in the south, was the first region to be extensively covered by villages. Immigrant villages also were founded on previously uninhabited land in the hills of the Jerusalem Corridor, in the northern part of the country, and then in the south, the region extending to Beersheba known as the northern Negev.

The following table lists (1) the total number of villages based on public financing [14] founded yearly between May 15, 1948, the date of Israel's independence, and the end of 1957; (2) the number which were founded as moshavim; (3) the number of settlements in existence as farming villages by the end of 1957; and (4) the number of moshavim in existence by the end of 1957. Annual figures are given according to the Hebrew year, which begins in September or October.

This table, constituted from statistics issued in January 1958 by the Land Settlement Department of the Jewish Agency,[15] illustrates the changing tempo of land settlement during the first post-statehood decade and the increasing ascendancy of the moshav over the kibbutz as the primary community type utilized for implementing the expanded land settlement program. Discrepancies between columns one and three and columns two and four involve vicissitudes in the histories of many of the villages founded.

These vicissitudes can be grouped into several categories,

[14] During this total period, fifteen middle-class moshavim were established.
[15] Jewish Agency for Israel, Land Settlement Department, Statistics Section 1958:35–39.

	Total No. of Villages	No. of Moshavim	Total No. by end of 1957	No. of Moshavim by end of 1957
May 15, 1948– a Oct. 3, 1948	25	4	23	4
Oct. 4, 1948– b Sept. 23, 1949	102	42	102	58
Sept. 24, 1949– c Sept. 11, 1950	122	84	118	101
Sept. 12, 1950– Sept. 30, 1951	32	21	31	24
Oct. 1, 1951– Sept. 19, 1952	15	11	15	12
Sept. 20, 1952– Sept. 9, 1953	46	37	42	38
Sept. 10, 1953– Sept. 27, 1954	10	7	10	7
Sept. 28, 1954– Sept. 16, 1955	16	10	16	11
Sept. 19, 1955– Sept. 5, 1956	20	11	18	11
Sept. 1956– Sept. 1957	6	6	6	6

a During this period 20 kibbutzim and 1 moshav shitufi were founded, but the 23 villages in existence by the end of 1957 included 16 kibbutzim and 3 moshavim shitufiyim.
b During this period 42 kibbutzim and 4 moshavim shitufiyim were founded, but the 102 villages in existence by the end of 1957 included 39 kibbutzim and 5 moshavim shitufiyim.
c During this period 13 kibbutzim and 5 moshavim shitufiyim were founded, but the 118 villages in existence by the end of 1957 included 11 kibbutzim and 6 moshavim shitufiyim, 3 of which had not been founded as moshavim shitufiyim.

according to the factors responsible for them. Changes in the community type of a village comprise one such category. These changes, which also occurred during the mandate period, could result from the decision of a village's founders to change the organization of their village from one community type to another. Although such changes during the period under review were most common in villages founded as kibbutzim which became moshavim shitufiyim, the reverse also occurred. Villages founded as moshvei ovdim also became moshavim shitufiyim, and vice versa. Such changes could also occur when villages abandoned by their founders were repopulated by another body of settlers.

A distinctive class of vicissitudes involves villages founded by the special army unit, Nahal. For no decision about community type usually is made when such settlements are initiated, and the founders usually live communally for the first few years. When the community type is decided, by members of the founding nucleus and/or by new recruits to the village, this adds to the total number of settlements of that type in existence in a given year. Of the some thirteen settlements founded by Nahal between 1951 and 1957, the majority of those which remained farming villages became kibbutzim.

The decrease in total number of villages reflected in column three as compared to column one mainly involves, although it is not confined to, settlements founded as kibbutzim in the classic tradition and those initiated by Nahal. For of the former, at least five founded during the period under review were no longer in existence by the end of 1957. This was also true of several villages founded as moshavim, possibly as moshvei ovdim rather than as moshvei olim. Village sites and fixed assets might be put to different use, most commonly becoming agricultural boarding and/or day schools for youth; and some sites were resettled as moshvei olim. Of the settlements founded by Nahal, at least three did not develop into farming villages.

The vicissitudes contributing the largest number of moshavim to the increase indicated in column four of the table, as compared to column two, entailed a shift in administrative jurisdiction over one group of immigrant villages. During the period of improvisation following Israel's independence, not all of the expanded program of land settlement drawing on new immigrants was carried out through the system of action involving the Land Settlement Department of the Jewish Agency. The Jewish National Fund, which had taken the initiative in founding the ma'abarot,[16] also initiated a

16 Cf. Bein 1952:527.

type of settlement termed the *kfar ha'avoda* (work village). Situated in mountainous regions, mainly in Galilee and the Judean Hills, these villages lacked the basic ecological resources for development into viable agricultural settlements under existing conditions. Agricultural potential was subordinate to security and other considerations in their founding and location; and village economy was based primarily on afforestation and land reclamation projects, on which the settlers were employed. Planning for the future of these villages, insofar as the consideration given to it can be termed planning, envisaged the creation of auxiliary farms as land was made arable. Ultimately, it was thought, these plots of arable land would expand sufficiently to provide the settlements with a viable agricultural base.[17]

Since afforestation and land reclamation were traditional activities of the Jewish National Fund, the policies it followed in founding immigrant villages involved elements of continuity with its role in the pre-statehood system of action, as well as improvisation and a stake in expanding its sphere of action.[18] However, lacking institutionalized links to the village federations and other resources for the administration and development of immigrant villages, the Jewish National Fund could not sustain this new role for more than a few years. Of the twenty-six work villages founded, twenty of them during the years 1949–52, some thirteen passed over into the jurisdiction of the Land Settlement Department of the Jewish Agency in 1956. Most of the others did not develop, even nominally, into farming villages.[19]

[17] Cf. Bein 1952:527–28.

[18] The role and sphere of action to be left to the Jewish National Fund became an open public issue by the mid-1950s, particularly since the state, after independence, had title to 76.5 percent of Israel's land, much of it in the Negev and nonarable under current conditions, whereas the Jewish National Fund held title to 18 percent (cf. Rubner 1960:101). In 1958 a National Land Company was formed to take title to both state and Jewish National Fund land. The Jewish National Fund has continued to engage in soil reclamation and afforestation work in Israel and to carry out its educational and fund-raising activities both in Israel and the Diaspora.

[19] For example, three *kfrei avoda* (pl. of kfar avoda) in the Judean Hills passed over into the jurisdiction of the Jerusalem municipality.

Thus, elements both of improvisation and of continuity with pre-statehood patterns of action marked the program of rural settlement of new immigrants from its inception. This combination of continuity and improvisation extended to the initial provisions for moshav olim development and immigrant adaptation to the role of settler. Although a guide or instructor (*madrikh,* pl. *madrikhim*) accompanied the immigrants to their village sites from the time the first moshvei olim were founded, his own role was undefined and its scope was pervasive: he was to concern himself with everything related to village establishment and the settlers' adaptation. Recruited, ideally from one of the veteran moshvei ovdim, by the moshav federation which had recruited the settlers and to which their village was affiliated, he was considered qualified for whatever his role might demand by virtue of his background.

His guidance was soon supplemented in many of the villages by that of an instructress (*madrikha*), who was supposed to help the women in their adaptation to the demands of moshav life. In addition, the moshvei olim, like the moshvei ovdim, were provided with teachers, insofar as they were obtainable, recruited and employed until 1953 by the Labor Trend school system of the Histadrut or the Religious Trend school system. The moshav olim was also supplied with a nurse, if one were available, recruited and employed by Kupat Holim, the Sick Fund of the Histadrut. The Army provided a military instructor to give the men basic military instruction and organize and supervise nightly guard duty. The moshav was also to employ a bookkeeper and a storekeeper.

The first moshvei olim, therefore, were organized as moshvei ovdim with the additional provision of an instructor, and if possible an instructress, to compensate for deficiencies in the knowledge and skills of the immigrant settlers. Possible problems of role-socialization beyond the learning of skills were not given consideration, nor were the instructor and instructress perceived as needing any kind of training.

This disregard of the magnitude of the role-socialization

demanded of the new settlers and of the magnitude of the role-innovation demanded of the people employed as instructors can be regarded as a manifestation of what I have previously termed the "ethos" or value system of Labor-Zionism. I will now attempt a further delineation of this ethos and of its expressions both in behavior and in the organization of relations widely prevalent in the nascent society in which the moshvei olim emerged and of which they have been a part.

ETHOS, POLITICS, AND ADMINISTRATION

While Labor-Zionism developed as a secular ideology with secular ends, it was presented and adhered to with religious fervor by its followers and was permeated with a religious redemptory character. For a total transformation of identity —of conscious values and behavior associated with these values—was demanded of the adherent. This transformation was seen both as instrumental and as an end in itself. The phrases "redemption of the homeland" and "redemption of the Jewish people," recurrent in ideological and programmatic statements, had the secular denotations of reclamation of the land and its restoration to fertility and of recreation of a Jewish society and nation in Palestine. But in Labor-Zionist ideology these goals also involved a nonsecular and quasi-religious identification of the redemption of land and of people, by and through each other. For the pioneer, by the labor of his hands for the homeland, also redeemed himself from the attributes of Diaspora Jewry.

Socialist ideology made possible the assimilation of a redemptory ethos to secular goals. For the Jewish occupational distribution in the Diaspora, associated with lack of a homeland, was perceived and felt as "parasitic." Associated with this parasitism, i.e., with the lack of a Jewish peasantry and working class as the productive base of the occupational "pyramid" of a "normal" society, were the material and social aspirations of Diaspora Jewry, and the values and behavior decried and despised as "bourgeois." These were considered not only to result from but to reinforce anti-

Semitism. Self-redemption and the redemption of the Jews as a people could only be achieved through immigration to Palestine and commitment to the arduous and self-abnegating role of the pioneer. The transformation of identity demanded by Labor-Zionism included acceptance and enactment of the values of the revolutionary movements current in late-nineteenth and early-twentieth-century Europe: Spartan simplicity as a means of identification with the working class, full sexual equality, repudiation of the "bourgeois family," etc., to which the Marxist kibbutz federation added a militant opposition to religion.

In analyses oriented to culture in relation to psychological processes, this ideology has been associated with rebellion against the father and his authority, as well as against the conditions of shtetl life into which so many of the Labor-Zionists had been born.[20] I suggest that this association can be extended to the many guilt-eliciting aspects of child-socialization in the shtetl and, indeed, of many of the shtetl's means of social control.[21] For Labor-Zionist ideology encouraged and reinforced adolescent rebellion, but both its verbal rhetoric and the rhetoric of action employed by the youth movements also utilized guilt-producing appeals to stimulate motivation and maintain adherence to values. There was also a transfer of the beleaguered intensity of the shtetl way of life and of its religious commitment in the intensity of the ideological commitment of Labor-Zionist adherents. The members of the youth movements who went to Palestine had the inner rewards of the elect in any redemptory movement, the companionship of their fellows, and freedom from the constraints of traditional shtetl or middle-class European Jewish culture to strengthen them against hardships and loneliness.

While the ideology and ethos just summarized reached their most total and revolutionary expression in the com-

[20] Diamond (1957) and Spiro (1956:38–42) discuss this in relation to the kibbutzim, and Kaufman (1949) notes the pervasiveness of anti-Semitic stereotypes in statements of Zionist ideology, which can be related to repudiation of the shtetl.
[21] Cf. Zborowski and Herzog 1952:296–306, 191–213; Joffe 1949.

munal settlement movements, particularly that of the Marxist kibbutz federation, less extreme versions of them pervaded much of Jewish Palestine by the 1930s and persisted past Israel's independence. The agricultural pioneers set the tone for the workers in the cities; and the urban youth movements and adult educational and social programs sponsored by the Histadrut propagated Labor-Zionist pioneer values throughout its membership. Even religious Zionist youth adopted those aspects not in conflict with religious law, easily synthesizing secular redemption and a religious orientation.

Many themes in the Labor-Zionist ideology and the transformation of identity it demands are clearly adapted to young people, drawing upon and feeding adolescent rebellion and the proclivity toward idealism with which it may be associated. And the majority of the pioneer immigrants have been young. In fact, it may be doubted whether older people, settled in their occupations and engaged in rearing their children, could be mobilized by such an ideology. Thus, the post-state opposition of the kibbutz movements to the recruitment of settlers from among the new immigrants in the transit camps and their stress on working with the youth may have expressed their awareness and experience that adults could not easily be resocialized to identify with and accept kibbutz ideology and institutions. However, when a Labor-Zionist orientation has once been acquired, as among the pre-state pioneers in all types of settlements and even in the cities, its values have usually been durable.[22]

The redemptory ethos of Labor-Zionism was transmitted to successive generations of immigrants from Eastern Europe during the mandate period.[23] But the pioneer immigrants did not wish to transmit it to their children and did not do so. For while they themselves were the "generation of the desert," they considered their children to be truly the elect,

[22] Cf. Spiro (1957:217–21) and Talmon (1961) on problems of aging in the kibbutzim. The behavior of veteran Labor-Zionists is described in this study also (e.g., Chap. VIII). It was in the cities that modifications of the Labor-Zionist ethos, particularly of its disdain for material possessions, developed during the 1950s among veteran Labor-Zionists, and much justification accompanied the acquisition of creature comforts.

[23] Cf. pp. 83ff.

a generation born and raised in the homeland, to be brought up free of the internal and external plagues of Diaspora life. And, in fact, the children of the pioneers are generally assured and offhand in manner and casually aggressive, with few overt expressions of emotional intensity.[24] Self- and peer-group reliance, deliberate stoicism, and matter-of-factness were values they commonly accepted and expressed in their behavior during the 1950s, as was the orientation toward youth. However, the deliberate blunting of sensibilities, self-inflicted in the case of their elders and reinforced by the hardships of pioneer life, seemed most evident during that period in the young people's outgroup perceptions and relations.[25]

[24] It would take methods developed in the study of group interaction, applied to some representative sample of the native Israeli descendents of the pioneer aliyot, to validate this statement; and the terms "assured," "offhand," "casual," "aggressive," and "emotional intensity" would all have to be defined in a way permitting reliability and replicability of observations and contrast to other definable qualities. Nevertheless, I do not think that many of those familiar with native Israelis during Israel's first decade would take issue with my statement, although they might use different language in describing *sabra* behavior and/or make differentiations that I do not. This description is offered as a generalization about style of interaction and has no implications as to psychodynamics. I felt that the range of personality variation was as great among the sabras as among any population segment of a large society.

[25] No one I encountered among the young adult sabras working in land settlement or in other public sectors and agencies expressed overt hostility toward immigrants from the Oriental lands in the terms described by Spiro (1957:101–2) as being used by the kibbutz adolescents he studied. However, I observed one group of kibbutz adolescents showing great discomfort at a synagogue blessing party in a moshav olim settled by immigrants from the Atlas Mountains, and these adolescents refused to eat the food offered them. They were on a visit to the moshav to teach Israeli songs and dances to the immigrant youth.

In my experience, as in Spiro's account, the general blunting of sensibilities in outgroup perceptions could result in a negative evaluation of immigrants of European background or, indeed, of anyone perceived as a different and inferior kind of person. Thus, even a young sabra psychologist, married and the mother of an infant child, who lived in a Jerusalem neighborhood of new houses (*shikun*), commented negatively on a neighboring older couple, post-statehood immigrants from Europe who had married after concentration camp experience and also had very young children: "They're different from us; they are old; we have nothing to say to them." The "we" referred not just to herself and her husband but to the other young Israeli couples, most of them also with young children, in the neighborhood. I found that sensibility in regard to the arts among adult sabras then in their twenties, and sensitivity toward each others' feelings, might be combined with great callousness toward the feelings of those perceived as different, including obviously deviant peers.

To their tasks as instructors in the moshvei olim, veteran settlers and their grown children brought the assumptions and values of their background. While ideology had become routinized in the veteran villages, apart from crises, and politicized in the country as a whole, it was the principal resource originally employed in the attempt to motivate the immigrants to accept and live by the Labor-Zionist ethos. The initial provisions for immigrant reception expressed the assumption that an initial period of hardship was to be expected, accepted, and transcended. If such privation was endured in the spirit of abnegation and devotion implicit in the Labor-Zionist self-redemptory ethos, role-socialization would be the result.[26] Even when the new immigrants re-

---

[26] The transformation of identity demanded by the Labor-Zionist ethos persisted during most of Israel's first decade, in somewhat diffused form, as a pervasive demand not only on immigrants from the non-European countries, but on all newcomers who sought to find work and take part in the development of the new society. Thus, professionally trained young people from the Americas, Western Europe, and South Africa supplemented the young immigrants from these lands recruited as adolescents by the pioneer youth movements and oriented to land settlement, primarily to founding new kibbutzim. A significant proportion of these young professionals, including some who had joined and then left kibbutzim, found anything but the professional norms to which they had been trained obtaining in their respective spheres of competence in the public agencies of Israel, particularly during its first half-decade, and little interest in or sympathy for such norms (see above, pp. 137–38).

For example, in the field of social welfare, funds for welfare allowances were provided by both the Ministry of Social Welfare and the local authorities to which the welfare offices were attached, with the Ministry allotting funds for welfare cases among new immigrants. However, such funds were channeled through the local authorities, and a district council head could delay transmitting part of such funds, including those designated for the social worker's salary, in order to use them for other immediate district expenses. The remaining funds could then be given to the social worker to allocate as she saw fit. Social workers then could face the interim choice between paying themselves in full or extending aid to needy families.

In most fields, administrative practices were similarly disorganized by modern Western standards during this period. Thus highly trained professionals had to carry out a range of clerical and manual tasks necessary to their work if these tasks were to get done within any reasonable period of time. More important, policy decisions within their accustomed sphere of competence might be made at a much higher level, often without their being consulted or even informed either of the fact that the issue was under review or of reasons for the decision made. Also, superiors without recent professional training or without any qualification beyond practical experience, might judge their performance according to their success at improvisation, regardless of criteria of professional effectiveness and efficiency. Those attempting to effect a definition or redefinition of their

mained unmobilized by appeals to ideology, such appeals continued to pervade the educational campaigns carried out not only in the moshvei olim but in the country at large, and they were part of the rhetoric employed by officeholders at all levels and by volunteers in the agencies and programs concerned with immigrant absorption.

Statements of ideology often took the form of a recapitula-

roles and tasks rarely met with a positive response from their supervisors and agency administrators, particularly in regard to professions whose legitimacy had not been established prior to Israel's statehood or even, in the case of agencies whose top administrators were veteran Labor-Zionists, had not been recognized in Eastern European shtetl culture. "You have been given a chance, and now go prove yourself," or "It's good for you," were not infrequent retorts by such administrators to protests by young professionals from the Western countries about unclear or inconsistent delegation of authority and responsibility, or lack of facilities for even minimally efficient utilization of professional skills. And protests, based on professional knowledge, concerning planning and policy decisions and the allocation of resources to implement them could be totally ignored. Personal acceptance, achieved through a period of self-abnegating hard work, whether or not professionally efficient and effective, together with other visible behavior expressing Labor-Zionist values and adaptation to Israeli norms provided the surest road by which young professionals from the Western countries, in the absence of political and/or personal connections, might finally gain an attentive hearing for professionally based suggestions involving changes in agency practices. Even in agencies where supervisory and/or middle-range personnel also had a modern professional orientation, politicization at the policy-making levels, reviewed above in the next few pages, impeded professionalization of many fields and services, unless special conditions could be created by a high-ranking expert adviser recruited from abroad, who could influence the flow of aid from the international agencies or the flow of contributions from a Zionist voluntary organization in the Diaspora.

The transformation of identity demanded by the Labor-Zionist ethos of all immigrants and pervasive in Israel during much of the first post-statehood decade may give perspective to the positing of "readiness to change" as a key variable for successful immigrant absorption by a leading Israeli sociologist in the early 1950s (Eisenstadt 1955:113–24, 143–67). For immigration policies of some other states, particularly in Latin America, historically have expressed their interest in attracting people with entrepreneurial and/or management skills, who, it was hoped, would help change the country. Indeed, Brazil is one of the countries that has attracted and admitted refugees from Europe and Egypt who could not adapt to Israel. By the beginning of the 1960s Israeli sociologists had added "cultural background" and "cultural similarity . . ." determining "whether the immigrant has actual knowledge of the most important elements of Israeli culture and/or whether he has intellectual attitudes and learning habits enabling him to acquire this knowledge efficiently" (Weintraub and Lissak 1964a:100) to "predisposition to change" as variables in immigrants' successful integration into Israeli society, at least their absorption into the moshavim. "Cultural background" began to receive official recognition in Israel as a factor to be taken into consideration in policies and actions directed toward the immigrants after about 1955, as is reviewed in Chap. VI.

tion of the ideals, sufferings, and achievements of the pioneer aliyot, and a comparison of the latter's hardships with the facilities that Israeli public agencies gave the new immigrants. Thus, in answer to complaints and protests over conditions in the moshvei olim or over the difficulty of sustained manual labor, as compared to conditions in their countries of origin and to their previous occupations, settlers would be told—by village instructors and service personnel, by the field staff and administrators of the Land Settlement Department, by representatives of the moshav federations, by the staffs of the various ministries, national institutions, and voluntary organizations who visited the villages, and even by members of the absorbing population whom they encountered outside the villages—of the fortitude and accomplishments of the pre-state pioneers. They, the new immigrants, such accounts would conclude, also had to learn the dignity of labor in their own country and rid themselves of the habits of the Diaspora, and they had the advantage of all the organizations that "worry for their welfare." The Jewish Agency pays their fare to Israel, gives them a dwelling on their arrival, provides them with organized opportunities for employment until they learn to be farmers. They have teachers, a nurse and doctor, the village workers to teach them if only they will learn, and yet they complain and protest. . . .

Repeated in many contexts, in greater or lesser detail, these utterances soon developed an almost ritual quality. Easily learned by the immigrants themselves, the recounting of past history and sufferings took on the quality of a performance, serving both settlement agents and settlers as a charter in pressing for or withholding compliance to some demand.[27]

27 Such "performances" occurred in all the contexts in which new immigrants interacted with officeholders of the national and voluntary organizations. I witnessed them in transit camps, offices of welfare agencies, government bureaucracies, etc., as well as in moshvei olim and Land Settlement Department and moshav federation offices. They also could occur in casual conversations between new immigrants and veteran members of the absorbing society as the latter responded to some complaint of the former concerning life in Israel.

The ideology and redemptory ethos of Labor-Zionism were accompanied by a disdain for professionalism,[28] apart from specific vocational skills. Devotion, commitment, and native ability were considered sufficient for the carrying out of any civic task, whatever its demands and magnitude, in an orientation almost analogous to the attitude toward the "gift of grace" in a religious community.

There were historical reasons for this attitude. The majority of the members of the Second Aliya had had little formal education besides their early religious education and extensive self-education. The youth movements which had recruited in the Diaspora tried to prevent their members from pursuing formal education beyond secondary school, lest they be diverted from ideological commitment, an identification with the working class, and immigration to Palestine. Nonetheless, the achievements of its Zionist population in developing Palestine during the mandate period had been largely the work of these pioneers, repeatedly disproving the predictions of experts. Reinforcing ideology with improvisation and devotion, they had reclaimed a countryside, organized an economy,[29] won a war, and proclaimed a state. The systematic procedures inherent in professionalism were considered dilatory and ineffectual, inapplicable to the problems facing Israel during its first half-decade. "We don't have time," was the constant answer at all levels to sugges-

[28] Such disdain is to be found in the militant civil rights movements, according to Dr. Mildred Dickeman, who is an anthropologist and has taken part in civil rights activities in Mississippi as well as under less perilous conditions. This suggests that there may be a correlation between activism intent on changing an established order and disdain for professionalism. A factor possibly explaining such a correlation, whatever the historic reasons in any particular case, is that professionalism is non-charisma-oriented by definition, and expert predictions may not take into account the power of commitment to effect change under nontotalitarian conditions as long as a movement maintains its élan in driving toward goals.

[29] However, Zionists of "Western" rather than Eastern European background tried to rationalize activities in Jewish Palestine before statehood. Brandeis' unsuccessful attempt to do so in the early 1920s included suggestions more than reminiscent of those proposed by expert advisers after statehood and/or increasingly adopted after 1953 in the rationalization that has been taking place in Israel. Cf. Halpern (1961:184–88) and Mason (1946:456–63) for somewhat different accounts of the Brandeis-Weizmann dispute.

tions that systematic analysis and evaluation should precede action. This attitude, general throughout the public agencies of Israel, dominated the land settlement sector, the bastion of the pioneers.

National policies toward the immigrants were permeated not only by ideology and the tradition of improvisation, but also by Zionist politics. Factional systems of action effected most of the pre-statehood nation-building activities, as recounted in Chapter II; and public services were offered through various politicized or politically-affiliated voluntary organizations, with the financial aid of the World Zionist Organization and partisan factions and sympathizers in the Diaspora.

With Israel's independence, Zionist traditions were maintained in the provisions for its government. A unicameral legislature, the Knesset, was established, elected by universal adult suffrage on the basis of proportional representation, with the country constituting a single constituency. Lists of candidates for each party, nominated by the parties themselves, effectively by their central committees, are submitted to the voters, who vote for a party list rather than for individual candidates.[30] The proportion of votes given a party determines the number of its victorious candidates, starting from the top of the party list. The president of Israel, elected by majority vote of the Knesset, exercises his principal non-symbolic function in asking a Knesset member and party leader to form a cabinet. In all the national elections through 1965, Mapai has been the party with the largest number of votes but, lacking an absolute majority, has governed in coalition with varying combinations of the other political parties, excluding Herut, the successor to the Revisionist Movement, and Israel's Communist Party. The politics of coalition government resulted in the continued politicization of national services after statehood.

Thus, education continued to be carried out by voluntary organizations until 1953, with four sectarian trends recog-

30 The use of the present tense refers to conditions known to still exist in 1965–66.

nized, each with its own school system, teachers, and curriculum. With the immigrant influx, the parties to which the trends were affiliated immediately began competing for the registration of the new immigrants' children, even offering gifts and promising benefits to children and parents.

To counter this, a law was passed in 1950 that the existing trend system would not apply to the immigrant camps. In 1951, a State Education program was proposed that created a state educational system. This system had a single administrative center, the Ministry of Education and Culture, constituted in 1949, but two categories of schools, teachers, inspectors, and curricula: a secular category, known as State education; and a religious one, known as Religious State education. This law was passed in 1953; and henceforth, students were registered according to place of residence rather than trend, with parents deciding between the two kinds of schools.

Nonetheless, political agitation over education continued in the moshvei olim, since the secular moshav movements sought to have the settlers of their affiliated villages choose the State education curriculum and teachers for the village schools. However, since most of the immigrants from the non-European countries were personally religious, representatives of the religious parties sought to influence these settlers to demand Religious State education. Such agitation generally provoked crises in the villages in which it occurred, and could be a factor in the abandonment of a village by part of its population.[31]

In the field of health, politicization has not involved the split between secular and religious factions but rather the vested interests of the Histadrut. Its members are insured with its Sick Fund, which maintains a network of outpatient clinics, hospitals, and convalescent homes throughout the country and has its own medical and administrative staff. Given the prior existence of the Sick Fund, the functions of the Ministry of Health were restricted to programs of public

[31] Cf. pp. 314ff.

health, preventive medicine, and mother-child care, and to maintaining a governmental network of hospitals, including mental hospitals. The Ministry of Health is one of the ministries that the dominant Labor Party has allocated to the non-Labor secular parties in its various coalition governments; its top-level policies have therefore varied, depending on whether the minister has been a member or opponent of the Histadrut.

The politics of the health services have affected the moshvei olim, since they are served by both the Sick Fund and the Ministry of Health. For members of all moshvei olim are automatically members of the Histadrut, or at least of its Sick Fund. The Sick Fund provides a dispensary in each moshav olim, as it does in the moshvei ovdim, to be staffed by a nurse and visited twice weekly by a physician. With the shortage of nurses in the country, the Sick Fund was not always able to recruit nurses and physicians willing to serve in the villages during the first post-statehood decade. However, it refused to relinquish its services in the moshvei olim, since these were the most immediate and obvious benefits the immigrants could see resulting from their membership in and payment of dues to the Histadrut. A village could be temporarily without Sick Fund personnel and have to rely on a neighboring settlement for curative services, even while nurses employed by the Ministry of Health were visiting it to carry out the public health and mother-child care programs of the Ministry. Conversely, the Ministry generally demanded its own dispensary in the village, a visible embodiment of its services and role. The public health nurse's program of mother-child care and health education and the other Ministry of Health programs of sanitation, epidemic prevention, etc., also tended to be uncoordinated with the activities of the Sick Fund nurse, except insofar as the village instructress could effect such coordination.

Furthermore, the division of responsibilities between the governmental agencies, national institutions, and voluntary organizations has been complicated by the interests of the many voluntary organizations besides those of the Histadrut that had served the pre-state Jewish community. In the field of health, a further organizational division of labor existed in the villages of the Jerusalem Corridor. For the preventive medicine programs which were under the Ministry of Health elsewhere were carried out there by the Hadassah Medical Organization, although environmental sanitation, etc., remained under the Ministry of Health. Still other voluntary organizations were responsible for the rehabilitation and care of blind, crippled, mentally defective, or otherwise handicapped immigrants. Should an immigrant family recruited into the moshvei olim include such a member, as frequently happened, the services of these organizations also had to be mobilized. This was generally accomplished through the social worker, employed by the Ministry of Social Welfare, of the district to which the moshav belonged.

The insistence of voluntary organizations on maintaining their own services could reflect either the special political interests of these organizations, as in the case of those affiliated with the Histadrut or a competing network, or, alternatively, the response of a nonpoliticized organization to the politicization of many of the governmental services. Thus, a nonpolitical social service agency, sponsored and financed largely by an American Jewish organization, retained into the decade of the 1960s its administrative autonomy in Israel in order to retain control over the services it offered and their quality. For while this agency, like Hadassah in the field of health, has had the policy of turning over its services to Israeli jurisdiction, it did not feel that conditions during the 1950s warranted this.

For the Ministry of Social Welfare, when first organized, was assigned under the coalition government to a religious party. Like most Israeli ministries when first established, it was then heavily staffed by party members, most of whom were later confirmed in their posts by civil service regulations on employment and dismissal. These functionaries were not always receptive to the values and practices of modern social work. By not turning over its services to the Ministry, the voluntary organization in question maintained its professional standards, even while contributing to organizational multiplicity.

Such organizational multiplicity had direct consequences for the moshvei olim. Israel's independence ended the pre-statehood competition in the land settlement sector for land for village sites. But with the mass immigration, the vast expansion of land settlement, and the scarcity of material goods, resources, and qualified personnel, the competition was rather for funds, resources, and personnel such as teachers and nurses. Since the administrative districts into which the country has been organized and reorganized have differed for various organizations,[32] the social instructor who had some problem concerning services in his village usually had to travel widely, cooling his heels in a variety of official waiting rooms. Frequently the harried administrator whom he finally got to see could do little more than promise that the instructor's legitimate request would be met when the needed resources were available. However, the instructor knew very well that dozens of similar requests were pending, and that the scarce resources were probably being siphoned off through intervention at a higher level as soon as they became available. Thus, he too would turn to the district and regional offices of the Land Settlement Department and to his moshav federation for their intervention with other agencies on behalf of his village, thereby contributing to the difficulty of routinizing the allocation of resources and services. The moshav federations, in turn, also exerted pressure on the Land Settlement Department itself, in the pre-state tradition; and if necessary they appealed to the representatives on the Executive of the Jewish Agency of the parties with which they were affiliated.

The importance of personal or political influence in cutting through the consequences of organizational multiplicity and the overlapping and frequently disorganized and haphazard bureaucratic procedures is expressed in Israel by the term *protektzia*. Having protektzia means having influence or

[32] Cf. pp. 148–49, 228–29.

power or access to persons of influence and power among the elite who determine policy and distribute resources. Networks of informal relations link the pioneer settlers, their associates, and adult children who have held leadership roles in the pre-state period and since. One-time membership in the same kibbutz or moshav, shared work in pre-state Zionist activities or those of the Histadrut, common participation in the illegal immigration and the War of Independence all made for personal bonds and loyalties among post-state officeholders and the nonofficeholding members of the veteran community. These bonds have been durable. When supplemented by political obligations or shared allegiances, they have provided informal channels of communication and influence for getting things done.

Also, the shortage of able administrators and the general politicization of administration resulted in intricate interlocking directorates in the top administration of government, of the national institutions, and of the Histadrut. As has been noted, the head of the Land Settlement Department of the Jewish Agency through Israel's first decade also was minister of finance. The father of the director of the Land Settlement Department was the most charismatic member of the Executive of the Jewish National Fund, and such instances can be multiplied almost indefinitely. Thus, organizational multiplicity and administrative confusion on the one hand, and the existence of informal channels for cutting through it on the other, were reciprocal aspects of Israel's politicization.

However, the disaffected who lacked protektzia always could stage a demonstration or turn to the newspapers to compel attention to a complaint. In fact, the staging of *scandalim,* disruptive scenes in administrative offices, was a means of gaining such attention which new immigrants soon learned and transmitted to more recent arrivals. A person who persistently made such scenes could have his case settled just so that the officials would be rid of him. A village instructor, through the judicious combination of scandalim in organizations where his moshav federation lacked political connections and the exercise of protektzia in other cases, would try to maintain the flow of resources and services needed by his village. A similar strategy was employed at successively higher levels within the Land Settlement Department, as will be subsequently illustrated.

It is in this general setting of Labor-Zionist ideology and ethos and of nationwide administrative improvisation and politicization that the moshvei olim had their inception and were planned and founded during the first half-decade of the state's existence. Against this background it is possible to chart characteristic features, variations, and changes in moshav olim organization.

INITIAL ORGANIZATION OF THE MOSHVEI OLIM:
THE PHASE OF IMPROVISATION

The first moshvei olim were organized on the model of the moshvei ovdim, except that an instructor and possibly an instructress were assigned to each of the villages (or, occasionally, to more than one of them) to compensate for the settlers' lack of skills and civic knowledge and to help them learn these and to adapt to their new roles. No definition or analysis of the role of these instructors was systematically provided or generally accepted until 1957, after many other steps toward systematization had been taken in land settlement and throughout the country. The people who filled these roles were expected to do what was necessary, in the prevailing tradition of devotion and improvisation.

The following description indicates the scope of their tasks, as these developed and were categorized by the settlement authorities during the first years of statehood. The description was prepared retrospectively [33] by a moshav federation spokesman. Upon establishment of a moshav olim, he writes, its instructor was to see to the election of the executive and other committees; to guide each of them; to supervise the obtaining of supplies; to set up the cooperative store and organize its functioning; to see that the proper bookkeeping system was introduced and followed; [34] to or-

[33] Assaf 1953:181.
[34] Cf. p. 95.

ganize the schools and find a place for them in the village; to find furniture and supplies for them; to find a place for the clinic and see that it was opened; to supervise the organization of outside work; to supervise the obtaining of supplies necessary for beginning agricultural work; to speed up agricultural planning by the settlers and decisions concerning land division; to guide the settlers in their farm work; to settle disputes between them; to foster leadership and self-direction; to give the settlers a sense of independence.

The list of duties cited for the instructress [35] is equally unsystematic, although more explicitly focused on value reorientation. She was to guide the women in their housekeeping, in developing a diet suitable to the local climate, in maintaining a "corner for culture" in the village, in health and hygiene, in habits of dress and cleaning, in work on the farm, in maintaining a vegetable garden and caring for chickens. She was furthermore to teach them to honor their men yet be independent, and, among immigrants with a patriarchal tradition, to teach them equality of the sexes.

As these lists indicate, value reorientation was seen as a necessary aspect of role-socialization, but it was to be accomplished together with the transmission of skills. Given the ethos previously described, all the duties cited were presumably within the competence of sufficiently devoted and able instructors. Classified according to their objectives and scope, the duties specified for the social instructor seem to fall into four categories: (1) the organization and supervision of the village cooperative organizations, self-government provisions, and municipal services; (2) supervision of the agricultural development of the village; (3) guidance of the settlers toward civic and agricultural autonomy; and (4) procurement of vital resources and services from the various public and voluntary organizations to which a moshav is linked. The instructor was to be concerned with the village as a whole, acting in place of the various committees until he could bring them into being and guide them to effective

35 Assaf 1953:181.

functioning. While the list of duties set forth for the instructress also can be divided into various categories, all except maintaining a "corner for culture" relate to the teaching and reorientation of the immigrant women rather than to corporate village organization.

In actual fact, during most of the first post-statehood decade the instructress as well as the instructor could be involved in maintaining liaison with the many organizations to which the moshav was linked. However, she was generally concerned with the nurses, social workers, the women's affiliates of the moshav federations, Youth Aliya, and the various youth and educational organizations, i.e., with the relationships implicit in the tasks generally carried out in the moshvei ovdim by the committees of health, education, culture, etc., as well as with the social welfare problems presented by the new immigrants. Conversely, the instructor would negotiate with the officials of the Land Settlement Department, with banks and credit institutions, with the Histadrut's Marketing Cooperative, Tnuva, and with the other agencies involved in the agricultural and economic development of the moshav, i.e., he would be concerned with the tasks carried out in the moshav ovdim by the executive, economic, and agricultural committees.

Early in the history of the moshvei olim, one or more agricultural instructors were added to the village team to supervise the agricultural development of the village and to help the settlers learn farming. For although the district offices of the Land Settlement Department maintained instructors in each agricultural branch who visited the villages of the district, their supervision was found to be insufficient to ensure that the settlers learned and carried out the branches of agriculture planned for their villages. Also, the social instructors were too burdened with organizational duties and with the "social problems" of the new settlers to be able to supervise and train them as farmers. Thus, those duties concerned directly with farming and implementation of the village's farming program became a separate category of activities with its own instructor. In fact, the division of labor between social and agricultural instructors was informally worked out between them and could differ from village to village and in the same village at different times. The instructress, too, frequently shared many of the activities of the social instructor, especially those concerned with village government.

Further description of the roles of the instructors and of other aspects of moshav olim organization involves dealing with changes which they underwent during Israel's first decade. It is also necessary to consider changes in the land settlement system as a whole and in the organization of the larger society. For their interconnectedness by now should be evident: the class of moshvei olim both manifested and can be seen as representative of transformations taking place in Israel. Furthermore, variations within the class, i.e., among the villages founded as moshvei olim at any given time, also expressed variables involving the larger society: the heterogeneity of its population, public policy regarding the new immigrants, the politicization of national development programs and of the public agencies, and variations among and within such agencies in their implementation of national programs.

As some indication of organizational variables of a public bureaucracy which could affect the moshvei olim, the Land Settlement Department of the Jewish Agency expanded greatly during the period under review, was divided into units, and both these and the central administration were then subject to reorganization. At the same time, the respective spheres of jurisdiction of the Land Settlement Department and of the Ministry of Agriculture, as of the Jewish Agency as a whole and the government of Israel, also had to be worked out. For purposes of land settlement, the country was divided into districts, each with its own administrative center; and with the expansion in the number of villages and districts, the districts were grouped into regions, each with its central planning and administrative headquarters.[36] Although variations in the country's climate, ter-

36 Cf. pp. 228–29, 233–35.

rain, water resources, etc. entered into the delimitation of the regions and districts, their number and boundaries also fluctuated according to decisions concerning new areas of land for settlement and the planning of village development. The Land Settlement Department's administrative units did not correspond to the units of self-government and local administration into which the governmental ministries and agencies divided the country. During Israel's first decade, administrative procedures, efficiency, and morale could vary among both the Land Settlement Department's regions and districts and the governmental units of administration. The governmental units also varied in their party affiliations, which depended on those of the elected local authorities. These variables and the protektzia of those holding posts of authority could influence the flow of resources to the moshvei olim under their jurisdiction.

The implementation of village agricultural and economic development and, in consequence, the resources available to settlers in the course of their uncertain commitment to farming, have also been influenced by many factors. Among these have been the size of the funds available in any year to the Land Settlement Department, a decision made at the highest levels of Jewish Agency and government; decisions about their allocation, usually made in accordance with national planning priorities at the headquarters and regional level of the Land Settlement Department administration; and the agricultural potential of the land assigned a village. Land settlement planning also underwent major changes during the period under review, and the layout of each moshav olim as well as other of its features still reflected in 1958 the considerations and specifications operative at the time it was founded and during its early years.

To deal with these changes and variations, I continue the use of types as a means of presenting data. In this chapter and the two that follow, I seek to describe transformations in the nationwide system of land settlement and in the organization of the moshvei olim as a class through distinguishing two major phases in their histories up to 1958. These phases are designated, respectively, the "phase of improvisation" and the "phase of rationalization." During the first of these, discussed in this chapter, modifications in the pre-statehood organization of land settlement were effected by improvisations under pressure, despite the new conditions and the expansion in scope of operation. Rationalization began in about 1952. However, since improvisation had hardly ceased when rationalization was initiated, I have used the term "phase," rather than "period" with its connotation of a clear temporal division.

During the phase of improvisation, each moshav was planned and founded as an independent economic unit, according to the pre-state moshav ovdim model, to be based on mixed farming primarily for direct consumption. Variations on this model, developed with the spread of irrigation during the 1930s, included: (1) the intensive farm of twenty-five to thirty dunams of irrigated land, growing fodder and vegetables, and including an orchard, a few milking cows, and poultry; (2) the partially-irrigated farm, consisting of ten dunams of irrigated land and forty dunams of unirrigated fields; (3) the farm of twenty-five dunams, six to ten of them planted with citrus groves, in the coastal plains favoring citriculture. In fact, during the pre-statehood period moshvei ovdim with irrigated land tended to specialize in dairy farming or market gardening.[37] Yet in the founding and development of moshvei olim until 1953, intensive mixed farming was the goal, in line with the national goal, not overtly rescinded until 1956, of Israel's agricultural self-sufficiency.

In principle, the new moshav settlers were to be given one cow, fifty laying hens, and land which included ten to fifteen dunams with irrigation facilities per family farming unit.[38] In practice, years might pass between the time a

[37] Cf. Rokach 1964b:23. Rubner (1960:107n.) cites the 1958 Bank of Israel report stating that veteran settlements engaged mainly in dairy and poultry production.

[38] Cf. Rubner 1960:108–9. In fact, some villagers were given two cows, the supply of laying hens might be replenished, and other variations occurred in extent as well as timing of allocation of livestock.

village was founded, particularly in the hilly regions of the Jerusalem Corridor and the Galilee, and the provision of irrigation facilities; and arable land, whether or not under irrigation, might not exceed fifteen dunams per family farming unit.[39]

Of the moshvei olim founded during the peak years of settlement, some included well over one hundred farming families, more than both the ideal and statistical norm of the pre-statehood moshvei ovdim.[40] Whether or not the reasons for founding such large villages involved then-current national goals, such as rural settlement of the largest possible number of people or security considerations, I do not know. In any case, such large villages were found to create many problems in settler utilization of common village services, in parceling out village land to the families, and in village agricultural planning. Problems common to most moshvei olim— settler role-socialization, factionalism, and replacement of families who left—also were aggravated. As a result, several such villages were divided and reconstituted as two or even three settlements during and after 1956.[41] Such settlements drew on services concentrated in a village center, according to principles of planning instituted during the phase of rationalization.[42]

Moshvei olim founded during the peak years also tended to have an extended layout, unlike the circular arrangement of the first moshav ovdim, Nahalal, which was designed to allow each settler household to be equidistant from the village center, in accordance with the basic moshav principle of family equality. In this circular layout of the village, land

[39] In their survey of "relatively well-established" moshvei olim, Halperin and Yaron found that the average settler plot in 1953–54 consisted of 11.5 dunams rather than the 26.5 which had been planned. The twelve moshvei olim which they surveyed and which they considered representative of a larger universe of thirty-six villages were all founded during 1949–51, and were all settled by immigrants from Europe. None of them was located in a hilly area (cf. Halperin and Yaron 1957:V, X).

[40] Cf. Halperin and Yaron 1957:VI–VII.

[41] Such division of villages further complicates the problem of determining the number of moshvei olim founded and in existence in any given year.

[42] Cf. pp. 177–79.

allotted to each family included both a plot near the house and the principal fields stretching out behind it.[43] This layout remained the ideal, which successive moshvei ovdim sought to approximate insofar as village terrain permitted. However, moshavim founded in the years immediately after statehood tended to have an extended layout. National security considerations constituted one factor in this lengthening of the village, since it was deemed desirable to minimize the distance between frontier settlements. However, Labor-Zionist ideology was also either a factor in or was used to justify this layout. For, it was claimed, locating the farm near the house rather than at a distance would make it easier to imbue the new immigrants with an attachment to the land and their new role as farmers.[44]

In fact, the "dispersed" villages, as the extended moshavim came to be termed, in contrast to the "concentrated" village layout initiated by the end of 1952, were found to pose their own security problems. The village sites were not sufficiently compact to facilitate nightly guard against enemy infiltration from across the frontiers. In addition, settler families were anything but equidistant from the village center. Those situated at a distance suffered considerable inconvenience, particularly during the rainy season, in utilization of common village services located in the center; and they might also feel more exposed than the others to enemy infiltration. In these respects, the dispersed village layout violated the moshav principle of settler equality, although division of village land into equivalent family holdings was supposed to be easier than in the more "concentrated" villages founded before the initiation of detailed planning.[45] During

[43] Irrigation was not originally practiced in Nahalal or other moshvei ovdim founded during the 1920s, and grain was a major field crop.

[44] Bein (1952:529) is explicit on this point, on which Land Settlement Department staff kept silent by 1955, giving security as the major factor determining choice of village site and village layout for such settlements.

[45] This was told to me by individual veteran members of the Land Settlement Department staff. In my direct observations between 1955 and the beginning of 1958, land parcellation proceeded piecemeal in many of the settlements founded during the phase of improvisation; village land devoted to specific agricultural branches often was not yet parceled and was worked by the settlers on a wage basis for the Land Settlement Department; and reparcellation of plots could occur. Weintraub and Lissak

the phase of rationalization, the Land Settlement Department included in such planning the future division of land among the settlers, determining holdings in advance.

The conditions of hardship that characterized the early years of the pre-state settlements also characterized the villages founded during the phase of improvisation. There might be no connecting road between a village and the nearest highway for two or more years, and settlers might have to carry in all supplies, including bread and water, from the nearest point of access by vehicle, often several miles away. This would be especially true during the five-month rainy season (approximately November through March), when unpaved or ungraveled paths turned into mud. The villages themselves might be miles away from any other settlement. Housing consisted first of tents and then of tin huts, with the construction of permanent dwellings and water pipes for each dwelling also delayed for two or more years. Linking a village with the national telephone system might be delayed still longer, as would its connection with the national electrical network. Moreover, the provision of electricity to the community does not mean its provision to the dwellings. The latter constitutes a separate item, for which the villagers have to pay to and through the village treasury. Permanent housing, when finally constructed, consisted of a twenty-four square meter cement-block house of one room,[46] with kitchen and shower recess partitioned off. Additional rooms, built onto and opening from the previous ones, would be added according to the size of the family. In principle, a third room would be provided only for families with nine or more members, but this rule could be relaxed if large families applied sustained pressure and were in a good bargaining position.[47]

(1964b:108) note that as of 1959 a citrus grove introduced by the Land Settlement Department into a moshav olim founded in 1950 had not been parceled. However, it should be noted that settlers in veteran moshvei ovdim sometimes practiced a branch of agriculture on a joint basis.

[46] Weintraub and Lissak (1964b:103) give thirty square meters, but my figure is that stated in an official 1956 Land Settlement Department publication (The Agricultural Settlement Department, 1956).

[47] Cf. pp. 217ff.

From 1951 on, the settlements began to suffer the continual depredations of infiltrators from across the borders. The most exposed moshvei olim were provided with lighting and security fences by the Land Settlement Department; but the principal means of maintaining security has been through rotating nightly guard carried out by the settlers themselves, under the training and guidance of the military instructor. Nonetheless, thefts of irrigation pipe, farm animals, and assorted supplies and equipment were continual in the more exposed settlements.

To these difficulties was added the problem of sustenance between the time the villages were established and the rehabilitation of the soil for farming and/or the laying of irrigation pipe. The classic pattern of moshav establishment had involved the settlers in an initial period of work outside the village to provide for current living expenses.[48] The availability of such work for the settlers of the early moshvei olim depended in part on whether their villages were established near older settlements and on variations in the natural ecology.

In isolated, hilly, and arid regions, the main sources of immediate employment were the Jewish National Fund's land reclamation and afforestation projects and the Land Settlement Department of the Jewish Agency itself. Employment provided by the latter included all kinds of work necessary to prepare the village lands for agriculture, such as drainage and laying irrigation pipe, planting orchards and vineyards that were later to be divided among the settlers, building roads within the village and constructing a road connecting it to the nearest highway, building fences, etc. The funds for this work came from the settlement's budget and constituted part of the Jewish Agency's investment in the farms, to be repaid by the settlers later as part of their long-term loans. Also, as funds for permanent housing became available, the settlers themselves would be hired as unskilled or semiskilled construction workers by Solel Boneh, the Histadrut's construction company, which carries out all building in the Labor-Zionist settlements.

48 Cf. p. 94.

In the settlements established in the more populated regions of the country, work could also be found in nearby moshavot and other non-Labor-Zionist settlements, in veteran Labor-Zionist settlements that had begun to employ outside labor, and in construction and development projects of all kinds. Such opportunities, together with work provided by the Jewish National Fund and the Land Settlement Department, were generally at least in part channeled through the district offices of the Land Settlement Department, which allocated them to the various villages in the district. The social, or sometimes the agricultural, instructor generally distributed the work among the family heads in their village and tried to wrest more work days for the village from the district office.

However, the moshav settlers had to compete with the transit camp populace for such work opportunities. As the public works financed by the Ministry of Labor did not employ moshav settlers, certain public projects might be carried out adjacent to a moshav while its settlers were in need of employment.[49] Since the wages paid by the Jewish National Fund and by the Land Settlement Department were consistently lower than the minimum wage scale at the Labor Exchanges of the Histadrut, the village settlers might consider themselves deprived in comparison with immigrants who had remained in the transit camps.[50] Also, wages paid by these organizations as well as by other public agencies could be delayed for months. In the meanwhile, the settlers might [51] have to subsist on advances that could be wheedled by the instructors from the district offices of the Land Settlement Department. Under these conditions, those settlers who

[49] Assaf 1953:186.

[50] Weintraub and Lissak (1964b:104) state that the government work projects paid a wage which amounted to no more than 65 percent of possible earnings in agriculture. The category of public projects to which they refer was notorious as "make-work" to provide employment for unskilled labor, and as not necessarily contributing to Israel's development.

[51] I use "may," "might," "could," etc., in the absence of statistics on frequency of occurrence in the universe of moshvei olim. There was no possibility of my carrying out survey research, and the Land Settlement Department could not be persuaded to sponsor such a project until the end of 1957 and then in regard to only a very limited number of variables.

could find steady employment, often at some distance from their village, took it. When the agricultural development of the moshav and of the farms could begin, they lacked ideological motivation to relinquish a steady source of income for the precarious business of farming.

And farming might seem a precarious business indeed to the recent immigrant. The initial investment for seeds, fertilizer, and tractor services was advanced by the Land Settlement Department as a short-term loan to the moshav as a whole, to be repaid after harvest and the marketing of crops. Settlers, in turn, borrowed on this loan, and the amount of their indebtedness was recorded on their account with the moshav. The Land Settlement Department also decided on the kinds of agriculture to be practiced in a village, the type of crops to be planted each year, and the number of dunams to be allocated to each crop. The latter decision was ideally arrived at jointly with the settlers, but practice was at variance with the ideal. The produce was to be marketed collectively through Tnuva, the agricultural marketing cooperative of the General Federation of Labor, or through the competing network of the liberal moshav federation, which set grading specifications. After sale of the crop and deduction for services, Tnuva forwarded payment to the village; and the settlers' debts were deducted from their returns.

Apart from the risk of crop failure, the total proceeds of the first harvest might be hardly sufficient to cover the cost of the initial investment, the water for irrigation, the advances for subsistence given by the Land Settlement Department during the months of active agricultural work, and the various village taxes. The new farmer might even find himself in debt. This was particularly likely when the settlements established in 1948, 1949, and 1950 were beginning to yield, and vegetables suddenly began to glut the market.[52] And in the villages where dairy farming was practiced, facilities for cooling, preservation, and transportation of the milk might

[52] Weintraub and Lissak (1964b:103, 105–6) note that all the villages in their sample of thirteen that were founded before 1952 had to dispose of produce at a loss and underwent a crisis as a result.

be inadequate initially, so that the milk would not be salable. Fowl provided as part of the agricultural development plan could die of the many diseases to which they are liable, as well as from inadequate provision of coops and runs and insufficient care.

Also, the expansion of the poultry flock beyond the initial investment by the Land Settlement Department called for capital investment by the settlers themselves. Without such expansion, the returns from poultry raising hardly justified the necessary intensive care.[53] Yet settlers might lack the necessary capital or consider such investment not economically justifiable in terms of returns. Indeed, many of the settlers from the non-Western countries were reported to have eaten their laying hens, this having become a classic example of their "primitiveness" in the stereotype assigned them by the larger society. In any case, recent immigrants who had stuck it out in the villages during the initial years of hardship and outside work might be crucially affected in their further acceptance of the demands of moshav life by the failure or success of their first harvests and by their gain or loss after marketing.

The planners and administrators of the Land Settlement Department also acknowledged in the mid-1950s that many of the moshvei olim hurriedly established during the early post-state years, especially in the hills of Judea and Galilee, were not well planned and lacked the resources for agricultural and economic viability. Arable land was insufficient, or submarginal to the extent that years of rehabilitation would be necessary before the full holding could be cultivated. The holdings themselves were generally too small to provide the farming family with a fair income, no matter how intensive its labor. Sufficient water for farming was unavailable without irrigation, although irrigation might not be economically justifiable in terms of the crop yield possible. The settlements themselves might be badly located for maximum utilization of the available arable land. Established and located prima-

[53] Weintraub and Lissak (1964b:105) note that a small dairy herd also is not profitable.

rily for reasons of national security, these villages have been especially difficult places for immigrant settlers. Most of them have been partially or wholly abandoned several times; and almost none of them were near economic consolidation by 1958.

The description thus far has focused on agricultural and economic variables and, secondarily, on variables related to the linking of the village to the administrative network of the country. For these were the factors to which the settlement authorities continued to direct their attention until at least 1955, apart from their provision of a team of instructors in recognition of the special characteristics of the moshvei olim. However, improvisation also characterized the peopling of the moshvei olim. In the recruitment of settlers, an initial attempt was made to organize settlement nuclei from among people of the same country of origin, preferably people already acquainted with each other. But when such nuclei were too small to populate an entire village, groups of diverse background would be settled together. Also, as families left a village, new recruits, often of a different country or subculture from those of any of the groups already there, would be brought in to replace them.

The operation of ideology and politics in recruitment of settlers was no small factor contributing to heterogeneity of village populations. For the assignment of villages to the various moshav federations meant that each could be settled only by recruits of that federation, regardless of other indices of compatibility and solidarity. Thus, many villages came to include settlers from three or more countries and/or distinct ethnic groups, and any combination of provenience and background represented in the mass immigration. Two extremely heterogeneous villages that I know of even included a few Karaite families, though according to rabbinic law (which they reject) they are not Jews and therefore can neither worship nor intermarry with other members of the village. The breakdown in the original attempt to maintain some kind of ethnic homogeneity in the villages was then rationalized by the national goal of "fusion of exiles."

Difficulty in recruiting instructors for the moshvei olim also made for significant variations in the development of individual villages. For while the moshav federations originally assumed that veteran settlers from the established moshvei ovdim would serve in these roles, in fact only a limited number of them seem to have volunteered for such service. While I have no figures on the number and proportion who did, the reasons for this limited response are easy to infer.

The practice of agriculture in the established settlements was extremely profitable in the years following the establishment of the state, and a developed holding in the veteran moshvei ovdim could support a two-generation family. Consequently, there was little motivation beyond ideology and patriotism to induce veteran settlers to leave home and family after years of sacrifice and accept the conditions of hardship in the new settlements and the demands of the instructors' roles, although a more than nominal salary went with the posts. Also, the labor of the older generation might still be necessary for the maintenance of the family farm. The pioneer settlers generally did not have large families, and service in the British Army, the illegal immigration and illegal defense army of Jewish Palestine, and especially fighting during the War of Independence had taken its toll among their children. A family left with a half-grown child and/or one undergoing compulsory military service had no one to spare. Furthermore, veteran moshav settlers who had displayed administrative and leadership ability and an interest in public life had open to them or were called to positions in national administration and land settlement much higher than the post of village instructor. Those who volunteered usually did so for idealistic reasons and rarely for over a year. Exceptions could, of course, be found among those in relatively straitened circumstances, to whom the cash salary would be a welcome addition to farm income, and among those who needed and found psychological gratification in the combination of service and authority involved in carrying out such a role.

From the peak years of village establishment onwards, the moshav movements were forced to recruit instructors from outside the ranks of their members. During the early 1950s the need was such that almost any adult who was an adherent of or active sympathizer with the political parties to which the moshav movements were affiliated, and who seemed sufficiently educated and literate in Hebrew to carry out the necessary paper work, might find a job as social instructor. Throughout the 1950s increasing numbers of settlers in the older moshvei olim, still in need of outside work, were also given posts as instructors in the newer moshvei olim. Graduates of agricultural secondary schools and of Youth Aliya were sought out and prized as agricultural and even social instructors, as were experienced agricultural workers in the moshavot. And almost any woman who seemed to know how to manage a household and to meet minimal Israeli standards of Westernization could be taken on as instructress, provided that her personal values and beliefs did not conflict with the minimal ideological and political commitments demanded by the moshav federations. Few of these recruits were themselves really familiar with the internal organization and role demands of the moshav ovdim, or with the country's organizational network.

Many of the nonmoshav recruits could not endure the difficulties of their jobs and would leave when new opportunities for employment presented themselves. Also, a minimal limit on inadequacy and/or delinquency in role performance was maintained by the Land Settlement Department and by the moshav federations, although this might be minimal indeed. Prolonged and conspicuous mismanagement and irresponsibility usually, but not always, resulted in dismissal. Then a veteran moshav member might be pressured to take over for a period of time "to bring back order" in the village. Also, dishonesty in the management of village resources was an unquestioned ground for dismissal, although hard to prove.

In fact, a chronic complaint of the new settlers, especially those of non-European background, was that the instructors stole. The delays in forwarding wages for work long since carried out, similar delays by the marketing cooperatives in forwarding returns for produce marketed, the complex system of moshav bookkeeping with its deductions when payment finally arrived for advances given long before, and the deductions for moshav taxes and for membership dues to the Histadrut all contributed to the new settlers' frustration on receiving less than the anticipated cash return and to their belief in the instructors' dishonesty.

Other factors contributing to such suspicion included their familiarity with corruption in their countries of origin, the fact that modern bookkeeping and other rational administrative practices were alien to most of them, the lack of order with which these practices were carried out throughout Israel and especially in the moshvei olim during the state's first decade, and the settlers' general anomie and frustration. The latter could find a handy outlet in expressions of hostility toward the instructors. Also, the suspicion of instructors' dishonesty, once generated, spread from village to village through the settlers' informal channels of communication. Even when not believed, it could be verbalized as yet another complaint in the recitals of grievances which accompanied crises.

Also, the non-European settlers had been accustomed in their countries of origin to offer hospitality, including lavish meals, to persons in authority as a prelude to asking favors or as a delicate form of bribery. This practice was continued in the Israeli villages, intermingled with hospitality as an authentic and basic value. Some instructors exploited the settlers' ready hospitality, whatever the motive behind it, and thereby left themselves even more open to settler frustration and hostility. However, others felt themselves caught in a dilemma, for the refusal of an invitation tendered without ulterior objective could be taken as an insult. Yet an instructor whose cultural background was alien to that of the villagers could not always distinguish such an invitation from one which did have an ulterior motive.

In any case, so many factors contributed to the common

settler complaint of their instructors' dishonesty that this complaint was given little heed in the Land Settlement Department. Or the settlers might be told that legal action would be taken against them if they persisted in making this accusation without offering proof.

Settler complaints against an instructor had in general little if any weight with the Land Settlement Department in a moshav olim's initial years. In fact, if the particular group of settlers had acquired the reputation of being trouble-makers and the instructors were well-regarded, such complaints even might be perceived as evidence of conscientiousness in role performance. "It is necessary to have a strong hand" became a proverbial saying throughout the Land Settlement Department and associated agencies in talking over problems of obtaining the settlers' compliance to the demands made on them. And in the common accounts by an instructor or district coordinator of a crisis quelled by a display of authoritarianism, the story often would conclude with the phrase "and then they were good children." That a process of socialization was involved was perceived; and the analogy with child-socialization extended to an implicit identification of the settlers with children in terms of the necessity of compelling socialization.

Only a sustained, all-out demonstration against an instructor by an entire village, in addition to the villagers' pressure on the moshav federation and the federation's and Land Settlement Department's own severe doubts about him would result in an instructor's being relieved of his post because of nonacceptance by the settlers. And then he might be sent to another village by the federation and Land Settlement Department, unless his rank incompetence and irresponsibility had been clearly demonstrated or perceived.

Nonetheless, many settlements experienced a repeated turnover in instructors, who varied considerably in their personal and sociological attributes and in their successive perception and acting out of their roles. The negative effect on village development of repeated turnover in the instructor team and/or of maintaining incompetent individuals in these roles was not lost on the Land Settlement Department and the moshav federations. The federations launched repeated attempts to mobilize members of their veteran settlements to serve as instructors, and, in about 1954, succeeded in creating among the young people of the veteran villages a volunteer movement for such service. For about the next three years, young people went to new settlements to serve as instructors after their army service.

These young people brought with them the attributes of their generation and background. Although raised in the moshvei ovdim, most of those I knew were not familiar, as were their elders, with the intricacies of its administration and of that of the country-wide organizations. Except for a few exceptions who were older, they had little experience beyond life in their villages and army service. Their provinciality and overt self-confidence were often reinforced by complacency,[54] for they had been brought up to regard themselves as the culmination of Zionist endeavor.

Their model for service in the moshvei olim was service in the Army's select units or the underground activities of the generation that had matured ahead of them. The physical hardships of the moshvei olim were accepted with romanticism and enlarged upon: thus, instructors' shacks or houses, similar to those of the settlers, were furnished with a minimum of furniture and equipment and were often allowed to accumulate mud and refuse as in a frontier outpost. Occasionally, boys and girls would share the same quarters, sometimes innocently enough in the tradition of the youth movements, but open to misinterpretation by the non-European religious immigrants. And liaisons were often enough formed, a legitimate prelude to the possibility of permanent mating in the secular value system of these young people, but a horrifying violation of religious law and decency to settlers from Moslem countries. Also, these young people gener-

---

[54] This term, like those used above, p. 133, denotes overt expressions of self-satisfaction, particularly in regard to standards of values and behavior. I make no judgment as to presence or absence of subjective insecurities and doubts.

ally assuaged their loneliness by gathering together in the evenings with service personnel of similar background and with similarly placed friends from other settlements to sing songs, drink coffee or orange juice, and chat until well into the night, to awaken after the settlers and just in time to hand out assignments for the day's outside work. They constituted each other's friendship and reference group, reinforcing habits and attitudes, and rarely mingling with the settlers on an authentically friendly and non-role-polarized basis.

To their work as instructors these young people brought their youth, provinciality, self-confidence, and complacent ethnocentrism. Thus, the non-European settlers were "primitive," a term applied indiscriminately throughout the country to immigrants from all the non-European countries, regardless of other differences between them. Those of rural background who were relatively untouched by Westernization were seen as the most primitive of all but relatively unspoiled, except insofar as they had learned bad habits in transit camps. Urban immigrants, especially those who had been caught up in an incomplete process of acculturation to European norms as these were presented in the urban centers of French North Africa and the Middle Eastern countries, were seen as the worst of all. Such habits of recreation as card-playing were despised, as was the drinking of alcoholic beverages, the wearing of jewelry or use of cosmetics by the women, and their hankering after urban amenities. Difficulties in handling moshav administration and negotiations with the network of relevant agencies would often shake the young instructors' confidence, and this could be admitted; but insecurities resulting from their difficulties with the settlers most commonly would be projected into a reaffirmation of Labor-Zionist ideology.

Thus, the traditional authority of elders among the new immigrants was disregarded or actively opposed. In the election of village committees, a concerted attempt would be made to promote young people. Although this was common policy in all the moshvei olim, the young instructors were particularly callous to the claims of ascribed authority. In the villages not affiliated to the religious moshav federations, the male instructors rarely if ever attended synagogue services, although the synagogue was a center for discussions among the settlers of public as well as religious matters. When settlers disputed their allocation of work or advances, or during village crises, it was common to see instructors in their twenties maintaining themselves poker-faced and adamant to the cries and pleas of middle-aged men with a host of dependents.

The instructress might sally forth from her own unkempt quarters, often shared with a young teacher, to remonstrate with the immigrant mothers of many children because of their littered beds and floors and unwashed babies. Instructress and teachers might cut children's hair during school recess or dress them in new clothes without consulting or informing parents, and regardless of cultural and religious values involved. Women might be told to eat with their husbands rather than after them, and any visitor to a settler dwelling during mealtime might scold the whole family for eating seated on the floor. Advice on family relations as well as on cleanliness, child-socialization, marriage, and even birth control would also be freely proffered.

While veteran instructors often did the same kind of thing, they tended to have a respect for wisdom and their own experience of life to guide them. Also, their authority was perceived by the settlers as more legitimate than that of the young people. "You have given us children to lead us," wept one delegation of elders from the Atlas Mountains to a regional director, who in this case could only privately sympathize.

The majority of the young instructors I observed fled home to their own villages as often as possible, and some of them found excuses to resign their posts before the year of service for which they volunteered had expired. Many of the district coordinators and directors of the Land Settlement Department privately expressed an overriding preference for instructors recruited from among post-state European immigrants with some agricultural experience. "At least they see it as a job and they stay."

A certain proportion of the instructors and service personnel consisted of quasi-acculturated immigrants from non-European countries and of the native-born children of the pre-state population of non-European background. Attitudes toward these instructors varied in the Land Settlement Department, the moshav federations, and among other members of the village teams. Regarding native Israelis who had Israeli schooling, army service, etc., the same set of attitudes and value criteria prevailed as in the case of native Israelis of European descent, except in one respect: negatively perceived deviations from accepted norms might be ascribed, in informal evaluations, to ethnic background.

However, quasi-acculturated post-state immigrants holding instructor roles were mostly "marginal men," subject to the ambiguities of identity generally associated with marginality. For few of these individuals were really acculturated in the sense of having assimilated the core values, behavior patterns, and traditions of the Labor-Zionist settlers and their children. Rather, they had learned the basic organization of Israeli society and could handle themselves within it. They had also acquired a knowledge of the ideologies and goals of the political parties and had become affiliated to one of them. They could speak Hebrew, were at least minimally literate in it, and had acquired the habits of dress standard in rural Israel. Many of them had spent some time in kibbutzim and/or were settlers of early moshvei olim; and all of the men had been in the Army. However, whereas the post-state immigrants of Eastern European background who had gone through such experiences and acquired the attributes could be considered largely acculturated, since their cultural baseline was essentially similar to that of the pioneer settlers, post-state immigrants of non-European background with the same qualifications can be considered socialized to Israeli society rather than truly acculturated to the Labor-Zionist ethos.

Recruited as instructors by the moshav movements, they could find themselves caught in the middle,[55] between the rest of the instructor team and their administrative superiors in the Land Settlement Department on the one hand, and the settlers on the other. Their lack of core acculturation could lead to complications in informal social relations with the other members of the team. They did not quite fit in, at least in many cases, and many of them suffered the attendant self-consciousness, susceptibility to real or imagined discriminatory treatment, etc.

Moreover, more serious problems could arise in relations with the settlers. For those assigned to villages peopled by more recent immigrants from the same country of origin [56] were in a difficult position as cultural intermediaries. They served as translators linguistically but might not be able to translate the demands of moshav role-socialization in a fashion acceptable to the settlers. However, as they were responsible for implementing the demands of the settlement plan, they had to try to impose these demands, even when they could not gain the settlers' willing acquiescence. Furthermore, the settlers might resent their authority and question its legitimacy, considering them not enough different from themselves to have the right to represent the absorbing society.

Of course, numerous factors could enter into such settler

[55] For an analogous problem in the very different socio-cultural setting of an Indonesian factory, cf. Willner 1963. The problem of the foreman as "man in the middle" has long been noted in research in this country (e.g., Gardner and Whyte 1945).

[56] Weintraub and Lissak (1964b:122) state that "it generally has been considered desirable to train a member of the moshav to fill the post" of instructor. In my experience this was not the case during 1955–57, although opinions and practices varied greatly among Land Settlement Department regional and district staffs. In the sample of some sixteen villages I visited, which were founded during the phase of improvisation, I found four instances of instructors chosen from among the settlers. Two instances involved agricultural instructors, and both instructors were graduates of Youth Aliya. One was a member of, as well as the instructor in, a village mostly settled by such graduates, and a social instructor no longer was considered necessary in this village. Another instance involved an instructress who had had secondary schooling in her country of origin, unlike almost everyone else in the village; and the other case was a "general" instructor, who, I believe, had served in the Army.

perception, including the settlers' previous experience and kind of experience with preceding instructors, the personality of the particular instructor, the way he got along with key figures among the settlers and his own behavior towards them. Thus, some instructors might become increasingly authoritarian in the style of power-holders in their country of origin, and/or might blame and attack the settlers for not adapting as they claimed they had earlier learned to adapt. Dissociation from and depreciation of their own ethnic group might develop in this situation among such instructors, with attendant problems in their own identity definition, reflected in increasingly tense relations with both settlers and other instructors.

Instructresses in the same situation might face fewer problems with settlers than the instructors, which can be ascribed at least in part to the differences in the demands the two roles make on the settlers; and some whom I observed achieved real success as cultural mediators, although this was not always appreciated by their superiors. However, some instructors also had striking success both in implementing the demands of the settlement plan and in serving as cultural intermediaries. Thus, opinions in the Land Settlement Department and moshav movements varied as to the advisability of making such assignments, although more were against than in favor of them. Those instructors who succeeded in carrying out their tasks to the relative satisfaction of their administrative superiors were esteemed and given full support. However, in the case of those considered dubious, the administrators might more readily acquiesce in settler demands that they be removed than when native Israeli instructors or those of European background were the objects of such demands.

In the assignment of quasi-acculturated instructors of non-European background to villages peopled by ethnic groups other than their own, fewer of these problems with settlers seem to have emerged, although my data on this point refer to instructresses as well as instructors and even so are scanty. However, the most negative stereotypic evaluations of their respective ethnic groups to be found in the absorbing community might be used by settlers and instructors alike in their characterizations of and complaints about each other in times of crises.

The key role of the instructors in the administration and development of the moshvei olim has been reflected in the amount of description I have devoted to categorizing classes of people filling these roles; for such variations could visibly affect role-performance and its perception. However, despite the importance of the instructor role, improvision persisted in the recruitment and assignment of instructors, in the definition of their tasks and responsibilities, and in their supervision, for years after rationalization had begun in the agricultural, economic, and administrative aspects of moshav planning and implementation. Only by 1956 were there the beginnings of a systematic attempt to define the various instructor roles and to give preservice and in-service training and more adequate supervision to the instructors themselves. A definition of their roles, formulated in 1957, is presented in Chapter VI in the context of other changes in the land settlement system and in the larger society.

V

THE PHASE OF RATIONALIZATION

This chapter and the following one discuss the rationalization of Israel's land settlement program. The term "rationalization," as used in this study, refers to the conscious development of procedures for adapting means to ends and/or the conscious adaptation of ends to the capacity of means.[1]

Features of the pre-statehood organization of land settlement which can be considered incompatible with the program's rationalization include: the scope and diffuseness of its goals; the dependence of the program on uncontrollable factors such as availability of land and settlement capital; and the diffusion of authority in a program carried out by a plurality of egalitarian voluntary movements.

The rationalization of Israel's post-statehood land settlement program involved the progressive detachment of its goals from the sphere of ideology and their reformulation as specific aims which could then be related to means according to utilitarian considerations. Such deliberate reformulation of aims and assessment of means did not begin until several years after statehood. For Israel's sovereignty had the most immediate consequences for sectors of national life which had been under the control of the mandatory government, such as the administration of justice, or which could not be left in the domain of voluntary organizations, such as the Defense Forces. Thus, Israel's judiciary, which had not been involved in the pre-statehood factional systems of action, and the Defense Forces, which were reconstituted from the voluntary armed bodies within months after statehood, were among the first areas of public life to be organized on a

[1] Underlying this definition is the point of view, discussed by March and Simon (1958:136–58), that what constitutes rationality is problematic under conditions of uncertain knowledge about the probable outcomes of alternative courses of action. Such uncertainty may be considered a characteristic of public action programs seeking to effect pervasive change, as was discussed in Chap. I.

thoroughly professional basis by the standards of any modern nation. However, land settlement did not fall into a category of public life subject to reorganization.

Therefore, Israel's sovereign status first affected the land settlement program through some of the changes that accompanied independence: the availability of land and increase in flow of capital; the scarcity of food in the country; the mass influx of immigrants, and the decision to draw on it in recruiting settlers. The manifold consequences of this decision for the role of pioneer were not foreseen, and the methods of settlement developed during the pre-statehood period were retained insofar as possible. Improvisation, in the pioneer tradition of action, marked the response to new conditions, as was reviewed in Chapter IV.

Israel's independence had additional implications for land settlement. These included: (1) the possibility of planning agricultural development on a national and regional basis rather than being restricted to the village as the unit of rural development; and (2) the necessity of linking land settlement to other aspects of national development and of relating agricultural production to the needs of the national economy. A cumulative recognition of this possibility and these necessities provided the major impetus for the rationalization of Israel's land settlement program.

The consequences of the recruitment of new immigrants into land settlement gave rise to other changes in the program, changes in policy toward the settlers and in the system of relations between the settlers and the settlement agencies. It is less easy to distinguish rationalization from improvisation in this area than in the ecological and economic dimensions of land settlement, partly because of the paucity of codified knowledge on planning socio-cultural change and achieving it according to plan.

The first index of rationalization I use has to do with compliance and the means chosen to get the settlers to comply with specific demands of the roles into which they were recruited. Insofar as the means were adapted to the ends, a policy may be considered a rationalization. The second index, applicable to policy regarding the settlers as well as to policy regarding the ecological and economic aspects of land settlement, involves the policy-makers' recognition that systematic, specialized knowledge could be relevant to their decisions, and their readiness to seek it. As the first social scientist to work with the land settlement program on a continuous and full-time basis, I may note that the first index has greater relevance to this case than the second and can be applied at an earlier stage in the post-statehood history of land settlement. Rationalization began in regard to the immigrant settlers with the extension of the land settlement agencies' legal authority to effect settler compliance in the absence of consensus.

The term "bureaucratization" has been used to denote the development or extension of bureaucracy's controls over areas of activity not previously subject to them.[2] The term can also refer to the development of bureaucratic features in an organization.[3] Both usages are relevant to changes which occurred in the post-statehood land settlement system as part of the cumulative, if only partial, rationalization of land settlement policy.

The term bureaucratization, used in reference to the development of bureaucratic features in an organization, generally denotes the emergence of such characteristics as: differentiation and delimitation of organizational roles and tasks; centralized, hierarchic authority; formalized, impersonal rules and procedures governing official decisions and actions; employment in the organization as the continuous and primary occupation of its members, with recruitment based on technical qualifications and with regular monetary remuneration for work. The term bureaucratization as applied to areas of action brought under bureaucratic control can be seen as involving: (1) the extension of legal authority to such areas; and (2) an organization's acquisition of power to demand compliance to norms set or regulations issued under such authority.

[2] This is the usage proposed by Eisenstadt (1959:303).
[3] Cf. Blau and Scott 1962:8, 10.

Rationalization of the ecological and economic aspects of land settlement contributed both to the bureaucratization of the Land Settlement Department of the Jewish Agency and to the partial bureaucratization of the larger land settlement system. Rationalization of policy regarding the immigrant settlers contributed to the bureaucratization of the Department as an aspect of its bureaucratizing consequences for the total system.

The remainder of this chapter discusses changes in Israel's land settlement policies which may be considered rationalizations and which took place during the first post-statehood decade, beginning in 1952. This year is taken as marking the inception of the phase of rationalization because two new organizational units were then brought into being. One unit was established in the interests of agricultural planning and coordination on a national scale, the other to administer legal controls over the settlers. Both units were created to carry out activities which have been here defined as rationalizations, in contrast to policies undertaken in a spirit of improvisation. However, neither the activities of these units nor other modifications in land settlement policy could effect more than the partial rationalization of Israel's land settlement program in the period under review, and limitations on rationalization are also discussed in this chapter.

Chapter VI focuses on the administrative hierarchy that developed to insure the implementation of the post-statehood land settlement program. Factors other than rationalization also contributed to the bureaucratization of the land settlement system, notably the expansion of the program, as was noted in Chapter IV. Nonetheless, the convergence of rationalization and bureaucratization is salient in their extension to the instructor roles, and this will be discussed in Chapter VI.

PLANNING, AUTHORITY, AND RATIONALIZATION

The Joint Planning Center was established under the auspices of the Ministry of Agriculture and the Land Settlement Department of the Jewish Agency to plan the development of agriculture in Israel and to coordinate the activities of the many organizations also involved in agricultural development. The Division of Contracts and Securities was a unit created within the Land Settlement Department to establish on a contractual basis the responsibilities of the settlers for the capital assets advanced by the Jewish Agency.

These two organizational units, one a publicly recognized national planning body,[4] the other an obscure administrative department, expressed in different ways a definitive break with the pre-statehood organization of land settlement. However, while the Division of Contracts and Securities gave administrative recognition to the break which had occurred years earlier when uncommitted and unprepared new immigrants were recruited into the settler role, the break in the ecological and economic aspects of land settlement was most marked after the establishment of the Joint Planning Center.

Prior to the creation of the Center as a permanent body in 1952, a Committee for Joint Agricultural Planning, composed of members of the Land Settlement Department and of the Ministry of Agriculture, had met intermittently. It issued in 1950 a Four-Year Plan for Israel's agricultural development over the period 1951–54. This plan had among its goals: (1) production of enough food for national self-sufficiency, apart from meat and grains; and (2) expansion of the rural sector of the national population from 13.1 percent in 1950 to 26 percent in 1954. The plan envisaged the achievement of these goals without major changes in the established pattern of mixed dairy and vegetable farming in each village. It assumed that mass immigration would continue, that water resources would be sufficient to meet the irrigation needs of the desired agricultural expansion, and that market demands would expand to absorb the planned quantity of agricultural products for direct consumption.[5]

By 1953, when the Joint Planning Center issued a new Seven-Year Plan, immigration had dropped to the point where, in 1952, the number of immigrants was exceeded by

[4] Cf. references to it in Rokach 1964c and Weitz 1963.
[5] Cf. Rokach 1964c:31–32.

the number of emigrants, a situation that has not since recurred. It was now known that water resources for irrigation would be developed far more slowly than the previous plan had assumed; and the current output of certain products, such as milk, practically met local market demands, including those of the flourishing black market, under existing income levels. Nonetheless, the new Seven-Year Plan retained many of the goals of the earlier plan and envisaged no substantial change in established agricultural policy.

Extensive criticism of the plan, particularly by foreign experts,[6] led to its revision and to the introduction of more careful methods of assessing Israel's resources for agricultural development and of forecasting the domestic market. Israel's extremely unfavorable international balance of trade and of payments also brought under review the goal of national agricultural self-sufficiency. Agriculture has been very heavily subsidized in Israel and prices have been regulated by the government. The cost of this self-sufficiency now began to be weighed against the economic advantages to be gained by promoting the cultivation of both products with a favorable export market and industrial crops for domestic processing, with the concomitant policy of maintaining imports of products substantially more expensive to raise domestically.

In determining subsequent goals, a compromise was reached between the demands of rationalization and the claims of ideology. The principle of mixed farming, particularly in lands to be brought under cultivation or those that were newly settled, was abandoned. This represented a break with ideology, since proponents of mixed farming maintained that attachment to the soil and to agriculture as a vocation demanded that the farming family be able to supply its domestic needs from the diversified output of its own homestead.[7] The decision not to include a small dairy herd in the

6 E.g., Black 1953.
7 E.g., Dayan's discussion of the moshav ovdim includes the following statement (Dayan 1947:31–32): "While diversification of crops is not peculiar to the Moshav, a cooperative smallholders' village is inconceiv-

new moshav farms, which meant that the farming family must depend on purchased milk, was particularly viewed as a betrayal of ideological values.[8]

The proposal to promote industrial crops, supported by experts, implied an even greater break with ideology. On the one hand, adherents of classic Labor-Zionism felt that it reduced the farmer to a producer of cheap raw materials and further undercut the emotional satisfactions to be derived from return to the soil. On the other hand, the economic production of low-value industrial crops calls for relatively large-scale mechanized agriculture and a labor force that can be flexibly deployed.

While the kibbutz and the moshav shitufi provide these conditions of cultivation, they were not community types which attracted many families from the non-Western lands. Indeed, such immigrants living in transit camps would work as wage laborers in established kibbutzim nearby but were not interested in entering them as members, in spite of the economic security that membership would provide.

Despite the development of wage labor in the classic kibbutzim and moshavim, land settlement policy-makers did not suspend the creation of new moshvei olim in favor of developing large-scale cultivation to be carried out by hired labor, as advocated by foreign experts. While this policy began in the mid-1950s to be followed to a relatively limited degree in the leasing of Jewish National Fund land to individuals or a few families with capital, the repudiation of ideology that its wholesale adoption would have involved was unacceptable in the political climate of the early 1950s. Moreover, the recruitment of new immigrants into the moshav federations increased the political strength of the

able without it because the plan requires a maximum of self-sufficiency. In other words, the primary purpose of the settler is to provide for the needs of his own household and his own livestock. Only after the necessary supply of bread, milk, cheese, fruit, vegetables and forage crops has been produced, is the rest exchanged for money with which to buy commodities that cannot be made on the farm. The marketing of surplus products is thus assumed to be of secondary importance. Nevertheless, it was always the purpose of the Moshavim ultimately to increase their surplus produce so as to supply the urban communities with basic foodstuffs."
[8] Cf. Rubner 1960:107–8.

factional systems of action. The economic risks entailed in placing expensive capital assets in the hands of unprepared and uncommitted new immigrants and the seasonal and concealed underemployment involved in small-scale farming under current conditions, although underlined by experts, were not significant considerations to those holding power in the land settlement system of action.

However, with the abandonment of the principle of mixed farming the agricultural development of Israel began to be planned on a basis that overcame, insofar as possible, the limitations of the moshav small holding for large-scale cultivation. Farm layout was designed to consolidate individual holdings in continuous fields behind the homestead dwelling, and agricultural planning was no longer bound by the size of the individual holding. However, such centralized planning eroded the moshav principle of managerial autonomy of the individual farming family, as noted earlier in Chapter III.

Even before the creation of the Joint Planning Center, rationalization of land settlement had begun. The Negev was the first region in which the founding of new villages was preceded by a soil survey, including a mapping of the region and assessment of the soil's potential for different crops. This survey was used in decisions regarding village sites, number of agricultural units in each village, and location of buildings.[9]

After the Center's establishment, its goals led to a survey of the agricultural resources of all the villages in Israel and to the planning of specialized farm types adapted to different climatic conditions, topographical features, and kinds of soil. Planning was directed to the most economic use of water possible, and to providing the farmers with incomes equal to the average income in urban occupations.[10]

[9] Cf. Rokach 1964c:35.

[10] Moshvei olim founded in the hilly regions of Israel during the phase of improvisation lacked the agricultural potential to provide such an income, and this was freely discussed within the Land Settlement Department during the years 1956 to 1958. By 1957, the director of the Department proposed that industries be established in these areas. Rokach (1964c: 33–34) reviews the types of farms planned and brought into being since 1955, and Weitz (1963:108–9) discusses some of these and other farm types and their changing specifications.

Shortly after the creation of the Joint Planning Center, clusters of villages, as well as individual villages, began to be founded and taken as the unit for provision of certain services. At the end of 1952 and during 1953, two clusters of several villages each were brought into being in the Negev. One of these groups consisted of three villages and the other of five, four of which were added in the neighborhood of a village created in 1949. The villages or *garinim* (sing. *garin, nucleus*) of each cluster were situated as closely together as possible, and a common service center was established within walking distance of each village.[11] The principle of regional settlement, extending well beyond the organization of such services as a tractor station and a school to serve each group of villages, was included in the major revision of previous settlement methods instituted in 1953 and put into practice in comprehensive regional planning initiated in 1954.

Comprehensive regional planning was introduced as a means of linking land settlement and agricultural development to the development of industry and of dispersed urban centers. First introduced in areas designated for specialization in industrial crops such as cotton, sugar beet, and peanuts, regional planning included the construction of plants to process such products in an urban center within the area. The location of these plants was designed to minimize the

[11] Rokach (1964c:35–36) views these villages as marking a second stage in the planning of land settlement. The intensive but unplanned creation of villages between 1949 and 1951 constitutes the first stage he distinguishes, and comprehensive regional planning constitutes the third stage.

In my view, however, the two groups of villages more resembled those founded during the peak years of improvisation than those founded after the inception of detailed planning. This view seems borne out by the evidence of Weingrod's study (1966) of two villages which clearly are two settlements of the three-village cluster. Yet village variability was such that there are grounds for classing the village founded in 1949 with the post-statehood moshvei ovdim rather than with the villages still termed moshvei olim in 1957 (cf. Chap. IX, pp. 433–34). For while this village was peopled by immigrants from the island of Djerba in Tunisia, they were young adults who had been in Youth Aliya before the settlement was founded. According to two informants, they came to the village site as an already organized group, knowledgeable about the conditions of moshav life. By 1957 the village had reached economic consolidation, and its only instructor was himself a settler.

cost of transporting low-value crops, and the plants strengthened the economic base of the urban centers.

Another basic aspect of comprehensive regional planning was the creation of new villages in clusters, each cluster including a rural center in which would be located services for the group of villages. This arrangement was intended to provide cheaper and better services than could be organized for individual villages. Determination of village size also need no longer be influenced by consideration of the number of families necessary to justify the cost of such services. Security considerations, never absent in the planning of land settlement in Israel, also would be served by the establishment of new villages in clusters, since this arrangement countered the vulnerability of an isolated settlement.

Services to be located in the rural centers included and went beyond those available in villages established as self-contained units. They comprised: a school, a youth center which provided agricultural and vocational training as well as general education, a cultural center, library, sports ground, general dispensary with medical and dental clinic, and such basic agricultural and economic facilities as tractor station, garage and repair shop, carpentry and metal workshops, cold-storage facilities, central cooperative consumers' store, marketing facilities, ice factory, granary, bakery, and emergency generators and installations for electricity. Each village was to be joined by a connecting road to its center as well as to the nearest branch of the national highway system.

Services to be located in the urban center included district offices of the governmental agencies, a secondary school, bank, theater, stadium, and the range of other facilities integrating the countryside with the national life.

Two somewhat different patterns of village and rural center clusters were planned and in large part carried out during the years 1954–56. According to one pattern, five or six villages, each to include eighty farming families, were to be served by a rural center like the one described above, with the service personnel making their homes in the center. Each village was to be located no more than two kilometers from its center, with service facilities within the village itself limited to the village office, kindergarten and first grade school, synagogue and ritual bath, armory, village cooperative shop for the purchase of daily necessities, and a village assembly hall. The settlers were to meet their vegetable needs from kitchen gardens and maintain a small poultry run and a small herd of sheep, including milking ewes.

The other pattern, known as the composite moshav, was to consist of three village units (garinim), each designed for sixty families, laid out around a center in which would be concentrated services similar to those in the rural center of the pattern just described, though on a smaller scale. Although the center would be within easy walking distance of all three units, each unit of the composite moshav would also have its own office, kindergarten and first grade school, synagogue and ritual bath, armory, and small consumers' depot for bread and milk. Both patterns included homes for the service personnel in the center. But whereas each village of the previously described pattern was to be provided with its own team of village instructors during its initial years, the composite moshav would be served by a single team.

The first pattern was the basis of the much-publicized settlement, during 1955 and 1956, of a region of some 700,-000 dunams, in which a new town was also created in 1956. In the space of one year, fourteen moshavim, six kibbutzim, four large farms, and the new urban center were founded, and two out of the four rural centers that had been planned were initiated. The second pattern was the basis of the settlement of one district, which included three such composite moshvei olim. A small nearby city served as its urban center.

With regional planning, the preliminary survey of an area to be settled included a detailed investigation of regional features and resources; studies were made of climate, chemical and physical properties of the soil, topography, water resources, flora and fauna, existing agriculture, market possibilities, and existing service facilities. The area would be mapped, the villages and farm units located, and precise decisions made on land utilization, farm parcellation, and the sites of all buildings. A plan would also be prepared on the use of water, and the irrigation network, main and subsidiary pipelines, and water meters located in advance. Village design included placement of roads, electric poles, and fences; village landscaping, and the trees and shrubs to be planted around each house.

Under regional settlement, the size of the moshav dwelling was increased to forty-five square meters, and each dwelling included three rooms and was provided with kitchen sink and bathroom recess. These homes were to be completed by the time the immigrant settlers arrived, except in the case of the first region to be settled under regional planning. In the villages of this region, settlers were first provided with a wooden shack, later to serve as storehouse. They helped to build their houses during the first months after arrival, and unskilled construction work provided one source of income until agricultural development of the villages got underway.

Modifications of previous settlement practices included an arrangement that both would ensure that the village passed through the initial stages of agricultural development according to plan and would provide the settlers with farming experience before they assumed the responsibility of working their own farms. Each of the moshav federations established holding companies jointly with the Land Settlement Department, through which village land was to be cultivated during the initial years after the founding of a moshev olim. These companies would administer and supervise implementation of the agricultural program, while the settlers would be employed by them as day laborers. Only after farming skills had been learned would the land be turned over to the settlers and divided among them; and this was to take place in stages, over a four-year period.

This arrangement, known as the managed farm, also took account of the demoralizing effect of insufficient outside work to sustain a settler family during the first stages of moshav development. By making initial cultivation of their own future farms on a wage basis a source of income for new settlers, land settlement policy-makers hoped to guarantee each family at least fifteen work days per month, even in slack season.

The establishment of these holding companies by the moshav federations was one of a number of changes in land settlement policy toward new immigrant settlers that accompanied or was included in comprehensive regional planning. These policies embodied an explicit recognition that the majority of post-statehood new settlers did not share the values and goals of those who had innovated and could sustain the pioneer settler role, and that ideological exhortation was unsuccessful in effecting commitment to these values and goals. The establishment of the moshav federation holding companies may be considered a rationalization of the methods previously employed for introducing new immigrants to the demands of the settler role. For it provided agricultural training and the security of a minimum income from agricultural labor without associating these with the managerial responsibilities of the family farm. However, this policy also extended the areas in which the settlement agencies exercised control over those recruited as settlers.

The progressive transformation of a system of relations based on normative consensus into one buttressed by the coercive power of formal authority began well before comprehensive regional planning. The establishment of the Division of Contracts and Securities within the Land Settlement Department in 1952 is here taken as marking the point of transition.

The Division of Contracts and Securities was set up to administer legally binding agreements specifying the precise responsibilities and obligations of the settlers in regard to the capital assets advanced by the Jewish Agency for the development of new villages and farmsteads. The fact of a contract between settlers and Jewish Agency was not discontinuous with pre-statehood practices after 1930. The discontinuity involved the terms and jurisdiction of the contracts administered by the Division.

Until 1931 the settlers of the Labor-Zionist villages received capital funds without contracts stating that these funds were loans and stipulating conditions of repayment. The idea of such a contract had been under discussion throughout the 1920s. However, the Histadrut's Agricultural Center endeavored to have the contract drawn up between Nir Shitufi, the Histadrut organization of agricultural villages,[12] and the Zionist organizations then allocating the funds. But the organizations refused to accept such an arrangement, insisting that the contract be made directly with the settlers rather than with Nir Shitufi as their representative. Protracted negotiations over the form of the prospective contract were resolved after the Labor-Zionist settlements assumed the status of cooperative societies with a legal corporate identity.

Starting in 1931, contracts were signed between settlements and the Foundation Fund, under the terms of which the funds of the latter were granted as loans subject to interest and repayment. Although somewhat different terms were granted to different settlements, and these terms were later modified, the most common contract granted the loan for forty-nine years at an interest of 2 percent, payment of interest to begin five years after receipt of the total amount of the loan, and repayment of capital to begin ten years after receipt. However, it was common opinion in Israel during the 1950s that the by-then-wealthy veteran villages founded during the early period of Labor-Zionist land settlement had not repaid the funds advanced for their initial capitalization and probably never would.

Whatever the erratic course of contractual agreements between settlements and settlement agencies during the prestatehood period, contract terms in effect during the decade of the 1950s involved the granting of a settlement loan for a thirty-year period at an interest of 3.5 percent, payment of interest to begin three years after the signing of the contract and repayment of the principal to begin ten years after the signing. However, the contract which grants the settler family title to the farmstead is not signed until 70 percent of the sum deemed necessary for the full development of the

12 Cf. pp. 64–65; Bein 1952:458–59.

farm has been invested. This 70 percent represents the total sum advanced from public funds, with the rest to be supplied by the settler family or through other loan arrangements. Before the contract is signed, a supervisory committee of the Histadrut visits the village to review the value of the assets stated in the contract, claiming deduction of those lost through drought, flood, etc.

This contract can be seen as continuous with the contract arrangements instituted during the pre-statehood period, and the terms seem designed to protect the settlers, insofar as possible, from the accumulation of legal responsibilities before their farms were consolidated and of liabilities caused by conditions beyond their control. Indeed, according to the contracts negotiated during the 1930s, only 65 percent of the Foundation Fund investment was subject to repayment, and the remainder was considered "expenditure on public amenities." [13]

However, in the contract in use during the 1950s, the loan advanced to the settlement included the costs of village planning and of preparatory work on the village lands, the development of water resources and of the irrigation network, road construction, deep plowing, initial construction of farm buildings and housing, the provision of livestock and implements, the planting of orchards and vineyards, the provision of electricity to the village, part of the initial working capital, and, on a pro rata basis, the cost of public buildings and common village assets. The investment of public funds per moshav farm unit was considered to be IL25,000 in the mid 1950s, IL30,000 by 1959. In the settlements established during the phase of rationalization, 65 percent of this investment was to be made by the end of the third year after a village's founding, and the stage of consolidation, i.e., the total investment, reached by the end of the seventh year.

According to moshav principles, reviewed in Chapter III, the loan of public funds is made to the village as a unit, and equal amounts of credit are to be advanced by the moshav to each of the settler families. A contract between settler

[13] Cf. Bein 1952:460.

families and the moshav federation stipulates the agreements entered into between the individual settler families and the moshav as a corporate entity. However, settlers signed the settlement loan contract directly with the Jewish Agency, at least during the period under review, as well as the contract with the moshav federation.

Among the contracts administered by the Division of Contracts and Securities was a contract between the Jewish Agency and each settler family entered into long before the settlement loan contract just described. The prior contract affirms the Jewish Agency's ownership of all the farm assets financed from public funds—livestock, equipment, and buildings—and holds the settler family responsible for these assets until the settlement loan contract transfers ownership of the farmstead to it. The creation of this preliminary contract by the Division of Contracts and Securities represented the response of the Land Settlement Department to losses suffered in allocating assets to the moshvei olim.

For immigrants had departed from settlements leaving property neglected and debts on the books for agricultural credit they had received. Their laying hens might have perished or been eaten, and larger animals might have died or gone astray. In fact, in one village I know of, settled by immigrants from North Africa, mules were allowed to run off across the frontier because the settlers feared them. Outhouse doors were burned for fuel in ovens built by immigrants from rural areas of Moslem lands for baking their traditional flat loaves of bread. Farming implements might be left broken or in hopeless disrepair. The dwellings might have deteriorated to the point of having to be renovated before new settlers could reasonably be asked to occupy them, particularly in cases where large families had occupied the twenty-four square meter concrete-block houses.

Furthermore, the moshav as a corporate entity might be heavily in debt to the Land Settlement Department for agricultural credit advanced it for a crop that had failed, or of which a good part had been sold by the settlers on their own, perhaps in the markets of a nearby town. And when the settlers disposed of crops privately, pocketing the proceeds, there was no way to deduct the debts they had incurred for water, seeds, and other agricultural supplies from these unregistered earnings. The moshav as a unit remained in debt to the Land Settlement Department, with only those crops marketed through the village marketing cooperative providing a return from which credit advances could be deducted. Should families leave without paying their debts, these remained as debts of the moshav to the Land Settlement Department. The Department had the choice of either transferring the full burden of these outstanding debts to families who had remained in the village and who had received credit at the same time as those who had left, or of writing off the debts of those who had left as a loss. Moreover, village bookkeeping had frequently been neglected during the early years of moshvei olim founded before 1952, making it difficult or impossible in many cases to ascertain exactly the amount of credit and supplies a family had received.

By imposing a special contract on the new settlers, the Land Settlement Department made it impossible for them to leave the moshvei olim without repaying their outstanding obligations and returning supplies and equipment in reasonably good condition. They were also obligated to pay rent for the period they had occupied a permanent dwelling in the village. The Division of Contracts and Securities carried out a detailed survey of all the assets of the Jewish Agency in the villages already founded, and opened files for settlers in such villages as well as for settlers in villages founded after the creation of the special contract.

Some of the responses of new immigrant settlers to the settlement contracts indicate the limitations of specific formal controls as a means of eliciting compliance to the demands of diffuse roles. For one effect of demanding that settlers sign the preliminary Jewish Agency contract was further to discourage already-discouraged newcomers to a moshav from remaining as settlers. Immigrants formerly urban but incompletely Westernized might understand just enough of what the contracts entailed to fear it. Unfamiliar with modern credit and interest practices, they might perceive the obligations they would incur in terms of the traditions of ownership and indebtedness familiar to them. "We would be their prisoners forever," was the not unique response of one group of newcomers from Tunis, who had been recruited as moshav settlers by the glowing accounts of moshav movement emissaries and who were already frightened and depressed by the demands and greater prospective demands of agricultural work and by the absence of urban bustle and urban amenities such as shops and cafes. As long as they did not sign the initial contract, such newcomers could hope to leave the moshav and be granted housing in a new development town or in a new immigrant quarter of an established city, or at least temporary quarters in a transit camp, with the right which all new immigrants have to the eventual provision of a low-cost permanent dwelling.

The reluctance or initial refusal of settlers to sign the first contract was generally perceived by village instructors as further evidence of the settlers' "primitiveness" and propensity to make trouble. A common practice was to try to collect settlers' signatures or thumbprints on the contracts without fully explaining what was involved, "to avoid trouble," i.e., to avoid the possibility of concerted opposition to signing and the crisis in the management of village affairs that this might entail. Instructors who attempted to push through the contract in this way were generally most successful, as might be expected, with new immigrants of rural background who had not passed through the transit camps or otherwise been "spoiled" by too much previous experience in the country. When concerted opposition to signing did arise, the moshav federation's representative to the villages and the Land Settlement Department's district coordinator, or perhaps even its district director, would argue with the settlers, both pressuring and reassuring them, until the majority could be persuaded to sign.

Conversely, however, immigrants recruited to the villages by the moshav federations not infrequently included families recognized after they arrived as unsuitable for agricultural life. These were usually families in which the family head was elderly or ailing and which had no adolescent son to take over the farm within a reasonable period of time. During the phase of rationalization such families were not allowed to sign even if willing to do so, and the Land Settlement Department might contribute to their resettlement elsewhere. However, should such families have relatives in the village, the Land Settlement Department's refusal to let them sign the contract could also precipitate settler opposition, although this opposition rarely reached crisis proportions unless it became linked to other issues.

All new moshav settlers, including those in the moshvei olim, also had to sign a lease with the moshav federation to which their village was affiliated. This lease stated the terms on which the moshav federation and the village as a corporate unit granted the settler family title to the farm. The lease of the principal moshav federation commits the family to membership in all the corporate village bodies and to all the obligations and regulations this may entail.[14] The contract of the religious moshav federation also commits the family to refraining from work on the Sabbath.

The settlers of one village, established in 1950, steadfastly refused to sign the contract of the federation to which their village was affiliated. They were from the island of Djerba in Southern Tunisia, where the Jewish community has maintained a tradition of Hebrew learning for hundreds of years. Land Settlement Department officials, commenting on the settlers' stand, attributed it to their literacy in Hebrew and consequent refusal to commit themselves knowingly to the terms of the contract. In fact, one of the Department's regional directors, who had joined an older moshav olim settled by immigrants of Eastern European provenience similar to his own, admitted privately that he himself would have hesitated to sign the moshav federation contract had he not been an official of the Jewish Agency.

[14] See Assaf 1953:287.

The area of contracts illustrates the limitation of legal controls for bringing about compliance to the demands of diffuse roles which by law are assumed voluntarily. The contracts between the moshav settlers and the Jewish Agency provided legal means for safeguarding the Agency's investment in assets allocated to moshav settlers. However, the settlers were not thereby obligated to desire these assets, to make use of them willingly and efficiently, or to accept the range of commitments involved in the role of moshav farmer.[15]

Thus, the area of contracts illustrates the limits to rationalization of land settlement policy regarding the immigrant settlers. Rationalization could take place in areas in which goals could be related to specifiable courses of action with known consequences or, at least, with established procedures for forecasting consequences.[16] However, land settlement policies toward the immigrant settlers could not be rationalized through recourse to a specialized body of knowledge, given the lack of codified procedures for rapidly effecting massive value indoctrination and goal reorientation. Yet legal authority, with its coercive provisions for exacting compliance, could not be extended to the range of behavior encompassed in the role of moshav settler. Founded as communities-in-formation, the moshvei olim could not legally be adminis-

---

[15] It might even be argued that the imposition of the contract could impede settlers' identification with the values and goals of land settlement and with the role of moshav farmer. For it added to the issues on which compliance was demanded, regardless of possible settler opposition, and around which a crisis could develop. In fact, however, so many issues could precipitate opposition and provoke a crisis in the course of a moshav olim's early development that I doubt whether any special significance can be assigned to the imposition of the contract. My impression was that the issue of the contract could crystallize and harden families' decisions to leave the moshvei olim, since the contract represented a legal as well as symbolic acceptance of obligations. However, all the settlers I knew who signified such a decision by persistent refusals to sign the contract had made this choice earlier, had persistently stated their desire to leave, and had expressed it by such nonverbal behavior as refusal to start a kitchen garden in the plots around their dwellings or even to unpack the majority of their belongings.

[16] As March and Simon have pointed out (March and Simon 1958: 137–39, 155–56), goals influence choices between alternative courses of action only if there is a means of evaluating whether and to what extent these alternatives would make for goal realization.

tered as total institutions whose inhabitants could be segregated from the larger society and treated as inmates subject to legitimized pervasive regulation.

The rationalization of Israel's land settlement program was limited also by the multiplicity of its goals, the intransigence of some of them to known means of implementation, and by the program's multiple links with the larger society. Rationalization, although progressive, could only be partial, as is further discussed below.

LIMITS TO RATIONALIZATION

Ideology and politics can be seen as the major factors which set limits to the rationalization of Israel's land settlement program. For the goals of Labor-Zionist ideology linked the country's agricultural development to the creation of new villages whose settlers would till the land.[17] Concomitantly, the politics of Israel precluded the dissociation of publicly financed new villages from the factional systems of action which were among the basic organizational units of the new society in formation. Therefore, rationalization could progress only insofar as new policies could be accommodated within the land settlement system of relations which had developed during the pre-statehood period. The system itself was not subject to basic reorganization, despite the strains placed upon it by the recruitment of new immigrants into settler roles created by the pre-statehood moshav pioneers.

Two policies, both instituted within two years of the beginning of the phase of rationalization, illustrate in different ways the limits to rationalization implicit in the land settlement system. The Law of Candidates for Agricultural Settlement, initiated in 1953, represented a rationalization as the term is used in this study. Designed to provide a legal basis for expelling from the villages those settlers whose sustained dissidence exceeded the land settlement authorities' limits of

[17] The negative value put on hiring agricultural labor, together with the stress on developing a population of Jewish farmers working their own land, precluded the large-scale development of commercially managed large holdings.

tolerance, this law, like the preliminary moshav contract, constituted an extension of legal controls over the settlers.

The "ship to village" policy, initiated in 1954, was concerned with getting immigrants who were arriving in Israel into villages as speedily as possible. Although designed to mitigate the consequences of previous improvisations, it may be considered no more than a procedural rationalization. It facilitated the execution of policies not susceptible of substantive rationalization within the system of relations through which land settlement was carried out. However, it effected no alteration in the conditions of settler recruitment which brought to the moshvei olim people whom the land settlement authorities had to take legal measures to expel, or in the conditions of village life which fed settler dissidence. I discuss the two policies in the order expressing the priority of recruitment to expulsion, despite the historical priority of the Law of Candidates for Agricultural Settlement.

The ship to village policy was initiated as part of a broader national policy, undertaken in 1954, of seeking to do away with the transit camps. For these camps had become demoralizing centers of discontent and anomie as well as unhygienic and dilapidated blights on the landscape. Veteran inhabitants of these camps, some of whom had dwelt in them for four or five years, had acquired much of their knowledge of Israel through the round of encounters with the personnel of the agencies allocating work, permanent housing, welfare services, medical treatment, etc., and with the representatives of the political parties seeking their allegiance and competing, until 1953, for the registration of their children in schools representing the politically affiliated educational trends.

The work available to such immigrants was largely of the unskilled-labor variety, except in the case of individuals possessing vocational skills needed in the society in formation. Older men or those formerly engaged in sedentary occupations, if unable or unwilling to engage in strenuous manual labor, could become social cases waiting to be assigned a kiosk or shop, licenses for which were allocated through the

Ministry of Social Welfare. Both such men and those prepared to work but unable to find more than intermittent temporary employment tended to become increasingly demoralized and/or to take to various forms of dissipation. Their wives in many cases tried to eke out the welfare grants on which the families depended for subsistence by seeking employment as domestics. Their babies would often be left in the care of older siblings and bigger children might be neglected.

The transit camp inhabitants quickly learned and transmitted to new arrivals a repertoire of techniques for circumventing the procedures of the various agencies for allocating limited resources. The more successful techniques included scandalim to compel attention to needs and grievances, affiliation with political parties seen as offering protektzia, and threats of switching political affiliation. Anomic rebellion, including physical violence toward those handling allocation, and anomic retreatism [18] also were common phenomena among immigrants dwelling in the transit camps.

The national policy of eliminating these camps involved practically all the public agencies engaged in national development and in the reception and absorption of immigrants. Through constant construction of permanent housing, efforts were made to accelerate the transformation into new towns of transit camps located in development areas, and to relocate the inhabitants of the camps which were to be dismantled. The flow of newcomers to Israel into the latter camps also was to be avoided insofar as possible through other provisions for their reception. One of these was the ship to village policy.

This policy involved the enrollment of prospective moshav settlers from among prospective immigrants still in their countries of origin or in the process of transit to Israel. They were then transferred to new villages or those with vacancies directly upon disembarking in Israel. This policy served the interests of the land settlement system as well as contributing

[18] Cf. Merton 1957:140, 153–55.

to the national effort to eradicate the transit camps, since it expedited the recruitment of new settlers while eliminating the effects of transit camp experience on newcomers.

However, the ship to village policy also involved prospective immigrants in the factional systems of action prior to their arrival in Israel, and it did so without necessarily providing them with information about the conditions awaiting them or the options and commitments involved in signing with a moshav federation. A not uncommon technique among emissaries of the moshav movements abroad seems to have been to show prospective recruits photographs of the flourishing veteran settlements, including the homes of the emissaries themselves, and to tell them that this would be what they would have, as indeed they could have—eventually. Another technique was to approach drowsing immigrants on the boats at night and hand them papers to sign, or so I was told by unwilling new settlers who claimed they had been recruited into the villages in this way.

Even new settlers from the Moslem countries who had participated in local Zionist activities before emigrating did not necessarily feel that they had been informed of the possibilities other than land settlement open to newcomers whose immigration to Israel had been financed by the Jewish Agency. A mature recent arrival from Tangiers, who claimed to have been active there for years in the local Mapai organization and who was literate in Spanish, French, and to some extent in Hebrew, said of assignment to a village rather than to a dwelling in a new town or in the immigrant quarter of a major city: "It is a lottery; none of us knew what our turn would be."

In fact, immigrants brought to the villages directly from the ships had been processed by the Jewish Agency's Departments of Immigration and Absorption before passing into the jurisdiction of its Department of Land Settlement. Representatives of the Department of Immigration in the various Jewish Agency offices abroad authorized and arranged their journey, applying the selection criteria instituted in 1952 to preclude the further descent on Israel of social cases, which some of the Mediterranean Jewish communities had been glad to pass on to the new state. On arrival in Israel, the immigrants passed into the jurisdiction of the Department of Absorption, which was in charge of the provision of immediate necessities including shelter. Only after arrival in the moshvei olim, which presumably were their permanent homes, did newcomers come under the jurisdiction of the Land Settlement Department.

Nonetheless, once registered for land settlement by a moshav federation, immigrants in transit lost the possibility of immediate assignment to anywhere other than a village affiliated with the particular federation which had recruited them. Representatives of the federations and of the Absorption Department assigned them to various villages of the federations during the voyage, according to the availability of places.

Thus, immigrants would be assigned to vacant new villages together with those traveling on the same boat; and extended family or friendship groups, arriving on different boats, might find themselves dispersed throughout the country. Where only a few vacancies existed in a village, as in the case of the older moshvei olim, some of whose previous settlers had left, newcomers might be settled with people of quite disparate provenience and origin.

The politics of land settlement affected assignment of settlers to villages even after land settlement policy sought to promote the peopling of new villages by culturally homogeneous groups. Although the main index of such homogeneity still was country of origin, finer distinctions were recognized in some of the recruitment activities of the settlement federations. Thus, in seeking settlers for the villages created in the framework of regional settlement, the federations recruited abroad, trying to organize groups of people of similar background, already linked together by kinship and friendship ties. Groups actually recruited included not only inhabitants of traditional rural villages in North Africa, but also several groups composed of European-educated or otherwise Westernized young families from the same North

African city, who had learned about and accepted moshav principles and the general ideology of the village federation in preparation for their new way of life. Nonetheless, if by the time their immigration could be arranged there was not room for all of them in one of the villages assigned the federation, the settler group would be split up and its members dispatched to more than one village, according to the number of places available.

However, the actual transporting of moshav recruits from ship to village was very efficiently organized. Buses and/or more usually trucks to move immigrants and belongings were waiting at the port when the ship docked, and the drivers knew just how many families to expect. After passage through immigration formalities and customs inspection, families and their hand baggage were loaded; and the trucks shot off, often on a drive of some hours, to their respective destinations. For some months after their arrival in the villages, discontented families might recount this trip, recalling with emotion their discomfort and anxiety.

On arrival at the village sites, immigrants recruited into land settlement between 1954 and 1956 generally found either several streets lined with temporary huts laid out around the village center, as in the case of the majority of newly founded villages, or, if the village had been settled earlier, permanent houses instead of huts. As might be expected, immigrants of urban background, practically all of whom at this period were from North Africa, experienced no small shock at the sight of such a village, often located kilometers away from other settlements and surrounded by the semiarid plains of a still-uncultivated part of the northern Negev or by the as yet hardly reforested slopes of the Judean Hills or another mountainous area.

Many of these immigrants, on catching sight of this "desert," refused to descend from the trucks until cajoled and persuaded by the experienced drivers, the village instructors, and/or other land settlement personnel, who assured them that matters would be straightened out once they got down, but that nothing could be done until then. However, once

the trucks left them in the village, they no longer were under the jurisdiction of the Absorption Department of the
Jewish Agency but under that of the Land Settlement Department.

As part of the allotments advanced to all new immigrant
families by the Absorption Department and to all new
moshav settlers by the Land Settlement Department, each
new family received beds and mattresses, a kitchen table
and stools, a primus-type cooking burner of the sort used
throughout Isreal, a pot or so, a food package for each member of the family, and a small amount of cash, graduated
according to family size, to tide them over the next few days.
With an initial crisis over descending from the trucks, and
an initial allocation of specified goods, life in the moshav
olim had begun.

The ship to village policy accomplished the immediate
goals of turning part of the flow of newcomers away from the
transit camps and of facilitating recruitment of new settlers.
However, it did not accomplish these goals through the
development of new means of securing the immigrants' knowing and willing acceptance of the role of moshav settler.
Rather, it extended the settlement authorities' means of inducting into a legally voluntary role people who might not
have assumed it under conditions of fuller information and
conscious choice.

But since the moshvei olim were not total institutions
whose inhabitants could be segregated from the larger society, new immigrant settlers could and did quickly learn
to challenge and test the extent of control which actually
could be exercised over them. Relatives and acquaintances
who had been in the country longer than they, representatives of political parties other than those to which they had
become affiliated through recruitment by a moshav federation,
even strangers briefly encountered on trips and visits passed
on their knowledge of how to wrest concessions from those
in authority. The ship to village policy could funnel people
to the moshvei olim, but it could not exact their compliance
to the demands of the settler role.

Even before the ship to village policy was instituted, however, a measure was enacted for expelling from the villages those settlers whose prolonged dissidence had proved impervious to other means of control. The Law of Candidates for Agricultural Settlement, passed by the parliament of Israel, enabled the Land Settlement Department to institute legal proceedings to remove from the moshvei olim settlers who would not work their farms, who violated the regulations of the moshav constitution, or who disturbed the peace or menaced other village inhabitants. This law can be seen as a measure by which the land settlement authorities sought to protect the interests of village development from some of the consequences of their own policies. In practice, however, the usefulness of the law was limited.

For it was not directed against people clearly unsuited to be settlers who were brought into the moshvei olim both before and after the ship to village policy. Such people included those who, because of their age or physical disabilities, were either incapable of sustained agricultural work or soon would be, and who might have a host of very young as well as some aged dependents but no one of suitable age to take over responsibility for the farm within a reasonable period of time.[19]

Brought into the villages through recruitment procedures over which the Land Settlement Department had little control, such people were referred by village instructors to the attention of the social welfare agencies of Israel. Nonetheless, years might pass until some more suitable accommodation for them could be arranged. In the meanwhile, the most needy would be given whatever work they could carry out

---

[19] Weintraub and Lissak (1964b:107–8) refer to a village where the settlers willingly worked their farms but in which demographic factors (including the presence of families with many dependents) made for poverty, default of payment on village taxes and on dues to the Histadrut, and the suspension, in consequence, of the medical services that the Histadrut's Sick Fund provided for members of the village. Given the corporate organization of the moshav as a unit, the presence of social cases in a village and their inability to pay village taxes mean that the tax burden falls on the remaining village families who may not be able to carry it.

within the land settlement framework, including such jobs as school janitor or school cook, and/or family members would seek outside work. Moreover, in some cases such families were part of an extended family which, in one of the Moslem countries, had constituted a single household and/or economic unit. Such units became dissociated into nuclear families in the villages, because moshav organization took the nuclear family as the basic economic and household unit, although there was no prohibition on joint cultivation of several family farms. The proposed removal of nuclear families physically incapable of working a farmstead effectively sometimes provoked the opposition of other members of the extended family whom the settlement agencies wanted to retain as village settlers. Although these relatives might lack the means and/or manpower for contributing to the support of their less able kin or helping to work their farmstead, the Land Settlement Department did not take action in such cases, at least in the instances I observed. Indeed, as of the mid-1950s the Land Settlement Department seemed resigned for the time being to the impediment that social cases posed to village agricultural development, although it was prepared to contribute to their resettlement elsewhere.

The Law of Candidates for Agricultural Settlement was applied only with the greatest of discretion to one of the classes of settlers specifically singled out in official explanations for its passage [20] as its primary targets: settlers who neglected their farms in favor of employment in adjacent towns. For the Land Settlement Department could not and did not oppose such outside work during the initial years of villages founded during the phase of improvisation, when these settlements were as yet insufficiently developed for their inhabitants to be able to earn even a marginal living from their farms. Moreover, in 1953, the year the law was brought before Israel's parliament, the Land Settlement Department could not disregard the impact of the 1952 de-

[20] E.g., Jewish Agency for Israel 1956:239.

cline in dairy and vegetable prices on settlers who had begun serious cultivation of their farmsteads but had not realized an income large enough to live on from them. Although the Department replanned the agricultural development of villages affected, it did not expel settlers who turned to outside employment. Indeed, many families it would have preferred to have retained in the land settlement sector left such villages of their own accord.

The other grounds for expulsion were also invoked with great care. I have been in villages which had seethed with scandalim for years as settlers expressed their frustrations over lack of work, lack of credit for immediate needs, the state of the village store, prices paid for their produce, loss of village office or dismissal from it by a village instructor or one of his superiors in the land settlement hierarchy, indeed over almost any issue of village life. Settlers who had struck each other in the heat of a dispute, even settlers who had struck a village instructor, had not been expelled, although striking an instructor frequently resulted in an official charge of assault. To the best of my knowledge, only men who had persistently engaged in acts of violence and/or were considered habitual delinquents would be subject to legal action for expulsion on the grounds of disturbing the peace or constituting a menace.

Moreover, it was easier for the land settlement authorities to talk of or threaten expulsion than actually to carry it out. Of the 220 settlers brought to action as of 1956 under the Law of Candidates for Agricultural Settlement, only 80 had been removed from the villages. Furthermore, according to the law, settlers could not be expelled from a moshav for violating the constitution of its federation unless provided with a farmstead elsewhere.

Both the moshav contracts and provisions for removing settlers from villages without their consent illustrate limitations on the rationalization of land settlement that are inherent in the extension of legal controls over the settlers. For the exercise of such controls could not extend beyond policies that the law of Israel would uphold. In contrast, ideology could justify, as being for the immigrants' own good, whatever measures were successful in inducting them into the moshvei olim. Ideology also gave moral sanction to any means of persuasion and control, short of physical force and the violation of civil rights, that succeeded in getting the settlers to do what the settler role required. Legal controls, on the other hand, could buttress only very limited measures in support of such diffuse claims.

The policies reviewed so far were not the only modifications of earlier land settlement arrangements introduced soon after the phase of rationalization began. Comprehensive regional planning included features which were designed to alleviate problems classed as "social" and/or which had specific "social" aims. Such features included the policy of populating each of the clusters of villages located around the proposed rural centers with an ethnically homogeneous settler body. Concomitantly, the centers themselves were also to constitute community units, to be settled by the service personnel staffing their centralized facilities.

These features were introduced into comprehensive regional planning in an attempt to avoid the undesirable consequences, manifest in the older moshvei olim, of earlier arrangements. First of all, it was widely felt by 1954 that populating a moshav olim with immigrants of diverse backgrounds made for greater problems in village development than arose in the homogeneously populated villages. Secondly, the majority of the personnel employed in the moshvei olim did not follow the approved policy of living in the villages, but rather made their homes elsewhere and traveled to the new settlements to work.

Conclusions about the peopling of the immigrant settlements had been reached without benefit of or interest in social research. However, the impressions on which they were based, insofar as I could sort these out from utterances of the land settlement program administrators, seemed to have involved two salient aspects of the settler factionalism endemic to the moshvei olim. First, such factionalism was pervasive in villages inhabited by people of obviously different provenience and background, and it commonly, although not invariably in my observations, was expressed in such villages in the idiom of ethnic difference. Secondly, the prevalence of kinship ties among members of village factions was also repeatedly evident in the universe of moshvei olim. The land settlement program administrators seem to have perceived these two sets of recurrent social facts as linked to each other.[21]

Both circumstances and the cultural climate of Israel favored such a link. A very evident circumstance was the actual coincidence of ethnic group and kin group in many of the heterogenously peopled villages, for the ethnically distinct population segments were frequently, although not always, composed of people related to each other. Moreover, it was extremely difficult in Israel during the 1950s to sort out the culturally significant social distinctions among people of exotic provenience and background.[22] Categorizing according to ethnic group membership was the usual way of making such distinctions, and country of origin was the most common basis for the ethnic classification of people and for stereotypic generalizations about their behavior. Dichotomous categories, such as European and Oriental or Ashkenazi and Sephardi, were the commonest ways of drawing broader distinctions within the population. As far as I could judge, the plethora of observable facts regarding social background and cultural difference simply could not be handled by members of the new society except through recourse to such modes of categorization. It was as if categories of cognition could not at that time expand to process in other terms the load of data available to perception.

21 As an example of such linkage, see the following statement by Rokach (1964c:36): "The patriarchal family structure of the newcomers from the Oriental countries, which is supported by the kinship groups (hamula), made it impossible to settle different ethnic groups in the same village. . . ."

22 For example, I encountered immigrants from the island of Djerba in southern Tunisia who had kinsmen in the neighboring area of Libya and who had lived there for a time themselves. However, the fact that immigrants from Djerba felt themselves closer to these immigrants from Libya than to people from other regions of Tunisia was known only to those administrators who had extended contact with them or who had this fact brought to their attention.

Furthermore, experience by then had led to a general recognition throughout Israel that kinship units larger than the nuclear family were of basic importance among immigrants from the Middle East. This experience tended to be assimilated, at least insofar as I could observe, to what was known of the importance of bonds of patrilineal descent in Arab society. The administrators of the land settlement program, in particular, included individuals drawn from veteran settlements who had had Arab villagers as neighbors during the pre-statehood period and/or who still had contact with the Arab population of Israel. In reflecting on the "social problems" of the moshvei olim, such administrators, in my experience, tended to equate moshav factions comprised of immigrants from the same country or region with the social groupings organized on a patrilateral basis already familiar to them.[23]

Thus, the solidarity associated with lineage segments and with the ideology of patrilineal descent in Middle Eastern society seems to have been extended to generalizations concerning Jewish immigrants from the same non-European country or region of origin. Moshav olim cultural or ethnic

[23] Weintraub and Lissak make the same equation in their usage of the term "hamula," justifying it as follows (Weintraub and Lissak 1964c:135–36): "Properly speaking, the origin of what is known in Israel villages today as hamula lies in the Mediterranean patrilineage, territorially defined (although the term itself is in use chiefly in Iraq, Israel and Jordan). In Israel, however, these criteria of membership have sometimes been blurred, and groups combining several families—not necessarily of common patrilineal descent and common former residence—have emerged still calling themselves hamulas. This has been due not only to changes in the original structure, begun already in some countries of origin, but also and chiefly to the fact of their having often been split in the process of migration and settlement. In this context, therefore, the term 'hamula' denotes the groups or 'cliques' actually functioning in the moshav rather than the historical hamulas."

While I do not doubt that settlers themselves used the term "hamula" to designate village factions or "cliques," as Weintraub and Lissak state, I did not hear this expression among newly arrived immigrants but only among those who had been in Israel for several years. I suspect that most immigrants who employed it in reference to village cliques and factions learned this usage in Israel as part of their acculturation. Indeed, the only immigrants of whom this might not have been true would be those whose native language included the word "hamula." It would be interesting to investigate their usage of the term in conversations among themselves in native speech.

homogeneity, equated with immigrants' common provenience, was seen by the settlement authorities as offering a means of reducing conflict among the settlers of an immigrant village.

The provisions of comprehensive regional planning for the residence in rural centers of service personnel employed in the moshvei olim expressed both: (1) the general Israeli ideology of transforming the immigrants as quickly as possible; and (2) the view that village workers were in a crucial position to serve as generalized agents of acculturation. Therefore, their residence elsewhere than in the moshvei olim was disapproved of, since it curtailed their daily contacts with the settler families and, correspondingly, their opportunities to influence them and serve as models.

Moreover, even the effective maintenance of moshav services, such as school, dispensary, and store, could be handicapped when village workers lived away from the moshvei olim. This was particularly evident during the rainy season, since personnel at the village level did not have access, except as hitchhikers, to vehicles that could pass through kilometers of mud. Not all of them were able and willing to trudge through rain and mud on foot day after day to reach otherwise inaccessible villages in time to carry out their jobs on schedule. Nonetheless, only the village instructors and the storekeeper (and in many cases not even they) could be pressured to take up residence, at least during the work week, in the immigrant settlements. The shortage of personnel and the administrators' recognition that the village workers had their own lives to lead, whatever the claims of ideology, made residence a matter of personal choice rather than an aspect of occupational role.

However, both ideology and concern with national solidarity prohibited that the national goals of "fusion of exiles" and rapid immigrant assimilation be abandoned or left to the workings of time. The framework of regional settlement was utilized to serve these goals through means that were considered workable. The cluster of villages around a rural center provided the opportunity for settling each of the villages with a homogeneous body of settlers and for establishing the center as a homogeneously "Israeli" community. Attractive housing, which elsewhere in Israel was at a premimum; the ready availability of congenial company with the same background and interests; and the centers' other facilities and proximity to work were considered inducements that would persuade service personnel and their families to make the centers their home. Concomitantly, the immigrants' propinquity and constant mingling with each other in the rural centers would lead to "fusion of exiles" and would accelerate their adaptation to Israeli customs and values as personified in rural center communities.

The politics of Israel, as they affected the land settlement system, impeded implementation of the policy of homogeneously peopling the villages founded in 1955 and 1956 in the framework of regional settlement. This policy could not be more than partially implemented, although all the moshav federations had recruited settler groups that could be considered culturally homogeneous according to finer criteria than country of origin, and whose members were already related to each other through ties of kinship or friendship.

The recruitment of such groups had come about in one of two ways: (1) through the enlistment of total communities or segments of them in such culturally homogeneous regions as the Atlas Mountains of Morocco and the island of Djerba; and (2) through the recruitment of relatively middle-class, Westernized North African urbanites by one or more families of the group itself, families who had been active in local Zionist affairs, had decided to immigrate to Israel, and, under the aegis of a moshav federation representative, had enlisted relatives, friends, and congenial associates for settlement together. Neither means of recruitment of immigrants was unique to the phase of rationalization, although the Israeli transit camps rather than the countries of the Diaspora had been the earlier locale of recruitment.

The politics of Israel made possible the disruption of these groups, given (1) the political affiliation, made in advance, of all new moshvei olim with one or another of the moshav federations according to agreements reached at the highest national policy levels; and (2) the fact that the immigrants recruited by each federation could only be settled in villages assigned to the federation. The political competition of the moshav federations could disrupt the homogeneity of more than one settler group, as in the following two cases.

Jews in the Atlas Mountains had been "discovered" and signed up for immigration to Israel by an emissary of Tnuat Hamoshavim, the principal moshav federation, as will be described in Chapter VII. However, since these Jews were devoutly religious, representatives of the religious moshav federation sought to get them to transfer their affiliation, both on their way to Israel and after their arrival there. The success of these representatives in one village led to the departure of fourteen of its first sixty families, as is described in Chapter VIII, and the replacement of these families by immigrants of somewhat different background brought to the new settlement through the ship to village policy.

The fourteen families who had changed their moshav federation affiliation were taken to another village in the same new settlement region, a village assigned to the religious moshav federation. However, this was a village which had been set aside for immigrants from Djerba, who, I was reliably informed, had been promised settlement together in a moshav expressly reserved for people from Djerba. The first contingent of some forty families from Djerba arrived in the village to find the fourteen families from the Atlas Mountains already there before them. Moreover, the families from Djerba had also had added to their number and, transferred from ship to village with them some five other families from cities of Tunisia. As it happened, this particular group of immigrants from Djerba grumbled about these five families but did not become engaged in a succession of disputes with them, as they did throughout the next year with the contingent from the Atlas Mountains.

Moreover, the settlement of these immigrants from Djerba in the specific village to which they had been sent was itself a modification of a promise that had been made to them when they were recruited, or so I was informed. For adjacent to the new settlement region were several older moshvei olim also peopled by immigrants from Djerba. The new recruits were reported to have requested and been promised the village of the new settlement region closest to these older moshavim. However, this village was the one assigned to the liberal moshav federation.

The settlement of this latter village illustrates still another way in which the disruption of a homogeneous settler group could take place. For it had been promised to one of the groups of relatively middle-class and Westernized young families who had organized themselves abroad, in this case in Casablanca. However, these families did not arrive in Isreal until some six months after the village was ready for occupancy. Although I know of a case, in the new settlement district, in which a village remained vacant for months awaiting the contingent of immigrants for which it had been reserved, this kind of delay did not occur in the new settlement region. Instead, the liberal moshav federation signed up and brought from ships to village assorted nuclear and extended families from Tangiers and from different parts of rural and urban Morocco. By the time the organized group reached Israel, only about half of them could be accommodated in the new village. The remainder of the families were dispatched to an older moshav olim affiliated to the liberal federation, many of whose earlier settlers had left.

The moshav federations also did not have a sufficient number of homogeneous groups of the two kinds characterized above to settle all the villages of the new region (although one village was peopled by recruits originally from Iraq and Iran, actually from the Kurdistan regions of these countries, who had been in Israel for some five years). Therefore, two of the villages were peopled by families and extended families recruited abroad and sent to the villages from the ships and by families recruited at some point in transit. One of these villages, briefly discussed in Chapter IX, was initially populated by three contingents of Westernized immigrants from, respectively, Tangiers, Tunisia, and Morocco; by immigrants from Morocco and Tunisia who were from the traditional urban Jewish ghettos of these countries; and by a few families from rural Morocco, although not from the Atlas Mountains. It seethed with factional disputes throughout its first two years, disputes which involved rival leadership claims. Although supporters of the factional leaders, in fact, included immigrants from all the countries represented by its inhabitants, these disputes were presented in the idiom of ethnic conflict between the Tangerines and an alliance of Moroccans and Tunisians. In addition, a number of families originally from Cochin (Kerala) in India, who had already been in Israel for several years, transferred from a kibbutz and from another moshav olim to this village about a year after it was founded. These new settlers, physically distinctive from all the others and sharing no point of pre-immigration culture with them besides Jewish identification and observance, achieved ready acceptance throughout the village.

Settler solidarity and village development were the goals the settlement authorities sought to achieve through the policy of peopling new moshvei olim with culturally homogeneous settler populations. However, even where this policy was carried out successfully, it did not necessarily lead to the desired goals, as is reviewed in Chapter IX. Other factors besides the cultural or "ethnic" homogeneity or heterogeneity of village settlers, however these terms be defined, influenced settler solidarity and affected village development, and variable settlement conditions and variations in the land settlement system of relations were not the least of these factors.

The politics of Israel also impeded the centralization of services that was one of the goals of regional settlement. The schools established in the rural centers were designed to serve the entire cluster of surrounding villages. But while the State Education Bill which became law in August 1953 abolished the previous trend system in education,[24] it pro-

24 Cf. pp. 66, 138–39.

vided for two classes of public schools, teachers, inspectors, and curricula: one, known as State education, predominantly secular, and the other, known as State Religious education, committed to religious values and observances. Two of the four rural centers planned for the new settlement region were constructed, one serving a cluster of villages affiliated with secular moshav federations, the other serving a cluster of villages affiliated with the labor-religious moshav federation. The schools of these centers offered respectively the State education program and the State Religious education program. In the new settlement district, similar arrangements were carried out in the two composite moshvei olim that I observed.

However, immigrants from the Atlas Mountains had been settled, as already noted, in villages affiliated with the principal moshav federation, although other such immigrants were also recruited by and settled in villages of the religious moshav federation. Representatives of the religious political parties had no difficulty in persuading the Atlas Mountains immigrants settled in the Tnaut Hamoshavim affiliated villages to exercise their legal right to choose State Religious education for their children. But since the settlers of the other moshvei olim of that particular village cluster in the settlement region and also those of one unit of the composite moshav in the settlement district preferred State education for their children, duplicate school facilities had to be constructed. Furthermore, the intermingling in school of children from the various villages, part of the policy of "fusion of exiles," also was more restricted than planned.

The land settlement program administrators were hardly unaware of the disruptive effects of the factional systems of action on the implementation of their policies as planned. Almost all of the officials of the Land Settlement Department were members of one of Israel's political parties, those at the higher levels mostly of Mapai. However, they had to cope almost daily with conflicts of interest between the Department's nonpartisan nation-building goals and the ideologically justified political aims of the partisan movements and organizations participating in the land settlement program.

For the Land Settlement Department has had as its primary goal the creation of viable agricultural settlements. In carrying out its program, it founded not only villages based on Labor-Zionist principles but middle-class settlements. By the middle 1950s, it even sponsored large farms to be managed on a commercial basis.[25] The members of the Land Settlement Department's permanent administrative staff were not committed to the ideologies and principles of village organization of any of the partisan village federations. Most of them, moreover, were personally critical of the policies and practices of the moshav federations regarding the moshvei olim, of the Histadrut marketing and supplier cooperative societies, Tnuva and Hamashbir Hamerkazi,[26] and of the general politicization of land settlement, all of which complicated the attainment of the Department's main goal.

Moshav organization and the moshav movements' policies not only demanded that all settlers of a village assume corporate responsibility in village economic transactions. They also demanded that produce be marketed exclusively through Tnuva, or, in the case of the small number of moshvei olim affiliated with the liberal moshav federation,[27] through the marketing society of the agricultural association to which the moshav federation was linked. Similarly, moshav organization and the moshav movements' policies allowed the cooperative store to be the only source of purchases in the village, and these stores could use only Hamashbir Hamerkazi as wholesaler, except in the villages of the liberal federation.

Under regional settlement, a wide range of supplies for the settlers of a village cluster were to be offered by a large

[25] Of the four large farms established in the first region that was developed according to the principles of comprehensive regional planning, at least two were leased to private individuals. Another large farm nearby, which I visited, was held and managed by six young families.

[26] Cf. p. 64.

[27] Halperin (1957:208) notes that seven moshvei olim were affiliated to this federation as of the years 1953–54.

store in the center, with depots for daily necessities in the villages. But for more than a year after settlement began in the first region developed, the stores in the centers were not yet constructed or ready for use, and each of the new villages had a store like those of other moshvei olim.

These stores were not consumers' cooperatives under the control of the settlers themselves, as in the classic moshvei ovdim, but rather were maintained and run by a special branch of Hamashbir created to service the immigrant settlements. This branch assigned as temporary store-keeper one of its employees, who was responsible to it rather than to the moshav. Not all of these storekeepers lived in the moshvei olim even during the week, and some of those who traveled daily from a nearby urban center might arrive late and leave early. Many of them were post-statehood immigrants from Eastern Europe, and often had little sympathy for the customs of non-European immigrants and were patronizing and irritable in their daily dealings with them.

The stores themselves were frequently poorly stocked, and basic provisions could be delayed for days during the rainy months, when it was difficult for trucks to get through the mud of the connecting roads. I have been in moshvei olim where the national rations of meat and fresh fruits and vegetables had not arrived for weeks, and the vegetables were in poor condition when they did arrive. Dairy products might spoil, especially in moshvei olim whose settlers were not accustomed to consuming them; and I have known store-keepers not to order fresh dairy products for families who wanted them.

The rule prohibiting purchases on credit in consumers' co-operatives was enforced in these stores, and occasional sympathetic storekeepers who had provided credit for needy families were censured by their supervisors and held per-sonally responsible for the amount owed. However, wages for work done for public agencies could be delayed for months, notably, according to my observations, in the case of the Jewish National Fund. Men with many dependents could have money owing them beyond the advances given to insure at least minimal subsistence, yet be unable to purchase on credit at the village store.

Toward the end of 1955, this situation was somewhat modified. The Land Settlement Department, the Jewish National Fund, and the special Mashbir branch for immigrants worked out a policy according to which advances on wages for work done or to be done for these two agencies would be given to the settlers partly in coupons, which could be used in lieu of money in the village stores. However, while this arrangement augmented settler purchasing power, it also increased the settlers' dependence on the village stores without making for any improvement in them. Indeed, I knew many settlers who complained bitterly that staple foods were dearer in the village stores than in the nearest towns and who could cite comparative prices item by item.

I also observed many cases in which the head of a family, when he had the money to do so, would forfeit the possibility of a day's employment in order to make the trip to town to bring back supplies. In several villages, groups of settlers purchased animals, particularly before the holidays, had them ritually slaughtered in their own village or in the nearest one with a qualified slaughterer, and divided up the meat. In one moshav olim an itinerant meat merchant even sold fresh cuts to the villagers without the interference of the instructors, although they subsequently prohibited this. Villagers of rural background commonly preserved supplies of vegetables by traditional means when they were plentiful and drew on them during other periods of the year. However, formerly urban immigrants, particularly those of middle-class background, were in a state of relative deprivation in comparison to Israeli urbanites and their own past experiences, particularly during the winter months, and they felt it keenly. I was in few new villages settled by former urbanites in which the village store was not a source of continual bitterness and complaints, feeding tensions and entering into village crises repeatedly as a subsidiary issue.

However, the Land Settlement Department staff could do

little in response to such complaints except exert pressure on the special Mashbir branch for immigrants. This led, at best, to a limited and temporary improvement in services. Even the stores instituted in the rural centers under regional settlement did not show a conspicuous improvement in services during their first year.

Less chronic than settler frustrations over the village stores but more threatening to village development and settler role-socialization were occasional refusals by Tnuva to accept the full quota of vegetables grown by a particular moshav olim. This could occur because of a glut on the market. In such cases the Land Settlement Department sided with the settlers and exerted all possible pressure on Tnuva to persuade it to reverse its decision. But should such pressure be unsuccessful there was nothing the Department could do. Even if it took on itself the loss of agricultural capital involved, such refusals by Tnuva precipitated village-wide crises and compounded the attrition of settler role-socialization.[28]

Even veteran members of the moshav movements might make compromises in such instances that conflicted with their own ideology. Thus, in a composite moshav that I studied, such a refusal by Tnuva had taken place in regard to a crop of tomatoes. Since this occurred during the first year after the moshav's founding, the agricultural holding company of the moshav federation and the Land Settlement Department, rather than the settlers themselves, faced the loss involved. However, earlier in the season a private dealer had offered to buy the crop and had been refused by the social instructor, in this case a pioneer settler of a flourishing classic moshav ovdim. Although long active in the affairs of his moshav federation and with high status in it, he tried after Tnuva's refusal to persuade the private dealer to accept the crop, only to be quoted, according to a reliable informant, a much lower price than the original offer. I could not find out how the negotiations ended, but the fields remained full of tomatoes to which anyone could help himself.

28 Weingrod (1966:91–94) discusses such a case in the village he studied.

Analogously, in the new settlement region during its first year, a most devout adherent of Labor-Zionist and moshav ideology declared that he was prepared to have private store-keepers open their own shops in the moshvei olim if conditions could not be improved in the existing village stores. The speaker was a pioneer settler of another veteran classic moshav ovdim, who had lost both his sons in Israel's War of Independence and who had left his farm, later donated to the national Defense Fund, to settle in the new region and live and work among the immigrants. He was appointed first head of the provisional local government body of the new region, and his wife worked as a full-time schoolteacher without accepting a salary. Despite their national prestige and protektzia, which included direct access to the President of Israel, and despite the power this man exercised in his official capacity, he was unable to bring about any noticeable improvement in the village stores of the moshvei olim of the region, much less the drastic innovation of which he spoke.

For the cooperative societies of the Histadrut, such as Tnuva, Hamashbir Hamerkazi, Kupat Holim (the Sick Fund), etc., had become powerful organizations in their own right, each with its own goals, interests, and also problems. Their services to the new settlements constituted only one aspect of their ramifying activities; and the Histadrut itself was the most powerful organization in Israel, able to influence government policy at the highest decision-making levels and able to ignore directives of governmental ministries.[29]

The rationalization of the land settlement program could be impeded by the policies and actions of the many agencies that were not under the control of the Land Settlement Department, but which were part of the system of action through which the land settlement program was carried out or which were essential to village development and the provision of services. The Land Settlement Department could only exert pressure through its top officials and through political chan-

[29] Cf. Rubner 1960:46.

nels, and/or these officials might use their own protektzia to try to compel other organizations to perform as desired. For example, the director of one settlement region threatened the Histadrut's Sick Fund with a public scandal in the newspapers unless it provided nurses for the dispensaries of the villages in the settlement region he administered. The same man, on another occasion, took a burning issue to the Prime Minister of Israel to secure his intervention.

Thus, the tactics which the new immigrants quickly learned to use in their dealings with Israel's public agencies were actually those employed, with inside knowledge and finesse, at every level of administration. When such tactics could not be used or did not work, the Land Settlement Department could only accept the situation and utilize its own resources, insofar as possible, to cope with problems in terms of its own goals.

However, policies and practices which the Land Settlement Department could not control were not the only ones acting as obstacles to settler role-socialization during the phase of rationalization. For most of the villages founded between 1948 and 1951 still had not by 1957 received the full capital investment of the Jewish Agency in their development or even most of it. Many of these settlements, moreover, lacked sufficient arable land and water to become viable without substantial expenditures on land reclamation and on expansion of water resources.[30] The allocation of funds for extension of the land settlement program and the uncertain income of the Jewish Agency itself impeded improvement of settlement conditions in villages founded during the phase of improvisation. This was particularly the case in villages where the optimum conditions that could be created at that time would not result in a level of agricultural productivity that might justify such expenditures. Thus, older villages could be considered underprivileged in comparison with the newer

[30] Weintraub and Lissak (1964b:102) state that nearly half the moshavim founded between 1948 and 1950 lack proper conditions for development. They evaluate such conditions on the basis of security factors, i.e., distance of the village from the frontier and its vulnerability to marauding infiltrators, as well as resources of land and water.

regions in which rationalized planning could be implemented only if the flow of investment was maintained according to schedule.

Priorities in allocation of the Land Settlement Department's funds were determined at the highest policy-levels. Within the limits of these priorities the various settlement regions were in a competitive position in regard to their budgetary demands, as is described in Chapter VI, and the directors of the regions used their skill and influence in negotiating and pressing their claims with the Land Settlement Department directorate.

However, when the Department revised earlier policies as part of the rationalization of its program, this could impede the settlers' identification with farming as a vocation in villages founded during the phase of improvisation. For example, the settlers of one moshav olim, established in the Negev in 1950, had received cows as part of the Department's capital investment in their farms. These settlers, who were from Libya, had not taken proper care of these animals. This may have influenced the Department's decision, after it began to curtail the further development of dairy farming in the country, to change the farm type of the village. It repossessed the cows and replanned the village's agricultural development in terms of field crops. However, the settlers remembered their cows and wanted them back. By 1957, many families had even purchased cows from their own resources and were trying to learn how to take care of them without the aid of the Land Settlement Department. They were still calling themselves dairy farmers, although the issue was a closed one for the Land Settlement Department.

Inconsistencies in land settlement policy experienced by settlers could impede role-socialization, but they also could encourage knowledgeable settlers to attempt to effect changes in or exceptions to policy in specific issues of concern to them. The politicization of land settlement did not discourage such attempts or the possibility of their success. For settlers could use the threat of switching the political affiliation of their village at the next election to bring the moshav movement to exert pressure on the Land Settlement Department. Or the settlers of an already well-developed border village close to economic consolidation could use threats of leaving the settlement as a very powerful bargaining point. Furthermore, the Agricultural Center of the Histadrut, while displaced from its pre-statehood importance in land settlement by the post-statehood transformations in the program, still held power in Israel's agricultural sector and exercised its pre-statehood functions for those new settlers who turned to it. If it brought an issue to the Land Settlement Department for review, the case could not be ignored.

For example, the Agricultural Center's intervention led to the reevaluation in 1957 of disputes that had been going on for years in a village founded in 1950 and seething with crises since then. The settlers of the moshav were mostly immigrants from India and had been placed together for that reason, but they actually represented three thoroughly distinct Jewish communities. The largest segment of families were descendents of Jews originally from Baghdad who had followed the British to India and established themselves there centuries ago, spreading out through Southeast Asia. The few families in the village not from India were from Burma, kinsmen of some of those from India.

One group of related families of this village segment controlled most of the village offices, both the elective positions and the salaried posts, apart from those of instructors, such as dispensary nurse. Furthermore, the members of this group of relatives were the most diligent and successful farmers in the village, according to the evaluations of the local district staff of the Land Settlement Department. The leader of the kin group, who was head of the village's Executive Committee, had the support of these administrators in his policies.

A gentle, elderly man and a middle-aged niece who kept house for him represented the Beni Israel, a large and ancient Jewish community of India. He had been an agronomist in India, had been active in India's struggle for independence as well as in its Zionist movement, and had come to Israel in fulfillment of his Zionist commitment. He had ended up in this moshav olim, which he had served as social instructor during a brief period in its early history. However, the Land Settlement Department had dismissed the appointment, which the moshav federation apparently had made. He toiled uncomplainingly on his farm to the extent of his limited strength and was respected by the villagers and by the instructors as well. But he held no post of power in the village and was regarded as an unimportant old man by the Land Settlement Department's district staff.

Some sixteen households from Cochin (Kerala) constituted the remainder of the village's settlers. It was they who turned to the Agricultural Center of the Histadrut, maintaining that they were discriminated against in the village both politically and in the allocation of village agricultural capital assets furnished by the Land Settlement Department.

Their complaints were not new in 1957, but at some point in the course of their dissatisfactions they had brought these grievances to the emissary who had recruited them for immigration to Israel. This man was a veteran Zionist with high prestige in the country. Their case then had gone to the Agricultural Center; it included a petition for resettlement in a village with other immigrants from Cochin; and the director of the Land Settlement Department was called on to make a decision.

As a detailed investigation in the village made clear, the idiom of ethnic difference clothed a range of disputes in which neither of the ethnically distinct major village segments constituted solidary contending factions. Indeed, one of the immigrants from Cochin, earlier one of their leaders and spokesmen and elected to the Executive Committee, maintained that the present complaints were unfounded. Some members of the "Baghdadi" body of Indian settlers had no love for the family holding power in the village, were so indifferent to the immigrants from Cochin as to seem unaware of their protests, and were full of their own grievances against the land settlement authorities and the demands of the settler role.

The immigrants from Cochin who wanted resettlement had

their petition granted, particularly since such immigrants in another village had made the same request and the two blocs of settlers could be brought together to constitute a village population. Thus, by 1957, the Land Settlement Department heeded protests that could be resolved through resettlement fostering village ethnic homogeneity, at least when discontented settlers knew the channels through which and terms in which to present their claims.

Given the land settlement system of relations, new immigrants whose grievances could be legitimized in terms acceptable to ideology and/or policy could find themselves protectors. The moshav federations and the Agricultural Center of the Histadrut could be brought to back them on certain issues in otherwise unavailing protests to the staff of the Land Settlement Department; and the Land Settlement Department would try to protect their interests in case of deficient services by other organizations essential for village development, such as Tnuva. Some issues, however, in which settler protests were seen as legitimate by the Land Settlement Department, such as those concerning the village stores, could remain impervious to reform for years. Other issues might involve claims that clearly were not legitimate, but the particular settlers might be powerful enough to get their way if they did not demand compromises beyond the power of the Land Settlement Department to effect.

Another village founded during the phase of improvisation illustrates this kind of situation as well as the concessions that could be gained by threatening to switch political affiliation. The village had been settled by two extended kinship groups from different parts of Yemen who formed feuding factions in the village. Nonetheless, the settlement was well along in its agricultural development when the Land Settlement Department decided to increase the number of farmsteads for reasons related to agricultural planning. The two factions then entered into a bitter competition for allocation of these farmsteads to members of their respective groups, lest one of them gain a numerical advantage sufficient to win control of the village offices.

The more beleaguered faction threatened to change its political affiliation to the moshav movement of Herut, should the desired proportion of new farmsteads not be allocated to it. It would have won its point had it been able to advance enough adult candidates qualified to be moshav members in their own right. Unable to do so, it tried to secure a farm for one member's son who was still in the Army and not eligible according to moshav movement and land settlement regulations; in this case it got its way. When, however, the faction advanced as another candidate a boy still below army age, this was too irregular to be countenanced, particularly since the other faction had eligible adult candidates. The weaker faction then tried to carry out its threat, and the ensuing crisis in village affairs had political implications that brought it to the attention of the Knesset, the national parliament.

Even less legitimate, but more successful, was an astute new settler's manipulation of the politicization of land settlement. This man was a suave, multilingual former cafe-owner from Tangiers, whose cafe there was said by those who had known him abroad to have included a brothel. Still in his prime and with sturdy adolescent children, he was recruited into land settlement by the liberal moshav federation and sent in 1955 to its village in the new settlement region. One of the first settlers of the village, genial in manner and obviously capable, he held a position of leadership among the others and also, initially, was seen as a settler leader by the village instructors. After about seven months in the village, he had had enough of land settlement and of the moshav federation and decided to seek resettlement in a town, where he planned to open a cafe. He wanted an immediate assignment to a permanent dwelling in town, rather than to have to wait for months or years in a transit camp dependent on the absorption authorities.

The village to which he had been sent already had a history of settler dissidence. The village rabbi, an immigrant from Morocco, had earlier tried to effect a switch in village affiliation to the religious moshav federation. He failed in this, since the majority of the settlers no longer kept or wished to keep the full range of religious observances. Nonetheless, the village seethed with discontent, including profound settler hostility to one of the instructors. Unable to persuade the representative of the liberal moshav federation to get him transferred to a town with immediate claims to housing, the former cafe-owner joined several other dissident Westernized settlers in circulating a petition to change village federation affiliation to the principal moshav federation. A majority of settler signatures to the petition was obtained, and the attempt failed only because the moshav federation refused to accept or act on the offer. Partner to the planning of regional settlement, it declined to be a party to its disruption.

The former cafe-owner was undaunted. He welcomed the arrival of the contingent of the organized group to whom the village had been promised, who had already had their morale shaken by the splitting of their group on arrival in Israel, as recounted above. He had no doubt that other discontents would follow. He openly declared that he would remain in the village until the next national election, if necessary, in order to work for a switch in its federation affiliation. He was reported to have received his house well before the election fell due.

However, the great majority of settlers recently arrived in the country did not know how to present their complaints and demands in a way that could elicit concessions from the land settlement authorities or even gain their serious consideration. Such information, obviously, was not disseminated by the instructor teams and could be so distorted in transmission from one immigrant group to another as to be useless. Settler rebellion at odds with the entire land settlement value system only succeeded in uniting all the agencies in a display of authority to quell protest. A very fine line made the difference between scandalim which promoted attainment of an objective and those which lost a protesting immigrant or settler group the chance of a review of the case in question. Barring luck, considerable acculturation was necessary before an immigrant could sense that line and learn what tactics might work in a given situation.

Newly arrived settlers, moreover, actually had very little power. The case of the cafe-owner involved the unique vulnerability of the liberal moshav federation as contrasted with the others. On the one hand, its ideology lacked the point of contact with new immigrants from North Africa and the Middle East which in the case of the religious moshav federation was supplied by the religious orthodoxy of those not yet exposed to Western influences. On the other hand, unlike the principal moshav federation with its links to Mapai, the liberal federation could not attract new immigrants through offering membership in the party holding power in the country. As a rule, until settlers had accepted farming as a vocation and had begun to play their designated role in the agricultural development of the villages, the investment they represented to the settlement authorities was not sufficient for their demands to carry much weight.

But by the time settlers achieved a bargaining position, they too had made investments, both material and emotional, in their village. Even if unable to get their own way, they did not lightly leave the settlement that had become their home.

The politicization of land settlement can be seen as having set limits to rationalization. However, it also can be seen as having served to integrate the changing post-statehood system, the pre-statehood interrelated components of which had undergone a partial dissociation.

For the expansion of the land settlement program and the change in its nation-building role and goals had parallels in the post-statehood history of other programs which had laid the foundations of the new society. For instance, of the manifold programs of the Histadrut, the development of industry increasingly came to the fore. Not only the Histadrut as a whole but its marketing and supply societies, Tnuva and Hamashbir Hamerkazi, expanded and assumed new tasks and pursued their own goals. The services of Tnuva and Hamashbir to new settlements more obviously served the interests of these organizations than those of the new settlers.

The agencies of the government also exercised a jurisdiction with which the pre-statehood organizations had to come to terms, however much their prior existence initially might have curtailed the scope of the governmental agencies. In fact, governmental authority has steadily expanded over areas of activity previously in the hands of the pre-statehood factional systems of action. Defense, education, social security, and the labor exchanges were successive areas over which the government assumed jurisdiction during slightly over a decade from the time it came into existence. Of the quasi-governmental agencies, the Jewish National Fund also lost autonomy with the creation in 1958 of a national land authority to administer both its land and that to which the state held title.

The system of relations through which the land settlement program was carried out did not undergo basic reorganization during Israel's first post-statehood decade or for years afterwards. However, the system was subject to strain as each of its interlocking organizational units adapted to the new conditions.

The system's politicization may be seen as having served to integrate its constituent units. The rationalization of land settlement took place in what may be termed the middle range of policy. Political and ideological considerations influenced both top-level decisions and village-level implementation. The politicization of land settlement also offered the immigrant settlers channels for gaining attention to their interests as they saw them, in spite of the authority that was exercised over them by the administrators of the land settlement program. Once sensitized to the politics of Israel and to their own bargaining power as the persons on whom the success of the program essentially depended, they could try their hands at the same game of politics, pressure, and organizational manipulation that was practiced at higher levels throughout the system. In so doing, they constituted more than a target population even prior to full socialization to other aspects of the settler role.

A BURGEONING BUREAUCRACY
AND THE NEW SOCIETY

The Jewish land settlement of Palestine was largely accomplished by people organized into movements. Indeed, movements founded Israel as new state and new society, as was discussed in Chapters I and II. The decline in the importance of movements to Israel's development had as its counterpart the growth of bureaucracies administering the country. This chapter focuses on the Land Settlement Department of the Jewish Agency as a bureaucracy during Israel's first post-independence decade, when the Department held a central role in the national land settlement program.

The Land Settlement Department may be considered a transitional bureaucracy. For the settlements it helps to found pass out of its jurisdiction when they achieve viability, more specifically when its full capital investment in their development has been made and the settlers have shown themselves able to work their farms effectively and manage village affairs.[1] Of the organizations cooperating in the land settlement program, the settlement federations are the ones to which the villages remain linked, while in matters of agricultural policy consolidated and viable settlements are under the jurisdiction of the government's Ministry of Agriculture. Given Israel's size and its dependence on advanced land reclamation technology for new resources of arable land, the Land Settlement Department's field of action is progressively foreclosed by the successful attainment of its goals.

Whatever the future of the Land Settlement Department, it assumed the central role after Israel's independence in im-

---

[1] According to the statistics of the Land Settlement Department, fifty-nine settlements that had achieved consolidation by 1957 were still receiving aid from the Department (Jewish Agency for Israel, Land Settlement Department 1958:29). Of these, twenty-six were moshavim and twenty-six kibbutzim. Some of these had been founded prior to Israel's independence.

plementing the land settlement program, and it developed into a large and complex organization in the process. Factors involved in its growth and differentiation as an organization include: (1) the multiplication in number of new settlements founded, and the resulting expansion in the size of the administrative and technical staff planning and carrying out the settlement program; (2) national agricultural planning after 1952, and the increased authority and planning responsibity acquired by public agencies at the expense of the traditional decision-making scope of the settlers of new villages; and (3) the areas of activity in the moshvei olim over which the Department assumed authority which it neither claimed nor exercised over new settlers in the pioneer tradition or those in middle-class villages.

The term "bureaucratization" was introduced in the previous chapter, according to current usage, to refer to: (1) the development of bureaucratic features in an organization; and (2) the development or extension of bureaucracy's controls over areas of activity not previously subject to them. The term in both these usages can be applied to related phenomena in Israel's post-statehood land settlement system. The Land Settlement Department developed bureaucratic characteristics as it assumed greater authority over new settlements than it had held over those settlements founded during the pre-statehood period. After the centralization of agricultural planning this new authority was not limited to the moshvei olim, although it did not extend in other kinds of settlements to areas outside the scope of agricultural planning and development. Years before changes in agricultural policy in the interests of national development, the Land Settlement Department assumed pervasive authority over the settlers recruited into the moshvei olim. This saliently contributed to its development of a major bureaucratic feature, the hierarchic exercise of authority.

The village instructors were the agents through which the Land Settlement Department exercised daily authority over the implementation of its program in the moshvei olim. The employment of such instructors substantially augmented its staff; of its 1,878 employees in 1957, 606 were village instructors.[2] The village instructors also constituted the lowest level of its extended hierarchy of authority, reviewed in this chapter, in both the administrative and technical spheres. However, the authority the instructors exercised, delegated to them by the moshav federations which recruited them as well as by the Land Settlement Department which employed and paid them, was vested in the settlers according to the moshav community type. In theory, the instructors held it only until they could prepare the new immigrants to assume the responsibilities of the moshav settler role. In practice, years elapsed, even after village self-governing committees had been constituted and began to function, before instructors fully relinquished village management to the settlers and ceased to exercise surveillance over the committees, particularly the crucial executive committee. I have been in villages which had passed the stage of economic consolidation and had been in existence for eight years or more, yet still had an instructor.

However, the instructor role became incorporated into a hierarchic line of authority rather than having been initiated as part of it. The initial assignment of instructors to the first moshvei olim, according to the accounts of veteran land settlement personnel, envisaged the instructors as guiding and training the new immigrants rather than as holding authority in their stead. This conception of the instructor role was not markedly discontinuous with the pre-statehood system of relations for implementing land settlement. The youth movements which recruited and trained future settlers in the pioneer tradition have had emissaries, often recruited from veteran villages, to organize, train, and lead the youth groups both abroad and in Jewish Palestine and Israel. The Hebrew word *madrikh* (female, *madrikha*), generally translated as "guide," has been the term used to designate both such group leaders and the village instructors. Indeed, a

---

[2] All figures for 1957 given in this chapter are those stated in Jewish Agency for Israel, Treasury Department: 1958.

madrikh occasionally accompanied new settlers in the pioneer tradition when they first went on the land.

The transformation in the instructor role in regard to the moshvei olim was reported to have been occasioned by the incapacity of most of the recruits to the immigrant villages to comprehend the responsibilities of the moshav settler role and to accept them. For example, some settlers elected to the executive committees initiated by the instructors were said to have put to their own use the Land Settlement Department's initial capital investment for village development. The obligations of committee members toward both the village as corporate unit and the totality of its settlers neither were easily grasped nor readily accepted by rivals for village leadership, particularly in moshvei olim peopled by immigrants unused to the principle of delegation of authority to elected village representatives. According to veteran land settlement administrators, managerial authority in the new villages had to be given to the instructors if the interests of village development were to prevail over imminent chaos.

The transformation in the instructor role was accompanied by an increase in the Land Settlement Department's power in regard to the moshvei olim, at the expense of that of the moshav federations. For while the instructors represented the federations at least as much as they represented the Department, the partisan federations possessed no more influence over the settlers than whatever they could gain through success in ideological indoctrination or through offering the settlers political or more tangible inducements in order to win their loyalties. However, the Land Settlement Department dispensed the material resources for village development, including housing and other daily necessities. The instructors, whatever their political and federation loyalties, had to turn to the Land Settlement Department rather than to the federations for the authority and flow of resources most significant to their relations with settlers as well as to the course of village development.

It may here be noted that the Land Settlement Department was not differentiated from the resource-dispensing Jewish

Agency of which it was part by the great majority of new settlers. The Sohnut, as the Jewish Agency is called throughout Israel, had paid their fare to Israel; the Sohnut had brought them to the new villages; and the Sohnut was seen as the agency on which they were most dependent in the villages, as in fact it was.

The transformation of the instructor role in regard to the moshvei olim was not the only manifestation of the hierarchic exercise of authority in the post-statehood Land Settlement Department. Additional administrative posts were created between the top policy positions and the village level, augmenting the administrative hierarchy that had existed prior to Israel's statehood. The total program was directed from a head office, centered in Jerusalem in the Jewish Agency headquarters building, while the areas of Jewish land settlement had been classed into districts which were administered for the purpose of the program by district officers and staff.

However, bureaucratic features had been relatively little developed in the pre-statehood Land Settlement Department, at least according to accounts I received. It had been a small organizational unit, and practically all the people it employed were supposed to have been personally acquainted with each other. Extensive professional training was not a necessary qualification for a post of administrative responsibility in it. It was part of a sector of action pervaded by the Labor-Zionist ethos, and relations within the Department and between its officials and villagers were markedly egalitarian. Formalized, impersonal rules were little developed in a system in which the allocation of resources largely was determined by politicized negotiations between partners working toward a common goal.

In the post-statehood bureaucratization of the land settlement system, rationalization contributed substantially to the differentiation and specialization of organizational roles and tasks and to the utilization of professional knowledge and formalized professional procedures in land settlement planning and implementation. Impersonal rules and procedures also marked the extension of legal authority over the settlers. Nonetheless, the organizational features of a bureaucracy developed at an uneven rate both within the Land Settlement Department and with regard to various aspects of its program. Some of the nonbureaucratic characteristics of the pre-statehood period were still evident in the years 1955–58, when I was associated with the Department, as is indicated below. Its mixture of bureaucratic features, as they developed, with nonbureaucratic characteristics was not atypical of other public agencies in the country during Israel's first decade.[3]

SKETCH OF A CHANGING ORGANIZATION

The apex of the Land Settlement Department's hierarchy of authority was (and still is) the post of head of the Department. This post, like the position of head of all the departments of the Jewish Agency, is explicitly political. All heads of departments are members of both the Executive of the World Zionist Organization and that of the Jewish Agency, and they are elected every four years by the World Zionist Congress. Since, however, the delegates to the World Zionist Congress are party appointees, the members of the Jewish Agency Executive are also, in effect, party appointees.

From before Israel's independence until after its first decade of statehood, the occupant of the office of head of the Land Settlement Department was a high-ranking member of Mapai. He simultaneously held other top-level posts including, successively, those of treasurer of the Jewish Agency and minister of agriculture and minister of finance in Israel's government. A member of the Second Aliya who had come to Palestine from Russia in 1914, he had a background characteristic of Israel's governing elite during this period.

It is not irrelevant to note here that in the allocation of ministries in the successive coalition governments since independence, Mapai consistently has retained for itself the crucial ministries of defense, foreign affairs, finance, police, and education and culture. In the allocation of portfolios in the Jewish Agency, that of chairman of the executive of the

[3] Cf. Arien 1956; Bernstein 1957: Chap. 6; Samuel 1956:59–75.

Jewish Agency in Jerusalem consistently has been held by Mapai, as have the posts of treasurer of the Jewish Agency and head of the Department of Land Settlement. Of the other departments of the Jewish Agency directly concerned with the mass of new immigrants, the Department of Immigration consistently has been headed by a member of a religious party, and the Department of Youth Immigration (Youth Aliya) by a member of the liberal Progressive Party. The Department of Absorption was headed by members of Mapai and Mapam and, after the formation of Ahdut Ha'avoda, by one of its members. A member of the General Zionists consistently headed the Economic Department of the Jewish Agency.[4]

Within the post-statehood Land Settlement Department, there have been three major administrative levels, in which all posts, except that of head of the Department, are appointive. These levels have been: the head office, the regional offices, and the district offices. The head office has had jurisdiction over publicly financed land settlement throughout the country. Basic policy has been decided by the department directorate, which also has apportioned budget and supervised the program. The regions and districts are territorial units into which the country was divided for implementation of the program. Their number increased during Israel's first decade as the expansion in number of settlements called for the redrawing of their boundaries. Each of them had its own headquarters and administrative and technical staff.

The region was the significant unit below the national level for land settlement planning and administration. It was a post-statehood unit of administration, made possible because of national sovereignty over the country's territory and considered necessary because of the expansion of land settlement and the different agricultural potential of different areas of the country. The country was divided into five regions by 1955, and their territories corresponded, insofar as was

4 Between 1961 and 1965, the configuration of Israel's political parties changed, with new mergers and splits taking place. Other changes occurred during 1967–68, after this book was completed. I touch on some of these changes, relating them to the main themes of this study, in Chapter X.

practical, with Israel's major geophysical divisions. Thus, the geographically discontinuous mountainous areas of the country, the Judean Hills and the hills of Galilee, were classed as subregions within a single administrative region. The district was the significant unit in the daily implementation of the program. During the middle 1950s, district lines were drawn to include an average of twenty to twenty-five settlements, and the regions generally included two or three districts.

The highest appointive office in the Land Settlement Department, as in all departments of the Jewish Agency, has been that of departmental director. During Israel's first decade, several departments of the Jewish Agency had two persons holding appointments as director. The Land Settlement Department was one of these, and for a time it even had three directors. However, generally only one of these directors was known to the public as such and was continually visible in the administrative line of authority. He is the person meant when reference is made in this study to the Department's director. His office was in Jerusalem, in the headquarters building of the Jewish Agency, whereas the person holding the second continuous appointment as director had his office in Tel Aviv. The Jerusalem-based director was a native Israeli of the generation that had reached adulthood during the last decade of the mandate period. He held a doctorate in agronomy and was an active member of the Mapai.

The highest policy body of the Department was its directorate, whose members included the head of the Department, its directors, and several deputy directors. After the founding of the Joint Planning Center, the one of its two directors who represented the Jewish Agency was also a member. The other director of the Joint Planning Center represented the Ministry of Agriculture. A Joint Guidance Center, created in 1954, also had two directors, one representing the Ministry and the other the Agency. Administrative posts within the head office included those of secretary and treasurer.

Most of the functional units attached to the head office came into existence with increased differentiation of departmental tasks after statehood. The Joint Planning Center and the Division of Contracts and Securities were created in the interests of rationalization, as was reviewed in Chapter V. Units might also be transferred from other organizations to the Department; and the expansion in scope of tasks accompanying expansion of the program might lead to the creation of new units by reorganization from within the Department. For example, the Department's Professional Division had previously been the Extension Department of the Agricultural Experimental Institute, first initiated in 1921 and financed by the Foundation Fund. One of its sections, as of 1951, dealt with special crops and projects, including tree nurseries and calf-raising. A separate Project Section was later created, to which calf-rearing and tree nurseries were assigned. By 1957, the tree nurseries were administered as a separate section. This kind of fissioning of specialized units was characteristic of the expansion of Israel's public agencies during the first post-independence decade.

However, it was easier to create new functional units than to consolidate existing ones in the interests of rationalization. In the Land Settlement Department, for example, the Professional Division continued, at least into 1957, to supervise instruction in specialized branches of agriculture, despite the creation in 1954 of the Joint Guidance Center and its development into an agricultural extension service. Also, by 1956, if not earlier, a proposal to amalgamate two other specialized units was under consideration, but it still had not been implemented by 1958. These two units were: the Absorption Section, with fifteen employees in 1957, which maintained liaison with the Absorption Department of the Jewish Agency and processed the removal of discontented settlers from the villages; and the Social and Security Section, with three employees as of 1957, which dealt with both the relocation of social cases and matters of village defense. The heads of both these sections were veteran Labor-Zionists in the pioneer tradition. The question of their relative ranks, should the two sections be merged in the proposed Division of Sundry Affairs, may have been a factor impeding its creation.

The Department's Water Division was one of its earliest specialized units, and had its analogue in the Water Division of the Ministry of Agriculture. In the division of functions between the Land Settlement Department and the Ministry of Agriculture, the former's Water Division remained responsible for the supply of water to new settlements, while the Ministry's Water Division assumed responsibility for water use in the country as a whole. The development of Israel's water resources was a major concern in national planning, and it also underwent rationalization, after a phase of improvisation during which Israel's underground water resources had been considerably overestimated. However, rationalization in regard to water resources involved the country as a whole rather than a single sector. The Land Settlement Department's Water Division, which came to include sections dealing with planning and implementation and such specialized activities as drilling and pumping stations, became part of a network of organizational units and agencies which crosscut organizational boundaries and had their own interagency coordinating bodies.

Of such agencies, Tahal, the Israel Water Planning Authority, was created in 1952, the same year as the Joint Planning Center. Unlike the Center, however, it was established as a corporation, with 52 percent of its shares owned by the government and the remainder divided between the Jewish Agency and the Jewish National Fund. As a corporation, Tahal has not only planned and designed Israel's water systems, but has carried out projects abroad.

Of the specialized units attached to the head office of the Land Settlement Department, some, such as the Water Division, engaged in central planning and direction of areas of activity that were worked out in detail at the regional and district levels. Others, such as the Absorption Section, worked on all administrative levels throughout the country. Still others, such as a Section for Middle-Class Settlement and a

Abbreviated Organizational Chart of the Land Settlement Department of the Jewish Agency, 1955–1957.*

* This chart has been adapted from a rather sketchy organization chart of the Land Settlement Department as of 1960–61. I have not tried to fit in all the organizational units attached to the head office which are referred to in the text, and there are other omissions.

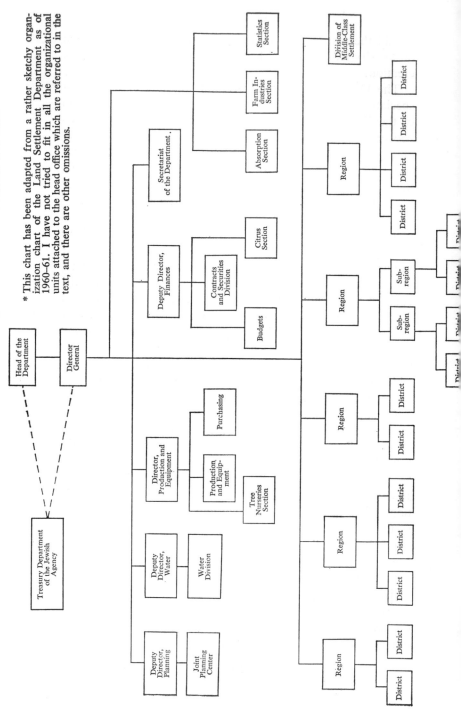

Section for Auxiliary Farms, operated outside the scope of regional and district organization. The Section for Middle-Class Settlement dealt with families able to invest some 35 to 50 percent of the funds needed for capitalization of their farms, and with the class of villages these families founded or joined. The Section for Auxiliary Farms worked with other agencies in providing capital and instruction for the cultivation of small plots by immigrants settled in housing projects near the veteran moshavim and in new towns, and by those who were employed by moshavim as salaried workers.

Each of the Land Settlement Department's regional and district units had its own director, directorate, and administrative and technical staff. The district offices were usually located in an urban center within the district, while the much larger regional offices most commonly were situated in the principal city of each region. Responsible for settlement planning within the region according to policy lines laid down at the head office, each regional office included its own technical units, such as a farm-planning section, water section, technical section, and financial section. The farm-planning sections were guided by the Joint Planning Center, the water sections by the Department's Water Division; and the technical sections maintained liaison with the Professional Department of the Jewish Agency, which was concerned with all construction carried out under Jewish Agency auspices. The regional offices have also included sections concerned with the principal branches of agriculture practiced within their areas, such as citrus orchards or field crops. Each region in addition had a transportation depot, in which vehicles assigned to it were kept and serviced.

The regional offices had autonomy in hiring all personnel employed within the region. Their employees were paid from their own budgets, over which they exercised authority. As of 1957, they averaged about 203 employees each, exclusive of village instructors, while the head office had 234 employees. The professional employees of the regional offices, like those of the head office, included agronomists, agricultural economists, engineers, accountants, and technical and clerical staff. Such categories of personnel were generally recruited on the basis of professional qualifications and were paid according to the various professional salary scales obtaining throughout the country.

The district offices generally included on their staffs a farm planner, water engineer, road and construction engineer, a clerk in charge of contracts, bookkeeper, and cashier. One of the administrative assistants of the district director usually served as office manager. District staff generally included instructors specializing in the various branches of agriculture. These instructors traveled constantly among the villages of the district, guiding the village agricultural instructors and also guiding and supervising the settlers directly. The farm planners, water engineers, and road and construction engineers worked according to plans executed by farm-planning, water, and technical sections at the regional level; the bookkeeper and cashier were linked to the financial section of the region, and the contracts clerk to the Department's Division of Contracts and Securities. The instructors were under the guidance of the Department's Professional Division.

Within each district, the settlements were generally grouped into subdistricts of some five to ten settlements each, their number varying with local conditions. Each of these subdistricts was under the direct supervision of an administrative field assistant to the district director. The title of this post may be translated from the Hebrew (*mrakez ezor*) as "district coordinator." This position was created during the peak years of land settlement, when the multiplication of new villages in the districts made for a gap in communication, felt on both sides, between the district directors and officeholders on the village level. The coordinators were constantly on the road, visiting each of the settlements of the subdistrict at least twice weekly and providing constant liaison between them and the district office. It was the coordinator to whom the teams of instructors in the moshvei olim first turned with their problems and complaints and from whom they were supposed to receive guidance. The district coordinator was also in touch with the heads of the village executive committees in the settlements which were not moshvei olim. He was supposed to maintain liaison with those in the moshvei olim as well, although the coordinators I observed generally did not speak to settlers before having conferred with the village social instructor, and did so usually in reinforcement of the latter's authority.

As I have tried to indicate in this sketch of the Land Settlement Department's organization, the growth of hierarchic authority was crosscut by the principle of decentralization and by the inclusion of professional specialists in the Department's policy-making bodies at all levels. Moreover, the administrative line of authority, from the head and director of the Department down through the regional and district directors and their assistants, was made up of people with farming experience and considerable technical knowledge.

The posts of regional director were held during the 1955–58 period by individuals whose background was characteristic of those holding authority throughout the agricultural sector and also in other areas of public administration and national development. The director of the Hill Region was a middle-aged agronomist who had immigrated to Palestine decades earlier from Russia. He had been associated with the Jewish National Fund for many years before joining the Land Settlement Department. Since the Jewish National Fund played a key role in land reclamation in the hilly districts and in the economy of its new villages, for whose settlers it was a major source of employment, the Jewish National Fund background of this director was no small asset in his work and had been a factor in his appointment. The director of another region was a native Israeli who had grown up in a veteran kibbutz and had previously held a high post in the military administration of a border area. The director of a new region, specifically chosen to establish it, was a young man who had been brought to Palestine, also from Russia, as an infant. He previously had been an aide of the head of the Department, had become a village instructor in preparation for his new post, and then had been sent abroad to study public administration. Most of the younger regional directors and members of the regional directorates had distinguished themselves in the pre-statehood underground activities and/or in the War of Independence. They were all members of one of the secular labor parties, or were identified with the general orientation of these parties.

The district directors included veteran employees of the Land Settlement Department, veteran settlers of long-established villages, adult members of the generation born into these villages, and young men, recruited through various personal and political connections, who had some background in agriculture and had in some previous capacity shown themselves capable of getting a job done. Given the expansion of the Land Settlement Department and a certain turnover in its staff, it was not difficult to advance through the ranks from one post to another. Young men who demonstrated ability were not infrequently sent to school within the country or sent abroad for special training.

The establishment of the Department's annual budget illustrates how the administrative line of authority meshed with the relative autonomy accorded each level in the hierarchy. Each district drew up the investment schedule it considered necessary for each village in the district for the next year. The pre-statehood relations of partnership between settlers and the Department were retained in new villages peopled by settlers in the pioneer tradition, since these settlers themselves formulated their villages' prospective budgets under the guidance of the district director and his staff. The total budget for the district, including the district office's operating expenses, was sent to the regional office. The regional office reviewed the budgets of its constituent districts, coordinated them, added its own operating expenses, and sent its total budget to the head office.

The head office, in turn, reviewed the budgets forwarded by the regions, added its own operating expenses, including the budgets of its specialized units, and forwarded the total departmental budget to a special Budgetary Committee.

This committee, whose membership was determined by the World Zionist Congress, or by the Actions Committee of the World Zionist Organization, reviewed the budgets of all the departments of the Jewish Agency before passing on them. The budget was then placed before the Actions Committee of the World Zionist Organization. According to one informant, perhaps 20 percent of the sums initially requested at each level was trimmed off by the time the Land Settlement Department's budget was approved. The Treasury Department of the Jewish Agency supervised budgetary allocations, seeking to insure that each department of the Jewish Agency did not exceed the funds at its disposal.

The directorate of the Land Settlement Department allocated the total departmental budget, but each region had full authority over the funds it was assigned. In carrying out the settlement program, the regional authorities shifted funds as the occasion demanded in their allocations to districts, as did the district authorities in their allocations to the villages. The departmental directorate could also reallocate funds and seek emergency appropriations. Budgetary negotiations were characterized by competition between equivalent organizational units from the village level on up.

As the formulation of the Department's budget illustrates, officeholders at every level in the Department's administrative line of authority participated in the making of policy. They retained considerable autonomy in executing it and could try to force reconsideration of decisions taken at a higher level. In the formulation of policy, meetings, consultations, and the free expression of opinion were characteristic preliminaries of decision-making. The departmental directorate met weekly, the departmental director held regularly scheduled meetings with the regional directors, and meetings were held between technical staff and administrative staff at all levels within the regions and the districts. Moreover, irregularly scheduled days of discussion cut across regional and district lines, and meetings of all kinds led up to the introduction of new lines of policy.

Meetings held to discuss new possibilities, as well as those called to resolve disputes and crises, could include representatives of the settlement federations and of other agencies active in the land settlement sector whose interests were involved. Indeed, the basis for participation in such meetings and, in fact, in many meetings (with the exception of the recurrent conferences of specific officeholders), was rarely made explicit. Decisions were left to the person or persons calling the meeting, and anyone who knew of a conference and felt it was his business to be there might put in a claim to attend.

To know when one might validly advance such a claim can be considered one index of membership in the land settlement system ingroup. The same index applies to membership in the country-wide policy-making and administrative elites. For in the maneuvering to extend or consolidate their jurisdictional scope, overlapping and partly competitive organizations commonly tried to get their representatives into interorganizational committees and meetings concerned with policies that had some bearing on their activities. Within the land settlement system, not only office but an individual's personal or political concern with the issues at stake, his general protektzia, and his personal prestige all counted in the advancement and consideration of claims for participation. In the country as a whole, analogous considerations also were important in bids for inclusion in interagency meetings to consider policy, as were the prestige and protektzia of the person advancing the organization's claims.

In the effective exercise of authority within the Land Settlement Department, prestige counted for as much as status. For the Labor-Zionist ethos and the way things got done in Israel during its first decade mitigated against hierarchic controls and impersonal rules even after the extension of the Department's line of authority. Prestige within the organization was contingent on work performance, and both ability, insofar as it could be judged, and devotion rated. Hard and sustained work without the need for administrative rewards and sanctions remained a basic value within the Department. The workday for all but clerical employees generally extended far beyond eight hours, depending on the needs of the situation, as determined by the officeholder himself in conformity with ideology and norms. Working facilities were improvised in terms of available resources, with almost no concessions to status and no regard for comfort.

The egalitarianism of the Labor-Zionist ethos and the stress on getting things done also influenced people's behavior regardless of relative status within the organization. As late as the period 1955–58, practically all the employees of the Land Settlement Department addressed and referred to the Department's director by his first name. Similarly, regional and district directors, their staffs, and representatives of the moshav federations would be called by first name or by last name unadorned with title. Status subordinates could originate interaction without being restricted to official organizational channels. In fact, taking a problem to the person most capable of solving it, regardless of respective status and formal intervening channels, might be seen as a sign of competence and initiative.

Weekly reception days at the district and regional offices and the head office as well augmented channels of communication within the Department and between settlers and officeholders at every level. These reception days generally coincided with those days on which regularly scheduled meetings were held at the offices, and the field staff reported.

The Jerusalem quarters of the head office, as of 1954 to 1958, consisted of a three-office suite at the end of a large corridor on the first floor of the Jewish Agency building, a few other rooms on the same floor, and two adjoining rooms on the second floor of the building. The central office of the first floor suite was that of the director, and it was a bare room furnished with desk, a few chairs, a bookcase, and a telephone. The doors of his office led on one side to an office that the secretary of the Department shared with a typist, and on the other to an office that the director's general administrative assistant and secretary shared. Both of these offices also had telephones and generally were open to the public. On reception days, the benches in the corridor and in an improvised waiting room would be crowded with employees from the districts and regions who had business at the head office, with employees of the technical divisions and sections, with representatives of villages in the pioneer tradition, and with moshav olim instructors. All of them jostled each other while waiting their turn to see the secretary and/or the director, with those at the head of the throng already spilling into the two outer offices.

The harried departmental secretary, transacting business with several people simultaneously while constantly on the phone, would periodically order those pressing in to leave his office, only to have it soon fill up again. Veteran members of the Department and those with high posts in the divisions and sections would crash in to offer their greetings and try to push their affairs. While waiting to see the director, they would start exchanging news in the corridors and conducting business they had with each other. Moshav olim settlers with grievances generally lined the corridors and sat on the floor, the women among them cradling and occasionally nursing babies.

Since the routine processing of papers, even employment forms, could take weeks, practically all business was presented as nonroutine and urgent by those directly concerned. The order of processing generally followed priorities assigned by the director and highest officials and, failing this, might be influenced by the intervention of those with greater status and protektzia than the persons involved.

The regional offices generally consisted of a collection of temporary wooden buildings situated slightly on the outskirts of the cities in which they were located. The district offices were generally a smaller collection of similar buildings, although other accommodations were used when obtainable. In the regional headquarters, an ordered bustle generally prevailed in the offices of the technical staff, but the administrative offices were often characterized by the same beleaguered atmosphere as the head office, particularly on reception days. The district offices, particularly those of the older districts, tended to be quiet, except on reception days; but practically everyone except the clerical workers might be traveling around the villages or in conference in some other part of the country.

However, early mornings at the district offices might be characterized by a jostle comparable to that of reception days. District coordinators, technical staff about to leave for the villages, and professional instructors might grab for available desk space to get out some clerical work or cluster around the district director's office for a last-minute exchange. Village instructors might burst into the office to announce a new crisis, preceded or followed by demonstrating settlers. In fact, settlers soon learned to get to the district and regional offices before they opened at 7:30 A.M., the beginning of the Israeli workday, in order to get to see the directors or key assistants. In relations between employees of the Department, as throughout much of Israel, casual aggressiveness was the normal mode of behavior in getting business done. The progressive rationalization of the land settlement program and the growth of such bureaucratic features as hierarchic authority and specialization of roles and tasks had not vitiated by 1958 the climate of improvisation customary in the land settlement sector.

Between 1955 and 1958, the Land Settlement Department developed new policies toward the instructors' roles and, secondarily, toward the utilization of specialized knowledge in the Department's relations with the moshav olim settlers. The development of these new policies can be seen in the perspective of changes taking place in the country as a whole. These changes included the slackening pace of immigration, and the sometimes-reluctant gradual recognition that the Labor-Zionist ethos and the tradition of improvisation were not effective substitutes for professional training and its efficient utilization. Moreover, in the land settlement sector stretches of unoccupied arable land were diminishing. Far more villages had to be consolidated than remained to be founded, barring radical innovations in large-scale reclamation of desert and land from the sea.

Efforts at professionalizing the instructors' roles contributed to the bureaucratization of the Land Settlement Department, as is reviewed below.

BUREAUCRACY AND THE VILLAGE LEVEL

The retention, after Israel's independence, of the pre-statehood system of relations in the land settlement sector made for a diffusion of power among the participants in the settlement enterprise. The Land Settlement Department's expanded scope of activity exceeded the areas over which it could successfully exercise controls. This was salient on the village level. Post-statehood settlers in the pioneer tradition, if not convinced of the soundness of the Department's plan for their village's development, could refuse to follow it. In such cases there was very little the Department could do, particularly if the settlers gained the support of their village federation, except try to influence the agricultural program they formulated. Even settlers of the moshvei olim could sway the Department's decisions, as was described in Chapter V.

However, it was the instructors in the moshvei olim who were the primary heirs to much of the administrative autonomy earlier possessed by settlers in the pioneer tradition. Furthermore, no one in the Land Settlement Department's administrative hierarchy could tell them what to do to bring about settler compliance to the demands of the moshav settler role. While incorporated into the Land Settlement Department's administrative hierarchy, the instructors retained considerable freedom of action and were subject to relatively little supervision during most of Israel's first decade.

This freedom of action did not mean that other organizations in Israel left the instructors and settlers in solitude in the villages. Apart from the service personnel of the village —teachers, nurse, military instructor, and storekeeper—and the agencies they represented, many organizations in Israel had business in the new settlements or made it their business to try to promote immigrant acculturation. The moshav federations, partners with the Land Settlement Department in the founding and development of new villages, also made claims to supervise both instructors and settlers.

The federations had representatives who traveled around the country, visiting affiliated villages. Representatives in the haphazard sample I observed sought to keep tabs on what was happening in the moshvei olim, and exercised no more authority over either instructors or settlers than they could win by force of their personalities. They served as liaison between villages and federation; they tried, with varying success, to handle such internal problems as bad relations between members of the instructor team and bad relations between settlers and instructors. They offered advice about village cooperative arrangements; and they arranged transfers of settlers and instructors from one to another of their affiliated villages across the boundaries of the Land Settlement Department's regions. They also appeared in the villages at times of potential or acute crisis to add their voice to those of the instructors and the Land Settlement Department administrators. I have seen village instructors disregard federation representatives for whom they had little esteem.

The women's auxiliaries of the various political parties or women's movements associated with such parties worked with the instructresses. The auxiliaries generally opened women's clubs and instruction centers in the moshvei olim, providing them with sewing machines and kitchen equipment and forwarding used clothes for distribution among the settlers. The instructresses were supposed to use these clubrooms to give the immigrant women lessons in housekeeping, child rearing, cooking, Hebrew, and general culture; and the women's auxiliaries had representatives who sought to offer the instructresses guidance. These representatives had as a goal the transformation of the immigrant women into persons who would act and think like the pioneer women of the moshvei ovdim. As of the 1955–58 period, the representatives were firm on ideology but bewildered and uncertain as to how it could be transmitted.

Although veteran village instructors might disregard

moshav movement representatives, the Land Settlement Department's administrators could not do so. For while the financing and administration of the land settlement program were under the jurisdiction of the Department, the federations, through their party affiliations, held political power. Indeed, as part of the resource-dispensing Jewish Agency, the Department not only paid the salaries of the village instructors but also contributed to each federation the sum of about IL 5–6 per year for each family in the moshvei olim affilated to it. This sum, officially given for "guidance in the villages" totaled IL 100,000 in 1957.

Other organizations also sent workers into the villages. The Absorption Department of the Jewish Agency had several field workers, also termed madrikhim, of the same ethnic groups as the settlers themselves. They traveled about the moshvei olim, spending a day or so in each, to explain the Israeli scene to the settlers and raise their morale. At least this was the way two such instructors I knew understood their job. A governmental Civic Education Service, which became a unit of the Ministry of Education and Culture, had representatives visit the villages to hold evening lectures, show films and slides, organize community singing, and take settlers on tours through the country. This service also contributed radios to the cultural centers of some moshvei olim, including villages not yet provided with electricity. The cultural center could be a wooden hut in bad repair and hardly used, and I have seen the radio intended for it end up in the room of one of the instructors. The Army occasionally assigned recruits to the moshvei olim for a month or so at a time. The men helped in such activities as sanitation campaigns, and the girls in educational activities. Youth Aliya also sent instructors to organize educational and recreational programs for the fourteen through seventeen age group, activities in which young adults also occasionally participated, and such instructors frequently took quarters in the villages.

In fact, a full catalogue of the people who visited the moshvei olim as part of their jobs or as representatives of voluntary organizations would lead to a catalogue of a good proportion of the organizations in Israel. Also, high-ranking administrators of many agencies visited the villages on tours of inspection. They might enter into only cursory conversations with the settlers, but many of them seemed to feel not only entitled but obligated to do their bit to promote immigrant acculturation. Thus, during even brief visits, they might instruct children barefoot during the rainy months to put on shoes, girls kept at home to go to school, women to stop suckling toddlers, etc., depending on whom they happened to meet and what struck them as needing immediate correction in terms of Israeli norms.

Agencies whose services to the new villages were only one aspect of their spectrum of activities were the first to be subject to a reassessment of attitudes toward the new immigrants and of the services they offered. Beginning in about 1953, a handful of people began defending the new immigrants' rights to retain elements of their traditional cultures and the intrinsic worth of such elements. Most of these people were specialists in education, psychology, social work, and public health who had been trained in their professions abroad. They included some veteran Israelis as well as immigrants and foreign experts from Western Europe and from what were termed in Israel the "Anglo-Saxon" countries. Israeli members of the service professions also began returning after graduate training abroad and sought to influence execution of policy in the organizations in which they worked.

A partly cooperative and partly competitive informal network developed among those preaching a more permissive approach to the problems of immigrant acculturation. The individuals in it used their varying connections and protektzia to influence policy-makers to give their ideas a chance or, at least, an audience among those dealing daily with the immigrants. Israel is a small country in which the administrative and policy-making elites have been linked through many informal channels. Once a new idea caught on, it could spread rapidly.

Moreover, by about 1956 a new respect for professionalism

began to pervade practically all the public agencies. Some two years earlier, various professional groups such as physicians had begun to exert pressure to raise their civil service salary scales. In principle, holders of the highest civil service ratings received salaries three times higher than those of employees in the lowest positions. With inflation, the assignment of living allowances, and the sharply graded income tax, the net income of highly trained professionals in public service came to approximate that of relatively unskilled employees at the lowest grades.[5] Salary increases were finally granted holders of higher grades, although not without an outbreak of strikes during 1955 and 1956. While the increases were far from substantial, they symbolized the increased status of the professions in the national ethos. By about 1957, a growing regard for efficiency had made substantial inroads into the traditional disdain for professionalism which had been part of the Labor-Zionist ethos. New civil service regulations began to demand specialized training and professional qualifications of all new employees in public agencies above a certain level. A public administration program had been set up in the Hebrew University and, by 1957, even veteran employees of the Jewish Agency began to take courses.

The new respect for professionalism, and especially for degrees, converged with the reshaping of attitudes in regard to immigrant acculturation. However, this reshaping of attitudes, as it was increasingly accepted and popularized, began to take on attributes of a quasi-ideology; and fadlike aspects contributed to its spread. By 1957, preservice and in-service training programs not only had mushroomed in the various services, but these programs also had to include lectures by those recognized as "experts" in the new approach. In fact, the various service organizations began to compete in holding such courses, which offered a new lever for expanding their influence and scope in interorganizational jockeying. Such expressions as "respect for the way of life of the immigrants" became catchwords, acceptance of

5 Samuel 1956:63–64.

which might or might not influence the behavior of those who worked directly with the public.

These combined pressures influenced both the Joint Guidance Center and the highest administrative levels within the Land Settlement Department. With U.S. technical assistance, the Joint Guidance Center developed training programs for instructors in the moshvei olim. By 1956, the Center's Home Economics Section delimited the role of village madrikha as that of instructress in home economics, sought to define the duties this involved, and developed in-service training programs in home economics which included some elementary social science. The Center also set up a five-month preservice training course for agricultural instructors, whose graduates committed themselves to serve as such for three years. The course included training in the various farm branches and in farm management, with a few lectures on relations with settlers thrown in at the end.

By 1957, a school for social instructors was created, financed by the Jewish Agency and cosponsored by the principal moshav federation. The job of the social instructor was redefined as that of village coordinator, and a five-month course was offered to instructors recommended by district directors and by the moshav federations. This course included training in administration and in the social sciences. The first class had an enrollment of somewhat over thirty, and its graduates were also to serve as instructors for three years.

Thus, rationalization of land settlement had extended, by 1957, to attempts to professionalize the village instructors' roles and tasks. What such professionalization involved can be illustrated in part by citing the definition of roles and listing of tasks prepared for the first course for social instructors by a district director of some twenty years' experience in the Department. Slightly condensed in translation, it goes as follows:

"The village coordinator is to direct all the economic and municipal institutions of the moshav olim, and is to give a portion of his time to educating the settlers and to developing civic activities in terms of the moshav cooperative framework.

He represents the village and its affairs both to the outside world and in the village. His authority thus derives both from the Land Settlement Department and from the village. Within the village, he is the representative of the Land Settlement Department, and is responsible for the implementation of directives received from the district office in regard to both economic and agricultural development. His duties include channeling municipal and economic affairs through the appropriate village committees and seeing that these committees function. Furthermore, he is to see that the other members of the instructor team carry out their tasks and duties. He is to prepare the village budget and see that it is implemented. He is to coordinate the activities carried out in the village by other organizations with the program and framework of the Land Settlement Department. He is to develop a local leadership to work with him, but also is to give guidance and attention to all the settlers. He is to supervise the village register and books kept by the secretariat and see that they are up-to-date. He is responsible for seeing that the settlers are properly insured in terms of life insurance and property. He is responsible that accounts are kept in regard to equipment and supplies granted the settlers through the various loans of the Land Settlement Department to the village. In working to further the social development of the village, he will concern himself with receiving suitable families for vacant farms and with getting unsuitable families out of the village, operating in this through the district office channels.

"The agricultural instructor is to devote all his time to teaching the new settlers farming skills. In so doing he should visit every farm in the village regularly and according to an established schedule; and he should examine the progress of the different kinds of crops and animals and the state of repair of the farm implements and buildings, instructing the settlers in their care. He should help the district farm planner and the specialists in the different farm branches in planning the crop rotation schedule of the village farms; and, before the beginning of each season, he should plan in detail what each

farm would need. He should see that the settlers carry out
this plan. In addition to his regular visits to each farm, he
should hold lectures and give demonstrations to all the
settlers before each agricultural season, using the facilities of
the Joint Center for Agricultural Instruction and distributing
and explaining its farming bulletins. He is to see that all the
necessary supplies arrive in time and supervise their
allocation. He is to keep check on the irrigation equipment
and its use. He is to watch over the progress of the ripening
crops, see that they are harvested carefully and at the right
time, and see that the harvests are brought to the appropriate
collection depot (often set up in the fields) for marketing
through the village cooperative."

The definition of the role of village instructress, now the
instructress in home economics, was worked out separately by
the Home Economics Section of the Joint Guidance Center
during 1956 and 1957. As incorporated into the list of role
definitions here reproduced, it runs approximately as follows:

"The instructress in home economics is to accomplish her
goal above all through the personal example she sets. Through
the example of a modest way of life, her appropriate dress,
her ordered room and becoming behavior, she is to gain the
confidence of the settlers. She is to develop in the settler
women a devotion to their homes, their farms and to making
their living through the work of their hands. She is to
encourage them to attain self-sufficiency in their private lives
and to participate in village affairs, in guarding public and
private property, and in mutual aid. She is to learn the
customs and way of life of the settlers and to respect their
customs and traditions. Her specific tasks are as follows: She
is to visit the homes of the village and also hold receiving
hours in her room; and she should try to spend some of the
holidays with the settlers. She is to make regular inspection
visits to the village dispensary, kindergarten, school kitchen
and secretariat, lending her aid as needed. She also is to
instruct the women in the use of the health, social welfare,
mother-and-child care, etc., services that are brought to the

village, and have the women waiting and ready when the outside service personnel arrive. She is to guide the women in their housework and agricultural duties; in setting up a household budget; in making out simple accounts and filling out forms, if they are literate; in infant care; in food preparation for infants and general family cooking; in home canning and preservation of farm produce in season; in sewing and mending for home and family; in decorating the home; in housecleaning, laundering and storing of clothes; and in the cultivation of a kitchen and flower garden. In her guidance she too is to give lectures and hold demonstrations, as well as visit the homes, as guided by the Joint Center for Agricultural Instruction and the regional coordinator of the Section of Home Economics." [6]

These definitions of the instructors' roles and duties may be compared with the lists of their tasks formulated during the phase of improvisation, cited in Chapter IV. The later definitions establish a clear division of labor between "village coordinator" and agricultural instructor, and establish the primacy of the former. However, a more fundamental difference is to be found in the conceptions of the instructor role expressed in the two sets of definitions.

The earlier definitions envisaged the instructors as supplementing the settlers. The duty of the instructors was to provide guidance and knowledge in getting village development underway. Settler role-socialization was assumed to be the automatic outcome, and the instructor roles were presented as transitory. Essentially, the village was still perceived as the domain of its settlers, as in the classic tradition.

The 1957 definitions, in contrast, present the instructor roles as ones of authority over the settlers rather than as supplementary. The village is not the settlers' domain. Rather, it is a trust held by the Land Settlement Department. The instructors, as part of the Department, administer this trust, receiving and transmitting directives. Not until the settlers achieve role-socialization will the village be granted to them,

6 These definitions appeared in Jewish Agency for Israel, Land Settlement Department: 1957.

and there are no assumptions as to how soon this will take place. In short, while the older definitions still imply a consensus-based system, the newer definitions are those of a system based on and maintained by authority. Furthermore, they make it clear that the hierarchy of authority includes the instructors.

The 1957 definitions were prepared by members of the Land Settlement Department and of the Joint Guidance Center associated with it, whereas the earlier ones were formulated by a moshav federation spokesman. However, this difference in the organizational perspectives of their authors does not alone account for the difference in emphasis. Rather, the change in emphasis corresponds to the expanded role assumed by the Land Settlement Department at the expense of the moshav federations. The federations acquiesced in the expanded authority of the Land Settlement Department, for it maintained the land settlement system. This system, in turn, served the interests of the federations, adding to their membership and strength. Indeed, the federations were long-range beneficiaries of the system. The villages, once viable, move out of the Land Settlement Department's jurisdiction, whereas their moshav federation affiliation is supposed to endure.

Moreover, in the maintenance of an authority-based system of relations, coercion cannot easily be exercised by political organizations dependent on the votes of those disputing the system. Authority can better be exercised by an administrative body. The expansion of the Land Settlement Department's authority over the settlers can be seen in this perspective.

The 1957 definitions of the instructor roles made it clear that the Department exercised authority over the instructors as well as over the settlers. For they too were to do as they were directed. In addition, the instructresses also were brought under supervision. A new post, that of coordinator of home economics, was created in 1956 at the regional level. These coordinators, in turn, were responsible to the head of the Home Economics Section of the Joint Guidance Center. The professionalization of the instructors' roles contributed to the growth of bureaucratic features in the Land Settlement Department.

The professionalization of the instructors' roles acknowledged, rather than glossed over, the discontinuity in the moshvei olim between their settlers and the land settlement system into which they had been recruited. This discontinuity, based on cultural differences between those who created the system and the majority of the post-statehood immigrants, ran through the new society.

Before turning to the microcosm of the society represented by an immigrant village, I turn to the preimmigration way of life of its settlers, Jews from the Atlas Mountains of Morocco. The discontinuity between Chapter VII and most of the chapters preceding it reflects the discontinuities between the kinds of worlds familiar to the majority of new immigrants and the organization of the new society. I seek to relate the way of life of Jews in the Atlas Mountains to the larger society of which they were a part, and to the particular tradition of orthodox Judaism which gave meaning to their lives.

JEWS IN THE HIGH ATLAS MOUNTAINS OF MOROCCO: A PARTIAL RECONSTRUCTION [1]

GENERAL BACKGROUND

The arrival of Jews in North Africa may go back to the period of the Phoenician colonization, but more probably can be assigned to the years following the destruction of the First Temple in Jerusalem in 586 B.C.[2] A flow of Jews from Palestine continued in subsequent centuries, particularly after the destruction of the Second Temple in 70 A.D., and it was augmented by immigration from other parts of the Roman Empire. As Jews dispersed throughout North Africa, exten-

[1] This reconstruction is based on field work carried out in Ometz from June to December 1955, with follow-up visits six months later. This field work was conducted by Miss Margot Kohls, a social worker with long experience of moshvei olim, under my supervision. I was able to supplement her observations in Shavur and Nishar, other moshvei olim settled by Atlas Mountains immigrants.

Miss Kohls' research in Ometz was sponsored and directed by the Henrietta Szold Foundation for Child and Youth Welfare in Jerusalem. It was one of several research projects of the Szold Foundation directed at understanding the transformations taking place in Israel among immigrants of non-Western origin. It was guided by the service orientation of the Szold Foundation and was focused primarily on the interaction of immigrants and the team of village workers, and on changes in the practices and habits of the former. In the gathering of data on the preimmigration culture of the immigrants, ethnology in depth was neither envisaged nor attempted.

Miss Kohls summarized her research in an article entitled "Culture Patterns and Adjustment Processes of Moroccan Immigrants from Rural Areas," published by the Henrietta Szold Foundation in its quarterly journal *Megamot*, Vol. 7, No. 4, 1956.

This chapter is a slightly expanded version of a paper published in *The Jewish Journal of Sociology*, Vol. IV, No. 2 (December 1962). It appears here by permission of the editors of *The Jewish Journal of Sociology*.

[2] This is the view of Chouraqui (1952:13–21) after a careful review of the available evidence, and Briggs (1960:89–90) also gives this date. Goulven (1923:317–26) reviews various discussions in the literature without reaching any opinion other than that Jews were established in North Africa several centuries before the Christian era, a view on which there is general consensus. Voinot (1948:99–101) suggests 320 B.C., when Jews were deported to North Africa by Ptolomy Soter, as the earliest verifiable date.

sive conversions to Judaism occurred among its Berber population until the rise and spread of Islam. The Jews of the Atlas Mountains are most probably descendents of ancient Jewish immigrants and of Judaized Berbers who did not become Moslems.[3]

They have lived in towns and villages scattered throughout the Atlas Mountains region.[4] In the towns [5] they generally

[3] Cf. Chaumeil (1953:228–29); Monteil (1948:157ff.); and Montagne (1930a:46) for indications of the often forced conversion to Islam in recent centuries; Flamand (1952:118, note 1) for the same process in recent decades; and Voinot (1948:102–3).

[4] Flamand (1950:368–76) gives a list of 155 settlements in which Jews were then to be found, with their approximate Jewish population, in the Atlas Mountains region between Marrakesh and Mogador (including these two cities). In addition, he lists (1950:377–79) 34 more settlements which were noted in earlier literature as inhabited by Jews but in which by 1949 they were no longer to be found. He derives the majority of these from the maps of Dresch (1941: Planche I, Feuilles 1–3) referring to the Central Massif of the High Atlas Mountains. In the commentary on his maps, Dresch briefly writes of the Jews (1941:10) that they are not shepherds and certainly not farmers. He goes on to say that they are mostly to be found at the edge of the Atlas Mountains, near markets, or on the main routes of passage, and rarely in the mountains proper. He then qualifies this observation by adding that in the eastern region Jewish families are to be found dispersed in villages, although tending to come together.

Whatever the accuracy of Dresch's observations for the Central Massif, there were settlements of Jews practicing agriculture east of this region, according to Flamand (1950:336, 372, 374–76). Among these settlements were the former homes of the immigrants who settled in Ometz and Shavur and who had engaged in farming previously, as is subsequently discussed in the text.

[5] Montagne (1930a:37–41) distinguishes several kinds of urban or quasi-urban settlements in the Atlas Mountains region. These are (1) cities on the plains around the mountains, e.g., Marrakesh, Mogador, and Taroudant; (2) towns or large villages at the foot of the Atlas Mountains, at the juncture of mountains and plains; and (3) large villages at the summits of the Atlas Mountains, inhabited during the winter but deserted during the summer when their settlers disperse to summer pastures and plots. Jews are to be found in settlements of all three kinds. Thus Marrakesh had a Jewish population of 18,310 in 1949 and a non-Jewish population of approximately 225,000 (Flamand 1950:381), as contrasted to a Jewish population of approximately 11,000 in 1920, 21,000 around 1930, and 26,000 in 1936 (Flamand 1950:371). Mogador, essentially a Jewish city in 1920, with a population of 9,500 Jews as compared to 9,000 non-Jews, had 6,500 Jews and 13,000 non-Jews by 1949 (Flamand 1950:371). Taroudant had a Jewish population of approximately 1,200 in 1920, and 953 (out of a total population of over 10,000) in 1949 (Flamand 1950: 374). Of the juncture towns cited by Montagne, two out of five, Amismiz and Imi n Tanout, are on Flamand's list. Demnat, another such town lying 120 kilometers east of Marrakesh, had a Jewish population of 2,500 in 1936, 2,200 in 1940, and 1,900 in 1949 (Flamand 1952:23). This population was studied and written up by Flamand (1952). As an example of

have had their own quarter, known as *mellah,* although they mingled freely with the rest of the population in the main streets and marketplaces. In the rural districts, Jews frequently have lived in separate hamlets or clusters of hamlets [6] (also termed mellah) adjoining or at a short distance from Berber villages, themselves often composed of separate sub-villages or hamlets.[7] Occasionally a few Jewish families would

---

the large summit villages of his third category, Montagne cites (1930a:40) Amasin, canton of Ikhozamen, near Sirwa. This village is pictured in another of his publications (Montagne 1930b: fig. 29), and has a special hamlet nearby, inhabited, according to Montagne's caption to the figure, by blacksmiths, Jews, and strangers. Its Jewish population, according to Flamand (1950:367), was 100 in 1949.

Another kind of quasi-urban settlement in the mountains, discussed separately by Montagne (1930a:124–27, 341–47; 1930b:11ff., figs. 59ff.), is the *kasbah,* the large fortified castle or complex of castles serving a great chief or the chief family as fortress, palace, administrative center, storehouse, etc., and usually rising above a village. Montagne (1930a:346–47) notes that a mellah might be established under the protection of such a kasbah, with the Jews lending money and engaging in commerce.

6 Flamand (1950:384–85) notes that the mellah in rural areas generally consist of a series of settlements named after the Berber tribes among whom the Jews live. He gives the names of a number of such mellah, particularly in the Dades region lying outside the area of his Marrakesh-Agadir list. In general, he states, there are no isolated mellah or even isolated clusters, but rather chains of mellah along a line of communication, with continuous relations between them. The few isolated exceptions to this arrangement he considers to be refuge mellah, with a Judaized Berber population practicing agriculture. The Jewish settlements I have termed Ait Adrar and neighboring Ait Rahhal, the previous homes of the immigrants to Israel whom this reconstruction concerns, consisted of four hamlets each.

7 Montagne (1930a:151–52, 218–20) considers the village (Berber, *mouda* [Montagne] or *lmud'a* [Berque 1955]) to be primarily an administrative unit, sharing a mosque, a common storehouse, pasture land, and a brushwood forest. A village assembly, in which the decisions are made by agreement of heads of extended families (although all men able to bear arms may participate) regulates such common matters as affairs of the mosque, hospitality towards strangers, guarding the fields, regulation of irrigation, usage of forest and pasture, etc. The assembly meets at the mosque. The village, according to Montagne, has practically no political functions; and Berque (1955:32) is even more emphatic on this point. The major political unit is the canton (Berber, *taqbilt*), usually composed of several villages separated by mountains from the neighboring cantons, and governed by an assembly of the heads of families from within the different villages. The major social unit is the extended family, the patrilineal lineage (Berber, *ikhs*); and two or three such families usually constitute a hamlet of twenty to thirty habitations. A hamlet may also consist of one such lineage or, as Berque indicates (1955:32, 61–92), the *ikhs-s* may be distributed among various hamlets and villages of a canton. Genealogical units from the level of the lineage to that of the tribe—

inhabit a corner of a predominantly non-Jewish village.[8] All the Atlas Mountains families I encountered in Israel undoubtedly had Berbers for neighbors, although they referred to them in Hebrew as Arabs.[9]

---

in which the assumption of descent from a common ancestor may be largely fictitious—are generally (although not in all cases) designated by the Berber form "Ait" or "Ida," followed by a proper name. "Ait" or "Ida" also may be used to designate territorial units (as on a map of the Atlas Mountains) which seem to be cantons, usually inhabited by people of diverse origins (cf. Berque 1955:63ff.; Montagne 1930a:34–35). This form usually is taken to mean "sons of," but Hart has suggested (1960:472–75) that the meaning to the Berbers is "people of," referring to territory as well as common descent.

[8] Flamand (1950:384), using the term "mellah" to denote any Jewish aggregation, refers to such instances as *"mellahs* reduced to one or two families," and cites several. He considers them to be neither vestiges of formerly larger aggregates nor the beginnings of new larger aggregates, but rather tiny Jewish outpost colonies ("comme des 'comptoirs', de miniscules colonies juives en terre étrangère").

[9] Flamand (1952:141–46) falls into this usage himself in describing the relations of the Jews of Demnat with their Berber neighbors, and I assume that he does so in paraphrase of the statements of the Demnati Jews. Demnat is but forty kilometers west of Ait Rahhal and ninety kilometers west of Ait Adrar (Flamand 1950:366), and had received into its mellah emigrants from both places (Flamand 1952:139, statements of informants). Therefore, it can be assumed that this usage on the part of the immigrants to Israel antedated their immigration, rather than having been adopted when they took up Hebrew as a spoken language.

The language of these immigrants was described by Moroccan immigrants from the northern cities as an Arabic dialect containing many Berber words and difficult to understand. I assume that this is the same Arabic dialect described by Flamand (1952:23–24), analogous to that of Marrakesh, spoken by both Moslems and Jews in Demnat, with both knowing and using Chleuh Berber in their relations with the mountain Berbers and the Jews using Hebrew only in their prayers.

As for the Jews in other parts of the Atlas Mountains, Chaumeil (1953:232–33) notes that the Jews of Tahala (about 180 people in 1951 [p. 239]) living among the Ammeln in the Anti-Atlas spoke Arabic among themselves (dialect unspecified), Chleuh with their neighbors, and an argot, composed of Hebrew and deformed Arabic vocabulary and Arabic syntax and grammar, when they did not wish to be understood by their neighbors. (In regard to this argot, Slouschz [1927:194–96] reports that the Jews of the Jebel of Tripoli had a Hebrew dialect of their own, which was slowly disappearing by 1908, and that most of its vocabulary was Hebrew spoken with a change in pronunciation. He lists words of Hebrew, Aramaic, and even Greek origin. He adds that elements of this language are to be found in Algeria and Morocco, but only as a few scattered words used by Jews among themselves in the presence of outsiders.) In discussing the origin of the Jews of Tahala, Chaumeil suggests (1953:285ff.) that at least some of them may be descendents of Jewish immigrants from Khaibar in Arabia who were expelled in the seventh century A.D. by the Caliph Omar. He cites their domestic use of Arabic as evidence in favor of this. Monteil (1946:394–95) reports the same use of argot and

Many of these villages, according to the testimony of Israeli and urban Moroccan emissaries who visited the Atlas Mountains, are situated at high altitudes, sometimes of over 2,000 meters,[10] and such villages may be accessible only by mule or on foot. They may be built against mountain slopes or on the tops of cliffs; [11] and the emissaries described some villages as being partly hewn into the mountainsides.[12] The villages are generally located near mountain streams,[13] and fruit trees were reported to grow in abundance near most of them.

Houses might be built of stones, mud, or even of mud and straw, depending on materials available in the vicinity, according to informants.[14] Dwellings could range in size from several rooms to several stories. Windows consisted of small openings in the walls, without glass. Entrances and ceilings

of Arabic domestically for the Jews (thirty-four families) of the mellah of Bani in the pre-Saharan oasis region along the Dra River. Among the various origins of these families (some claiming descent from ancient immigrants from Palestine, some from Debdou in the northeast [cf. Slouschz 1927:388–429], some from the Anti-Atlas), Khaibar also is set forth as a possible ancient provenience of some of them.

I can do no more than signal the suggestiveness of the general domestic use of Arabic (whatever the dialect) among Atlas Mountains Jews for the question of their antecedents and/or for the general problem in Moroccan ethnology of the Berber-Arab division (cf. Hart 1960:458).

10 Dresch (1941:5) states that the highest villages in the Central Massif of the Atlas Mountains are located at an altitude of 2,000 to 2,400 meters.

11 Pictures of a sample of Atlas Mountains villages are to be found in Montagne (1930b: fig. 6, figs. 22–33). Cf. also Berque (1955: pls. IX, XI, XII).

12 Slouschz (1927:450) describes the mellah of Tazert, west of Demnat, as having been built in this way.

13 Cf. also Montagne 1930a:41.

14 Slouschz (1927:449) reports that the houses of Sidi Rahal, a juncture town at the foot of the Atlas Mountains southeast of Marrakesh, were made of baked mud. The houses of the mellah of the village of Oulad Mansour, eighty kilometers east of Sidi Rahal (Flamand 1950:372) and to the west of Demnat, Slouschz (1927:450) describes as being mud huts. Still further east, he found fortified houses (material unspecified), with forty Jewish families divided between six such dwellings (Slouschz 1927: 451). A brief resume of house types in the High Atlas Mountains is to be found in Montagne (1930a:41–43; 1930b:5, figs. 17–21) and, for the Seksawa, in Berque (1955:30–31, pls. I, III). According to their descriptions, houses of beaten earth without upper stories are to be found primarily in the valleys, usually well-fortified, whereas storied houses of stones are characteristic of the high mountains. A monograph on houses and villages in the Anti-Atlas is also available (Adam 1951).

were low, the latter made of roughly worked rafters. In build-ings several stories high, access to the upper stories would be through inside stairs or outside ladders. Houses were gen-erally built against each other and around courts. Most of the cooking would be done in the courts. People lived very close together, according to the description of an Israeli emissary; he reported that in one case fifty families occupied a ground space of about fifty to eighty square meters.

In such villages the Jews have generally been artisans and traders, the traditional occupations of Jews throughout North Africa.[15] In some localities they have also engaged in money-

[15] Various combinations of crafts and trade are reported by Slouschz (1927) for the Jews from Tripoli west, by Briggs (1960) for the Sahara, and by Chouraqui (1952:222–26). The Jews of Ait Adrar practiced a fairly wide range of crafts, as is reported subsequently in the text, but this does not seem to have been true in all parts of the Atlas Mountains. Chaumeil (1953:233–34) reports that the Jews of Tahala in the Anti-Atlas engaged only in small-scale commerce—the sale of sugar, tea, oil, and cloth—in competition with Chleuh shopkeepers; in jewelry-making, which about half the men practiced; and in the itinerant vending of jewelry and cloth in the various weekly markets of the countryside. They are not moneylenders, he writes, "the Chleuhs having superior mastery of the art of usury," and they have no access to land whereby to engage in farming. He adds that they are very poor. Monteil (1946:395) gives the traditional occupations of the Jews of Bani as those of goldsmith and trader, but adds that the number of goldsmiths had been reduced to four by 1945. He also notes that they manufactured date brandy. Flamand (1950:382) mentions that a Jewish mattress-maker was allowed to practice his craft among the Ida ou Tanan, the westernmost tribe of the High Atlas Moun-tains, but that he could not obtain permission to settle among them.

As for the Atlas Mountains towns, Slouschz (1927:499) gives the fol-lowing occupational distribution for the Jews of Sidi Rahal as of 1913: of a population of 462, 214 of whom were adults, 40 were merchants of woolen goods, cloth, etc., 7 perfumers, 10 jewelers and metalworkers, 57 cobblers, 12 blacksmiths, 8 vendors of oil, 4 vendors of grain, and 25 beggars. In Demnat, the occupational distribution of Jewish males as of 1949 was as follows (Flamand 1952:29–30): 2 bakers, 36 makers of Turkish slippers, 2 doughnut makers, 9 jewelers, 5 butchers, 7 harness makers, 1 blacksmith (not a native of the town), 13 ropemakers, 25 shoe-makers, 1 hairdresser, 3 limekiln repairers, 60 merchants, 2 bicycle and sewing machine repairers, 3 domestic workers, 4 processors of oil, 3 teach-ers (who had left by 1950), 7 millers, 4 carpenters, 9 mattress makers, 3 notaries (a post for which no qualifications were necessary), 27 walnut grinders (casseurs de noix), 1 painter, 4 fishermen, 8 porters, 9 rabbis, 7 bookbinders, an unknown number of metalworkers, 2 makers of bellows, 3 makers of sieves, 19 tanners, and 19 tailors. Of these occupations, the highest in prestige was that of merchant, followed in descending order by tailor, tanner, butcher, mattress maker, bicycle repairman, shoemaker, maker of furniture, and maker of doughnuts. The lowest position was that of maker of Turkish slippers, with harness makers, sieve makers, millers,

lending,[16] and in distilling fig or date brandy for their own consumption and for illegal sale to the Moslems.[17] They could not own land, and the practice of agriculture was excep-

and metalworkers holding successively higher ranks. Rabbis, teachers, and domestic workers were not included in Flamand's list, and the rabbis also engaged in other activities, i.e., ritual slaughter of fowl, shoemaking, or tailoring (Flamand 1952:95, note 1). This practice of several trades simultaneously or according to season is characteristic of most of the population. Flamand (1952:52) considers the level of knowledge and skill in all crafts to be very low; he reports that people worked very long hours but with neither attachment to any one occupation nor pleasure in the work. Of the 370 families in the mellah, 10 were "rich," 5 of these merchants; 100 were indigent and partly sustained by the Jewish Community Committee (an 8-man elected body functioning under the administration of the French Commandant des Affaires Indigènes); and there were 25 beggars, of both sexes (Flamand 1952:50–52, 122–26).

[16] Moneylending and commerce are the sole activities that Montagne (1930a:126, 347) ascribes to Jews in the Atlas Mountains in his few references to them. Clarke (1959:93) speaks of them as moneylenders and as blacksmiths, tailors, and carpenters, many of them itinerant. In referring to the former activity, he says that it helps stabilize the economy, in that the Berbers are improvident, and there might be widespread starvation in late winter and early spring were it not for the moneylenders. He does not specify the source of these statements. Flamand (1952:38, 41) refers to usury conducted at an interest rate of 24 percent among Jews within the mellah of Demnat, but adds that the subject is complex and secret. How widespread moneylending was in the villages I cannot say, especially given Chaumeil's contention that the Jews of Tahala were not moneylenders, cited above in note 15. The immigrants to Israel had lent money to Moslems to buy and care for animals for them and also in return for use of land for farming or for a share of the crop, as is subsequently discussed in the text. Inquiries about usury were not made, but there was some evidence that it had been practiced.

[17] This seems to have been a general pattern throughout North Africa, cited by Slouschz for Tripoli (1927:37, 126) as well as Morocco (1927: 455ff.), and by Briggs (1960:89). Clarke (1959:92) refers to it among Jews of Telouet, the seat of the Glaoua tribe; and a rabbi, one of the immigrants to Israel from Telouet, had laughingly informed me of it.

Telouet, southeast of Marrakesh and southwest of Demnat, is the site of a great kasbah (cf. Clarke 1959:61–63; Montagne 1930b: fig. 7) of the former ruling family. Four of the villages in the valley, according to Slouschz (1927:463–67) had mellah in 1913 containing, in all, about 800 Jews. Slouschz gives the figure of about 300 Jews for the principal mellah of Ighilbein, and Flamand (1950:374) gives the figure of 150 for this same mellah as of 1949.

By 1913, the time of Slouschz' trip to the Atlas Mountains, the Glaoui were far along in the expansion of power and territorial conquest through which they finally achieved, in alliance with the French, a domain extending over both sides of the Atlas Mountains, east to the Dades and south to the Sahara. An account of their rise is to be found in Montagne (1930a:320–32, 334–41). At the time of Slouschz' visit, the nephew of Si el Madani, the Glaoui ruler under whom this conquest was achieved, was caid of Telouet and had as his intendant a Jew, of whom Slouschz

tional but not unknown.[18] They might own cows and/or sheep, cared for by neighboring Berbers, to whom they gave the money to purchase the animals.[19] Newborn animals would be divided between Jew and Berber.

Women's work in the villages included food preparation and child rearing; and wives might help their husbands in such trades as shoemaking and tailoring.[20] In the villages where agriculture was practiced, women may have aided in some farming tasks.[21] In Ait Adrar and Ait Rahhal they all

---

writes (1927:465): "A clever Talmudist, he has a cunning and subtle mind. He plays up to every caprice of the Kaid, and knows the art of making himself indispensable to the courtiers. He is very friendly with the black eunuchs who are so influential in Musselman courts, and he is even admitted to the Harem . . . he has been able to monopolize all the export trade, dividing the profits with the Berber chiefs, and he often comes into conflict with other Jewish merchants, who fear and detest him. An undying feud exists between him and his rivals, who only wait for the moment when he will fall from grace to exact their revenge and take his place." El Hajj Thami, younger brother of Si el Madani, and his successor as pasha of Marrakesh from 1919 until his own death in 1956, also was reported to have employed Jews. Montagne, writing of the kasbah Jews (1939a:346–47) who "facilitate commerce and conclude with the Moslems all the transactions which the caid would not be able, without blushing, to negotiate directly," must have had such figures in mind.

[18] All the villages reported to practice agriculture (Slouschz 1927:450ff.; Flamand 1950:366–76) seem to be east of the Central Massif of the High Atlas, the subject of Dresch's study (1941), and in territory that came under Glaoui rule.

[19] Flamand (1952:141–42) reports this practice by Jews in Demnat. The Berbers have the right to use the animals (bulls, cows, sheep, goats) in working their fields, and milk, butter, and wool are divided equally. When the Jew wishes to realize his capital, the animals are sold and all gains above the initial investment also are divided equally. Flamand adds that the "Arab" does not always act in good faith in these transactions, but that competition among such guardians of flocks serves the Jews as one means of control.

[20] In Demnat the following occupational distribution, listed in descending order of prestige, was reported for women in straitened circumstances (Flamand 1952:30): 1 dentist (meaning puller of teeth, who also was nurse for the newborn, and leech), 8 midwives, 113 seamstresses, 45 knitters, 19 thread makers, 2 sieve makers, 24 makers of brandy and wine, 7 laundresses, 16 domestic servants, 15 water carriers, 19 rugmakers, 8 embroiderers. Also noted were 3 makers of black soap (Flamand 1952:34).

[21] Some informants in Israel denied that women had ever worked in the fields, but some of the women from Ait Adrar were observed in Ometz hoeing their gardens with real proficiency from the first days of their arrival, and in Shavur I saw an old woman from Ait Rahhal carry home, with the ease of obvious long experience, a huge load of grain tied to her back.

practiced weaving, both for domestic needs and to fill an occasional commission from the neighboring Berbers. Throughout the Atlas Mountains villages, women rarely left their homes except to fetch water,[22] sometimes from a spring or stream an hour's distance away by foot; and they never went to market.

Jews could be identified throughout the Atlas Mountains by the black skullcaps worn by the men.[23] Berbers too may wear skullcaps, but these are in colors.[24] Otherwise, the dress of Jews approximated that of their neighbors. Principal garments for the men traditionally included a long-flowing shirt, over which would be worn the *djellaba,* a loose outer garment sewn up the middle and provided with a hood. The women traditionally draped lengths of woven woolen cloth several times around their bodies, securing them at the waist with coiled woolen girdles. In recent decades this costume was being replaced by long, shapeless dresses made of manufactured cotton cloth. All married women would keep their heads covered, as dictated by Jewish law.

Within the Jewish villages, both wealth and religious learning and piety conferred status, and old age was honored. Marriages were arranged by parents, and young men would be married between the ages of seventeen and twenty. Girls could be married as early as their seventh or eighth year,[25]

[22] Women in Demnat also carried water home from the public fountain of the mellah (Flamand 1952:37). Flamand notes that any Jewish male in Demnat, unlike the Moslem men, would feel dishonored if he were to fetch water or carry bread. Women who could afford to do so paid carriers to bring water to their homes. Chaumeil (1953:37) notes that in the mellah of Tahala women leave their homes only to do laundry and fetch water.

[23] Prior to the arrival of the French, sumptuary restrictions applying to Jews also included their wearing black footgear (Turkish slippers) and walking barefoot in the towns. The possession of horses and arms also might be prohibited (de Foucauld 1888:395ff., as cited in Chouraqui 1952: 93). Informants claimed that the wearing of black djellabas also had been erratically enforced prior to the French protectorate (cf. Briggs 1960:92, and pictures of Jews in black djellabas in Tahala [Chaumeil 1953: figs 3, 8] and Ifran [Monteil 1948:pl. I]). However, the wearing of black by Berbers as well as Jews is reported for Telouet in 1913 (Slouschz 1927:467), and the immigrants to Israel stated that they had worn outer garments of whatever color they pleased.

[24] Cf. Clarke 1959:92.

[25] Slouschz (1927) cites cases of such early marriage from all over North Africa. Flamand notes (1952:57, 64ff.) marriages in Demnat be-

but the age of thirteen or fourteen also was customary. The marriages of those who had wed as children usually would not be consummated until they reached their teens, at least this was the case in Ait Adrar. Monogamy was general.[26]

The prescriptions of Jewish law and ritual were scrupulously observed, although the general level of Jewish learning was low. North African Judaism has been suffused with mysticism and magical beliefs and practices,[27] which permeated the observances of the Atlas Mountains Jews. Various customs also were common to Jews and Berbers. Particularly noteworthy among these is the cult of the saints, the veneration of holy men, at whose tombs offerings would be made and favors asked.[28] The same tombs could be the objects of pilgrimages by both Moslems and Jews.[29]

---

tween girls of nine and men close to or over thirty, the usual age of marriage for males in this town. Girls might be engaged by the age of eight years, and some even by the age of six. A girl who had reached the age of seventeen unmarried was an old maid. In 1934, the president of the High Rabbinical Court of Morocco had the French protectorate forbid the marriage of Jewish girls below the age of thirteen. This law was largely ignored in Demnat and probably even more so in the villages. One result in Demnat was the frequency of deaths among young girls unable to survive premature motherhood. Conversely, girls aged ten might already be widows.

[26] This is true of the Atlas Mountains Berbers as well (cf. Montagne 1930a:43; Berque 1955:34), in contrast to the Arabs of the plains.

[27] The influence of the Kabbalistic tradition, particularly the mystic Book of Zohar (the "Book of Splendor"), has been particularly strong (cf. Chouraqui 1952:276ff.). The Zohar, written in Aramaic and purported to be composed in the second century A.D. by Rabbi Shimon bar Yochai after the defeat of the final Jewish rebellion against the Romans, is a work filled with allegory and mystical exegesis, actually written in the thirteenth century. The itinerant rabbi from the Holy Land, the *haham* (wise or learned one) traveling from village to village, collecting money to send back to the Palestinian academies, and dispensing cures, blessings, and Kabbalistic formulas (cf. Chouraqui 1952:279; Slouschz 1927:96–103) was a common figure from the fifteenth century on. Such rabbis introduced the cult of Zohar, with its Messianic aspect, and other Kabbalistic doctrines and practices to the most remote communities in North Africa.

[28] This practice is an aspect of North African Judaism which may largely derive from the influence of North African maraboutism (Chouraqui 1952:293–301), and it flourishes throughout Morocco, particularly among the Berbers of the Atlas Mountains. Voinot (1948:107, 121ff.) suggests that it derives from ancient Berber beliefs and practices which antedate Islam and became systematized after the introduction of Sufism into Morocco.

[29] Voinot (1948:16–92) lists one hundred sites throughout Morocco that are the object of such double veneration. He divides them into three cate-

Each Jewish village had one or more representatives to mediate relations with the French and Berber local administration.[30] The Jews of Ait Adrar lived in virtual symbiosis with their Berber neighbors, and enjoyed excellent relations with them and a high subsistence level. However, it was reported that this was far from being the case in some other parts of the Atlas Mountains,[31] where Jews had to work desperately hard to maintain a bare subsistence level.[32]

gories: 1) those of holy men whose origin is claimed by both Moslems and Jews, each of them having a legend in reference to the alleged person involved; 2) those of Moslem origin also visited and revered by Jews; and 3) those of Jewish origin also visited and revered by Moslems. He finds thirty-one sites to belong to the first category, fourteen to the second category, and fifty-five to the third category. Of these one hundred sites, the greatest number, thirty-seven, are in the High Atlas Mountains; of these, twelve fall into the first category, three into the second, and twenty-two into the third (Voinot 1948:85). There is no relation between the number of such sites in a region and the density of its Jewish population.

30 According to Israeli emissaries and their urban Moroccan assistants who had visited the Atlas Mountains, these were generally the richest men of the communities. The chief informant among the immigrants from Ait Adrar, a thoughtful young rabbi, denied this. He claimed that in Ait Adrar the villagers chose the mediator for his truthfulness and reliability as well as ability, lest he distort communications or use his position to further his own interests. He gave as an example of this the case of a clever young merchant who had traveled often to Casablanca and was also the son of a rich and respected man. He had been given this position but was allowed to hold it only for a few months, since he was found to be unreliable.

In Demnat there had existed a position of sheikh of the Jews since before the French protectorate (cf. Slouschz 1927:454). Chosen by the Jewish community, as of 1949, he arbitrated lawsuits insofar as he could, and served as intermediary between the Jewish population and the local judicial power (meaning the caid and his khalifat, aided by an official of the French administration) in the regulation of misdemeanors (Flamand 1952: 126–27). His duties included investigating cases and giving his advice before judgment was passed, attending the sessions of the court held on the twenty-second day of each month, and aiding the tax collector in fixing and collecting taxes. Unlike his Moslem counterparts, who received 5 percent of the money collected, he served without remuneration. The administration of justice was "rickety" where the Jews were concerned, according to Flamand. But this was tempered, he adds, by (1) the equality of treatment given to Moslem and Jewish defendants; (2) the general absence of Western-style guarantees in the administration of justice; (3) the existence of the right of appeal; and, above all, (4) the infrequency of appearance of Jews before the court.

31 The Atlas Mountains are part of the traditional *Bled-es-Siba* of Morocco, the "land of dissidence" of the Berber mountain tribes, resistant to the sultan's authority and administration, as contrasted to the *Bled el Makhzen*, the plains area subject to the control of the central government. Of the Jews of the Bled-es-Siba, particularly of the Atlas Mountains,

AIT ADRAR

Ait Adrar is situated ninety kilometers east of Demnat, at an altitude of over 2,000 meters. The Jewish villages were located near a mountain stream; and cold springs, which never froze in winter, were also nearby. Olive trees, plum trees, and other fruits were reported to grow there in profusion. The region is known for its beauty, and French tourists visited it during summers, camping near the banks of one of the streams.

The Jewish community lived in four hamlets, situated from one to several kilometers apart. Itkaalan had a popula-

---

in 1883–84, de Foucauld wrote (de Foucauld 1888:394ff., as cited in Chouraqui 1952:93, 95–96) ". . . they are the most unfortunate of men." He describes not only the sumptuary restrictions to which they were subject, cited above in note 23, but also a series of special taxes levied against them, and, most particularly, the state of vassalage in which they lived. "Every Jew of the *bled-es-siba* belongs body and goods to his lord, his *sid*. If his family was already established in the countryside, he has come to him (the sid) as part of his inheritance. . . . If he himself (the Jew) has come to settle down, he must constitute himself, as soon as he arrives, the Jew of somebody. His homage given, he is tied forever, he and his posterity, to the one he has chosen. The sid protects his Jew against strangers as one defends his property. He makes use of him in the way he manages his patrimony, according to his own character." De Foucauld continues with this analogy, contrasting the wise and economical Moslem's treatment of the Jew with that of the prodigal: the former requiring as annual tribute no more than the Jew can afford; the latter demanding excessive sums, taking the Jew's wife as hostage for what he cannot give. De Foucauld piles detail on detail: should violence break out, everything the Jew earns is snatched from him; his children are taken away; finally, he himself is put on the market and sold at auction. Or else his house is pillaged and destroyed, and he and his family are chased away. "No one protects a Jew against his lord; he is at his mercy."

By 1913, the year of Slouschz' visit, such conditions of vassalage still obtained in the Dades region (Slouschz 1927:483), which had not yet been conquered by the Glaoui. In the region of Telouet the Jews suffered from very heavy taxation and might have to engage in slave labor (Slouschz 1927:470), but this was no less true of the Berber subjects of the great Berber chieftains newly risen to power (cf. Montagne 1930a: 348ff.), who despoiled their subjects, formerly organized in independent canton (taqbilt) states (cf. Montagne 1930a:147–241).

By the 1920s, Jews still remained, according to Montagne (1930a:45), "the most despised class in Berber country"; but they could move around freely under the French protectorate, unlike former times when, according to de Foucauld (as cited in Chouraqui 1952:96), the men needed the authorization of their overlords in order to travel and their families were compelled to remain behind to guarantee their return.

Informants from Ait Adrar spoke of the time, before the arrival of the French, when they needed a protector in order to enter a Berber village.

32 Cf. Chaumeil 1953; Flamand 1950:390–93.

tion of about sixty families, Taabant of about fifteen families, Ait Ouriat of about twenty-five families, and Ait Imi [33] of about twenty families. Each village had a synagogue, but only Itkaalan and Taabant had living in them men able to carry out the duties of ritual slaughterer (*shohet*), performer of circumcisions (*mohel*), and teacher (*mori*), meaning teacher of Hebrew and minimal Jewish learning. These functions, for several years prior to emigration, had been performed in the other two villages by a rabbi from Itkaalan, the son of its own rabbi. In addition to its rabbi, Itkaalan had a shohet-mohel. A single Jewish cemetery, situated next to Taabant, served all the villages.

Taabant also adjoined both the site of the weekly market, held on Sundays, and the district office of the French administration. Also located there was the seat of the Berber subdistrict to which it and Itkaalan belonged. Ait Ouriat and Ait Imi were under the jurisdiction of another subdistrict.

Houses in Ait Adrar were built of small stones and clay, with ceiling and roof made of wooden beams on which a special kind of red clay was poured. This hardened sufficiently for another story to be built on top of the first, and houses might be three stories high. Roofs might also be covered with tar, to keep out the rain. More recently, cement, purchased in the cities, was reported to have been used occasionally in building. Houses were painted according to individual taste.

Extended families lived either around courtyards or in adjoining houses. Each nuclear family generally occupied one room, where its members lived, slept, and worked at their trades. In summer many people would sleep outside. The women of an extended family generally cooked together in the courtyards, and one or two ovens might serve about ten nuclear families. Since water was nearby, women seldom left the vicinity of the house. Food would be brought home by the men, or neighboring Berbers would bring it to the house. Some houses seemed to have had small gardens, in

[33] These are the true names of the hamlets, all of which, with the exception of Ait Imi, I was able to find on the Index Map of Morocco.

which hot peppers, *nana* (a mint plant used in brewing tea), and other vegetables were grown. Some people might keep chickens, goats, and sheep, although the latter were mainly held and tended by the neighboring Berbers, according to the arrangement previously described. Some families also kept donkeys or mules, although these were generally farmed out to the Berbers also.

The villagers were carpenters, blacksmiths, tinkers, jewelers, shoemakers, leatherworkers, tailors, dyers, makers of millstones, and processors of oil for the surrounding countryside. Some of them also knew building trades. Most, if not all, of the men seem to have known and practiced more than one craft; and specific skills were differentiated. Thus, shoemaking was differentiated from shoe repairing, and the practice of trades would be qualified as "for the Arabs." Sons often, but not always, learned and practiced their fathers' trades. The only craft practiced by women seems to have been weaving, both for family use and for the neighboring Berbers. However, only widows or women of very poor families would weave habitually for the Berbers, according to informants, although a very rapid and skilled weaver might do so occasionally. Girls generally began to learn to weave at about the age of eight. Tailors might be helped by their wives, who held the threads in the fine sewing required for djellabas and women's traditional robes. However, no woman could sew or repair garments until, a few years before the time of emigration, two women purchased hand-run sewing machines and learned to use them. Also, women did not know how to knit, although many men possessed this skill.

The raw materials for all the crafts could be purchased at the weekly market, at which cows, sheep, chickens, cloth, finished craft products, and manufactured goods from the cities were also sold. While everything needed by the villagers was available at the market, purchases might also be made in Demnat, Marrakesh, and even, in the case of those specializing in trade, in Casablanca.

Subsistence, apparently, was assured, since most of the year's supply of basic foodstuffs could be obtained by working in agriculture during the summer months. Jews might work for landowners as laborers, receiving part of the harvest in exchange. The portion they received was usually enough to last for the rest of the year. Also, a group of Jews might take over a field and work it, receiving part of the harvest in return. Finally, Jews might receive land as security for loans. Until the debt was paid, they received part of the harvest from the real owners, who continued to work it.

Additional food would be received as payment for craft work, and informants described how they were given baskets of eggs, strings of chickens, and sacks of grain in exchange for work performed. Food was also given as a gift, in addition to the price agreed upon. Fruit was free, as was salt, which was available in crystal form at a nearby salt mine. Those unwilling to dig it out and fetch it themselves paid a trifling sum to a Berber to bring them several months' supply. The women ground the crystals in mortars. Thus, food hardly entered the money economy of the Jews of Ait Adrar, and minimal subsistence needs could be satisfied by all. When purchased, food was bought in quantity: grain by the sack and meat in the form of animals for slaughter.

Work was carried out by each according to his own tempo. The villagers might labor long hours during peak agricultural periods, but otherwise men might ply their trades for only a few hours a day. A full day's work began after morning prayers and would extend to about 11:00 A.M., to be resumed at about 4:00 P.M. and continued until sundown.[34] Every religious holiday or life-cycle ceremony usually was observed for several days, with work put aside.

Meat had a central place in the Ait Adrar diet. Even the poorest families were reported to have eaten meat, fried in oil, every day, together with bread baked in the outdoor oven. Beef and chicken were preferred, and the meat of sheep and goat also was consumed. Another item of daily consumption

[34] The workday in Demnat for Jews was: in winter, 7:00 A.M. to 2:00 P.M. and 3:00 P.M. to 8:00 P.M.; in summer, 6:00 A.M. to 1:30 P.M., 2:30 P.M. to 8:30 P.M., and 9:00 P.M. on even to 2:00 A.M. (Flamand 1952:42). Subsistence in Demnat was far from assured, according to Flamand's description, a situation which is reflected in these hours.

was couscous,[35] whose basic ingredient is generally wheat, millet, or barley flour, rolled into tiny balls and steamed. Couscous might be served with meat, fried pepper and other vegetables, or with cooked chickpeas, and always with a highly seasoned sauce. It was so freely available and eaten so often that the old rabbi from Itkaalan once remarked that he would forget to say the blessing on food over it. Fish could be caught in the nearby river, and eggs were abundant. Beans, corn, potatoes, tomatoes, and melons, as well as fruit from the surrounding trees, entered into the diet. Milk was purchased by some women from a Jew who had many cows, but mainly children drank it. However, sour milk was prepared, as was a kind of cheese, and these were consumed by adults.

Upon arising, adults drank tea, and ate or not as they chose. Meals seem to have been eaten around noon and in the evening. Ceremonies usually included a festive meal, with large quantities of meat. The entire community, and usually neighboring Berbers as well, would be invited to life-crises ceremonies and parties. While milk and meat were eaten separately, separate sets of dishes do not seem to have been kept.

Men were accustomed to taking wine with their meals; and brandy, made in the village, was also consumed. Women as well as men drank wine and brandy, especially on festive occasions, but they drank, as they ate, apart from the men, and they never took strong drink while among women only.[36] Strong, very sweet green tea prepared with mint was drunk at all times, as it is throughout Morocco, and it was served to very young children. In Ometz, the settlers continually spoke of the very cold water they had had in Ait Adrar, and purchased iceboxes as soon as they could to continue drinking cold water in Israel. During the winter months in Ait Adrar, when the snow lay on the ground, people were reported to

35 In Demnat, meat and couscous were eaten by the vast majority of Jews only on holidays (Flamand 1952:42, 78). The usual meal consisted of barley bread and vegetables prepared with a highly seasoned sauce.

36 In Demnat, homemade wine and brandy were on all tables (Flamand 1952:80–81). Wine was made of local grapes, and the brandy or *mahya* of grapes, raisins, figs, and dates, with grains of aniseed added.

have rarely gone out. They would sit together, drinking wine, brandy, or tea, and gossip.

The customary dress for men was the djellaba. In Ait Adrar these were made and worn by Jews in blue or brown cotton or white wool. They did not care for black and did not wear it, except for their black skullcaps. Conversely, black was frequently worn by the neighboring Berbers. The hood of the djellaba would be worn on the head only during cold or rainy weather or during periods of mourning. Generally, it would be used as a pocket. Men ordinarily went barefoot, but might wear Turkish slippers on trips or holidays. While working, especially in the fields, men often might wear the loose, baggy trousers with hanging seat, fitting closely around the lower leg, which are worn throughout North Africa. Long or short shirts would be worn over these trousers. Under the djellaba, the men generally wore long shirts without trousers, and some were reported never to have donned them.

The traditional woman's dress was woven of fine white wool, and in its weaving narrow strips of cotton, often tufted, were added at about six-inch intervals. The coiled rope girdles, usually of red and black, would be wound several times around the waist. The traditional headdress of the Jewish women of Ait Adrar consisted of a small (forty to forty-five centimeters long) piece of rectangular silk cloth, around which a very long, narrow silk shawl, generally dark red, with a fringed edge, would be wound four times and then tied. Its ends would fall to the waist or even lower. However, beginning about two generations prior to the time of emigration, women had begun to replace the traditional costume with long, shapeless gowns. Material for these gowns generally would be purchased at the weekly market, and the gowns would be made by men in the village who specialized in this. Women would often wear one gown on top of another, the number varying in part with the weather; and the outer one might be used to tie an infant on the back. Silk kerchiefs in all colors, also to be purchased at the weekly market, were worn increasingly, rather than the traditional headdress. Most women ordinarily went barefoot, donning embroidered leather or silk slippers only on holidays or at ceremonies. Recently, some women had begun to wear Western-style dresses or skirts and blouses, which could be purchased at the weekly market or in Marrakesh.

Toddlers were dressed in small shirts. From about the age of four, boys would wear small djellabas and girls would be dressed in long gowns like their mothers. Bead bracelets and necklaces containing amulets were fastened around the arms and necks of the children to guard against the evil eye.

New clothes were supposed to be made or purchased for everyone before the Day of Atonement, Yom Kippur, and before Sukkot, the harvest festival which occurs within a week after Yom Kippur. Clothes made for Yom Kippur were supposed to be white, and those for Sukkot in colors. New clothing was made or purchased at other times of the year according to need, means, and taste.

Jewelry worn by the women consisted of silver bracelets with incised geometrical designs, and silver rings, colored bead necklaces, and earrings made of strings of beads. The bracelets and rings were generally made by jewelers in the village, and the beads for necklaces and earrings would be purchased at the market or in the towns. Threaded in among the beads would be metal amulets, of which more will be said later. These were made by the village jewelers and could be passed on for generations. More recently, cheap costume jewelry purchased in the market, usually imitation gold or silver chains and bracelets, might also be worn.

Henna would be smeared on the head or on other parts of the body at various times. It would be placed on a baby's head when its hair was first cut and on weaning; on a boy's head and hands at his confirmation ceremony, his Bar Mitzva; on the head, hands, and feet of a bride; and on a bridegroom's hands.[37] A bride's face was also washed in henna water. According to one young man in Ometz, henna

[37] According to a description of a wedding which took place in Demnat in 1932 (Flamand 1952:57–60), the bride's hands, arms, and feet were stained with henna.

strengthens the hair and is put on the heads of children of every age. A woman returning from the hospital also had her head smeared with henna. The most general explanation given was that henna is used for beauty, against illness, and when a child stops nursing. It also seems to have been used as protection against the evil eye. Soot was also used on various occasions. A boy being confirmed had his eyes blackened, as did brides and bridegrooms. A black spot of soot was observed on the forehead of a sick baby in Ometz, and women were seen with their eyes blackened on festive occasions. Thus, soot too seems to have been used for beauty and against illness. A black band of cloth also was once observed bound across the forehead of a sick man.

These customs were but elements in the body of beliefs and practices concerning health and illness held by the Jews of Ait Adrar. The central beliefs and practices seem to derive both from local tradition, shared with the Berbers, and from part of the vast body of ancient Jewish tradition that does not come within the binding law. As explained by the old rabbi of Itkaalan and his son, also a rabbi in Ait Adrar and the principal systematic informant for this reconstruction, demons (*shedim,* singular *shed*) cause many illnesses, and apparently all the sudden ones. Every human being has a shed who goes with him wherever he goes. Men walk on the earth and shedim under the ground. There are additional shedim everywhere, and precautions must be taken not to step on them lest they revenge themselves by bringing on illness. They cannot be appeased, only guarded against. Said the rabbi: "As a man takes care of himself, so also must he take care lest his shed cause him ill." Beliefs about shedim are ancient in Jewish tradition, and discussions of them are to be found in the Talmud.[38]

As the rabbis further explained, ditches of standing water are one of the places where shedim congregate, and should not be stepped into. Also, there are shedim in the

---

[38] Clarke's brief description (1959:71–73) of beliefs concerning spirits, *djnun,* in a Berber village north of Telouet shows parallels.

fire, and water should not be poured on it. Thus, after an evening of songs and instruction for young people in Ometz, led by the youth instructor, a young man was asked to pour water on the bonfire around which the group had sat. He answered in terror: "I have a wife and children and they still should live." Shedim are particularly prevalent on Tuesdays and Fridays, the third and sixth days of the Jewish week.

Against the shedim are the angels (*malakhim*), whose protection can be invoked with the help of the Kabbala. Special prayers and amulets containing the Holy Name invoke such protection. It is thought that angels sit in the entrance to the house, so that water never must be poured out there. The settlers from Ait Adrar did not believe that one human being could put a spell on another, as is held by other groups of Jews, such as those from Yemen. When asked about this, the younger rabbi in Ometz seemed amazed and said that the power obtained through learning Kabbala could be used only to heal.

Among the illnesses caused by shedim are fainting, insanity, and sudden paralysis of a limb. These are healed by people with special knowledge, which is to be found in the Kabbala. The two rabbis in Ometz, father and son, modestly admitted to having this knowledge. Special prayers are said in such cases, special charms are written and fastened to the sick person or sick limb, and bands are tied tightly on aching parts of the body. Prayers also are said over water, are written in the hand of the sick person or on his forehead, and a charm might be put in his ear. Further details were not forthcoming from the rabbis. There are also prayers and amulets for journeys and, indeed, for every occasion.[39]

Thus, there are amulets for pregnant women, worn on the girdle or in a necklace. It is also believed that a pregnant woman will miscarry if she steps on fingernail parings, a belief to be found in the Talmud. However, in talking about childbirth, women would say that they weren't afraid; what

[39] The ritual of Judaism includes prayers for every occasion.

happened would be as God willed it. As observed in Ometz, in cases where labor had started before the woman was taken to the hospital, she stood or sat on the floor supported by two women and holding on to a rope suspended from the ceiling. Children of all ages might be in the room. It was reported by the Ometz instructress that none of the women cried out while in labor.

After the birth of a child, talismans are written and fastened on the wall; in Ometz they were placed above its sleeping-place and around the room.[40] These talismans generally consisted of pieces of paper on which horizontal rows of lines of graduated length were inscribed in several patterns, together with blessings. Up to five such talismans were observed in rooms containing newborn babies in Ometz. Their purpose, explained the younger rabbi, is to render powerless a *sheda* (she-demon) who has many names, the most important of which is Lilith, and who puts to sleep the mothers of newborn children and then kills the child. In addition to the other amulets worn by children, their ears are pierced and wire amulets inserted. This might be done immediately after birth, but some families waited for years. Thus, the children of the young rabbi had their ears pierced at the age of five, but a customary age seems to have been between six months and a year. These ear amulets rarely remain on for more than a year.

There are different names for the different illnesses and different names for the shedim causing them, but the names of the shedim should never be pronounced. Thus, when the fieldworker forgot this injunction and repeated with recognition the name of Lilith [41] after the rabbi had spelled it out, he blanched and told her never to say that name. Also, it

40 Flamand (1952:101–8) reproduces printed talismans used in Demnat against scorpions, to protect a male infant on the day of his circumcision, and to protect women during childbirth. The maker of talismans, while at work, must guard himself by wearing a ring engraved with the name of an angel, the name formed by the final letters of the first five verses of the Bible. Before engraving the ring, the engraver should purify himself in running water.

41 The career of Lilith in Jewish thought, her evolution from a demon who mated with Adam to consort of God, is presented by Patai (1964).

is wisest not to talk about shedim and not to discuss past illnesses, since the shedim might return. Thus, it was not until seven months after the settlers had come to Ometz and ten months after they had arrived in Israel that the instructor team received the first indication that a seemingly much-respected old woman had had attacks of insanity in Ait Adrar. She had appeared ill for several months and had been sent to a hospital for diagnosis. When the hospital could find nothing wrong with her, her son admitted that every year at about that time she would become ill and dispirited. Later it emerged that she had periodically suffered spells of madness in Ait Adrar, during which she would run around the village naked. Also, she had once bitten another woman, who then went mad too. The latter had died in Ait Adrar prior to the emigration. When the old woman's attacks of madness were once talked about later in the presence of the old rabbi, he stopped the discussion, saying, "What is buried is buried." During their attacks, the insane in Ait Adrar were kept locked in their homes and had their legs chained, since people feared them.

However, not all illnesses are caused by shedim. Some, like diarrhea, were considered to have entirely natural causes, and both natural causes and shedim might enter into others. Such ailments were treated with herbs, as prescribed by the old rabbi. The herbs used, he said, are those specified in the Shulhan Arukh.[42] However, he stated that all the old women also knew how to use herbs; and a few of them who were then in his presence smiled.[43] The settlers had brought these herbs—such as a special kind of mint for stomach

[42] The Shulhan Arukh, which can be translated as "The Set Table," is the code of Jewish law and practice summarizing the Talmud. It was composed by Joseph Caro in the sixteenth century in the holy city of Safed in Palestine. Since it embodied the Sephardi tradition, certain modifications were made in the Shulhan Arukh by scholars in the Ashkenazi tradition to bring it into accord with Ashkenazi practices. The Jews of the Atlas Mountains, of course, followed the Sephardic tradition.

[43] Flamand (1952:96, 99) notes that in the mellah of Demnat inhabitants turned to the old women for formulas of exorcism and to the Berber magicians (he writes "Arab") for charms against illness, etc.

pains—along with them to Ometz, and the old women would bring them out on request.

The old rabbi also pointed out that it is written in the Torah, the Five Books of Moses, that "each goes to its kind." Therefore, heat could expel heat, as in the use of hot compresses for fever, and cold could expel cold. However, he thought little of the custom of burning an aching part of the body with a hot iron, as is practiced throughout the Arab countries, and did not prescribe it, although the treatment was known in the villages.[44]

But whenever herbal or other practical remedies were applied, prayers and amulets were used as well. As it was impossible to be certain whether or not shedim were involved in an illness, it was necessary to take precautions against them. Amulets were also used for toothaches; if relief was not forthcoming, the tooth was pulled. The rabbis did not pull teeth; but a number of people, among them a carpenter, knew how to do so.

Practices against the evil eye included fastening a right hand carved out of wood to an infant's sleeping-place. A handprint also might be painted on the outside wall of the house, near the entrance, as is the practice throughout the Arab world.[45]

Five, in general, was considered a lucky number. A baby's hair was first cut in Ait Adrar when the baby had five teeth. Henna then was rubbed on its head, and the mother invited all female relatives with small children—in effect most of the women of the community—to a celebration. In extending the invitation, the mother sent out a plate of food to each of the prospective guests. In returning the plates they sent back five eggs if the child was a boy, so that many more would come, one egg in the case of a girl, to discourage the birth of

[44] Clarke (1959:21) reports that piercing with red-hot skewers was used as a cure for lassitude combined with pain in the joints in Ait Rbaa, the Berber village where his party worked. He states that the pain is believed to be caused by djnun, who are made uncomfortable by the treatment and depart.

[45] Laredo (1954:100) considers the use of the sign of the right hand to be a custom going back to the Phoenicians.

more daughters. Instead of eggs, they might send five pieces of money. Women mentioned that fifteen and two are also good numbers. They knew no unlucky numbers.[46]

Whatever the provenience of the beliefs and customs described so far, those central to the way of life followed by the Jews of Ait Adrar derive from the tradition of Judaism, binding on the orthodox everywhere.[47] Social control was exercised largely within its framework, at least as locally understood and adapted. The synagogue was the center of religious life, and apparently of community life as well. However, it might be a very simple building, in which the scrolls of the Torah would be placed on a few boards. Every male received a fixed place in the synagogue at the time of his religious coming of age or Bar Mitzva, on his thirteenth birthday. This place would remain the same, regardless of later attainments in terms of learning and/or wealth. Fathers could seat their sons next to them. Only if a man went to another village would his place in the synagogue be determined by learning, the most honored places being the seats in front, nearest the Scrolls of the Law.

If a man did not appear for a day in the synagogue, this would be noted; and the next time he came he would be asked where he had been. Unless he gave a good reason,

[46] There is an aversion to even numbers in the Talmud. Its advice against doing certain things twice ("There is a teaching: A man should not eat or drink in a company where there is an even number, or wipe himself twice or attend to his needs twice." [Pes. 109b, as cited in Cohen 1949: 294]) may not have been known by the Jews of Ait Adrar, certainly not by the women.

[47] Jewish religious law, as laid down in the Talmud, includes 613 ordinances, the majority of them nonoperative, since they cover agricultural and criminal law and observances in the Temple. In addition, the Talmud and other writings which remain from the Talmudic period include vast bodies of nonbinding discussion, speculation, and narrative. Since the Talmudic period, successive generations of rabbis in all the centers of learning in the Diaspora have added commentaries and rulings, interpreting and adapting the Talmudic ordinances to changing local conditions. Thus, details of practice differ from one subtradition of Judaism to another and even from community to community within these subtraditions, and variously included are beliefs and customs drawn from parts of the tradition outside the ordinances. Judaism as a "great tradition" has many "parochializations" (Redfield 1956:70–94). Nonetheless, the basic observances of the law are the same; and the devout Jew observes them according to the tradition of his fathers and the rulings of his rabbis.

he would be warned by the important men of the community.[48] Should he continue not to attend, the community would ostracize him: no one would talk to him, no one would trade with him, and the ritual slaughterer would refuse to slaughter for him. This had never happened in Ait Adrar in the memory of the immigrants to Ometz. Sons of the community had been leaving Ait Adrar during recent decades to work in Casablanca. Some had settled there and had become less observant. But they fell back into the practices of the community whenever they returned to Ait Adrar.

Observances of the yearly cycle of religious holidays included some holiday periods of longer duration than ordained. Also, no work was carried out on days when post-Talmudic law does allow it, such as the days intervening between the first two and last two days of Passover and Sukkot or Booths. Of the holidays decreed in the Torah,[49] Rosh Hashana, the New Year, was observed for two days, and was considered the most important holiday of the year. The mood was profoundly serious on the first day,[50] lighter on the second. Yom Kippur, the Day of Atonement,[51] was of course a day of fasting on which the mourning abstentions were observed.[52] Nonetheless, some of the gladness that is supposed to accompany Yom Kippur according to the an-

[48] This was not the case in Demnat. Flamand (1952:118) reports that many adults went to the synagogue irregularly, except for Sabbath attendance.

[49] Jewish holidays fall into two categories: those decreed in the Torah, and those which developed later in Jewish history; the former are seen as the ordinance of God.

[50] Rosh Hashana and Yom Kippur are decreed together in the Torah (Lev. 23:24–29). The ten-day period beginning with the former and ending with the latter is called in the Talmud the Ten Days of Repentance. This period begins on the first day of the Hebrew month of Tishri, falling sometime in September or October. In the preceding month, repentance prayers are said each night. Rosh Hashana is the Day of Judgment according to Jewish belief, in which the destiny of every human being for the forthcoming year is decided by God.

[51] Yom Kippur is the day on which the judgments made on Rosh Hashana are sealed. It was the day on which the high priest entered the holy of holies (Lev. 16). As a day of afflicting the soul, it is a twenty-four-hour fast day, and the mourning abstentions are observed.

[52] The mourning abstentions involve abstaining from sex, from bathing, from anointing the body with oil, and from the wearing of leather footgear.

cient codes seems to have been maintained in Ait Adrar. White garments were worn, and some women were found dancing and laughing on the morning of the first Yom Kippur in Ometz. The men spent the entire day in the synagogue, and the women gathered outside it, at least for part of the time. Sukkot, the festival of Tabernacles, was fully observed, with no work done during the entire period.[53] Pessah, the Passover, was celebrated for eight days, with no work carried out during this time.[54] Shavuot, Pentecost, was observed for three days, with no work carried out.[55]

Of the post-Mosaic holidays, Purim, the Feast of Esther, was celebrated for two days, with no work done, although this is not demanded by the law. Similarly, the observance of Hanukka, the Festival of the Lights, included abstention from work for two days.[56] Oil was burned in the Hanukka lamp, rather than candles. The reason given for this was the ordinance in the Torah referring to the burning of oil before the Tabernacle. Simhat Torah, the day of Rejoicing

[53] Sukkot begins on the fifteenth day of the Hebrew month of Tishri, following Yom Kippur, and lasts for seven days. Decreed as a harvest festival (Lev. 30:33–44; Deut. 16:13–15), it involves, among other observances, eating all meals in a specially constructed outdoor hut. The first stake of the hut is supposed to be driven into the ground immediately after the close of Yom Kippur and this was done by the Jews of Ait Adrar. Only on the first and last days of Sukkot is work prohibited, but the Jews of Ait Adrar seem to have refrained from labor for the entire period from the beginning of Rosh Hashana through Simhat Torah, a one-day holiday immediately following Sukkot. Also, the observance of Sukkot may have lasted an extra two days.

[54] The law prohibits work only on the first and last days of Passover (Num. 28:16–25), although the prohibition against leaven is observed for the entire period.

[55] Shavuot is the festival of both the First Fruits and the Giving of the Law. Seven weeks after Passover, in ancient days, the first fruits were brought to the Temple (Num. 28:26–31; Deut. 16:9–12). Since the revelation of the law on Mount Sinai was supposed to have occurred on the same day, fifty days after the second day of Passover, the two occasions are combined in the same holiday. Shavuot is, in the Diaspora, generally a two-day holiday.

[56] Hanukka commemorates the revolt of the Jews against the Seleucid Greeks and the victory of the Maccabees in 165 B.C. It is one of the most minor of the religious holidays, marked for eight days by the burning of lights, one on the first day and an additional one on each succeeding day, in commemoration of the eight days during which the Temple was restored from desecration. Work may be carried out during Hanukka.

in the Law,[57] included in its observance the bringing of lighted candles into the synagogue by the women and children. All the holidays were marked by the serving of festive meals, and gifts of food customarily were given. A common festive meal was also eaten by the men on Rosh Hodesh, the first day of every Hebrew month, after the special prayers prescribed.

The five days of fasting in the Jewish calendar, in addition to Yom Kippur, were all observed by the entire community. These include four fast days connected with the destruction of the Temple. The most important is the ninth day of the Hebrew month of Av, when the destruction of both Temples occurred.[58] It also was forbidden among the Jews of Ait Adrar to wash from the first through the ninth days of the month of Av. In addition, they considered as an obligatory fast day the seventh day of the Hebrew month of Adar, which is supposed to be the day of the death of Moses.[59] A number of fasts which are voluntary, according to the law, were also kept by many people, both men and women.[60]

[57] This is a post-Talmudic festival which falls on the ninth day after the beginning of Sukkot and marks the completion of the yearly reading of the Torah and the initiation of the new cycle.

[58] The Ninth of Av commemoration calls for a twenty-four-hour fast and the observance of the mourning abstentions, although work may be carried out and travel undertaken, as on all the post-Mosaic holidays. The other fast days connected with the destruction of the Temple are: the tenth day of the Hebrew month of Tevet, which was the day on which the Babylonians circled the city of Jerusalem in 588 B.C., beginning its siege; the seventeenth day of the Hebrew month of Tamuz, the day on which the Romans broke the wall of Jerusalem in 70 A.D. and entered the city; and the Fast of Gedalia on the third day of the Hebrew month of Tishri, falling between Rosh Hashana and Yom Kippur, when Gedalia, the Jewish governor appointed by the Babylonians after the fall of Jerusalem, was killed. The fifth ordained fast day is the Fast of Esther on the thirteenth day of the Hebrew month of Adar, commemorating the fast set by Queen Esther (Esther 4:16).

[59] This is not an ordained fast but is considered a fast day by the righteous.

[60] These include the evening of Rosh Hashana and from sunrise to sunset during the period between Rosh Hashana and Yom Kippur; the first day of the Hebrew month of Elul, on which the repentance prayers begin; and the second and fifth days of the week during the period between Passover and Shavuot, which is a period of semimourning except for the thirty-third day (Lag B'Omer).

The Sabbath was fully observed,[61] although the women in Ometz sometimes were seen still cooking and cleaning on Friday after the men had left for the synagogue, and they could take their time about lighting the Sabbath candles.[62] In addition to the candle lit for the Sabbath, a candle was lit for every dead member of the family. Further candles might be lit for holy men. Once the practice of burning a candle for someone was initiated, it had to be kept up on all successive Sabbaths; to have done otherwise would symbolize that the dead had been forgotten. On Sabbath (Friday) evenings after the Sabbath meal, groups of men would come together, and the rabbis and old men would read from the Book of Zohar. On Sabbath mornings the men would visit each other and partake of festive foods, including meat in abundance and wine or brandy. The women would serve and then sit separately in a corner, as at all festive gatherings. The women might visit each other in the afternoon, but no formal meals were served. Women generally wore everyday clothes on the Sabbath.

Family relations and the life-cycle observances of the Jews of Ait Adrar were organized in terms of Jewish law, within a cultural tradition not markedly discontinuous with that in which the Talmud was framed. Marriages were arranged by parents, although it was reported that they were not carried out if the children objected strongly. Girls generally brought a dowry of household goods with them but could get married without one.[63] Community endogamy was preferred, but girls did marry out of Ait Adrar and brides

[61] Travel, work, and the kindling of fire are prohibited on the Sabbath.

[62] Lighting the Sabbath candle and saying the blessing over it is one of the three religious observances specifically required of women, in addition to the prohibitions binding on both men and women and the prohibitions related to uncleanness. The other two observances are: to burn a bit of dough with a blessing when the Sabbath bread is baked; and to go to the ritual bath or *mikve* of running water before marriage and following every period of uncleanness after marriage. All three were observed by the women of Ait Adrar, with the mountain stream serving as *mikve*.

[63] In Demnat, a dowry of at least the following objects was required of the bride: a rug, a woolen cover, a copper basin, a pestle, two mattresses, a collar of seven pieces of gold, and bracelets of gold or silver (Flamand 1952:56).

were brought in from neighboring Jewish settlements. Although according to Jewish law it is permissible to marry cousins, marriage between close cousins was not favored in Ait Adrar. It was reported to have taken place occasionally, however, although statistics could not be gathered on this point given the conditions under which the research for this reconstruction was carried out. As a young couple was not supposed to be acquainted before marriage, apart from unavoidable association in early childhood, this may have been one factor in the attitude toward marriage between cousins.

Structural factors also may have entered into this attitude, in that affinals were not regarded as real kin, whereas consanguineal kinship ties were recognized for at least four generations, together with kinship rights and obligations.[64] These meant mutual assistance and rights in each others' homes, although economic sharing, apart from financial assistance in times of emergency, seems to have been limited to a father and his sons when it did occur. Nonetheless, whenever people left Ait Adrar to study or settle in the towns, they immediately went to relatives, with whom they could live as long as they wished, sharing household tasks and responsibilities. Orphans might stay with various relatives, going from one to another. However, should a woman with young children be widowed, she would generally bring up the children herself, earning a livelihood by weaving for Berbers, and helped by both her relatives and those of her dead husband until the oldest son reached the age when he could assume the responsibility. In the very rare cases in Ait Adrar in which a widow had no relatives to help her,

[64] Kinship relations could not be looked into in detail, given the conditions under which the data for this reconstruction were gathered. It may be that the consanguineal relationship involved rights and obligations difficult to reconcile either with potential sources of tension between affinals or with the other kinds of roles in which potential affinals might stand in regard to each other. Thus, the women's practice of running home to their own families, their recourse against mistreatment as is subsequently discussed in the text, could possibly be seen as a factor mitigating against marriage between close consanguineal kin. However, the consanguineal relation equally could be seen as reinforcing the marriage bond, at least for the families involved, so that inference from this point is double-edged. Without additional data, the whole subject cannot be pursued further.

money would be collected in the synagogue from all the villagers; and neighboring Berbers were also reported to have contributed.

The woman's place was in the home; and as springs and streams were close to the villages in Ait Adrar, the women apparently never went far from their houses, until, in recent years, some girls went to Casablanca. It was forbidden for a woman to go out alone, to be alone with a man who was not a close relative, or even, it was reported, to talk to one. Fear of rape or adultery was not the reason; these were not even thought of in Ait Adrar,[65] as responses to questions made clear. Rather, it was explained, it just was not right for women to be alone with men or for girls to talk to boys; they would be ashamed. However, an unmarried girl in her teens might sleep in the same room as her grown brothers and cousins.

A woman, ideally, was to obey her husband in all respects and never question his judgment or talk back. If she did, he had every right to beat her, and he also could beat her if food was not prepared on time or to his liking. The accepted retaliation by a woman was to run away to her own relatives, generally taking at least the smaller children with her. Then the rabbi would be called in to make peace. Second wives were taken only if a woman remained barren through ten years of marriage. After that period her husband had the right to divorce her, as prescribed by Jewish law, unless she agreed to his taking a second wife. However, if a man waited until the ten years had passed before complaining of his wife's childlessness, he then had to

[65] However, adultery is reported to be frequent in Demnat (Flamand 1952:87–88). One of the reasons suggested for this is the disparate ages of the spouses. On the one hand, the young men, generally unmarried until after the age of thirty, seek sexual partners. Reciprocally, young women married to much older men are not unreceptive to advances from the younger men.

As for rape, it was reported that Jewish girls were often carried away by Berber men when the latter pillaged a mellah prior to the period of the French protectorate (Slouschz 1927:448); and Chaumeil reports that the women of Tahala in the Anti-Atlas were afraid to leave the vicinity of their homes (Chaumeil 1953:233).

wait another four years before divorcing her and/or marrying again.

Jewish law provides a considerable number of grounds on which a man can divorce his wife, provided that she accepts or can be made to accept the writ of divorce; and divorces for reasons othen than barrenness did take place in Ait Adrar, although neither case histories nor frequencies were collected. However, it is almost impossible in Jewish law for a woman to get a divorce unless her husband is willing to give her one. In Ait Adrar those rare women who asked for one lost their property rights, stipulated in the marriage contract. In Ometz, two cases occurred during the first year in which the families of young wives tried to get them divorces; the husbands demanded large sums of money as the price of giving the divorce, alleging that they had spent this amount on their wives. In Ait Adrar divorced women were not well regarded and could hope to be remarried only to widowers. This was also the case with widows; and second wives, including previously unmarried girls, could be fifteen to thirty years younger than their husbands.

Should a widow with small children marry again, it had to be written in the marirage contract, the *ketuba* of Jewish law covering the obligations of marriage partners to each other, that the new husband would take care of the children. "Otherwise," said the young rabbi in explaining the practice, "how could one be sure that he really would?" When a widower remarried, which he could do after the thirty-day period of mourning enjoined by Jewish law, his new wife was expected to care for his children. However, it seems to have been accepted that this care need only be minimal. Thus, it happened in Ometz that one man's two school-aged children by his dead wife went around particularly dirty and ragged. When the village instructress asked his present wife why this should be so, she shrugged and answered: "Poor things, they are orphans, they have no mother." In the meanwhile, she most carefully tended her own baby son. Young children whose mothers had died might be taken in and brought up by married siblings or by siblings of the dead woman. If a woman died in childbirth or soon after, the infant would be suckled by those relatives or neighboring women with milk. If no such woman was available, the baby generally died. The survival of one such infant, nursed in this fashion during the day and fed cow's milk and tea by his grandmother at night, was recounted as a miracle.

After the birth of a child, its mother is unclean for a stipulated period.[66] As during all her periods of uncleanness, she could not serve her husband food, nor could he touch her, her clothes, or covers, lest he be contaminated. At the expiration of this period, the woman bathes in running water. In Ait Adrar, the women then dressed in their best clothing and the day was one of rejoicing within the family, with a small family celebration. This custom was retained in Ometz. Thus, the youth instructress, herself a young married woman, once entered the house of a recent mother to find her washed, dressed in her finest clothes, and very happy. The unclean bed was outside the house airing, and the wife said joyfully: "It is now two and a half months after my son was born and I can sleep with my husband again." After he came home from work that day, she would serve him food for the first time since before she had given birth. In the meanwhile, she made tea for her guest and served it ceremonially on a round brass tray used to serve tea to guests on the Sabbath. Furthermore, she did not allow the youth instructress to sit down until she had covered the chair with a pretty spread.

Eight days after the birth of a son the circumcision ceremony marking the covenant of Abraham with God is carried out, as among Jews everywhere. It could be delayed,

---

[66] Beliefs and practices in Ait Adrar regarding the uncleanness of women were those of Jewish law. Women are considered unclean during menstruation and for seven days after, and must purify themselves by immersion in running water (Lev. 15:19–28). The period of uncleanness after the birth of a child varies with its sex (Lev. 12:2–5); in Ait Adrar this period was two and a half months after the birth of a son and three months after the birth of a daughter. In Ometz a special bed, the unclean bed, was to be found in every house, and men never sat on it or touched it. It was put outside to air after each period of uncleanness.

however, as is allowed by the law, if the infant was ill or underweight. If a member of the family was a ritual circumcisor (mohel), he had the privilege of performing the circumcision, although this was not obligatory. As observed in Ometz, the house was decorated with prized spreads and blankets before the ceremony, and the grandmothers put their hands in the water in which the infant first had been washed.[67] After the circumcision, the mother was forbidden to leave her bed for fifteen days.

Boys receive their names at the time of circumcision; and in Ait Adrar the circumcision ceremony was celebrated with a festive meal and celebration, to which all the relatives and usually the whole community were invited. For a female child, a festive meal and celebration would be held anytime from four to forty days after birth, depending on the means and inclination of the parents. This was obligatory, and only then could the girl be named.[68] As is customary among Jews, children could not be named after living relatives.

Babies were wrapped in cloths after birth, and their legs might be tied up to the knees and their arms wrapped with a piece of string over the covering cloth to guard against their scratching their eyes and face. From about the third or fourth month, their torsos were tightly wrapped to the hips to keep their backs straight. A baby was nursed until the age of two, although weaning might take place earlier if the mother become pregnant again. However, children below the age of two were observed being nursed even

[67] In Demnat special talismans were considered indispensable on the day of circumcision (Flamand 1952:104), and this may have been the case in Ait Adrar also, although such talismans were not noted at the circumcisions reported on in Ometz. On the day of birth in Demnat, a red and black cock was slaughtered and a soup made of it for the laboring woman (Flamand 1952:60). The head and neck of the cock were nailed to the door frame together with five small crown-shaped loaves of bread. Festive meals were served both on the Saturday which preceded the circumcision and after the circumcision (Flamand 1952:64, 65).

[68] In Demnat a small celebration was held for girls, much less elaborate than that for boys (Flamand 1952:60). Flamand (1952) cites neighboring mellah in which the birth of a girl might be celebrated equally with that of a boy and, conversely, mellah where the day of a girl's birth would be treated as a day of mourning.

after the birth of a new infant. The moment an infant became restless it was given the breast, and it was felt that infants never should be allowed to cry. Within a few months after birth children would be given additional food; pieces of bread to chew, strong mint tea, highly seasoned tidbits, or anything else that might keep them contented.

Babies were constantly with their mothers. They slept with them, were held in their arms or laps, or were tied to the mothers' backs. It was said that small children must never be left alone because of snakes or scorpions. Fear of shedim may also have been a factor. Mothers made infants sit up by the age of two weeks, supporting the torso while the baby was held in the lap. By that age infants also were encouraged to urinate and defecate on the floor by being held in the hands and fondled patiently. However, the moment a child began to toddle about, no attention whatsoever was paid to toilet training, as observed in Ometz. Young children were allowed to urinate and defecate whereever they wished, inside or outside the house.

Weaning ideally took place at the age of two, often patiently and gradually. While some mothers might put hair or pepper on their nipples or put henna on their breasts to frighten the child, many older women were opposed to this. Small children ate constantly; and a child reluctant to eat, as after sudden weaning, was tempted with anything he might like. However, no forcing took place.

The birth of a new baby did not involve displacement of older children. Mothers in Ometz were observed walking around with the smallest infant in their arms, the next oldest one tied or clinging to their backs, and another one hanging on their skirts. A woman who had just lately given birth and was not yet allowed to leave the unclean bed was observed keeping five children quiet and contented on a rainy day without toys or diversions. The newborn baby was in her arms and two elder children were snuggled up against her lap; two others were nearby on the bed, and she occasionally fondled them. A girl of about twelve brought tea and was doing the cooking and housework. Only after an intensive campaign of infant care and cleanliness by the Ometz instructress and nurse, which focused the mothers' attention and time on the care of their newborn babies, were children, presumably older infants and toddlers, ever heard to cry in the village. Young children were never spoken to loudly by their parents or forced to do anything they did not want to do. Although sons were culturally more valued than daughters, fathers were observed fondling and playing with young children of both sexes with equal affection.

Infants might be talked to, or crooned to in Arabic melodies, the form of singing women were allowed. Men sang religious songs in Hebrew on all ceremonial occasions after the festive meal. Women were forbidden to sing when men were present.

On the first Shavuot, Day of the Giving of the Torah, after his first haircut, a boy would be taken to the synagogue by his father. A piece of board on which the first two letters of the Hebrew alphabet were written would be put into his hand, and his father and all the men would encourage him to say them. Thereafter, he would be taken to the synagogue frequently. On reaching the age of four, he was taken regularly and was supposed to sit quietly and listen. This was also the age at which he would be sent to study with the mori, the religious teacher and only formal teacher of the community.

According to the ideal pattern described, the mori first treated the child patiently, perhaps giving him sweets occasionally, and the boy was not forced to spend many hours with the teacher. But as soon as his intelligence, *sekhel,* was considered sufficiently developed to understand right and wrong, his education began in earnest. He was expected to spend most of the day, from about 7:00 A.M. to noon and from about 1:30 to 6:00 in the afternoon with the mori, returning home to eat. While with the mori, he was to sit quietly and obey. Otherwise the mori would beat him with a stick or, if he did not wish to do so, he would tell the father and the father would beat the boy. A boy would also be beaten for absenting himself from study. The boys studied the Torah, together with the commentary by Rashi.[69] They memorized the prayers by rote, and did not have to understand their meanings. Except for those who wanted to be able to write books, i.e., make copies of the holy writings, they learned to write Hebrew script in block letters and only as an aid in learning to read. The Talmud seems not to have been studied except by those who went to centers of religious learning (*yeshivot,* singular *yeshiva*) in the towns.

In fact, many of the men seem to have studied with the mori for about two years only, with an additional period of intensive study before the Bar Mitzva. Their level of literacy, as manifest in Ometz, was low. Except for the rabbis, a few "learned" men, and some young men who had studied in Meknes or Casablanca, they had to learn to speak Hebrew in Ometz, and read and wrote with great difficulty. Most of them signed documents with a thumbprint. All the men knew addition and subtraction, but few of them could multiply or divide. Distances were measured in hours walked or ridden, or might be given in comparison with known distances, e.g., from one village to another.[70]

A few men had studied for about six years in Ait Adrar and met to read the Zohar which, however, they did not understand. In the adult literacy courses given in Ometz they were found to have a much greater facility in reading and writing than the others. Also, those who had spent some time in Casablanca, even without having studied further there, seemed to grasp and learn more easily than those who had lived in Ait Adrar all their lives. Teachers in Ait Adrar included the young rabbi, but there had been others as well who, in Israel, were settled in villages other than Ometz. They had been paid for their services by the parents until

[69] Rashi (Rabbi Shlomo Itshaki [the great commentators of Jewish learning and law are generally known by names composed of their initials, i.e., "the Rambam" for Rabbi Moses ben Maimon or Maimonides]) was a French rabbi of the eleventh century (died 1105) who wrote a commentary on the Torah and a monumental exegesis of the Talmud.

[70] Berque (1955:14) notes that in the mountainous landscape of Seksawa, distances were calculated according to the amount of time necessary to get from one place to another.

about four years prior to the time of emigration, when an international Jewish aid and relief organization in Morocco apparently began to pay them regular salaries.

The Bar Mitzva (plural Bar Mitzvot) was a major ceremony in a boy's life. He was dressed in new clothes, his head and hands would be stained with henna, and his eyes were blackened with soot. After the service in the synagogue, the parents would give a festive meal, to which all relatives and generally the whole community were invited. Bar Mitzvot occasionally were organized for several boys of approximately the same age, but this was an optional pattern.

After his Bar Mitzva, a boy was considered a man, but a man as yet of little understanding. His opinions would begin to be heeded when he reached the age of about twenty, contingent on the maturity of his intelligence and understanding, his *havana*. This acceptance was not dependent on whether or not he was married and had children. However, after the Bar Mitzva, he would begin to practice one or more trades, generally learned during the preceding years. Also, a boy who had lost his father would at this point be considered capable of supporting his widowed mother and younger siblings.

Little girls began to imitate their mothers at an early age. From about the age of four, they watched over their younger siblings and could be seen in Ometz carrying them around on their backs. They also had begun to help with the housework. A five-year-old was observed in Ometz washing clothes in a tin tub and sweeping the floor. While she was washing, her two-year-old sister brought water in a tin cup. By the age of eight, girls in Ait Adrar also knew the rudiments of cooking according to the dietary laws and were learning to weave. Their marriages were sometimes arranged at this age.

Such a marriage took place between the young rabbi, who was then about sixteen, and his wife. Some old women gave the following account of it, about a year after Ometz was founded, with a girl in her twenties (who by then could speak Hebrew) translating. Saada was about eight when the boy's mother came to the girl's mother and said: "I want your Saada for my Avraham." Saada's mother agreed. Then Avraham's father, Rav Shlomo, his wife, and their oldest son came to Saada's parents to ask officially. A date for the betrothal ceremony was set at this time. The young Avraham brought a goat and many chickens, which the bridegroom always provides, as well as a dress, a kerchief, a pair of slippers, a ring, and a head of sugar for his bride, all of which also were obligatory.[71] He also bought a bracelet and additional gifts, and sent them to her through his family. Saada's family prepared the food and invited all the relatives on both sides to the betrothal ceremony, which lasted one evening. It included a festive meal and drinking, prayers by the men, and their singing of religious songs in Hebrew.[72] At this festival, the date for the wedding was set, some three or four months later in this case, although any interval of up to a year was customary. It was agreed at the betrothal that Saada would remain with her parents until the wedding, although it was sometimes arranged that the betrothed girl would live with the bridegroom's family.

Weddings in Ait Adrar began on a Monday and lasted until the night of the Sabbath.[73] Before the wedding, the

[71] The gift from bridegroom to bride's family or bride, the *mohar,* is an ancient Jewish custom. The custom of giving a dowry is later, although of pre-Talmudic origin. The amount of the dowry and of a sum settled on the bride by the husband are recorded in the ketuba or marriage contract, and belong to the wife if she is widowed or divorced. In Demnat (Flamand 1952:55–57), a go-between is used by the boy's family to approach the girl's family. Once the boy is accepted, negotiations over the dowry begin. For the betrothal party the fiancé brings only a plate of henna and another of dates and brandy. As the notary draws up the contract, further squabbles over the amount of the dowry might take place, with the girl's father usually conceding.

[72] It possibly also included arrangements in regard to the dowry, but the old women said nothing about this and were not questioned in regard to it.

[73] Weddings in Demnat began on a Tuesday and lasted until Sunday (Flamand 1952:59), although the betrothal ceremonies generally took place on Mondays or Thursdays (Flamand 1952:56). Tuesday also was the favored wedding day in the Eastern European shtetl (Zborowski and Herzog 1952:277), "because when God was creating the world, at the end of the third day He said twice, 'It is well.'" However, Monday there was considered unlucky, since He did not say this even once at the end of that day.

bridegroom provided the bride's family with a cow for the wedding feast.[74] The bride's family provided quantities of chicken and other food. On the Monday of the wedding the bride was dressed in white, in Saada's case white silk; a kerchief was put on her head, and she was daubed with henna, etc. The bridegroom and relatives on both sides also stained their hands with henna. The marriage contract was written, and the ceremony performed according to Jewish law. The whole community would generally be invited to the wedding feast, and the neighboring Berbers as well, as in the case of the wedding of Avraham and Saada. During the festivities the bride sat on a thronelike arrangement covered with colored material, and neither bride nor groom could eat or drink until long after everyone else. Women, as always, would eat after the men and in their separate corners. After the feasting the men would sing and the women might yell, a whooping yell for which Berber women are famous, and which is sounded by Jewish women in Morocco on such occasions. Men and women might dance, but quite separately; and women could dance only with their husbands' permission. Steps are quite simple, and the woman dances holding her body stiff, like a wooden doll, arms pressed to her sides. If a woman danced well, she could be given money. Before midnight the young couple would retire to the house of the bridegroom's father, and shots then would be fired into the air by the young men.

In Ait Adrar, feasting and dancing would continue for the rest of the week, during which the men did not work. On the Sabbath the community would bring presents to the young couple in their own home, and the father of the bride was obliged to present a considerable gift. The wedding ended with a feast given in their own home by the newly-weds, helped by relatives on both sides.

Since Saada was so young when she married and Avraham was studying in Meknes, she divided her time for the next few years between her parents' home and his parents' home,

[74] In Demnat the bride's family must provide the cow (Flamand 1952:58).

staying with her family when he was away. While living with his family she was treated like one of their daughters. She was given responsibilties only as her intelligence developed, when she had enough sekhel. The young couple first had intercourse about five years after they were married. According to the old women, a child bride took up her duties as wife when she had enough sekhel to be one; whether or not she had begun to menstruate was irrelevant. Families sometimes sought child brides for their sons, in order to be able to educate the girls as they liked.

In a small community like Ait Adrar the young couple knew all about one another before the mariage, even though they were not supposed to have known each other. According to the old women, however, it could happen and had happened in other villages that the husband saw his wife for the first time at the wedding only to discover that she was blind, lame, or deaf. The women laughed uproariously in recounting this and obviously relished the thought.

Even after marriage a boy was supposed to obey his father. He could not undertake any journey, except to the Holy Land, without his father's permission. Any disobedience or neglect of religious duties and observances could be punished by beatings, a practice begun at the time of the boy's education. It was reported that fathers would often beat their children during the latters' childhood and youth, girls less than boys since girls had fewer religious obligations to perform. A father might also tell a disobedient son that he would kill him for further disobedience, and this was reported to have been believed. It was, in fact, considered permissible for a father to kill a child for violating the religious law, but this had never happened in Ait Adrar in anyone's memory. Mothers were reported to have beaten their children rarely, if at all.

The young rabbi, a man in his thirties by the time he settled in Ometz and by then the father of three boys, was asked what he considered the most important qualities to develop in a boy. He answered: "He should not despoil the Sabbath, he should not shave his beard, he should go always to the synagogue, he should keep all the commandments" (*mitzvot*), i.e., "he should be a good Jew." When further pressed, he hesitated questioningly; and when prompted to talk of the character of a boy he added: "He should be straight, he should learn a trade, he should look after his parents." Being a good Jew obviously included these and all other desirable traits. Other parents, when questioned, also emphasized that a boy should be brought up to be a good Jew. The ideal bride to choose for a son would be a girl who did not roam around, did not quarrel, and was a good worker. Beauty was not important. In choosing a bride or accepting a bridegroom it was important that they come from a good family, not necessarily wealthy but well-regarded and known not to quarrel.

Like all other life-crises, death was handled within the framework of Jewish law; and in Ait Adrar custom carried mourning abstentions beyond those enjoined in the Shulhan Arukh.[75] A bereaved family sat on the ground in a circle during the seven-day mourning period. Mourning customs were first observed in Ometz a few weeks after its founding, when two women received word that two of their sisters had died in Morocco. In the center of the circle of women, where they sat crying, had been placed a covered cup containing a small loaf of the traditional flat bread, *pitta*. Next to it was a plate containing salt, eggshells, and a broken piece of pottery.[76] This practice was not seen again among bereaved families in Ometz or in other Israeli villages settled by people from the Atlas Mountains. What was observed, however, was the differential behavior of men and women. In the case of a dead child, the women, the mother and grandmothers, wailed, wept, gashed themselves, rocked back

[75] For seven days after the death of parents, children, siblings, or spouse, an observant Jew does no work, sits at home on low stools or on the floor, and is forbidden to read anything but the portions of the Mishna, such as the Book of Job, that refer to suffering. In addition, the abstentions previously indicated must be observed and the requisite prayers said. For an additional twenty-three days, hair cannot be cut nor new clothes worn, and marriage is forbidden.

[76] Placing eggshells on the eyes of the dead was an ancient Jewish custom.

and forth, moaned a mourning chant, etc., while the father neither cried nor talked, although obviously grief-stricken. A bereaved husband, after his wife's death, also accepted his sorrow almost wordlessly.

During the seven-day mourning period, houses of the bereaved accumulated refuse and filth; and the mourners remained unwashed and unkempt and did not change their clothes. Then, on the seventh day, relatives and friends were observed in Ometz to come to the house and clean it thoroughly, scrubbing corners and washing all clothing and bedding. They also prepared food for the mourners, who washed themselves before eating. It had been forbidden in Ait Adrar to wash with warm water or soap or to travel during the remainder of the thirty-day mourning period. Furthermore, children and grandchildren of the dead were forbidden to wear new clothing and even, according to some informants (though not the rabbis), to wear clean clothing for a year. Those who wished to honor the dead did not cut their hair for a year. In practice, however, this could mean that relatives wore new or clean garments for a few moments, after which the mourner could don them. Also, if a friend told a mourner that it was not fitting that he go about so unkempt, he could cut his hair. It was reported that only the minimal mourning ordinances had been observed after the death of a small child in Ait Adrar, since so many died.

On the death of a man, the legacy would be divided after the children were grown. Girls inherited only if they were not married when this took place. Inheritance is a subject covered in detail in Jewish law,[77] and disagreements would be adjudicated by the rabbi. It was reported that quarreling members sometimes turned to the French administrator; but in this, as in other internal disputes, he would refer them back to the

[77] A tractate of the Talmud is devoted to the subject of inheritance. Sons and daughters inherit equally from a father's estate, except that the firstborn son inherits a double portion. Daughters do not inherit from the mother's estate. A wife does not inherit from the husband, although he inherits from her. The marriage contract provides for her in case she is widowed.

rabbis. One administrator was quoted as having said: "These are your customs, and we are not concerned."

In addition to the cycle of yearly and life-cycle observances, prayers were said and a festive meal served to relatives and friends whenever a family moved into a new house, at least this was the case in Ometz. On such an occasion, passages from the Book of Zohar had to be read aloud by the men.

Within the Jewish community, both riches and learning conferred status, and deference was accorded to age. The possession of wealth could confer status, as was true throughout the Jewish communities of the Atlas Mountains, even without learning. For it was assumed that a man had to be clever to make money. Once acquired, status could not be lost even if disaster overtook an individual. Said the young rabbi regarding this: "We used to honor him; how could we do otherwise now?"

Status was partly inheritable, at least status derived from learning and holiness. Thus, in one of the other mellah of the Atlas Mountains there had lived a rabbi who was considered a holy man. He had been in the Holy Land, Israel, in his spirit, apparently in a dream or trance.[78] The son of this holy man, although not himself outstandingly learned, held status from his father (*zkhut avot*) and had been fed and clothed "because of his father" by the local Jews wherever he had gone in the Atlas Mountains. He used to spend part of each year in Ait Adrar. In Israel he traveled from one to another of the villages settled by Atlas Mountains immigrants and collected a considerable sum of money, reputedly IL 100–200, each time he visited a village. He settled in one of the older moshvei olim, some of whose settlers were from the Atlas Mountains, but would not till his land. According to

[78] The Hebrew term used in the telling of this story, *kfitsat haderekh,* can be translated as "contraction of the road" and is to be found in the Talmud (San. 95a). There it refers to the experience of three Biblical personages for whom the earth was supposed to have shrunk so that distances could be rapidly traversed. These three persons were: Eliezer, servant of Abraham, on his trip to find a wife for Isaac (Gen. 24:42); Jacob on his trip from Beersheba (Gen. 28:10); and Abishai, the son of Zeruiah, who succored David (II Sam. 21:17).

reports, when the land settlement agencies for this reason would not give him permanent housing, the other villagers bought seeds and worked his land for him so that he would remain in the village.

The father of the old rabbi in Ometz had also been considered a holy man, as well as both learned and wise. It was reported of him that an itinerant rabbi from the Holy Land had invited him to come to Jerusalem, since his learning was being wasted in the Atlas Mountains. After his death, people from distant communities were reported to have made pilgrimages to his grave, where they prayed, lighted candles, and slaughtered sheep. Also the object of veneration was the grave of another holy man, an itinerant rabbi from Palestine who had died in Ait Adrar.[79]

Rabbis were generally the sons of rabbis. Sons of other families could go off to study and become rabbis, explained the young rabbi, but they found it so much more difficult. The wife of the old rabbi was considered a wise and righteous woman in her own right. She sat outside the Ometz synagogue during holiday and Sabbath services, and had been a principal midwife in Ait Adrar.

While the round of life of the Jews of Ait Adrar was governed by Jewish law and tradition, the discords and passions the law was designed to regulate were hardly absent. It was reported that men often lost their tempers and shouted, although they loathed being shouted at. One young woman informant admitted that fights had taken place between men in which the participants had struck one another. But, she

---

[79] Voinot (1948:61–62, 90, 95) lists a site in Ait Adrar as one of the objects of pilgrimage by both Jews and Berbers. Candles are lit there and animals sacrificed. There is no tomb, but according to legend this site is the burial place of one of ten Palestinian rabbis of ancient times who came to participate in the conversion of the Berbers to Judaism. His intervention is asked in cases of fever, whooping cough, eye trouble, possession by spirits, and sterility. Girls desiring husbands attach to a fig tree at the site a thread from their girdles, then wash their bodies with water brought for the purpose. After marrying, they come to thank the saint. Berber girls desiring more abundant hair comb it at the site; this is supposed to be an infallible remedy. On the twenty-fifth of December a grand public feast or *moussem* is held there, and the meat of sacrificed animals is divided with the poor.

The rabbis in Ometz did not speak of these practices.

added, people shook their heads at this. Peace was made by the rabbis, or could be made, apparently, by anyone deeply respected. For reconciliation was an expression of the honor due him. If men refused the peacemaking offices of the rabbis and continued to sustain a bitter quarrel, the French administrator might intervene and imprison both disputants. The young rabbi laughed in relating this. Rumors that one Jew, now in Israel, had murdered another in Ait Adrar reached the instructors in Ometz, but neither they nor the settlers wanted the subject to be discussed.

Public quarrels observed in Ometz included shouting and hitting between old women, shouting among men, and a reported attempt to beat up a work foreman. Bitter hatred between husband and wife was also observed in more than one case, apart from the recurrent pattern of men shouting at or hitting their wives and the wives then running away to their own families. In accusations, particularly against instructors, veracity was not always respected.

It was reported by the young woman mentioned earlier that even if a Jew shouted at one of the neighboring Berbers, the Berber would not shout back. This is but one detail in the symbiosis between Jews and Berbers in Ait Adrar that seems to have been exceptionally felicitous for the former. In addition to the economic arrangements previously described, it was reported that a Jew in time of need could go to a Berber and would always receive help. The arrangement was reciprocal, and Jews had to give Berbers money when asked. But it was never taken by force, or at least had not been since the arrival of the French. It frequently was said by informants: "We lived like brothers, and Arab property was like Jewish property." As guests at Jewish weddings, neighboring Berbers brought many gifts. Wages for work performed by Jews in Berber fields would be paid on the same or the following day.

It was also related that when Jewish parents beat their children, the children might run to the Berbers for comfort. The latter then would say: "Do not hit him; he is only a child." It also was reported that on one occasion some Jewish children ran after a Berber and threw stones at him, drawing blood. The man appeared before the father saying: "Look what your sons have done." The father commiserated but concluded: "What can I do? They are only children." And the Berber was appeased. Recounted the young woman previously cited: "Honestly, our Arabs weren't like Arabs; they were so good it is hard to believe. To my father's house often came one Arab who was very well off. He used to say of me: 'She is my daughter.' And when we visited him he always said to me: 'Tamu, take what you want.' I was small and really pointed to things and said that I wanted them, and he always gave them to me."

The Berbers respected the Jewish religious customs, and they did not enter the Jewish villages on the Sabbath. They knew the meaning of the Jewish festivals, and one old man who admired the old rabbi of Itkaalan brought him every year his best chicken to use as *kapara,* the Yom Kippur scapegoat. The young rabbi also was informed that after the departure of the Jews from Ait Adrar, the Berber subdistrict official, who lived close to the Jewish cemetery, would burn candles there every Friday evening.

But it could happen, on the death of a Jew who had lent money to a Berber, with land as security, or whose livestock was tended in a Berber's flocks, that the latter denied the existence of such an arrangement to the heirs of the deceased. Nonetheless, this was a rare occurrence in Ait Adrar. The French administrator (or administration) had forbidden the taking of interest in financial transactions and punished it with prison at hard labor. Some five years previous to the time of emigration, the administrator had annulled the economic agreements then obtaining between Berbers and Jews, resulting in considerable losses to the latter. The Jews of Ait Rahhal were also affected. For the most part, however, the Berber subofficials were bribed by the Jews not to inform the French administrator of such arrangements, which were part of Berber as well as Jewish local economy.

Also somewhat at odds with the idyllic state of Berber-Jewish relations usually described was an incident that had occurred some years previously, toward the end of World War II. Strife had broken out between Jews and Berbers when some of the Berbers accused some of the Jews of polluting a spring, and demanded that they build a fence separating it off from their village. The Jews refused, saying that the Berbers could buy their houses and land, and they would move elsewhere. A delegation of twenty-six of them went to the French administrator, and all were put in prison. They remained there for two months, had to work at hard labor, and had their beards shaved off. The young rabbi, who had been away when the men were imprisoned, had to go to Casablanca to get them freed. They still had to build the fence. During this incident, a number of the younger boys had left Ait Adrar for the cities.

Emigration to the cities, particularly Casablanca, had been in progress for several decades, as was the case in all the mellah of the Atlas Mountains.[80] When Jews from the villages passed through Casablanca on their way to Israel, they were often joined by members of their families who had settled there.

EXODUS

Knowledge of the establishment of the State of Israel only gradually seeped into the Atlas Mountains mellah.[81] For

[80] Chouraqui (1952:164–65) notes the great increase in the Jewish population of Casablanca because of migration from the interior. Marrakesh also was the object of migration from the Atlas Mountains. Flamand (1950:389–97) attributes this emigration to economic fluctuations, to which the mellah of southern Morocco were extremely sensitive. He notes at least 15,000 departures from these mellah between 1940 and 1949. Movement toward the great cities might be made by stages. Thus, the Jewish population of such juncture towns as Amismiz and Imi n Tanout had left them between 1930 and 1950, being replaced by Jews from the Atlas Mountains villages, who in turn passed on to Marrakesh and then to Casablanca. But the high birthrate kept the Jewish population of the villages relatively constant, although some mellah had disappeared.

[81] As of the years 1949–50, the Jews of Demnat were well aware of Israel's existence. Flamand (1952:145–46) reports that Berbers teased Jews as follows: " 'You are afraid of us, you Jews, you need us to protect you,' to which the Jew would answer in the same tone: 'We have beaten you well in Palestine, and now we have our homeland, our government, our flag.' Then the counter-retort: 'It's not true. America which is Jewish helps you, but you are only cowards, we will chase you from Palestine,' . . . Occasionally, the Jews would be told: 'Let them fight in Palestine, it's not our affair; we are brothers.' "

some years, in Ait Adrar, money had been collected for the Jewish National Fund by one of the community's influential and learned men, a copier of sacred writings and a ritual slaughterer. He made collections within a large district, which included Ait Rahhal. It was reported by the Israeli emissaries and their urban Moroccan assistants who visited the Atlas Mountains that many of the villagers did not understand what was involved, although in Ait Adrar a periodic newsletter from the Jewish National Fund was read in the synagogue. The villagers gave money as a contribution to the Holy Land. In about 1951, the collector of funds first approached the Jewish Agency offices in Casablanca, suggesting that his people emigrate to Israel. He was told to bring the signatures of all family heads, and did so. The villagers paid the expenses of his journeys. In 1952 he led some Jewish Agency officials to the Atlas Mountains, but they never reached Ait Adrar, because the local Berber officials forbade their entry. Nothing more seems to have happened until 1954, when an emissary representing the principal moshav federation visited Morocco to recruit potential settlers for the villages of the federation.

On a trip through Morocco accompanied by a physician from Casablanca, he encountered in the pre-Saharan town of Tagonit two Jews loading grain. Entirely ignorant of the existence of Jews in the Atlas Mountains, he asked where they were from, and was given the name of a district some four hours' walk away, in the southern part of the Central Massif. Sixteen Jewish families lived there, practicing agriculture. Much excited at the discovery of Jewish farmers, the emissary consulted a rabbi; it was September, the period of holidays, just before Simhat Torah. The rabbi gave him permission to travel, since he was doing holy work; and he set out immediately for the village. He was welcomed by its Jews as an honored guest. They knew of Jerusalem and the Holy Land, but nothing of the State of Israel. On learning of it, all wanted to leave immediately and signed up for immigration. Two days later, the emissary set out with a list of twenty-six Jewish villages, a villager to guide him, and two mules provided by the community. One hundred and eighty Jewish families lived in these villages, and all were eager to depart. Their general state of health was so good and the number of potential social cases so low that the Jewish Agency gave the emissary permission to recruit all the Atlas Mountains villagers, who had less than a 10 percent social case level, without the usual prior medical and social examinations. After about seven hundred families had come to the camps set up to process immigrants, this permission was rescinded. It had not been known that there were so many Jews in the Atlas Mountains.

Ait Adrar was in the third district the emissary visited, and he never reached it, although he got to Ait Rahhal. The French administrator was opposed to the emigration of Jews, not wanting the district to be emptied of its artisans, and the Berber subdistrict administrators forbade the emissary to enter. Arrangements had to be made through local intermediaries, and there were conflicting stories as to just what happened.

Whatever the other factors that may have influenced the exodus of the villagers, the primary motivation for immigration to Israel was religious fervor, with no clearly formulated secular expectations. "We had expected to find learned rabbis with beards and join them in the study of the law," answered one young rabbi from Ait Rahhal to questions put to him in Shavur. The Jews of Ait Adrar may have suspected that the life awaiting them might not be quite that simple; before leaving Ait Adrar, they had taken a vow to do as they were told in Israel. About a year after Ometz was founded, when the discontinuities of modern Israel with their ancient tradition were abundantly evident, the rabbis were questioned further. Asked why they had come before the advent of the Messiah, the old rabbi answered very solemnly: "We are the first generation and then the Messiah will come. We wait for him daily."

The Berbers of Ait Adrar were bitterly opposed to the Jews' departure. Some were reported to have said: "Remain here, and I will share all I have with you." They were also quoted as having said: "What shall we do now when we have nothing? To whom can we go?" At one point the Berber administrator put about twenty-five Jews in jail to prevent their departure. It was recounted that a Berber woman, generally considered mad, then said, "Let the Jews go. Their time has come to go back to their own country." The opposition to their leaving then relaxed somewhat.

Jewish Agency officials had advised the people to convert all they owned into cash. They did so at great loss, as prices in the local market crashed. Almost all their tools were left behind in the villages, and the young rabbi buried his books in the cemetery. Families left in small groups, sometimes by night, in order not to risk the possibility of last-minute detention. Within two months Ait Adrar was practically emptied of its Jews.

Three families were reported to have remained behind. One came as far as Casablanca, saw the sea, and, frightened, returned. These three families lived together with the Berbers for about a year. But they had no one to slaughter for them, and not enough men even to form a congregation for prayer. By 1956, they had left for Marrakesh.

OMETZ: THE FIRST YEAR OF A
SUCCESSFUL MOSHAV OLIM [1]

This chapter, like the previous one, describes a micro-universe; but the situations under review differ, as do the goals of the description. The reconstruction of the way of life of Atlas Mountains Jews before they came to Israel and settled in Ometz and elsewhere deals with a stable and integrated way of life, or at least one susceptible of description as stable and integrated. The first year of Ometz, indeed any interval in the history of practically any moshav olim prior to the role-socialization of its settlers, represents a situation neither stable nor integrated. The previous chapter attempts to depict the background of one group of immigrant settlers, complementing Chapters II and III, which depict the pre-state backgrounds of land settlement in Israel and of the moshav ovdim as model for the moshav olim. This chapter seeks to present the confrontation between land settlement system and immigrant settlers as acted out on the stage of one village.

The roles imposed on the settlers and their instructors by the land settlement system can be considered recurrent; within the range of variation indicated in Chapters IV through VI, they could be found in the organization of any moshav olim, particularly between 1954 and 1958. The goals of the settlement authorities also applied to all the moshvei olim within the range of variation that emerged in the post-state land settlement program. Specific to the first year of Ometz were the individuals filling the roles, their personal and group attributes, and the specific sequences of events that took place in the early history of the village. This chapter is a partial chronicle of this uniqueness, including changes in the village and its settlers.

[1] The field work on which this chapter is based was carried out initially by Margot Kohls, under my supervision, from June to December 1955, with follow-up visits six months later. I joined Miss Kohls in Ometz in October 1955, and visited the village regularly for the next six months.

The history of Ometz is the story of a success. Even by the end of its first year, there was every indication that it would survive and develop into a stable farming community with a stable settler population. But underlying its particularity and success is the pool of possibilities inherent in the moshav olim as a type, from which a different selection of alternatives could have resulted in a very different outcome. This case study of the first year of a village also maps out the dimensions of a village type.

THE SETTING

Ometz was the first village established under the program of regional settlement.[2] It is one of over twenty-five settlements established during 1955 and 1956 in the southern part of Israel. The geographical region thereby settled stretches from close to Migdal-Ashkelon in the west to the Judean foothills in the east, extending south to meet the region known as the Negev. To locate it in relation to the principal cities of Israel, it is approximately in the middle of the triangle constituted by linking Jerusalem, Tel Aviv, and Beersheva. In terms of the borders of the State of Israel,[3] it stretches from the northern tip of the Gaza strip on the west to the frontier with Jordan on the east. It includes an area of about 700,000 dunams, of which approximately 280,000 are arable, with the rest utilizable for natural pasturage or afforestation.

Prior to the new colonization project, only nine settlements existed throughout what I shall term the Daroma Region. One of them is a veteran kibbutz, and most of the others then were moshvei olim established during the phase of improvisation. A new administrative region, the Daroma Region, had been established within the Land Settlement Department of the Jewish Agency to plan and carry out the new regional settlement program. It included two districts: one approximately coterminous with the Daroma geographical region; and a second covering an area where the Judean

2 Cf. pp. 177–81.
3 Prior to its Six Day War in June 1967.

foothills began to rise. In the latter several new settlements, including four moshvei olim, also were established at this time. After the first year of settlement, the borders of the administrative Daroma Region changed. The new settlements in the hills passed over into the jurisdiction of the Hill Region, while a series of settlements around Ashkelon and leading into the Daroma, previously under the jurisdiction of the Central Region, passed over into that of the Daroma Region.

After the first year of settlement, the Daroma regional office of the Land Settlement Department was shifted from Ashkelon to the newly established urban center, Kiriat Mizug. Kiriat Mizug by then had a population of several thousand. Nine months earlier it had been a field on which the first buildings were being raised.

The transfer of the Daroma regional office to Kiriat Mizug also marked the point at which the Department's regional office relinquished the last of various affairs of local administration which it had assumed as part of regional planning and settlement, but which belonged in the province of local government. The first head of the provisional Daroma Regional Council, appointed by the Ministry of the Interior, was a pioneer settler of a veteran moshav ovdim, who settled permanently in the Daroma, establishing temporary residence in the village next to Ometz until the adjoining rural center was built. He was in constant touch with the Land Settlement Department regional directorate from the first days of settlement, and assumed the fuctions of his office as the governmental administrative and service network was implemented in the area. However, not all the Daroma villages were incorporated into this unit of local government when it came into official existence. Those settlements affiliated to the religious moshav federation were attached to the regional council, religious in party affiliation, of a previously settled area.

Ometz is located in the Daroma geographical region, its north side adjacent to the main road which runs between Ashkelon to the west and Kiriat Mizug to the east. Several kilometers on either side of Ometz run two north-south highways, which lead to Beersheva. Just north of it, across the east-west highway, is an older moshav olim whose settlers came from Hungary. The other new villages in the cluster of which Ometz is a part are located southeast and southwest of it, and the local rural center is directly adjacent to its south side. The rural center was not yet under construction at the time of Ometz' founding.

Ometz' careful planning included all the features of regional settlement. It was planned and built to include eighty-five family farming units and about eight nonagricultural units. The village layout is relatively compact: several rows of streets are set at angles allowing maximum land use and converging at the village center. The houses face the street, each set in its dunam of land, with the fields stretching behind and around the village. The region's topography is slightly undulating.

Permanent buildings had not been constructed by the last week of May 1955, when the first settlers arrived and the village officially was founded. Instead, relatively spacious one-room huts, later to serve as storehouses, had been put up as temporary dwellings; and classrooms, consumers' store, synagogue, office, dispensary, etc., also were housed in temporary huts located in the temporary village center. A water pipe with spigot brought water to the front of each dwelling, and each hut was provided with adjacent outhouse. Several temporary wooden huts also were provided for members of the instructor team and service personnel.

It was to this setting, swarming each day with workmen, supervisors, professional personnel from the Land Settlement Department regional office, trucks bringing supplies, etc., that the first contingent of settlers was brought. It consisted of sixty families from Ait Adrar. They had arrived in Israel several months earlier, and had spent the intervening period in a new transit camp nearby, to which they had been brought from the boat. However, their involvement with the organizational framework of Israel had begun before they left Morocco.

THE ROAD TO OMETZ

In the processing of families for immigration, not all the Jews of Ait Adrar or of the other Atlas Mountains villages were accepted for immigration to Israel, given the principles of selective immigration introduced in 1952.[4] Those families lacking a responsible male head in full possesion of his faculties, i.e., social cases or potential social cases, were not allowed to immigrate, despite protestations by their relatives that they would remain responsible for them in Israel. Instead, an international Jewish relief organization, active in Morocco, made itself responsible for their care, providing them with housing in the cities and a substantial sum of money through which to reestablish themselves. Further fragmentation of the Atlas Mountains communities occurred as families were assigned to different boats and/or, upon arrival in Israel, to different settlements in the country.[5]

Another basis of fragmentation and of continuing dissension in Israel was the competitive recruiting carried out by representatives of different moshav federations. Meir Grossman, the Israeli emissary who had traveled through the Atlas Mountains in 1954, was a settler of one of the first moshvei ovdim and went to Morocco as a representative of the principal moshav federation, Tnuat Hamoshavim, which was affiliated with the Labor Party (Mapai). The Atlas Mountains villagers whom he signed up for emigration were, thereby, also scheduled for settlement in moshvei olim assigned the federation. Given the religious commitment of these settlers, representatives of the principal religious moshav federation lost no time approaching them on their arrival in the immigrant processing camps.[6]

4 Cf. p. 118.
5 Cf. pp. 190–93.
6 According to Meir Grossman and an exchange of correspondence he had in March 1955 with the Casablanca office of the Immigration Department of the Jewish Agency, a representative of the religious moshav federation, together with the director of the camp in Casablanca (himself a rabbi), sought to persuade newly arrived Atlas Mountains villagers, including people from Ait Adrar, to transfer their affiliation to the religious moshav federation. They were described as having threatened to use reli-

Some families may have affiliated themselves with this federation while still in Casablanca. Others became affiliated with it on their arrival in Israel as a result of an agreement between the Israeli political parties. This agreement assigned 80 percent of the immigrants to villages affiliated with Mapai, and 20 percent to villages affiliated with Hapoel Hamizrahi, the religious political party. Upon their arrival in Israel, the immigrants were taken to transit camps under the political jurisdictions of the respective political parties, to wait until the Daroma Region village sites would be ready for occupancy.

While still in Casablanca, the villagers heeded the advice of Jewish Agency officials not to bring money to Israel, but instead to buy radios, sewing machines, bicycles, clothing, etc. They arrived in Israel with almost none of their possessions from the Atlas Mountains, apart from some items of traditional clothing. Scrolls of the Law, some seeds and dried herbs, mixing bowls for preparing couscous, and brass teapots and tea trays.

The sixty families from Ait Adrar who came to Ometz arrived in Israel in February 1955. They were brought directly from the boat to a special transit camp, which was under the jurisdiction of Tnuat Hamoshavim and had been constructed to accommodate immigrants destined for settlement in the Daroma villages. Representatives of the religious moshav federation once approached them there but were immediately chased out by the camp staff.

The future social instructor and instructress of Ometz

---

gious sanctions against those new arrivals who refused to be persuaded. Grossman also claimed that he left off recruiting in the Atlas Mountains at the request of the Immigration Department, so that villagers already in the camp could be dispatched to Israel before new ones arrived. However, according to Grossman, the representative of the religious moshav federation then began his own recruiting in the villages.

Upon the request of Grossman that the representative of the religious moshav federation be excluded from all recruiting activities among the Atlas Mountains Jews, the Morocco office of the Immigration Department held a hearing, at which both sides presented their cases. The Morocco office then decided to suspend the activities of the representatives of both federations; and the representative of the liberal moshav federation was not allowed even to begin recruiting activities in Marrakesh and in the Atlas Mountains.

first encountered the immigrants in the camp. Aharon Barzel and his wife Hava had come to Israel from Russia immediately after World War I. Members of the Third Wave of immigration to Palestine, they were among the founding members of a flourishing veteran kibbutz, Mapai-affiliated. Grandparents now, with their children stout members of the same kibbutz, past holders of kibbutz office, they personified both the successfully realized self-transformation of classic Labor-Zionist ethos and its continuities with Eastern European style of action and response.[7] They also were personally religious.

Aharon, sand-colored, stocky, physically still powerful, was a taciturn man, brusque and blunt of speech and manner. Hava, dark, thickening, luminous of eye and expression, was committed to the welfare of others, unremitting in their service, and as openly emotional and verbal as her husband was unexpressive. Both had the habit of work from early morning until late at night and Hava, who had attended a university in Russia, somehow also found time to read humanistic literature. They, of course, turned over their instructors' salary to their kibbutz.

Aharon once mentioned that several groups of new immigrants at the camp had asked him to be their instructor, but these were composed of former urbanites whom he felt would not remain in the village and become farmers. When approached by the immigrants from Ait Adrar, he accepted and began preparing the group for settlement. Hava, in the meanwhile, worked in the camp kitchen and became acquainted with the families.

Yitzhak, a young man of urban Moroccan origin who had immigrated to Israel seven years earlier, had served in the Army, and was a founding settler of a moshav olim established in 1950, was assigned to work with Aharon as translator and assistant instructor. This arrangement was made while the immigrants were still in the camp.

---

[7] They worried over Ometz, he silently and she expressively, in the same style that shtetl parents are reported to have worried over their children (cf. Zborowski and Herzog 1952:294).

During their period in the camp, the men began to work, largely engaging in afforestation for the Jewish National Fund. Aharon once mentioned that the first time they were called upon to do work paid according to productivity rate rather than by the day, they went on strike and wanted to stage a demonstration at one of the Jewish Agency offices. He argued with them and tried to influence them, Yitzhak serving as translator and mediator, and finally told them to go. But on his asking whether a few of them would try the work anyhow, one offered. The others then threatened to kill this man, but still another then consented. A few finally did go to work and saw that they could earn no less and perhaps even more than they had by working at a set rate per day. After that there was no more trouble over this issue, and in Ometz piecework came to be preferred to daily wage labor.

The young Ometz rabbi, Rav Avraham, also once mentioned that in the camp wool had been promised to the women so that they could continue weaving. Nothing came of this promise. Months later, a systematic investigation of the possibility of establishing cottage industries in the Daroma Region was carried out,[8] but no action resulted. Moshav movement representatives were opposed to the introduction of any activity that might divert interest and energy from farming. Also, in regard to Ometz, the Israeli organization supporting the maintenance of traditional crafts among the new immigrants decided that the traditional weaving techniques of the women could not produce a commercially worthwhile product.

Aharon and Yitzhak accompanied the settlers to Ometz, and Hava arrived within ten days after it was established. The military instructor was in Ometz on the day of settlement, as was the first keeper of the future village cooperative store, the driver of the village truck, and a youth instructor. A temporary nurse was available on the day of settlement, and the first Ometz nurse arrived the next day.

[8] See Willner, 1956.

Rahel, the nurse, was a single woman then aged sixty-two who had volunteered for the job. Also from Russia and a member of the Third Aliya, she lived in a veteran moshav ovdim with a brother and sister, neither of them married, and a young immigrant girl from Syria whom they were bringing up. Rahel had been a registered nurse before she left Russia and had worked for the Sick Fund throughout her life in Israel, resisting promotion to an administrative post. Since the beginnings of the mass immigration, she had worked by preference among the new immigrants, although never previously in a moshav olim. Another of her sisters was a member of the same kibbutz as Aharon and Hava, and they and Rahel were old friends. Rahel was tiny and slender, with the lively movements of a girl. Although worn and lined, her face was piquant and pixieish. As devoted and self-abnegating as Hava, she was less sentimental. Her sense of humor, sometimes mischievous, sometimes astringent, was constantly evident.

Rahel was housed at first in a wooden shack with water supplied by a pipe outside, as were Aharon and Hava. By August, a one-room hut with kitchen partition, sink, shower, and cardboard insulation, a replica of the housing provided for nurses by the Sick Fund in all the villages of the new settlement region, was built. It was located right next to the two-room shack then constructed for Aharon and Hava by the Land Settlement Department. Their shack differed from the immigrants' temporary housing, and from the identical housing assigned instructors in the other villages, in that a partition had been installed, making an extra room, and a floor, indoor sink, and shower had been provided. These were the only concessions made to Aharon and Hava's marital status and age, and the only ones they would have accepted. These three people formed the core of the team of instructors and service personnel in the village, and Rahel's house became the center of visits and informal meetings among most of its members.

Yehoshua, a lieutenant in the Army, was military instructor and also served as agricultural instructor during the first four months of the village's existence. A tall, big-boned young man in his twenties, with a brash yet engaging manner, he had been born in Greece and had come to Israel as a boy through Youth Aliya. Before joining the Army he had learned farming in veteran moshvei ovdim. During his first month in Ometz, he shared a shack with the driver of the village truck, a cocky young Israeli, who soon left. The village armory, a wooden shack surrounded by barbed wire, with water spigot outside the wire, was completed at the beginning of September; and Yehoshua then moved into it.

Each of the villages of the new settlement region was provided with a pickup truck by the Land Settlement Department. Running and maintenance expenses and the driver's salary were to be paid for from the village treasury. Since Ometz adjoined one main road and was relatively close to two others, Aharon soon decided to share the truck and driver with a neighboring village about five kilometers away, Ba'aya, where they came to be stationed. Instead of using them for his frequent trips on village business, as did the other village instuctors, he resolutely walked or hitchhiked to the nearest point of public transportation, whatever the weather, or timed his trips to take advantage of the daily round of the villages made by the district coordinator and other regional personnel. He expected his wife, the nurse, and other members of the village team to do the same, pointing out, if anyone dared to complain, the saving of village funds thereby effected.

A not-infrequent occurrence during the following months was the onset of labor on the part of one of the pregnant settler women in the middle of the night. Rahel would hurry to her side, while Yehoshua or another young man would bicycle to Ba'aya, a hand grenade tucked into his belt as protection against the appearance of infiltrators from across the border, to bring truck and driver to take the woman to the hospital. Rahel invariably accompanied the woman on such trips and occasionally Hava went along also. Husbands rarely went with them, and under no circumstances would touch their wives' clothing or blankets. Women in labor were already unclean, and men feared defilement.

The first storekeeper was a man of urban Moroccan origin, well in his forties, who had been in the country for about five years and previously had served as storekeeper in other immigrant villages. He shared a hut with Yitzhak, the young Moroccan instructor, and with Robert, a soft-spoken young bookkeeper who had arrived in Ometz a few weeks after settlement. Robert had come to Israel some years previously from Iraq, where he had completed secondary school.

The first youth instructor remained in Ometz only a few days, since he was transferred by Youth Aliya with the emergence of the first village crisis. But within a week, Tnuat Hamoshavim sent a young teacher to the village. Batya, a native Israeli born and raised in a veteran moshav ovdim, was then a certified schoolteacher who had taught previously in moshvei olim. Known to the instructors and nurse, she was "one of them" in values as well as affiliations. She organized classes for the children and Hebrew lessons for the youth, helped Aharon with the office-work, fed the pair of work mules sent to the village, worked with her students to plant the village wood when the seedlings arrived, etc. She spent about a month in Ometz, departing under the circumstances described below.

FIRST WEEKS AND FIRST CRISES

Once the day of settlement was decided on, Aharon and Yitzhak arranged for the future settlers, then still in the transit camp, to draw lots for their houses and land. On the day of settlement they were brought to Ometz in three successive groups. Some of them at first refused to alight from the trucks and had to be argued and persuaded into doing so.

It then became clear that they had not grasped the meaning of the earlier assignment of houses by lot. Successive arrivals sought dwellings next to kinsmen, matrilateral as well as patrilateral, and tried to avoid settlement in the outlying reaches of the village. Families shuttled from site to site; and

all the energy of the instructors was devoted to getting everyone housed before nightfall. The instructors did not insist on
maintaining the allocation of sites earlier established; insofar
as conflicts between settlers did not arise, family preferences
were respected. *Mezuzot*,[9] provided by the Ministry of Religious Affairs, were immediately distributed to the families.

The day on which Ometz was established marked the
opening of the new settlement region. Journalists and representatives of the various Israeli organizations involved in the
settlement program visited the village for the occasion.
Throughout the hot and dusty day, the village store, located
in the temporary village center between the dispensary and
the village office, was thronged with people. Instructors,
settlers, drivers, and visitors jostled and talked as they purchased juices, cold sour milk (a favorite food throughout
Israel), and soda. Fruit and bottles of sour milk were distributed to the families by the instructors and village workers.
The settler women did not appear in the store. Within a few
days this changed. From early morning, even before the shop
was opened, women and children stood in line or sat on the
ground outside it, and women did much of the shopping.

During the first day's bustle and confusion, representatives
of the Hapoel Hamizrahi-affiliated moshav federation slipped
into the village. They established contact with the settlers
through a brother of one of them. This brother had been in
the country for a number of years. Within a day, agitation
was well underway. By the third day, settlers were demanding
that the affiliation of the village be transferred to the religious
moshav federation. By the fourth day, about forty of them
staged a demonstration at the head office of the Land Settlement Department in Jerusalem. Within a week, the case of
Ometz was under review at the policy-making levels of the
head office. The decisions reached there were transmitted to
the settlers at a meeting in Ometz a few days later.

[9] *Mezuza* (pl. mezuzot), literally meaning "doorpost," is the name given
to a rectangular piece of parchment on which the words of Deut. 6:4-9
and 11:13-21 are inscribed. The parchment is rolled up and inserted in a
wooden or metal case. Such a case is affixed, in a slanting position, to the
upper part of the right-hand doorpost of the home of every observant Jew.

At this meeting, at which representatives of both moshav federations were present, the Land Settlement Department regional director explained that the moshav federation affiliation of Ometz was not subject to change. If the settlers insisted on changing their affiliation from Tnuat Hamoshavim to the religious moshav federation, they would have to leave Ometz and move to a village assigned to that federation. Such a moshav olim, Nshima, also in the Daroma Region and about ten kilometers from Ometz, was available for settlement.

About a dozen family heads had already committed themselves to remaining in Ometz; they formed a group a little apart and laughed as the meeting progressed. The other settlers (only men were present) were reluctant to accept what the regional director told them. One of the strongest supporters of the religious moshav federation began to object as the director was speaking, and was told by the latter to shut up. The other men then shouted that they all would go over to the religious moshav federation and started to walk away. When the director and moshav federation representatives paid no attention, they drifted back and the explanations continued. After the director finished speaking, shouts broke out: "We don't want to be near the border." When the representative of the religious moshav federation repeated, in his turn, the information just given by the director, one young man began screaming: "We don't want Nshima; you have plenty of other villages; if you haven't, take us back to Morocco." This too was ignored by the speakers; the regional director reiterated his points and left. Significantly, most of the older men were quiet during the meeting. At its conclusion, they clustered around the representative of the religious moshav federation and finally decided that a delegation of them would inspect Nshima.

This inspection took place the next day, and about twenty-six families then announced their intentions of transferring. But during the next week, most of these families, as well as others, remained subject to daily changes of mind. As the decision-making process continued, the power of kinship ties became evident. Not nuclear families but family blocs aligned themselves, following the lead of the most influential member. One such family authority, who from before the meeting had no intention of quitting Ometz, collected prized objects—rugs, bedspreads, and brass trays—from a group of his near relatives to guarantee that they would remain.

In several last-minute decisions to remain in Ometz, the influence of women seemed to play no small part. When one family head found that the husbands of both his sister and his eldest daughter were not to be persuaded to leave Ometz, he capitulated to the women's pleas and stayed on. In another case, their first baby was born to a young couple on the weekend before the scheduled date of departure. The young mother had begun labor in the middle of the night and was rushed to the hospital. The husband's old mother, who had been a midwife in Ait Adrar, expressed the family's gratitude to Yitzhak and announced that they were remaining in Ometz. A group of women had also gone off independently to inspect Nshima. They preferred Ometz and were heard to nag and scream at their menfolk. These families also remained. One of these women, an old widow, had two grown but unmarried sons, one of whom had been a leading agitator in pressing the shift in federation affiliation. After this old woman had worn her sons into acquiescence, she turned her attention to the instructors. Despite a ruling that agitators in the crisis must leave, they finally gave in to her vociferous and unremitting pleas; and the family remained.

Of the original sixty families who had settled Ometz, fourteen left some three weeks later for Nshima. As they departed from Ometz, their female relatives who were remaining behind broke into despairing lamentations.

This did not conclude the immediate involvement of the settlers in the politics of Israel. Education became the next focus of conflict. The plan of regional settlement envisaged a school in each rural center, serving its surrounding cluster of settlements, with only a kindergarten and first-grade school to be built in each moshav olim. However, while superior educational facilities and instruction thereby could be provided, the staff and curriculum of each seven-grade school could represent only one of the two public education trends: State education or Religious State education. Until the rural center school could be constructed, classes would be held in each village. A day center for youth between the ages of thirteen and eighteen also was to be constructed in each rural center, and in the meanwhile Youth Aliya tried to supply the moshvei olim with youth instructors.

During the period of agitation over moshav federation affiliation, the settlers had been informed that the Ometz school would follow the program of State education, but that the schoolchildren could receive additional religious education from their own rabbis as part of their curriculum. But a week after the fourteen families had left, Aharon felt compelled to inform the settlers that Israeli law gave them the option of voting for either school trend. In any case, representatives of the religious parties would have made sure that this information reached them.

Yitzhak had been the interpreter and intermediary for Aharon and the Jewish Agency officials in disseminating the earlier information. He had visited the immigrants in their homes and engaged in long discussions with them. In fact, on the weekend just before the date of departure for Nshima, Aharon returned to his kibbutz, and Yitzhak remained in Ometz together with Rahel and the driver. During this weekend, he was invited by the young rabbi, Rav Avraham, to meet with six families who had signed up to leave for Nshima but were reconsidering their decision. In his conversations with them, following the instructions he had been given, he had included State education as one of the conditions to which they would have to agree if they wished to stay in Ometz. All six families plus two others had decided to remain.

Aharon informed the settlers of their right to choose between school trends on a weekend that Yitzhak had gone home. Upon his return, he heard settlers again muttering that they would leave Ometz, and he felt that he had been branded as a liar in their eyes.

The first reaction of the settlers to the new decision thrust upon them was not to vote at all. Aharon insisted that they do so; and he scheduled a formal election to be held under the supervision of a clerk from the district office of the Ministry of Education. Rav Avraham, who had staunchly supported remaining in Ometz during the previous crisis, was ashen-faced as he led the line to vote. The outcome of the election was a unanimous choice for State Religious education.

Given the outcome of the election, Batya was forced to suspend teaching, and she soon afterwards departed from Ometz. Within the next two weeks, three pairs of teachers representing Religious State education successively appeared, taught for a few days, and disappeared. Although a fourth pair of teachers then remained in Ometz for about two weeks, the children no longer voluntarily attended school and had to be rounded up from their homes by each new set of teachers.

However, it was on Yitzhak that the settlers focused their resentment at the renewal of conflict over the issue of the school; and during the following weeks other resentments were directed against him. In carrying out his duties, Yitzhak sometimes made immediate decisions which Aharon did not always uphold; conversely, Aharon did not always keep Yitzhak promptly informed of actions and decisions he had taken. While Yitzhak's authority with the settlers was thereby being undermined, he himself began to be increasingly authoritarian with them.

One such occasion was a dispute between the young rabbi and a settler who had come to Ometz from the transit camp with the immigrants from Ait Adrar, although actually not one of them. This settler helped out in the synagogue, and one day had taken possession of its key. The young rabbi claimed that the responsibility of the synagogue rested with him, that he had signed for its furniture, and that the key should remain with him. He added, furthermore, that Ometz was a village for immigrants from Ait Adrar—indeed, on the official sign at its entrance, "Immigrants from Adrar" was written under the village name—and pointed out that the other settler was not even from Ait Adrar, and that he could leave. When the dispute was brought to Yitzhak's attention, he became furious with the rabbi. He told him that he and Aharon, not the rabbi, had signed for the furniture; that Ometz was a village for immigrants from North Africa and not just from Ait Adrar, that all the settlers had equal rights, and that he, the rabbi, would have to leave Ometz if he didn't respect these rights.

By then, new settlers had been brought to Ometz. The first five new families, who had arrived just before the school crisis, were relatives of those already there. These five families had arrived in Israel before the others and had been sent to other settlements. But over twenty other families had come during the second week of July, two weeks later. Some of these were also of rural Moroccan provenience, although not from the Atlas Mountains. However, the majority were former urbanites, many of whom immediately left and were replaced by additional families of urban background, including five families from Tunisia. Among the settlers of urban Moroccan provenience was another rabbi, like Rav Avraham actually a shohet, or religious slaughterer. Yitzhak claimed that the settlers were turning to this rabbi, who was more learned than Rav Avraham, that as a result the latter was trying to assert himself as leader of the village, and that he had to be put in his place. A gentle man suffering from occasional attacks of migraine, Rav Avraham had responded to Yitzhak's words in the dispute over the key to the synagogue by saying that henceforth he would pray alone in his home. As leader of the congregation, he did not carry out his threat, and the dispute was settled by the other man returning him the key.

The arrival of the new settlers had made for other sources of tension in the village. The immigrants from Ait Adrar had hoped to replenish and fill Ometz with relatives who had been settled elsewhere or who were still in Morocco awaiting their turn to immigrate. Although they helped the newcomers unload their belongings on arrival and welcomed them to Ometz as a good place in which to live, the general attitude toward them was one of distrust and reserve. The urban newcomers, in turn, although obviously from the mellah rather than from the Westernizing segment of the Jewish population of Morocco, tended to look down on the Atlas Mountains Jews. Furthermore, the old parents of some of the settlers from Ait Adrar had hitherto occupied separate dwellings, although neither able nor eligible to claim independent farms. With the arrival of the new families, they had to vacate these dwellings and move in with their children.

Although he had had a few years of French schooling and had worked in Morocco as a bank clerk, Yitzhak's own early background was not unlike that of the urban newcomers. He quickly formed ties of friendship with some of them. This seems to have been regarded by the settlers from Ait Adrar as his final betrayal of their interests.

Before the end of July, they sent a petition to the Daroma regional director asking that Yitzhak be removed from Ometz. They claimed that he had taken bribes to allow their aged parents to occupy separate shacks, had made advances to their women, and was leading their young people astray. The regional director, a Tnuat Hamoshavim representative, and Aharon immediately held a public meeting with the settlers. They demanded that the latter either retract their accusations or else lodge a formal complaint with the police. The settlers chose to do the latter, although individuals admitted privately that all the accusations were unfounded. The case dragged on for two months, and Yitzhak was finally exonerated.

However, the settlers from Ait Adrar persisted in their demand that he be removed from Ometz. This was not immediately acceded to, but by the end of August they knew that their proposal was receiving serious consideration. Soon afterwards, Yitzhak left Ometz for several weeks for his yearly period of military service. He returned and remained, although with little status and less authority, until early October. Then he was transferred to another new moshav olim as its instructor. But the young man, who first had taken up his duties with unbounded idealism and enthusiasm, had been deeply wounded in Ometz. He left an embittered man, and his spirit did not recover. He did not survive many months in his new post.

INITIAL ORGANIZATION OF VILLAGE INSTITUTIONS

The organization of village activities began with the establishment of Ometz and did not slacken through the weeks of crisis. Even with the improvisation attending the beginning of a village and the uncertainty and emotion associated with the Ometz crises, a routine was instituted to implement the village development plan and its provisions for the settlers' needs. In this section I will try to delineate the principal areas of moshav olim organization, as first effected in Ometz by its particular group of village workers, and as first responded to by its particular group of settlers.

Employment and Wage Distribution. From the day after their arrival in Ometz, the settlers were provided with work. During their first week in the village, the work was in Ometz itself: digging ditches for water pipe, working on various installations, etc. The main employer was the Jewish Agency itself. It paid at the rate of IL 4.60 per day or slightly more, with payment made approximately two months later.

Over the next four months, the principal employers were two large farms nearby, leased by the Jewish National Fund to private individuals [10] and run by managers. They paid a daily wage of IL 4.60 for adults and IL 3.45 for youth below the age of eighteen; and some kinds of work, such as harvesting, were paid on a piecework basis. Payment was made the same month the work was carried out. Next in providing work days came the Jewish National Fund's various land reclamation projects. Here also the daily wage was IL 4.60, with a delay of one to two months in forwarding payment. Construction of the settlers' permanent houses began, offering a daily wage of IL 7.33, with payment made every month. All the construction in the moshvei olim was carried out by Solel Boneh, the construction company of the Histadrut.

[10] Cf. p. 208, note 25.

Nightly guard duty in Ometz, as in all moshvei olim, fell into two categories: rotating four-hour shifts, which the settlers stood in turn, without payment; and paid shifts of eight hours. For the latter the Army paid IL 5 per night, and wages arrived within a month to six weeks. From May through September 1955, 5,546 work days were divided among the settlers of Ometz.

Arrangements with the employing organizations, including the various divisions and sections of the Land Settlement Department which hired settlers as unskilled labor, were negotiated by Aharon. With the assistance of Yitzhak, he allotted work to the settlers and paid them their wages when the money arrived, after deductions for taxes and for any advances they might have taken.

The principle of work allocation in all the moshvei olim was equal distribution of work days among the families. In practice this was often modified, especially when work was scarce. Family heads with many dependents might occasionally receive more work days than those with few dependents; steady part-time positions within the village, such as school janitor, might be assigned to older men or to the wife or half-grown daughter of a large family; and certain employment possibilities were limited to the possessors of specific skills or aptitudes. Thus, the woman taken on as school cook, to prepare the daily lunches served to the schoolchildren at a few cents' cost to their parents, had to be minimally literate; the well-paying construction work required dexterity and the ability to master simple skills quickly, though there was also a limited need for unskilled labor; paid guard duty could be allocated only to settlers who already had undergone some military training. When many of the settlers of a village were eligible for such employment, the particular assignments made by the instructors could and did lead to accusations of favoritism by disappointed candidates and become issues in village factionalism.

This did not occur during the initial months of Ometz. Those who possessed skills relevant to the Israeli context were few, and employment possibilities for the unskilled were plentiful. Indeed, by the middle of June the demand for workers in the cotton fields of one of the large farms nearby was so great that the instructors started offering such work to women and adolescents. Women also soon began to work in the fields of the adjacent older moshav olim, earning about IL 4.30. Work opportunities in this moshav were negotiated directly, without being transmitted through the Ometz office, and the wages were handed directly to the women. They began possessing money of their own, some for the first time in their lives, and not all of them turned it over to their husbands. In some cases, domestic complications then ensued, as is set forth subsequently.

During the fall harvests, which paid on a productivity basis, women came to earn more than men, since they worked more rapidly. Some men wanted wives with infants to go to work, which the instructors did not allow; but when employers expressed a preference for women, whom they found more reliable than the men, the latter protested. Aharon then adopted the policy of giving work assignments to women only at periods of peak employment.

Wage deductions covered insurance, according to the provisions of the national insurance plan in effect in Israel; obligatory contributions to the Jewish National Fund and the Foundation Fund; dues to the Histadrut; and a village tax of 5 percent of all earnings. This village tax was used to pay the cost of maintaining the village pickup truck and its driver's salary (on which Aharon had economized), the bookkeeper's salary and those of any other village employees hired, the cost of office supplies, and all other current village expenses. It resulted in an average monthly return in Ometz of IL 400 and reached IL 700 during one month of exceptional employment.

In some moshvei olim, a settler literate in Hebrew was appointed by the instructor as village secretary. Such an appointment generally confirmed or conferred leadership status. In many of the moshvei olim established during the phase of improvisation, the position of secretary, a salaried post in classic moshav ovdim organization, was combined with elective office on the executive committee. Generally there were two posts of secretary: secretary for internal administration (*mazkir pnim*); and secretary for external affairs (*mazkir huts*). Each of these was a leadership and decision-making office within the executive committee, and each carried a salary.

Although not only the Ometz rabbi but several other settlers were sufficiently literate in Hebrew to carry out such routine secretarial tasks as making out identity cards and the village register, Aharon did not appoint a secretary in Ometz. All such tasks he carried out himself, toiling at them until late at night and utilizing the help of whomever he could recruit from among the other village workers.

He did not express his reasons for this or for most of his decisions, unless to members of the Daroma regional directorate, and he had little tolerance for inquiries about them. These reasons might emerge in reminiscences months later, during the convivial half-hours he permitted himself on rare occasions. In regard to not having appointed a village secretary, the possibility of doing so may not have occurred to him, and any suggestion of it undoubtedly would have been dismissed. He was determined to curtail all outlay of funds not contributing directly to village development, and a secretary's salary would have had to come out of the village treasury. Also, he postponed for as long as possible the involvement of the settlers in activities that might give any of them new pretensions to leadership. He felt that only more trouble could come of this.

During their first month in Ometz, while the crises over moshav federation and school affiliation were in progress, the settlers accepted their work assignments with few disputes. Early relations with foremen at the various places of employment were less smooth. The immigrants from Ait Adrar, although accustomed to agricultural labor, had previously worked at their own tempo. They resented the foremen's constant injunctions to work faster. They also took off time in the fields for midday prayers. Aharon generally visited each new place of employment to arrange special breaks for prayer with the foremen and to check complaints and accusations made by the settlers.

The first real disturbance over work occurred toward the middle of August. Sixteen men from Ait Adrar quarreled with a foreman in the cotton fields of a large farm, and one of them tried to hit him. The thirty-two workers from Ometz then employed by the farm immediately were dismissed. On reporting what had happened to Aharon, the workers who had not participated in the fracas asked that he get them reinstated. Aharon refused; he wished to impress them with the notion of mutual responsibility. He hastened to the farm to try to get all the settlers rehired, but his immediate efforts were unavailing. For about a week there was unemployment in Ometz, and then other work was found for these settlers. Within three weeks the farm again was accepting workers from Ometz.

The first payday, in the latter part of June, passed peacefully, although it occurred just after Aharon's announcement that school elections would be held. Late in the afternoon, after the men had returned from work, they lined up at the village office. Aharon and Yitzhak handed them their pay envelopes, which included daily work tickets from each place of employment as well as a statement of the various deductions made. Most of the men, unable to sign for their pay, stamped a thumbprint on the required receipt.

Unlike many instructors in other moshvei olim, Aharon did not hold regularly scheduled monthly or bimonthly paydays, accumulating until then the wages received from the various employers in the interim. Instead, he made it a policy to schedule paydays as soon as the wages arrived from any employer; and he, Yitzhak, and the bookkeeper worked until late at night on such days to make payment on the next day possible.

Therefore, the second payday occurred a week after the first; and this time a clamor erupted. On the previous week, the settlers had received payment on work carried out and paid on a daily basis. This payday was the first for work carried out and paid on a piecework basis. The settlers were confused by the unequal rates of pay they received, and most of them loudly demanded repeated explanations. In the meanwhile, the vote over school affiliation had taken place; and its outcome had been taken by the instructors as a repudiation of themselves. As the settlers continued to argue over the amounts they were paid and over such matters as snapshots previously requested, necessary for their identity cards, Aharon's patience dwindled and his voice became louder and gruffer.

When one settler refused to sign for work tools he had received, Aharon's control snapped. He yelled at the man to return the tools and get out of the village. "Who needs them?" he shouted to his associates in the office, Yitzhak and Batya, who was helping to make out the identity cards. "I am not your instructor," he raged at the settlers. "Beasts don't need an instructor, pigs don't need an instructor." The settlers fell silent, accepted and signed for their pay, and quietly left the office. Later that evening, outside the store, one young man complained that Batya no longer was holding classes. When reminded of the school vote, he lapsed into shamed silence.

On subsequent paydays, settlers continued to demand explanations, but no more such scenes occurred. Aharon's policy of handing out pay as it arrived soon began to be appreciated. By the middle of September, the settlers were in agreement that Aharon was "good," citing as a reason that he never delayed their pay. By the end of October, paydays in Ometz had become cheerful events. Good-natured disputes occasionally occurred, but no one ever questioned or challenged deductions Aharon made, such as for clothing purchased from Hava. The settlers from Ait Adrar hardly ever requested advances on their pay, and none of them accumulated debts.

In some other Daroma villages, during these months, pay distribution often took place amidst howling scenes and even led to blows among the settlers. Constant pleas by the settlers for advances and mass scenes centering on this subject were commonplace in the intervals between paydays, especially given the employers' delays in forwarding wages.

Military Instruction and Guard Duty. In Ometz, as in the other moshvei olim, all male settlers able to bear arms received military instruction. This was given by Yehoshua to small groups of some ten to twelve men, in courses lasting about two weeks. While attending the courses, which included one hour of Hebrew instruction daily, the men received IL 4.60 per day from sums made available for the purpose by the Land Settlement Department. After completing the course, the villagers began standing nightly watch, and they were eligible for employment as paid village guards. A few young men who had undergone military instruction while still in the transit camp were able to work as guards from the second week of Ometz' existence on.

The immigrants responded enthusiastically to military training. At the end of each course its participants gave a party, to which each contributed IL 2. Yehoshua quickly became the most popular member of the instructor team, although he shouted at the men and boys in giving training, cursed them, termed them fools and donkeys, and cuffed them. To the other members of the instructor team he described the immigrants from Ait Adrar as slow learners. Those who had spent some years in Casablanca and the immigrants of urban provenience learned much more quickly but also were more troublesome: they were argumentative and not amenable to discipline. The older men were the most attentive. Among the immigrants from Ait Adrar, both a young man and his father were enrolled in one of the earlier courses. The son, a far better pupil, laughed at his father, terming him fool and idiot, but protested when Yehoshua did so.

The first paid guards standing eight-hour watch could not keep awake through the night; they made friends with the construction company night watchman, who would rouse them if they fell asleep. As more settlers became eligible to stand guard duty, they would remain awake by keeping each other company, and their chattering went on all night. Yehoshua made initial allowances in enforcing discipline; infractions he witnessed met with blistering reproof, but he made no attempt to catch them out.

During the summer of 1955, infiltration from across the border intensified, and the settlers were fearful. They barred their doors and windows; some extended families slept together in the hut of the member closest to the village center; women would come to the dispensary claiming to have been frightened by Arabs; men on guard duty also maintained that they had seen Arabs. For weeks the guards shouted and fired at every shadow, and news of infiltrators nearby once almost caused a panic until Yehoshua cursed the men into silence.

By August, morale had begun to stiffen, although settlers still reported seeing Arabs. Early in September, shots were heard in the vicinity; the next morning a woman appeared in the dispensary with the familiar complaint: "I am sick; I was frightened by Arabs." But she added: "Yehoshua shot bum, bum, ten Arabs." After having finished their period of military instruction, the best students were allowed by Yehoshua to keep their rifles and take them home. This was never disputed or questioned by the others. By the middle of October, one young man from Ait Adrar, who had spent several years in Casablanca, said: "I never touched a gun until I got here. Then I had something to be frightened of. Now we are equal to the Arabs. I can shoot at them. It's their brains against mine."

Distribution of Goods. In theory, the village store was supposed to supply all the needs of the settlers. In practice, its stock depended on the particular storekeeper and rarely included more than staple foods, unless the settlers ordered other articles. The Ometz store, throughout the first year, was open from about 8:00 A.M. until well after dark from Monday through Thursday. On Fridays the first storekeeper left early, returning late on Sunday. He soon instituted an arrangement with the young rabbi whereby the latter received bread in his absence and sold it as well as wine, soft drinks, and beer. Occasions arose when bread arrived almost on the eve of the Sabbath and remained unsold, to the rabbi's quiet amusement, since the women had already baked their traditional loaves. The storekeeper hired helpers from among the settlers, changing them daily, and preferring those who already knew some Hebrew and previously had lived in the towns. His language with the settlers was Arabic, and his voice was constantly raised.

Ice first had been delivered to Ometz about a week after it was founded. Most of the settlers purchased it, despite a price of IL .52 per block. They immediately ordered iceboxes from Hamashbir through the village store. "We had very cold water in Ait Adrar," they explained. Some of the women soon began carrying ice home from the village center in stools turned upside down. Hava occasionally adopted this practice.

Soon after their arrival in Ometz, the women gleaned the harvested fields of the nearby older village. They brought home stalks of grain that had been left standing, dried them in the sun, and ground the kernels into meal. This meal was used in making couscous.

Settler complaints about the store began in August. The villagers had discovered that such staples as sugar could be purchased in Migdal at two-thirds the price charged in the store. Men often went to Migdal after work, and they could be seen bringing home grains and vegetables by the sack. They also went to the Beersheva market to purchase animals for later slaughter. As the high holidays approached, almost every family acquired sheep, and some also purchased goats. These were sent to graze on uncultivated village land, and the wife of one of the settlers was paid by the others to herd them.

At the beginning of the second week of August, the first quarrel in the village store broke out. Two old women began screaming at each other, and the women around them took sides. The storekeeper said that the quarrel was over their respective places in line. Until then, settlers of both sexes had displayed great patience in standing in line, and the queue often extended out of the store and halfway to the village dispensary. Women filled the store during the mornings and early afternoons, although they had done no marketing in Ait Adrar. In the late afternoon men entered, on their way home from work, to buy and consume soft drinks and exchange the day's gossip.

Quarrels between women in the store led to violence in October, when one young wife struck another in the chest with a bottle. The worst scene occurred on the first weekday of November, when the storekeeper did not arrive at all, and bread was delivered only in the late afternoon and was brought to the synagogue for distribution. As the impatient women grabbed for loaves, two of them started hitting and throwing stones at each other, and one also struck the other's child. The youth instructor [11] separated them, getting her shirt torn in the process. Finally, three young men handed over the loaves, while she kept the accounts. On the following day, the storekeeper still had not arrived, and several young men helped unload a truck which brought in supplies.

Two weeks later the first storekeeper left Ometz, to be replaced by an energetic young man from Iraq, who had also been in the country some five years. Many more food items, including foods on ration to which the settlers were entitled but which the previous storekeeper had not thought that they would buy, suddenly appeared in the store. Monthly sales jumped from about IL 3,000 to about IL 5,600, and eventually settled down to about IL 4,800, with an average monthly expenditure per family of IL 60. Hamud, the new storekeeper, decided to educate the settlers, speaking to them only in Hebrew and in even louder tones than his predecessor.

Used clothing was made available to the settlers of Ometz and the other new villages by the Ministry of Social Welfare, the women's affiliate of the Histadrut, and the moshav federations. In addition, Hava collected substantial amounts of clothing from her kibbutz and through her friends. Free distribution of used clothing in the transit camps and villages had begun with the mass immigration, and the immigrants had been pressed to put aside traditional habits of dress. The free distribution of clothing had often provoked intense

[11] Cf. p. 341.

competition among the recipients, demands for more, and violent public scenes. By 1955, the social agencies discouraged it.

From the first days of Ometz, Hava did not give anything away to the settlers except under special circumstances. Rather, she sold clothing at nominal prices, using the money to provide layettes at token cost for every newborn infant and to support other services to the settlers. The first distribution of clothing occurred toward the end of June and was open to the entire settler population, including the newly arrived families of urban provenience. Confusion reigned as the settlers bought indiscriminately, and the stock was sold out before all the families had had their turn. On the advice of the Daroma social worker, Hava then tried to limit the distribution of used clothing to the most needy families, i.e., those with many members.

The next clothing sale, run on this principle, took place in early September. Hava notified the families she considered most needy when to come to the hut used as warehouse and clothing distribution center. The news spread throughout the village; and on the day of the sale, she was constantly stopped by other settlers who asked for clothing. Those with few children she told to purchase clothing at the shops in Migdal. Nonetheless, many people besides those invited turned up at the clothing hut that afternoon. Not allowed in, they stood outside and peered through the windows. Only one woman, an immigrant from Casablanca, made a scene, screaming that if she weren't given clothing she would bring Hava before the Jewish Agency. A few weeks later several more cases of clothing were sent to Ometz, and the smaller families were given the opportunity to purchase. There was no more trouble over this issue, although Hava occasionally broke her own rules by giving pleading mothers clothing for their children.

In a neighboring village, at about this time, the first clothing sale touched off such a scene that the sale had to be stopped and the storehouse closed. The settlers of this village, originally from the Kurdistan regions of Iraq and Iran, had been in Israel in transit camps for about five years.

Houses and Gardens. The one-room painted temporary dwellings provided by the Jewish Agency had floors of earth. Within days after their arrival, the settler women took cement from the supplies of the construction company (Solel Boneh), mixed it with sand and water, and made floors. Beehive-shaped ovens also appeared next to many of the houses, and the women continued intermittently to bake their traditional flat loaves of bread.

During the first four months, furniture in the shacks generally was limited to that supplied by the Jewish Agency. Its arrangement was relatively standardized. Two adjoining beds were set up near one wall for the parents. In another part of the shack would be the "unclean" bed, reserved for women during menstruation and after childbirth. Beds for children and other members of the family were distributed around the room against the walls. Over the mattresses would be spread army-type blankets, also supplied by the Jewish Agency, or rough woolen blankets woven in brilliant colors, which the immigrants had brought with them from Morocco. Only after they moved into their permanent houses were there Italian-made bedspreads, purchased in Casablanca, and silken table rugs, unearthed from their boxes and suitcases. In the shacks, these boxes and suitcases were stacked against each other in one corner of the dwelling, and clothing and other belongings were kept in them.

One area of the shack, generally near the entrance, was reserved for cooking. It was usually shielded from the wind by a low wall of blocks, also taken from the supplies of the construction company. The one-burner kerosene stoves used throughout Israel were placed on the floor, and the women cooked crouching over them. The unpainted wooden table and stools, also provided by the Jewish Agency, were used by the men for their meals, at least in the presence of visitors, and for serving visitors. Women and children ate sitting on the floor. Kitchen utensils, glasses, etc. would be set against the wall on the ledges formed by the protruding boards of the frame of the shack. Other articles were hung on nails that had been driven into the walls, and fish and other foods were strung up to dry near the ceiling.

Throughout the period in which the settlers inhabited the shacks, the visitor was assailed on entering by an odor compounded of cooking smells, drying fish, and urine. Rags, vegetable parings, and pieces of bread littered the floor. Young children, partly or wholly naked, contentedly sat or lay in their midst or rolled on the unclean bed, invariably chewing on a piece of bread or vegetable. The women might sweep out their houses in the afternoon. Hava's constant admonition of "soap and water" and her active participation in cleaning out under the beds had some effect as the months passed.

As the building of their permanent houses proceeded, settlers began to make use of them. During the hot summer months, people sat on the cool ground beneath the raised foundations. A betrothal party given in August was held in the shell of the unfinished future home of the girl's father; and a wedding party in November was given in a still-unfinished house.

From their first days in Ometz, the immigrants from Ait Adrar needed no urging to cultivate the garden plots around their dwellings. Using seeds they had brought from Morocco, they planted corn, beans, melons, tomatoes, sharp pepper, mint, and other herbs. They planted the seeds in narrow, crooked rows that were very close to each other. The agricultural instructors, Yehoshua and later Amos, showed them new methods of cultivation and supervised their planting of potatoes, garlic, carrots, radishes, cucumbers, and other vegetables. Over the months, seeds and seedlings were exchanged among neighbors and with relatives in other villages. Fruit trees were scheduled to be planted around the houses at the appropriate time of the year, but the settlers did not wait and planted the seedlings of whatever kinds of trees they could find, much to the exasperation of the instructors. Since most of the seedlings died, they did not have to be later uprooted. Men, women, and children worked for hours in their gardens and took great pride in showing the progress to the village team and to visitors.

Disputes over housing broke out at the beginning of August. Several new shacks had been constructed, bringing the number of settler units in Ometz to eighty-eight. A few families from Ait Adrar requested Aharon's permission to move to these units. Aharon refused, fearing that this could set a precedent for a mass reshuffling of dwellings. One family, that of the older brother of Rav Avraham, desired a new house located next to that of the wife's sister. Aharon had promised that they could have it when their grown son, still in Morocco, would arrive in Ometz and take over the house and prospective farm unit they occupied. Unwilling to wait, they broke into and occupied the new dwelling. When they defied his order to move back, Aharon summoned the police. They then started to move, only to return as soon as the police had left. The settler also sought out Aharon in the village office, tried to strike him, and had to be pinioned by the other men present. Again the police were summoned, and this time the man was taken to the police station, and his wife went along. As he was escorted from the village, he screamed that he would kill Aharon and that Aharon had accepted IL 50 from him for permission to move. He spent two days in jail.

After he was taken away, the family moved their possessions from the shack, but they sat outside it until evening. Finally, old Rav Shlomo intervened and persuaded them to return to their previous dwelling. None of the other settlers interfered in the case. Village gossip assigned the blame for the incident to the wife. It was said that her husband, usually a rather gentle man, had left her several times but had returned each time after about a week.

Another request to move into a new unit came from a sickly woman whose dwelling was in a far corner of Ometz. Although both Hava and Rahel privately acknowledged that her request was reasonable and could be justified as an exception, they were reluctant to take issue with Aharon. However, he raised no objection some days later when a number of the later arrivals, frightened by the security situation, moved into some still-unoccupied older dwellings in a corner of the village away from the main road.

Health Services. The dispensary was open morning and afternoon, with Rahel in attendance; and a Sick Fund doctor was supposed to visit twice weekly. In fact, visits by a physician tended to be erratic until late November, when a young physician, born and educated in Iraq, arrived to live in the rural center and serve the Daroma villages. In the Daroma Region, an agreement had been reached between the Sick Fund and the Ministry of Health that placed the latter's program of mother-child care under the Sick Fund nurse. The nurse also checked all children for eye and skin diseases. In addition to carrying out these programs, holding dispensary hours, visiting the sick, and being on twenty-four hour emergency call, Rahel joined Hava in an intensive program of infant welfare.

Unlike most nurses and instructresses working with immigrants from the non-Western countries, Hava and Rahel interfered as little as possible in traditional child-rearing and health practices. The mothers were not told to wean their children earlier than had been customary, nor was any attempt made to introduce new habits of toilet training or to suppress the use of amulets or recourse to the rabbis' traditional counsels. But from the day after the establishment of Ometz, Hava made daily visits to every home in which there was an infant, checking on the babies' health, giving them daily baths, and instructing the mothers on the virtues of soap and water, the use of diapers, and the boiling of drinking water. She made sure that the infants were brought every week to the dispensary for checks on weight and development.

The moment an infant fell ill or started losing weight, a rigorous round-the-clock regime was instituted. Hava would visit the homes of such infants every four hours to prepare and administer formulas, instructing mothers and grandmothers in such procedures. Infants who were suffering from diarrhea or toxicosis but were not ill enough to be taken to the hospital might be kept by Hava or Rahel for a few days under their hourly supervision. At any sign of serious illness, the child was rushed to the hospital as soon as transportation could be obtained, always accompanied by Hava or Rahel or both. They rarely took a child to the hospital, particularly for the first time, without bringing a parent along on the trip to show him or her where the child was being taken. This practice was considered unnecessary trouble by some of the younger nurses and instructresses in other villages.

The dispensary was actively patronized from the first days of Ometz' existence, and Rahel had her own version of the stages through which the village passed during its first ten weeks. The first stage consisted of the period during which the women made the cement floors of their dwellings and came to her with deep cuts in their hands. This was followed by the period during which the prickly cactus fruit was ripe, and the children and many adults came with infected scratches on their hands. The smaller children also had such scratches on their bottoms, since they wore only chemises; and their mothers had them on their breasts, since the children wiped their hands on the mother's dress. The third stage occurred in July, between the first and ninth days of the Hebrew month of Av, when the immigrants from Ait Adrar scrupulously observed the religious prohibition against washing.

During their first months in Ometz, illnesses involving fever, fainting, vomiting, and diarrhea created panic among the immigrants, for such symptoms often had proved fatal in Ait Adrar. They told of an epidemic marked by vomiting and diarrhea which, about ten years previously, had wiped out half their community within a few days. Never previously having been treated with antibiotics, they responded to them magnificently. A marked preference for injections over pills and other medicines soon developed.

During July, one of the settler women became very ill. Taken by Rahel to the hospital, she refused to remain and had to be returned to Ometz. The next day, Rahel and

Hava remonstrated with her for hours and the old rabbi joined them. Finally, she consented to go again and this time was accompanied by her husband as well as by Rahel and Hava. Clutching Hava's hand, she sat stiffly through the trip with a determined expression on her face. When she returned, she recounted proudly to Rahel: "The doctor came every day and said, 'Hello, madam' " (*Shalom, geveret*).

The settlers received treatment with repeated expressions of thanks and tried to press gifts on Rahel and Hava, whose roles they often viewed as interchangeable. One old man, after receiving an injection in his home, took out his Bible and kissed Rahel's hand and then the book as an expression of gratitude. The women soon believed that Hava's touch would help cure a child, and Rahel quickly became the personification of medicine. When the same sick woman had to be rehospitalized in August, her husband refused permission until Rahel repeatedly assured him that she could do no more. He and his brother as well as Rahel and Hava accompanied the woman to the hospital, and the brother begged Rahel to remain there with her. When Rahel left, Ometz, some six months later, the villagers continued for months to address her successors by her name.

Deep respect was also shown the physician. On one of his first house visits, to the same woman, her family put clean sheets on her bed before his arrival, washed and dressed her carefully, covered the bed with a silken spread unearthed from their boxes for the occasion, and put pieces of light blue cloth on the stools, all "to honor the doctor." Before being brought to the physician, children always were washed and dressed in clean clothes. Questioning of the young rabbi later revealed that in recent years a French physician had regularly visited Ait Adrar, but that the Jews had not taken advantage of his services. When asked why the settlers so freely sought out and listened to the Ometz physician, the young rabbi seemed astonished. "But this is Israel!" he exclaimed.

With all their faith in Rahel and in Israeli medicine, the

immigrants from Ait Adrar did not relinquish their previous practices. The use of amulets, henna, soot, bands around aching limbs, etc. continued, as did such practices as cleaning pus from running eyes with the tongue. Whenever Rahel was called to a bedside, she found the old rabbi leaving, or he would arrive as she departed.

Women's Instruction Room. In early September, an instruction room for the women was opened in Ometz. A wooden shack, it was sponsored and equipped by the women's affiliate of the Histadrut. Hava began holding daily classes there from 10:00 A.M. to noon, teaching the women the preparation of supplementary foods for infants, new recipes and methods of general food preparation, elementary sewing (which had been a male skill in Ait Adrar), the elements of literacy, etc. Such instruction rooms were provided in many moshvei olim by the women's organization associated with the particular political party to which the moshav federation was affiliated

The opening of the Ometz instruction room was marked by a dedication ceremony typical of such occasions. Scheduled in advance, it was attended by the district supervisor of the Ministry of Social Welfare, an official of the Ministry's Child and Youth Welfare Division, the Daroma social worker, a representative of the Daroma regional directorate of the Land Settlement Department, and, arriving late, the representatives of the women's organization. Summoned early, the settler women had dispersed and had to be called back to the instruction room. They were newly washed for the occasion and were dressed in gowns of all colors, obviously their best, purchased in Casablanca on the way to Israel and worn for the first time in Ometz. The ceremony included a speech given by the representative of the women's organization, dealing with the nobility of Labor-Zionist pioneering, the role of women, and the activities of the Histadrut and of its women's affiliate. Although the speech was translated and adapted by Yitzhak, the immigrant women obviously missed the point. For after Hava had answered for them and refreshments were served, they chorused their appreciation: "Many thanks, Jewish Agency!"

Education. Of the organized village institutions, provisions for education were the most erratically implemented. During the summer of 1955, the period of repeated turnover of teachers, volunteers supplemented their work. A university student arrived to teach Hebrew under the auspices of a national campaign organized for this purpose. During his vacation, until the end of October, he taught Hebrew during the hour set aside for this in the courses in military instruction, taught Hebrew to the children in the intervals between schoolteachers, instructed the youth, and tried to set up evening study-groups for the adults in the settlers' homes. During July, several pairs of young people from Aharon and Hava's kibbutz each spent ten to fifteen days in Ometz. Not allowed by the State Religious Trend teachers to help in the school, they taught the youth Israeli songs and sports.

When they departed, another youth instructor was sent by Youth Aliya to work in Ometz and two neighboring villages. A native Israeli of Yemenite descent, he organized a series of recreational activities of an educational nature, such as trips, sports, and club activities, through which knowledge about Israel could be transmitted. He left at the end of September because of illness in his family.

Early in September, three new teachers were assigned to Ometz for the regular school year. One of them was a girl of Hungarian descent from Tel Aviv. Although given a shack of her own, she was frightened or reluctant to live in Ometz and took a room in Migdal. The other two teachers were young men from a moshav near Migdal, established in 1950 and settled by immigrants from the island of Djerba in Tunisia. Both had attended a religious teachers' seminary in Israel. They planned to commute daily from their village to Ometz. During succeeding months, a day on which all three teachers arrived to hold classes was more infrequent than commonplace. Of the three teachers, only one of the young men, the teacher most regular in attendance, established more than formal relations with the remainder of the village team and with the settlers.

School attendance, initially irregular, became much more so during the period of repeated turnover of teachers. After each change of teachers, many children stayed home and had to be sought out by the new teachers. Furthermore, many older children went to work during the cotton picking season, and older daughters were often kept at home to care for younger siblings while their mothers went to work. The irregular attendance of the students, however, was more than matched by that of the teachers assigned for the school year. Often pupils could be found hanging around an empty classroom, commenting disappointedly, "No school today."

The children soon began to speak Hebrew, and the five- and six-year-olds learned more rapidly than older children. The boys were proud of their progress and cheerfully showed off their notebooks. The girls were modest. By September Hava's constant admonitions about "soap and water" began to have results; and most of the children came to school clean and cleanly dressed.

The kindergarten was first opened when one of the young transient teachers rounded up some thirty children who were between the ages of three and six. A regular kindergarten teacher arrived early in October. Yehudit, a native Israeli of Bokharan descent, was enrolled as a State Religious Trend teacher. However, she had not claimed exemption from military service on the grounds of being religious,[12] and she immediately took up village residence, inviting a rather deviant immigrant girl of her own age [13] to share her hut. In addition to her own work, she helped Aharon in the office. She soon achieved acceptance by the other members of the village team.

The solidarity of siblings initially was conspicuous in both the school and kindergarten. When one child was sent away from school, his siblings followed, although they thereby forfeited their share of the candies later to be distributed. A similar incident occurred in the kindergarten. But after about

[12] The law of Israel grants young women exemption from military service on grounds of religious orthodoxy.
[13] Cf. pp. 349, 355–57.

seven months, quarrels between siblings began to be observed.

Israeli songs were snatched up by all age groups, and organized group play in school and kindergarten included children of both sexes and all ages. All young men, including married men in their early twenties, joined in the activities organized for the youth. In August a sightseeing excursion was arranged by the youth instructor for the adolescents of Ometz and two neighboring villages. No girls from Ometz joined. But young married men gaily went along, singing Israeli songs, although they forfeited a day's work in doing so.

The school kitchen, partly subsidized by the Ministry of Education and Culture, with the parents also contributing to its support, was first opened in the second week of July. A girl from Ait Adrar, who had spent several years in Casablanca, was made cook under Hava's supervision. Since the girl was illiterate, Yitzhak did the accounts. Only cocoa, bread and jam, and tomatoes and cucumbers were served to the children during this period, and the kitchen closed down when the cook married a young man from another village and left Ometz. It was reopened at the beginning of November, with one of the women of urban provenience serving as cook, and hot lunches then were served. School attendance immediately doubled. The parents promptly and uncomplainingly paid their share of the cost of the meals, IL .50 per month for each child.

Early in October, a young couple arrived in Ometz from one of the veteran moshvei ovdim. Amos served as agricultural instructor; Shulamit took over as the new youth instructor, instituting informal lecture and discussion classes several evenings a week. She also taught Hebrew in the military instruction courses, replacing the student volunteer, and she helped Hava. Gay, energetic, and hard-working, Amos and Shulamit associated closely with the initial instructor group both in their work and informally. They occupied a vacant hut in the line of dwellings near the road to the rural center. Of available locations, this one was chosen as best reinforcing village security, while allowing the widest possible dispersion of the households that could serve the settlers as models.

Religion. The shack housing Ometz' temporary synagogue was located in the temporary village center near the dispensary, and the men entered it daily for their morning and evening prayers. Benches were arranged against the walls and in rows facing the Ark.

The most honored seat, against the left wall and nearest to the Ark, was occupied by Rav Shlomo, the old rabbi of Itkaalan. Next to him was his son, Rabbi Avraham, who led the services. All other men with places in the row along the wall and in the front line of benches were old or middle aged, and important visitors were seated on the front bench. The other places in the Ometz synagogue were less rigorously assigned, since not all the men appeared regularly for daily prayers. However, the temporary synagogue overflowed on the Sabbath, with the younger men seated outside, on benches placed next to the door and against the windows. On Sabbaths the wife of the old rabbi generally sat on the ground outside the synagogue listening; and Hava also sat outside, on a corner of one of the benches, while Aharon joined the men inside. In the quiet of the Sabbath, the chant of the services was audible throughout much of the village.

A mikve was installed in Ometz at the beginning of September. Prior to that, the mikve of a nearby older moshav olim was open to the women of Ometz according to an arrangement worked out by Aharon. However, separate public showers for men and for women had been installed in Ometz by the time it was settled. When Hava first informed the Ometz women of the interim mikve arrangements, two of the younger women answered that they had no need to go; they had just taken a shower.

Once its initial administrative arrangements were effected, the organized religious life of Ometz was handled almost entirely by the settlers. In fact, when Aharon got around to informing Rav Avraham, during the High Holiday season in September, that a committee to deal with religious matters (*va'ad dati*) was needed in the village, the young rabbi answered that one already existed. A representative of the Ministry of Religious Affairs had told him weeks earlier to form such a committee. As the rabbi subsequently recounted the conversation, he first had answered that not all the expected immigrants from Ait Adrar had arrived in Ometz, and that he had to wait in order to ask them what they wanted. The Ministry's representative replied that it was not necessary to wait; the rabbi should appoint the most learned men already in the village. And he had done so. He headed the committee, and its four other members were men in their forties. Three of them occupied seats in the synagogue in the honored row against the wall, and the fourth had a seat in the front row. After the High Holidays, this committee was officially registered by Aharon; and the head of the provisional Daroma Regional Council [14] worked with it in arranging such matters as the budgets for the synagogue and mikve.[15] The membership of this committee remained constant throughout the period of research in Ometz.

Rav Avraham received his Israeli certification as shohet and village religious instructor from the Ministry of Religious Affairs in July, and no question ever arose of replacing him as the official religious leader of Ometz. Whatever the tensions created by the arrival of Rav Yosef,[16] both rabbis led, in alternation, the Sabbath and High Holiday synagogue services. Shortly before the High Holidays, both rabbis as well as old Rav Shlomo had participated in the Brit Mila held for the newborn son of a young couple from Casablanca. The circumcision itself was performed by Rabbi Avraham, while Rabbi Yosef said the blessing which then was repeated by Rabbi Shlomo. Both immigrants of urban provenience and those from Ait Adrar attended the ceremony.

However, the *modus vivendi* of the rabbis was disrupted in October, at least as indicated by complaints Rav Yosef made to Yitzhak shortly before the latter's departure from

14 Cf. above, p. 305.
15 The Division for New Immigrant Settlements of the Ministry of Religious Affairs contributed to these budgets in all the immigrant settlements.
16 Cf. above, p. 319.

Ometz. The rabbi of urban provenience claimed that he had not been honored in the synagogue on the previous Sabbath; he had not even been able to get into the crowded building, and henceforth he intended to go alone to the fields to pray. The matter was resolved among the settlers without further recourse to the village workers. Some time later Rabbi Yosef left Ometz.

THE WOOF OF VILLAGE LIFE AND SETTLER ACCULTURATION

The organization of village institutions, outlined above, channeled but by no means comprehended the flow of events in Ometz, and the settler responses described constituted only segments of their changing way of life. In this section, I seek to describe shifting values and relations among the settlers in their manifold interactions with the Israeli scene.

Experimentation with new modes of behavior was evident among the youth from the initial weeks of Ometz' existence. One of the areas affected was religious observance, and a range of variation was apparent in the behavior of both settlers and village workers. During the height of the first Ometz crisis, Yitzhak remained in the village on the Sabbath before the departure of the families leaving for Nshima. He thoughtlessly plucked the head off a flower while walking to a house, and a cluster of young men accompanying him, all members of families remaining in Ometz, pointed out that this constituted a violation of the Sabbath. But on the same day some young men did not attend the afternoon synagogue service. "We are Mapai," they told Yitzhak. "We are nonobservant." Their absence elicited no known response from the older men.

Four weeks later, on the last Sabbath of July, the new youth instructor [17] played games, including ball, with the younger adolescents, and the adults did not complain or intervene in any way. Late that afternoon, Yehoshua involved some of the older boys in a game of football. He reported that they hung back until he kicked the ball among them.

[17] Cf. p. 339.

When the sun set, marking the end of the Sabbath, all the young men joined the game. No complaints were raised by the older settlers then or afterwards.

This was the period that settler bitterness toward Yitzhak was at its height, and the public meeting over the petition to have him removed [18] took place the next afternoon. When Aharon asked the settlers the basis of their accusation that Yitzhak was leading the youth astray, several men shouted that he wanted to take the boys on a tour of kibbutzim on the Sabbath, leading to quarrels between son and father. The incident to which they referred concerned a proposed visit, under the auspices of the Government Civic Education Service,[19] to a religious agricultural training school near a religious kibbutz. The boys were to have been picked up on a Friday afternoon, and, were to remain at the school overnight and visit the farms of the school and kibbutz during the Sabbath. In fact, the truck in which they were to travel did not arrive, and the visit was called off. When Aharon reminded the angry settlers of the facts, they screamed that there was no need to travel anywhere before the Sabbath, and they continued their abuse of Yitzhak.

The next outbreak occurred on the following Sabbath. In neighboring Ba'aya a baby had fallen ill the previous day. His symptoms had increased by nightfall, after the departure of the Ba'aya nurse for the weekend. He was brought to Rahel in Ometz then and again at noon on the next day, both times in the pickup truck shared by the two villages. The immigrants from Ait Adrar accepted this violation of the Sabbath with little protest; religious law permits the breaking of various prohibitions when the saving of life is involved. But at the time of afternoon prayers, the truck returned with the baby, its mother, and an escort of more than half a dozen boisterous young men, all immigrants from Tangiers settled in Ba'aya. As they noisily jumped from the truck, they were met with a shower of stones, and a clamorous fight ensued. Among other damages, the wind-

[18] See above, p. 320.
[19] Cf. p. 244.

shield of the truck was broken. The police were summoned, and four young men of Ba'aya were taken to the station and charged. The cost of replacing the windshield was shared by the contestants from Ba'aya and Ometz.

However, on the following Sabbath a few cars entered Ometz without incident. On the same day, Yehoshua, who of all the village workers made the fewest concessions to the settlers' traditions, took five young men from his course with him on a trip to the nearby police station. They also drove to a kibbutz where pigs were raised. One of the young men, who had distinguished himself from Ometz' first days by refusing to work and appearing almost daily at the dispensary crying, "I'll die, I'll die," reacted to the sight by declaring, "I want to eat pork." The others, however, made no comment. The excursion had no known repercussions among the other settlers.

Two weeks later Bar Mitzva ceremonies were held for five boys, and a party was given in their honor that evening. Tables and benches for the party were placed on the foundations of the prospective permanent home of one of the boys, and children of all ages performed dances and songs they had learned in Ometz. On the same evening, a program under the sponsorship of the Government Civic Education Service was held. An accordionist played before the youth clubhouse and there was singing and dancing followed by films on Israel. One of the boys who was celebrating his Bar Mitzva went to the film-show and had to be called away from it to attend the party. The instructors were not invited to this party, but they were asked to another one held on the following day, at which a few settlers also were present. Several days earlier, however, Aharon had been invited by the settler men to join them at their customary festive meal celebrating the first day of the Hebrew month.[20]

At the end of September, one of the settlers of urban provenience worked in his garden on the Sabbath before Yom Kippur. The immigrants from Ait Adrar complained

[20] Cf. p. 279.

about this indignantly among themselves, but they did not molest the man in any way.

From these incidents, admittedly an incomplete record, it would seem that the elders' response to violation of religious law and to the secularization of the young followed an erratic course. Under pressure of agitation or flagrant violations, the settlers could become aroused, but much was overlooked in daily life. The behavior of the village workers also varied with the individual, as did settler responses to it. Thus, when Yitzhak became the focus of hostility, alleged violations of religious law was but one of the accusations mobilized against him, whereas Yehoshua with impunity involved the young in repeated Sabbath desecrations.

It is possible that rigorous, detailed observation, impossible under the conditions of field work, would have detected differentiated patterns of behavior among the settlers, e.g., consistent resistance to secularization by some young men, its consistent welcoming by others, and vacillation by still others, depending on context and company. The reactions of the elders also might have demonstrated consistent variation. Previous residence in Casablanca did not appear to be a significant variable in these respects, but this was only an impression.

Yet while granting the inadequacy of the data, I believe that the erratic course of behavior they chart corresponds to a basic fact of moshav olim life: the unpredictability of daily events. I have discussed this point in Chapter I in reference to all situations of directed change which involve more variables than constants, and I return to it in Chapter IX.

A period of renewed tension over religion, stimulated by activities of representatives of the religious movements, began during October. Rabbi Avraham was known to be in regular contact with the religious labor party. Toward the end of the month, the new youth instructor, Shulamit, was told by settlers not to hold meetings with the youth on the Sabbath, since the village was religious. Devout herself, Hava was indignant that the settlers could distrust an activity Aharon and she countenanced, particularly since recent infractions of the Sabbath had been seen among the Ait Adrar immigrants. Rahel had noticed a man shaving on the Sabbath about ten days earlier; and a week later one of the women had come to Hava and had led her to a home where a group of young men, most of whom attended Shulamit's classes, were playing cards for money. A few days later, another young man in the class told Shulamit that Rabbi Avraham had written to Jerusalem asking for a religious instructor in the village. The boy added that he and the others would continue to attend her classes. The next evening Shulamit led the students to talk of recreation and suggested that card-playing was a poor use of free time.

Two weeks later, in November, the State Religious Trend kindergarten teacher, Yehudit, was told by her supervisor to begin teaching the youth herself despite the presence of Shulamit, representing Youth Aliya in the village. She declined to do so, but Rabbi Avraham went around to the young people to tell them to discontinue their studies with Shulamit. In response, they thronged the clubhouse where she held her lessons.

In the weeks during which these events occurred, many other developments were taking place in the village. The young men were being called to register for army service. The permanent houses were nearing completion, and only settlers willing to sign the contract with the Land Settlement Department's Division of Contracts and Securities [21] were to be allowed to occupy them. The moshav federation holding company [22] was due to begin the cultivation of the village land. The first rains had fallen by the end of October, transforming dusty earth to mud. By then Ometz had been in existence for five months, and a new phase of village development was underway. I return to this period in the next section.

The daughters of the Ait Adrar settlers had not been implicated in the process of religious secularization as had

[21] Cf. pp. 181ff.
[22] Cf. pp. 180–81.

their brothers. However, secularization in the sense of trans-formation of their traditional roles was inherent in moshav olim organization, and it progressively affected most of the settler women.

Attending school was a radical innovation for female children, but this was not in any way opposed by the parents. Nonetheless, girls of an age to help their mothers often stayed home in the course of the year, and the changes in and absences of the teachers encouraged this. The only girl of the Ait Adrar settlers to participate in the youth activities in the village was Tamar, the deviant twenty-one-year-old already mentioned, who had spent some years in Casablanca. Indeed, most other girls past puberty were already mothers, and Tamar's history, recounted below, included a marriage in childhood.

Among the women, such nontraditional actions as shop-ping at the village store and working for wages in the fields of the neighboring village took place early in Ometz' history, without the intervention of the village instructors or even their realization of the discontinuities involved. These dis-continuities, however, may have been mediated by the experience of those who had lived and worked in Casablanca and/or by experience on the trip to Israel and in the transit camp. Nonetheless, the instructors soon became involved in the settlers' domestic life and were agents of further change.

Their first encounter with the patterning of domestic disputes among the Ait Adrar immigrants [23] occurred shortly after the first village crisis. The instructors discovered that the wife and two small children of a man who had gone to Nshima had remained in Ometz with her brothers and mother. At first, Aharon saw the situation as one calling for action on his part. He wished to send them to Nshima with the district coordinator [24] on the latter's daily rounds, but all concerned evaded this. The woman's presence then became a subject of discussion with the Nshima instructor, who was visiting Ometz on other business concerning the

[23] Cf. p. 282.
[24] Cf. pp. 234–35.

settlers. The latter had already considered turning to the social worker of a neighboring district for his mediation, but had decided that the matter should be left to the settlers to resolve. The woman told Yitzhak that her husband had to come to fetch her and, as the days passed, Aharon allowed Yitzhak to give her IL 10 of the pay owing her husband. About a week later, the Nshima pickup truck brought him. He had come for the children, he claimed. He told his wife that he would beat her every day, that he did not want her but would take another wife. He was furious that she had been given a portion of his wages. Finally, they all left.

In the meanwhile, the registration of the villagers was in process, and Yitzhak discovered a girl of seventeen living with her brother in one of the houses, although she was married to a young man in the village. She had wanted a divorce while still in the transit camp. Yitzhak questioned her, but she blushed, hung her head and would not answer, behavior typical of most young women at this period when addressed by outsiders. She was "ashamed." Two older women who were in the shack with her, a mother and her married daughter, said that she was still a virgin. The rabbis had been unable to make peace between the young couple. Over the next few days, Yitzhak spoke to the young man, then brought the two together and the girl agreed to live with her husband. Fifteen days later she ran away again. After a few months the couple got a divorce, and within a year both young people had remarried.

As other domestic disputes reached his attention, Yitzhak regularly intervened in them. One quarrel involved a husband aged twenty-one and a wife of sixteen. Several weeks earlier the girl had demonstrated her readiness to embrace new possibilities of behavior. The ice-truck had arrived in the village, and Rahel had prevented a pregnant young woman with a weak heart, who had suffered four previous miscarriages, from lugging the big block of ice home. Turning to the husband, lounging in the village center after work, the nurse had told him to carry it. After some demurring he did so. The other girl then turned to her husband, demanding that he do the same. When he refused, she dropped the ice and walked off. After some hesitation, he had picked it up. Now he had beaten her severely, and she had run away to the home of an uncle. To Yitzhak's inquiries the young husband explained that his wife did not prepare food to his liking, and that she made little of him and had cursed him.

Describing the case the next day, Yitzhak recounted that he had summoned two neighbors as witnesses and concluded the following agreement with the couple: if either one of them began to curse the other, the latter was not to answer but to come with a witness directly to him. He hoped by this means to contain prospective quarrels before they became acute.

However, in the worst domestic case that came to light during this period, Aharon as well as Yitzhak stepped in. The parents of a young man had moved in with him after the arrival of the new settlers.[25] One day in July, they thrust his young wife, Mazal, out of the shack, took the baby from her, and locked her out. Both instructors hurried to effect a reconciliation, but by evening the young woman again had been thrown out. Again peace was made, but the girl continued to be abused by the others. Lacking family of her own in Ometz, she ran away a few days later to her brother in Nshima, taking the baby with her. She returned, but continued to be tyrannized and beaten. Her breasts soon went dry, and forcing husband and mother-in-law to provide food for a formula became a constant preoccupation of Hava's.

With Yitzhak's loss of status, Aharon and Hava inherited the role of domestic peacemaker initiated by him. Women would seek them out, weeping that their husbands had beaten them; less often, men would come to complain that their wives had run away. The incidence of women running away after a beating, if only to relatives next door, was far greater

25 Above, p. 320.

than it had been in Ait Adrar, according to remarks made by the settlers. Before the year had elapsed, almost all of the younger wives had run away at least once. When called upon in domestic disputes, Hava consulted the rabbis; and the traditional peacemakers were supplemented rather than displaced by the new authorities.

As time passed, the reasons given for quarrels showed changes in domestic relations brought about by the Israeli scene, particularly the decreasing submissiveness of the women. As early as September, one woman complained to the police after being beaten by her husband. Some of the wives refused to hand over their earnings to their husbands, and a few were severely beaten for it. Conversely, however, one man in his forties told his wife of thirty-one to go to work in answer to her request for money. He ended the quarrel by locking her and their four children out of the house. "She can go to her parents," he told the youth instructor, who, in this case, became the peacemaker.

In December a woman of twenty-one, whose infant daughter had recently died of pneumonia, asked her husband for permission to visit her parents in one of the new villages in the other Daroma district. When he refused, they quarreled; he struck her and she hit him back. Her husband took the children and put her out of the house. She came weeping to Hava. All her things were in the house and she had nothing. Her husband had never given her money for anything more than bread, although she had worked. Even while pregnant, she had herded the villagers' goats.[26] Now she had nothing to eat. She wanted to lodge a complaint with the police and go to court. Hava cautioned her that courts cost money, and sought out the peacemaking offices of Rav Avraham. "But she hit him!" cried the rabbi. Eventually, however, he spoke to the husband, who took her back. But three months later, the husband discovered that she had saved IL 300 and hidden it with an old woman to whom she was related. She ran away after he beat her, and this time she refused to return. Aharon

26 Above, p. 329.

finally effected a reconciliation, and he had both partners agree in a written contract to terms on which they would remain together.

Making out such a contract became Aharon's policy in all further domestic cases in which his intervention was sought, and sometimes its terms were honored. As the months passed, however, new grounds for disputes arose. After the families had occupied their permanent dwellings, for example, one young man beat his wife because the windows in the house were very dirty.

Although they intervened in marital relations only when called upon to do so, the instructors tried to effect a divorce in several instances. In the case of the unfortunate Mazal, Hava suggested a divorce to the husband and even considered bringing the parties before a rabbinical court. The second pregnancy of the wife made this impractical. However, in the case of two child wives, both aged thirteen, the instructors were more active. As soon as Batya arrived, the girls were urged to attend school, and they did so wearing the married woman's kerchief. Both ran away from their husbands' homes to their fathers; both begged for a divorce, and were supported in their pleas by the instructors.

By the end of July, the twenty-year-old husband of one of them told Hava that he was ready to give her back to her father. "In Israel she is no wife; she is only a little girl." The formalities of the divorce were to be arranged by Aharon after the High Holidays in September, but he was too much occupied by other matters to take action. In November, influenced by the prospect of induction into the Army, the boy changed his mind. His wife, weeping bitterly, was returned to him a few weeks later, but she promised Hava to continue school. She ran back to her father several months later; village gossip had it that her husband had tried to have intercourse with her. She admitted only that his father's new wife had worked her very hard, which her deceased mother-in-law had not done. Her father finally decided to force the issue of the divorce, which previously he had not been willing to do. In Ait Adrar girls were often married at the age of ten, he explained, "But here it is different." The young husband then demanded more than IL 100 before he would give the divorce, claiming that he had given this for her, which her father indignantly denied. A year after Ometz was founded, Aharon put serious pressure on the boy. The divorce was scheduled but not yet finalized when Aharon and Hava left Ometz.

In the case of the other wife, nothing could be done. She dropped out of school in the autumn of 1955, began attending Hava's classes for women in the instruction room, then also ceased attending these. She had been teased at school by the other girls; it was not certain that she was still a virgin. By December Hava and Shulamit persuaded her to return to school, but she soon dropped out again. She oscillated between her husband's home and that of her father, but the young man refused to consider a divorce.

A break with tradition was also apparent, in different ways, in the behavior of two young women who had spent some years in Casablanca prior to immigration to Israel. A happy blending of new attitudes with the claims of her traditional role was exemplified in the case of Simha. A strapping lass, clearly different from the run of Ait Adrar women, she had been given work in the transit camp kitchen, and already knew some Hebrew when she arrived in Ometz and became its first school cook. Although she was betrothed to one of the young men from Ait Adrar, the marriage was delayed pending revision of her legal age. It had been listed as sixteen on her father's identity card, but she and her family claimed that she was nineteen and the Ometz physician certified her as seventeen, the minimum age for marriage in Israel. But while the wheels of bureaucracy slowly ground, her hand was asked in marriage by a young man from Casablanca, settled in one of the older moshvei olim where she had relatives.

She happily reported on the change in fiancés in August, while returning from a shopping trip to Migdal. Her first fiancé had not wanted her to step outside of Ometz. He had not even given her a ring. This one promised her a ring and earrings and a necklace of gold. He had a separate house with furniture and a radio. "He is rich!" she exclaimed in joy, mentioning nothing of the personal qualities of the two men and still ignorant of the family name of her new future husband. And his parents did not live with him but had their own house and farm next door. The old mother of the first boy still came every day to her house to ask her to change her mind; but then she would have to live in the same house with her and the young man's brothers, she said, "and that isn't good." At first her father had not wanted her to leave Ometz, and in Ait Adrar she could not have married without his consent. But already in Casablanca it was different, like Israel. Now that she did not want the first boy, her father did not want him either.

The young couple wished to marry quickly, but not until October was the revision of Simha's legal age effected. While waiting she related to Hava that her future husband did not want her to wear a kerchief after marriage. One of the Ait Adrar wives was frequently seen in the village without a kerchief as early as September.

Tamar, unlike Simha, was in search of a new identity. A beautiful girl of twenty-one when she arrived in Ometz, she dressed far better than any other woman there, including the village workers. She attended the activities for youth, learned to understand and speak Hebrew very quickly, and distinguished herself in the fields as a rapid and reliable worker. She became attached to the researchers and readily volunteered information, although initially reserved about herself. The settlers gossiped about her: she talked to young men freely, she walked around the village. By August the young men in Yehoshua's courses told him that she was divorced, and other village workers heard the same report.

Tamar at this time said of herself only that she did not want to get married, she did not want to be like her mother. She added that when a family had no money they should not have children. She recounted how a young man from Migdal had recently visited her father and asked for her hand. She had run away from home briefly to live with relatives. She said that she had lived for four years with relatives in Casablanca. They had worked her very hard, and she left them to live with a friend and work in a factory. During that period she associated with other girls her age and had not visited any relatives, although she did so now in Israel. She had attended evening classes in Casablanca but, unlike a friend, did not learn much there. In Israel she studied Hebrew and hoped to join a Hebrew workshop in a religious kibbutz.

Her brother later told Yehoshua that she had been married at the age of nine for seven months, but had run away and gone back to her parents; she had then been taken to Casablanca by relatives, and had not wanted to return to Ait Adrar. When her brother had taken an apartment in Casablanca years later, she lived with him.

As the months passed in Ometz, she became fluent in Hebrew, but literacy defied her efforts. She spoke no more of going away to study Hebrew in a kibbutz, but instead talked of joining the Army. Her father opposed this, and when called up to register in November, she claimed exemption on religious grounds. From October on, she lived with the kindergarten instructor, Yehudit, continued contributions to her parents' household, and maintained her wardrobe.

Although all the women from Ait Adrar had great difficulty learning to read and write, Tamar's total block in that area dispelled the initial expectations of the village workers that she could be assimilated into the absorbing society with its many possibilities for a woman. The subject of her future perturbed Hava and Rahel. Work at a nearby Jewish Agency tree nursery, which was under the jurisdiction of Rahel's brother, was arranged for the girl around the turn of the year. She quickly and easily learned the skills involved, and soon was given permanent employee status.

During the first analysis of the Ometz data, Tamar's case was discussed with an eminent Israeli psychoanalyst, who suggested the following possible diagnosis. Tamar's early marriage seemed to have effected a lasting trauma in that area. In regard to her learning block, literacy in Ait Adrar was strictly a masculine prerogative. Having rebelled against her mother's way of life, the girl suffered from guilt and conflicts over her rejection of the traditional functions of her sex and over wanting to invade the masculine sphere. Her inability to learn to read and write was one expression of these conflicts.

Interestingly enough, both Tamar's mother and her older married sister lived in peace with their husbands, according to the best knowledge of the instructors and researchers. Indeed, Tamar's sister happily told Hava at the end of the first year that she and her husband always pooled their earnings and held everything in common. Moshe, the brother who had been in Casablanca, knew Hebrew on arrival in Ometz, had the first working radio in the village, and could be seen after work reading a paper in easy Hebrew to other young men. Outstanding in the military instruction course as well, he was the first settler to be given tasks with leadership implications by the instructors. The consequences are recounted below.

THE NEXT PHASE

Problems in the legitimation and transfer of authority plagued the moshvei olim and, indeed, can be considered a constant feature of the moshav olim as a type. In theory, land settlement policy favored the rapid creation of the usual moshav self-governing institutions, particularly the village executive committee, and the progressive transfer to the settlers of decision-making and managerial responsibility. In practice, decisions in this area were left to the village instructors, particularly the social instructor, with whatever advice or intervention that the land settlement hierarchy could provide. In this section, I continue the chronicle of Ometz' first year, turning to (1) modifications in its initial organization, and attempts to include settlers in the management of village affairs; and (2) concomitant events relevant to village development.

Aharon continued the practice, begun during the weeks of crisis, of calling occasional meetings of all the settlers over matters of common village concern. This practice was usual in the moshvei olim and had its precedent in the institution of the general assembly in the moshav ovdim and, indeed, in all Labor-Zionist community types. But whereas the general assembly of all members is the basic governing body in the classic settlements, meetings of settlers in the moshvei olim were initiated by the instructors and any participants from the moshav federation and/or Land Settlement Department hierarchy for purposes of explanation and/or clarification.

Meetings might be held prior to some new step in village development to inform the settlers of it, explain its necessity and their role in relation to it, and, hopefully, to gain their willing acquiescence. Meetings also could be called over some misunderstanding or discontent in regard to a village institution. Some instructors in my experience did not hold such meetings, either because they did not think of doing so, or because they feared that this would provide an occasion for a possible mass display of settler rebellion. However, in times of crisis, as during Ometz' first weeks, a Land Settlement Department district or regional official and/or moshav federation representative might join the instructors at a meeting called in the village to clarify choices open to the settlers or to quell settler dissidence in areas where land settlement policy allowed no choice.

Whatever the reason for such meetings or a particular social instructor's policy in regard to them, they were subsidiary as a moshav olim institution to the regularly scheduled meetings of the village executive committee; and they bore little similarity to the general assembly of the moshav ovdim. For the authority vested in the general assembly passed over to the settlers of a moshav olim only at the discretion of the land settlement authorities, after years of successful village development and the transformation of the immigrant settlers into relatively capable and committed farmers knowledgeable in the management of the moshav self-governing institutions. Key evidence of the latter was a stable and effective executive committee, with its members duly elected, a history of at least some rotation in office, and the decision-making powers vested in the office seemingly understood and accepted by the body of settlers. Until this state of affairs could be achieved, whatever the underlying power situation among the villagers, a series of instructors might work with a procession of unstable executive committees, with occasional meetings of all the settlers serving as one device in trying to effect their role-socialization.

In the case of Ometz, after its initial crises Aharon held intermittent meetings with the settlers long before he initiated an executive committee. Such meetings took place in the synagogue, and only the men attended. During two meetings held in October, guard duty was the principal subject under discussion, although the second meeting also dealt with the newly instituted national Defense Fund, to which all Israelis were asked to contribute. The Ometz village workers each gave IL 10 and the settlers accepted without a murmur Aharon's suggestion that each family contribute IL 5 to be deducted from the men's wages.

Guard duty had become, by October, an area of unrest in the village. Grumbling had developed over the nightly four-hour shifts that each man stood in turn, whereas the paid eight-hour watch was a job in great demand. Moreover, guard duty was the first area in which any settler had been given authority over the other villagers. Village security provisions included a part-time post for one of the settlers, assisting the military instructor in the upkeep of military supplies and the roster of the guard. It paid IL 50 per month. In the second week of August, Yehoshua had assigned the job to Moshe, Tamar's brother.

About nineteen years of age, Moshe had left Ait Adrar as a boy of eight. Just previously, the controversy over the fence had occurred,[27] and his father was one of the men imprisoned. The boy then had to help support the family, and he found work carrying building materials to the roofs of houses under construction or repair. When his father was released, he ran away to Casablanca, attended a religious school there, then transferred to a better one in Meknes, where Rabbi Avraham had studied. He remained there until the age of thirteen, the age of manhood according to Jewish law. He then returned to Casablanca and spent another year or so at a school sup-

[27] Cf. p. 299.

ported by a Jewish voluntary organization in France, the Alliance Israelite Universelle. At the age of fourteen he began
to learn and work at such trades as sewing handbags and
shoemaking. He then found work in a French-owned candy
factory, and learned to repair its machinery and drive a car
in addition to learning the processes of candy manufacture.
He became a supervisor in the factory and had taken an
apartment with Tamar before they joined their family in
migration to Israel.

Looking toward the future, Moshe had said in July that he
did not want to be inducted into the Army, since his family
needed his help. He was the oldest son; his father was close
to fifty; and there were five younger children. By August he
expressed the hope of learning a trade in demand in Israel,
such as mechanic or tractor operator. From Ometz' first
weeks, he impressed the village workers with his reliability and
sense of responsibility. Given his other qualifications and the
general Labor-Zionist orientation toward youth, he was an
obvious choice in the eyes of the instructors for a role in village leadership.

He was not so in the eyes of the settlers. As long as
Yehoshua was present, no negative reactions to the appointment were made public. However, when Yehoshua left the
village briefly, a few weeks later, Moshe's guard roster was
not accepted by the settlers called on to serve their turn on
unpaid watch. They refused to do so, and one of them,
Mazal's husband, who had made many loudmouthed scenes
in the course of Ometz' crises, threatened to kill Moshe.
Finally the boy was forced to call on relatives and friends to
maintain the village watch, although it was not their turn for
duty.

By the middle of October, Yehoshua transferred the task
of posting the guard roster from Moshe to Rabbi Avraham.
Previously, the villagers had asked that the rabbi be excused
from guard duty in general. Now they accepted their watch
assignments from him without protest.

Neither this incident nor the concomitant discovery that
Rav Avraham had already created a village Religious Com-

mittee convinced the instructors that he was the obvious leader of the settlers. On the contrary, Aharon maintained that the rabbi was listened to only because he spoke Hebrew, ignoring the relative fluency of Moshe and a few other young men by that time. Indeed, the instructors attributed a weak character to the gentle young rabbi, and were sure that his old father was looked up to much more by the villagers.

Although the latter unquestionably was true, the young rabbi as well as his father was called on continually by the villagers in his traditional capacities. By the end of October he confided to the researcher that he might have to leave Ometz, since he could not continue daily labor in the fields, given all the duties he had to perform on his return from work. He thought that Aharon should find him work that was less physically exhausting, such as paid helper to the storekeeper.

Rabbi Avraham's correspondence with the religious labor party and his attempts to keep the young people from attending Shulamit's classes for youth further decreased his standing with the instructors. They feared that the religious moshav federation would make another attempt to gain control of the village, and they saw the young rabbi as working toward this end. For example, he attended one of the youth classes and told Shulamit that he was not in agreement with what she said. This was on a day when she taught such time concepts as "yesterday" and "tomorrow." The rabbi also told Aharon: "In the village will be whom we want," and this was seen as a threat against all the instructors rather than as referring to a religious instructor for the young people. The day after the rabbi warned the youth against attending Shulamit's class, Aharon did not assign him work. Village gossip reported that the instructor had said that this was because of what the rabbi just had done. Aharon denied it, and the next day the rabbi was asked to substitute for the storekeeper, who had fallen ill.

In their anxiety over the possibility of new crises, Aharon and Hava alerted the Daroma regional director. Their apprehensions were not fulfilled. In regard to the youth, an agreement was reached at some higher level that one of the schoolteachers would join Shulamit in teaching them. The teacher who did so, starting in the first week of December, was the one most regular in attendance and closest to both settlers and the instructor group. He and Shulamit maintained friendly relations.

Even before this happened, the first storekeeper left Ometz, and Rabbi Avraham was taken on as paid helper by the new storekeeper, Hamud, probably on the instructors' advice. Although Hamud soon began to wonder whether he should order new goods, such as rubber boots, in addition to the wide range of foodstuffs he immediately made available to the villagers, he did not initially bother to ask his helper's opinion as to what the settlers would buy. By the middle of December, however, he spoke of the rabbi's reliability and had become somewhat less condescending toward him. More important, the turnover of goods in the store reached a high enough level to warrant the creation of a permanent post of helper, paying a daily wage of IL 5.5 plus fringe benefits. Within a few months, Hamud and Rabbi Avraham were on excellent terms. And by the end of November, even before the religious schoolteacher joined Shulamit in the instruction of the youth, villagers reported that the rabbi had visited the houses to inform the youth that they should attend Shulamit's classes.

During the period of unrest over guard duty and youth instruction, other developments took place in Ometz. By the end of October, army registration forms were distributed. Young men were liable for conscription, whereas the older men were to be enrolled in the reserve forces. Most of the bachelors welcomed the prospect of army service or claimed to, but the young husbands were filled with gloom. "What will happen to their farms?" asked Rabbi Avraham, adding, "What will happen to their wives and children?" Allocation of land to the settlers, as contrasted to its initial cultivation by the moshav federation holding company and the settlers' working for the holding company on a wage basis, was not scheduled to begin for another year. Nonetheless, there seemed to be a fear that draftees might lose their right to a farmstead in Ometz.

A few weeks later, after the young men were called to Beersheva to register, Moshe and another unmarried boy with an old father and many younger siblings expressed more worries: "We have to join the Army, and when we get back we will have to pay the debts of our families. It's not worth it to stay in the village or return to it after finishing military service." And they went on: "What will happen to the old ones without us? Someone has to help them. They can't work their farms alone." Moshe added that he knew people who had been in Israel for two years and had not yet been recruited by the Army. "Only in Ometz are people called up so fast." In fact, not until the following June was the first contingent of young men, all bachelors, actually drafted.

While army registration was taking place, an air-raid shelter was built in Ometz, as in all the new villages. Whatever their attitudes toward the prospect of conscription, the young men showed high morale in regard to Israel's security situation. "We're not afraid of the Arabs," they boasted. "We'll beat them." On a morning soon after registration, Shulamit, who had served her full time in the Army, not only gave her usual Hebrew lesson in the military instruction course but also drilled the men. She reported that they listened to her attentively, willingly obeyed her orders, and, when she relinquished the job to Yehoshua, they did not want her to stop. They complimented her, with amazement, on how much she knew.

By the beginning of November, one row of permanent houses was nearing completion. The instructors, in concurrence with the land settlement authorities, decided to let the settlers occupy the houses as they became ready, in staggered groups of about fifteen families at a time. By then only four of the eighty-eight farm units in Ometz remained unallocated, and there was no dearth of candidates for these.

For relatives of the original contingent of Ait Adrar immigrants had been seeking and had been granted admission to Ometz since the resolution of its first crisis in

June. Some of these families had arrived in Israel at about the same time as Ometz' first settlers but had been taken to older villages; others had been recruited by the religious moshav federation and had gone to its transit camp and then to a village affiliated with it in the second Daroma district; and others had arrived in Israel after Ometz was founded. By the middle of October, Ometz' official settler population consisted of sixty-three families from Ait Adrar, twenty-two families from other parts of Morocco, and five families from Tunisia; and families from Ait Adrar were living in the homes of relatives in the village, hopefully waiting to be assigned a farm unit. Other relatives were candidates for admission should the families from Tunisia and some of those from Moroccan towns leave Ometz, as they had declared their intention of doing.

On the last Monday of November, representatives of the Land Settlement Department's Division of Contracts and Securities visited Ometz, bringing contracts [28] for the settlers to sign preparatory to their occupying the permanent houses. Only the five families from Tunisia and one from a town in Morocco refused to sign, and one of the Tunisian families departed on the following day. Of the immigrants of urban provenience, only two families had left Ometz up to this time, apart from those who had departed within days of their arrival in July. The others from Morocco had by now established neighborly relations with the settlers from Ait Adrar, although a few of them continued to express in private occasional denigrating remarks about the latter. Only the families from Tunisia had remained a separate enclave in the village, adamant in their intention to leave.

Occupying five consecutive houses at one end of Ometz, these families consisted of two unrelated nuclear families, named Levi and Bitar, and one extended family made up of a couple in their fifties with two unmarried grown children and two married sons in their twenties. Of this family, named Aflalo, one of the young couples had a boy two

[28] Cf. pp. 184–85.

and a half years old; both young wives were pregnant; and the unmarried daughter of eighteen was no slimmer than her sisters-in-law well along in their pregnancies, in accordance with the Arab ideal of female beauty also traditionally held by urban North African Jews. The young women spoke French poorly but fluently; of the men, the middle-aged father spoke it brokenly. He had been a funeral porter for the organized Jewish community of Tunis. The unmarried son, who was thirty-two, was referred to as a "rabbin" by his family but actually had been a traditional teacher of elements of Hebrew and Judaism to small boys; one of the married sons had been a tailor.

Of the two nuclear families, the Levis were a couple in their late thirties with five children, the oldest a girl of fourteen. They were from the city of Sfax in Tunisia; all spoke French well; the husband was a tailor, his wife a dressmaker. The oldest daughter, Annette, had been in secondary school at the time of immigration. The other couple, in their thirties, had three small children. Suzanne Bitar spoke French well. She was a dressmaker and, on her arrival in Ometz, had informed Rahel that a brother of hers was a physician in Tunis. Her husband, Robert, spoke broken French. He announced that he had been wounded when the Germans had occupied Tunis; he had a bullet in his leg and could not do heavy work. In October, when he was asked in French what his profession was, he answered that he was an "industrialist." In further conversation, he said that he had been a shoemaker before the war, and that afterwards the French administration had gotten him a job "supervising the Arabs" in the port.

Differing from each other in background, manner, and extent of assimilation to French colonial culture, differing in these respects within the same family, as in the case of Robert and Suzanne Bitar, the immigrants from Tunisia were as one in their repudiation of Ometz and in their goal of settling in a city. Their complaints about Ometz, typical of immigrants of urban provenience dispatched to the moshvei olim, were similar, but the emphases of these complaints varied somewhat.

The heavily-fleshed Aflalo daughter, speaking raucously for her family, bitterly complained of the limited range of food available at the village store, its poor quality, the absence of milk, the impossibility of working on such a diet, and the need to go constantly to Migdal to shop. She went on to the kindergarten: the boy of two and a half had not been accepted. In Tunis he would have been in a kindergarten from the age of two and everything he needed would have been given gratis by one of the Jewish organizations. They had expected to go to a well-established village, like one near Tiberias where an older brother, who had been in Israel for six years, was settled; instead they had been sent to Ometz where there was nothing. "In the middle of the desert," lacking all "distractions," it was fit for the immigrants from Ait Adrar but not for persons such as they. Her father was too old to engage in agriculture; it was not suitable work for the "rabbin"; the whole family had to live on the wages of the two married brothers, and this amount was insufficient. As to their prospects for employment in a city, she and her father angrily brushed aside the question. They seemed to think that the men could engage in their former occupations or easily find other work.

The couple from Sfax, in their calm and quiet manner, stressed the need of an urban center for the continued education of their children and also spoke of Ometz as a desert, suitable for the immigrants from Ait Adrar but not for them. They added that moshav settlers should have grown sons to aid in the work in the fields. Their children were still small, but they had professions which could be exercised in town. Mme. Levi added that she was a woman to do work in her home but never in the fields. They, too, had relatives already established in Israel.

Suzanne, the physician's sister, was the most emotional, and she and her husband were the first of their families to come to Israel. Dark, slim, and intense, she too spoke bitterly of the village store and the state of the schools. Her daughter of seven and son of five had been in school in Tunis for years; here they would only grow up to be peasants. She had nothing in common with the "primitives" from Ait Adrar. She showed her sewing machine, the exquisite lacework and embroidery to which she devoted her afternoons "in order not to think," the children's toys and books. In town, she claimed, she could add to the family income by sewing; here her husband's wages were insufficient to support even a decent diet, and he was too exhausted after guard duty even to go to work. Indignantly she recalled how they had been summoned at 1:00 A.M. on the last night on the boat, spoken to in Hebrew, which they could not understand, and made to sign a paper. That was how they had landed in Ometz. They had asked to be sent to a city. Now they begged at least to be transferred from this desert to a ma'abara, a transit camp.[29]

All these families maintained their shacks in scrupulous order; their children were clean and neatly dressed; they spoke of the nice clothes, for which there was no use in Ometz, packed in the suitcases they had stacked against the wall. And by October, when these conversations were held, they all were almost entirely ignored by the instructors, apart from work assignments and military instruction for the men and treatment they sought at the dispensary.

For their repudiation of life in a moshav had alienated the senior instructors. Despite initial visits and encouragement by the latter, they had refused to start gardens around their shacks, they disdained Ometz and had refused to consider transferring to Ba'aya or another moshav olim with large numbers of Tunisian settlers. Moreover, their complaints and pretensions, in their fragmentary Hebrew, had irritated Hava and Rahel, who dismissed them, saying: "They are not for Ometz, it was a mistake to have sent them here. They probably have means, and they will find places for themselves in a town." Furthermore, the puritanical aspects of the Labor-Zionist ethos, so profoundly a part of these otherwise compassionate women, were brought out by the "bourgeois"

[29] Cf. pp. 119, 190ff.

values of the Tunisian women. Their household skills freed Hava from the duty of visiting their homes, without eliciting any respect for them as persons.

Only toward Annette, promptly renamed "Hanna," was any liking shown. The fourteen-year-old daughter of the Levis attended Shulamit's classes and was acknowledged by all the village workers to be pleasant and highly intelligent. She began helping Yehudit with the kindergarten children, and regrets were expressed that such "good material" would be lost to agricultural settlement. Her quiet, good-humored family was the first of the Tunisians to leave Ometz. Mme. Levi's brother had found an apartment for them in Acre, for which they paid IL 700 as key money, supporting the instructors' contention that the Tunisians had resources of their own.

Interestingly enough, Mme. Levi's verbalizations about the immigrants from Ait Adrar showed a change between October, when their cultural inferiority was stated as one reason for leaving Ometz, and the time of the family's departure. She was present when Suzanne Bitar was then being asked to reconsider going to Ba'aya with its contingent of middle-class Tunisians, and she indignantly remarked: "What is wrong with the people of Adrar? They are good people. It is the life of a moshav that is wrong for us."

With the departure of the Levis, Suzanne became even more depressed. The coming of the rains already had turned her indignation over being in Ometz to misery. She was again pregnant, and she aged startlingly. By December, streaks of gray had appeared in her hair, deep lines on her face. She became unkempt and slovenly. Whatever the emotional tie between husband and wife, Robert obviously was no source of strength in the family. And of all the Tunisian men, he was the only one to give "trouble" to the instructors. He complained about his wound and the difficulty of the work; they found him lazy and a nuisance to deal with.

Early in December, he outraged them further by forcing his way into the courtyard behind the locked village store, where Aharon caught him taking kerosene from the supplies stored there. When the instructor told him that this was theft and had to be reported to the police, Robert trembled and pleaded that he would not steal; there just had been no kerosene left at home for cooking. Rahel, on hearing the story, took pity on the man and, typically, found a way out for all. She arranged to meet Robert "accidentally" and asked the obviously downcast man what was wrong. When he spilled the story, she advised him to tell Aharon how sorry he was and to say that he would never again do such a thing. Although Aharon first refused to exonerate Robert, he let the man's apology serve as an excuse when Rahel herself then begged him not to make a police case of the incident.

By then Suzanne's continued deterioration had won Rahel's and Hava's concern, but they did not know what to do. Therefore, they were shocked to learn, two weeks later, that the continued presence of the Tunisians in the village was actually Aharon's doing. The Jewish Agency did not insist that immigrants brought to moshvei olim through the ship to village policy [30] remain there or else forfeit all immigrant claims to housing and other assistance in getting settled. Those determined to leave could be transferred to a transit camp, and the Land Settlement Department's Absorption Section had representatives visiting the villages to arrange this. The head of the Absorption Section, Aharon suddenly recounted, had come to Ometz several times and had asked for a list of the families to be taken out of the village. But Aharon had not given him any names. He considered it his duty to keep people in Ometz. He would let the Tunisians go to another moshav olim, he declared righteously, but he would not be responsible for helping villagers go to transit camps.

He was not to be dissuaded, and Hava came to share his point of view. As the weeks passed, Suzanne, on her side, rejected the thought of a transit camp and became fixated on getting to a city. In her desperate tirades against life in Ometz, she cried out that they had sold her husband's bicycle,

[30] Cf. pp. 190–95.

everything of value they had brought except her sewing machine, even the children's toys. Around March, all four Tunisian families left Ometz, having found housing they could afford in Jaffa. Hava proudly spoke of their departure as vindicating Aharon's stand. "In the end, they took care of themselves, at no cost to the Jewish Agency."

In the meanwhile, Ometz' development had continued. Toward the end of November, the moshav federation holding companies began cultivation of the Daroma fields. Another agricultural instructor, responsible for the operation of the labor federation's company in Ometz, arrived in the village. Oded, although born and raised in a veteran moshav ovdim founded by pioneers from Russia, was not personally accepted by the instructor group. Introspective and interested in such exotic subjects, for one of his background, as Wilhelm Reich's orgone theory, he was considered "complicated" and queer by the others, particularly Amos and Shulamit, who also accused him of laziness. Nonetheless, the values and moral authority of the senior village workers precluded open rifts or quarreling among the other members of the village team. Except for an occasional shrug or muttered comment, even gossip about each other was discouraged.

Renewed work problems with the settlers had engaged Aharon and Amos before the holding company's operations began. During the peanut harvesting season in October, workers from Ometz left the fields when they discovered that the rate of pay per kilo (IL .10) was lower than that they had gotten in harvesting cotton. It also turned out that they had not been properly instructed in the peanut harvesting procedure, and they earned next to nothing for their small yields. Aharon persuaded a few settlers to return and had them observe experienced workers; they then earned a normal day's wage, although remaining discontented. When peanuts again were harvested, at the end of November, they refused the work since the wage was even lower. Although the rains had begun, making for a shortage of work, and grumbling over unemployment was constant in the village, Aharon justified their decision.

A week earlier than this, settlers went on strike when the Jewish National Fund foreman hired only twenty-five of the thirty-eight men then without other work who had been sent to him for employment. Insisting on a policy of "all or none," the settlers walked off. Always concerned about maintaining employment, Aharon hurried off to try to win more days of employment for Ometz from the Daroma regional headquarters, and he also sought out possible sources of work among private employers in the area.

The instructors' efforts to keep them employed did not stop settlers from turning on Amos two weeks later when he handled the work roster alone in Aharon's absence on other business. Again, not all the men who reported to the Jewish National Fund had been accepted. The first two to return from the recruitment point near the road were given a special job digging cesspits for new outhouses. But as the other settlers without employment returned to find the two men working, they started screaming: "We have no work! We have no bread! Give work to all or none." Even Moshe, who had not before been unemployed, joined his usually quiet father in raising a scene, and the older man pushed at Amos in his agitation. The angry men continued: "You are no good as an instructor. We don't want you. Get out of Ometz." The young man stood his ground and finally succeeded in quieting and dispersing the settlers. Scenes such as this, a rarity in Ometz, were almost daily fare in other Daroma moshvei olim; and the Ometz settlers, thanks to Aharon's assiduousness on their behalf, suffered less from unemployment than the inhabitants of most of the surrounding villages.

Once the moshav federation holding company began cultivation of the village land, there was full employment again on days that the rain did not pour down. But new sources of trouble emerged. The holding company paid a daily wage, whereas the settlers by now well knew the benefits of piecework. They dawdled through the day's work and planted in crooked lines unless continually supervised. Amos and Oded were indignant that the settlers would not understand that they were "working for themselves," and that the moshav federation holding company was set up for their instruction and to protect the investment made in the village, for which they eventually would be responsible. The young instructors also resented being regarded as foremen and could not grasp the fact that this had become a very real aspect of their role toward the settlers.

Even when piecework was forthcoming, settler discontent with the terms of employment could erupt. For example, when the time came to plant additional trees in the village, in the middle of December, the minimum day's work was digging holes for 100 seedlings. When Amos first announced this, the men reporting for work demanded that the minimum be reduced to 60 holes. Some started shouting and brandishing their spades. When Amos refused to yield, twenty men set out for the Daroma regional headquarters office in Ashkelon to protest to the assistant director of the region. Seven people remained and worked, and they each finished 130 to 150 holes before noon, earning about IL 8 apiece. The demonstrators, who included settlers not previously "trouble-makers," did not get to see the assistant director, and they returned home to hear of the achievements of those who had stayed to dig. This put a temporary end to such incidents.

Moreover, during most of December and on through February, the attention of the settlers was largely directed toward settling in their permanent homes. Preparatory to moving into the houses, almost every family purchased furniture, of which the essential item seemed to be a large wardrobe. Wardrobes are standard items in Israel, where most dwellings lack closets. The settlers from Ait Adrar usually hung clothing over the rack intended for hangers and might store sacks of food or herbs on the wardrobe floor.

The first family to purchase furniture did so as early as August, spending IL 250 on a double bed, wardrobe, and icebox. Most of the other families delayed such purchases, except for iceboxes, until shortly before occupying their houses, and many of them bought wardrobes costing IL 200 or more. The first families to buy wardrobes and other furniture did so at stores in Migdal. Then dealers began hauling six or more wardrobes at a time to Ometz and selling them right in the village. Families who still had their purchases to make were then influenced by the village team to order wardrobes through the village store from Hamashbir, the Histadrut's wholesale cooperative.[31] A few men unsuccessfully sought loans from Aharon to buy furniture, and one family refused to move into its new house until it could afford to purchase a wardrobe. A few families also bought double beds and glass-topped, finished wood tables. Net curtain material was purchased by most of the families, and Hava sewed curtains for many of the women on the sewing machine in the Women's Instruction Room. She also began to teach the women to sew by hand, man's work in Ait Adrar, and giggling young wives could be seen trying to make seams, with one end of the material held between their toes.

The first group of settlers moved into their houses during the last week of December. The day after they received the keys, they scrubbed out the houses; and they moved in on the next day, holding a housewarming party that night. This pattern was repeated over the next two months, as the other houses were progressively finished and occupied. At the housewarmings, traditional behavior asserted itself: the old men, seated at the table in the main room, read the Zohar, surrounded by male relatives and other guests; the husband served heaping platters of food; the women sat on the kitchen floor, eating after the others were finished. The instructors generally were separately fêted in the smaller room, where the younger people served them. This treatment seemed to combine elements of traditional deference to authority with a shame the younger people suddenly expressed at the manners of their elders.

In executing the contracts dealing with the houses, Aharon insisted that the head of the family, his wife, and the oldest son, where old enough, all sign. This made them all responsible, while ensuring that no one of them could put another out.

About thirty families had purchased radios in Casablanca,

[31] Cf. pp. 64, 209ff.

but only Moshe's was battery powered and could be played while the village still lacked electricity. Some families also had brought bicycles with them, and other young men in Ometz began buying bicycles around December, paying well over IL 100 for them.

When Shulamit asked them when they would use the bicycles, a few young men answered, "On the Sabbath." To the youth instructor's chiding that this would cause a tumult in Ometz, the boys answered that they did not care, and they did not care what the elders would say. A few of them later actually did ride the bicycles on the Sabbath, although out of the elders' sight. The latter either did not know that this was happening or did not want to know. At least no public demonstrations resulted.

Intensive observations in Ometz ceased at the end of December 1955, but intermittent visits over the next three months and in June and July elicted the following events, relevant to the course of settler role-socialization being traced here.

A visit to Ometz by the Sephardic Chief Rabbi of Israel early in February passed peacefully, but an attempt had been made to use it for purposes of political subversion. Shortly before the scheduled visit, the man who had initiated agitation in Ometz at its very beginning, a brother of one of the settlers, again visited the village and spoke to the settlers whom he had influenced earlier. These settlers then approached Rav Avraham and demanded that he tell the Chief Rabbi that the instructors were cruel and unjust. The rabbi refused, answering that they knew that this was not true. But Rav Avraham was saddened. He told the instructors that his people were liars and deceivers, and that he wanted to leave Ometz.

The visit of the Chief Rabbi was not the first contact of the Ometz settlers with an eminent national figure. In the middle of October, a delegation including Rav Avraham joined delegations from all the Daroma villages on a trip to Jerusalem, where they were received by the President of Israel. While not significant to the progress of moshav role-socialization, such receptions and visits impressed the immigrants and probably contributed to their sense of national identification.

Problems of guard duty again developed around February. The rabbi's roster was no longer accepted by the settlers, probably another symptom of the breakdown of diffuse traditional authority. Yehoshua decided to take responsibility for the roster on himself again to avoid further trouble.

But religion still could be used as a rationale in evading role compliance. For when the Regional Youth Center, sponsored by Youth Aliya and by the Ministries of Education, Labor, and Agriculture, was finally opened in the rural center in April, only one boy and one girl of the Ait Adrar settlers regularly attended. The girl succeeded, after a stiff fight, in winning her parents' acquiescence, for her mother worked and they wanted her to remain home with the younger children. However, four other Ait Adrar boys had begun attending the classes when the Center first was opened, only to drop out and go back to work full-time. They told Shulamit, who no longer held classes in Ometz but taught in the Youth Center together with the youth instructors of the neighboring villages, that they had left the Center because it was not religious. She considered this to be an excuse, and their desire to earn money the real reason. The planners of the Youth Center had tried to forestall this problem by paying each student slightly over IL 1 for his or her half-day's work in its fields and workshops, where agricultural and associated vocational skills were taught after morning classes in general education.

Around April the settlers also suddenly stopped purchasing bottles of sour milk in the village store. Previously it had been a very popular food and, in addition to purchasing it to take home, settlers would drink it right in the village store even when the store was most crowded. The storekeeper tried to discourage this habit and was relieved when the settlers seemed to have complied. But he soon noticed that all purchases of sour milk had stopped. To his inquiries, settlers said that they had heard it was made of donkey's milk. Hava, however, was told that a representative of the extreme religious political party had visited Ometz and had informed the settlers that milk powder was used in its manufacture, rendering it unclean according to religious law. Whatever it was that had happened, both reasons were countered. Hava obtained a certificate from the rabbinate stating that the sour milk was kosher; and the storekeeper pointed out to the settlers that there were not enough donkeys in the country to yield the necessary milk. The villagers soon started purchasing sour milk again and continued to consume it in the store.

During the spring of 1956, the village's agricultural development proceeded according to plan. Sheep were brought to the village and quartered in a common village pen, and one settler was made shepherd, all without eliciting resistance. In fact, the immigrants from Ait Adrar welcomed having sheep again, and were much perturbed when some of them died. The Daroma Region's sheep-breeding specialist later said that the loss in Ometz was only 10 percent, compared to the normal 22 percent. The moshav holding company's operations expanded, and another agricultural instructor was added to the team of village workers. The settlers from Ait Adrar labored for hours after work in the dunam of land around their houses, and they asked that more land be given over to their personal cultivation before the first additional allotment was scheduled.[32] They purchased egg-laying poultry from their own funds, and happily drew on their gardens for vegetables.

This smooth course did not extend to the village's "social development," at least its self-governing aspects. Although Aharon admitted by early May that it was time to set up an executive committee in Ometz, he delayed doing so and the settlers finally effected its creation. Having lived for over a year in Ometz and being by now informed of their rights to such an institution by relatives and fellow-workers in other villages, a delegation of settlers approached Aharon early in June 1956 and told him that they wanted an executive committee or va'ad in Ometz. Aharon immediately agreed, and

[32] Cf. p. 180.

asked them whom they wanted as its members. This they had not considered, and it was left to Aharon to draw up a list of possible candidates. Most of his suggestions were married men in their late twenties and thirties whom he had found to be hard-working, reliable, and "progressive" in their adaptation to Ometz. Three such men were chosen; and the fourth, whom Aharon specifically suggested, was young Moshe.

Once the committee was chosen, Aharon sat with it and explained his principles of work distribution and the system of moshav finances. He told the members that they had to be an example in the village, and they accepted this with great seriousness. Over the next few days, they examined accounts in the moshav office, and they went to the village store and sought out explanations on its operation. Intense suspicion over the store had been developing in Ometz, even though the village rabbi worked there, and the committee members carefully examined the scales. They were suspicious over the holes in the weights, and were reassured only when shown the government stamp on them.

This Executive Committee lasted little more than a week. Within days after it was formed, other settlers were saying that its members worked only for their own interests. On the Sabbath of that week, when Aharon was away, the majority of men assembled, deposed the committee, and elected another. According to the report of a disgusted settler from a village in the Moroccan plains, they said that they would be their own instructors, that the storekeeper and the rabbi should be thrown out, and that they would run the store themselves. On the second committee, one member from the first one, the oldest man, was retained. Three other men in their thirties, belonging to different family groups than those of the deposed members of the first committee, were chosen; and in place of Moshe, another boy of twenty, who also knew Hebrew well, was named.

Rav Avraham and Moshe both expressed themselves bitterly about the overturning of the Executive Committee and the meeting which had brought it about. Moshe termed the settlers from Ait Adrar stupid, speaking of them as "they" and dissociating himself completely. Rabbi Avraham was deeply hurt at the suspicion that had been shown toward him. He felt that an executive committee was still unnecessary in Ometz; Aharon looked after them all well. He added that he had not even attended the meeting which overthrew and changed the committee. He claimed that none of the members of either the first or second committees had been men who had influence in Ait Adrar, and that such men, when approached, had not taken an interest in being members. They felt, he said, that everyone who wanted to be on the Executive Committee should have his turn and get tired of it, and then they would form a "real" Executive Committee.

Six weeks later, when the last follow-up visit to Ometz was made, the second Executive Committee was still in existence, except that Aharon himself had dismissed its youngest member, apparently because of insolence. Nothing further could be learned about the frictions and factions associated with issues of village leadership, because all the settlers were united in sorrow over the imminent departure of Aharon and Hava.

Ometz by then had been in existence for just over fourteen months, and it was considered by the land settlement authorities to be one of the most stable of the Daroma villages. Of its original team of village workers, whose reputation had spread beyond the Daroma Region, Rahel had been the first to leave. She had volunteered for six months and then had remained three months longer. But she was turning sixty-three, and her spirit could no longer cloak her weariness. She left at the beginning of March, to be succeeded by a woman of early middle age who remained for only three months and then was replaced by a girl in her twenties. Yehoshua was the next to leave, in June. He had married during his year in Ometz, and a baby already had been born. The young officer was reassigned within the Army, and a successor appointed.

The land settlement authorities were concerned over finding successors to Aharon and Hava who could maintain at least something of the standards of service they had set. In the case of Hava, Shulamit, although by then pregnant, was the obvious replacement. She had known this and had been working at Hava's side since June. A member of Aharon's kibbutz, a somewhat younger man, agreed to succeed him, and he was prepared to bring his wife and children to Ometz. By then the school in the rural center was in operation. Children from older moshvei olim, such as the village across the road from Ometz, were also scheduled to attend it, although Ometz would retain its own school subscribing to State Religious education.

Aharon and Hava's departure coincided with the resignation of the Daroma regional director who had carried the first regional settlement program from the stages of planning through its inception and first year. The boundaries of the Daroma Region were changed, with some villages passing out of its jurisdiction and older moshvei olim entering it. Ometz, the first of the Daroma villages, had cleared its initial hurdles.

According to reports by the regional director on Ometz' development some two years later, about eight families of urban provenience had left, to be replaced by relatives of the Ait Adrar settlers, not one of whom had departed. Village agricultural development was progressing as planned, although the settlers still were far from good farmers by Israeli standards. As to Ometz' social development, the regional director shrugged and told the story of a recent discovery: one settler had stored under his mattress IL 10,000 in single bank notes of IL 1. It was a long way from Ait Adrar to a moshav ovdim.

VARIABILITY IN VILLAGE DEVELOPMENT

The relatively smooth course of development experienced by Ometz during its first two years was rather rare among moshvei olim founded during Israel's first decade. In this chapter I seek to illustrate other kinds of village histories which emerged from the confrontation of immigrants and the land settlement system. Thus, the chapter focuses on contrast and variation at the village level. But these are not its only themes. For the land settlement system set limits to the consequences of the variability it generated. It is the play of variability within these limits that I attempt to indicate here.

CONTRASTING VILLAGE HISTORIES: SHAVUR AND NISHAR

Shavur and Nishar are two of the three village units of a composite moshav [1] founded early in 1956 in a new settlement district in the northern part of Israel. Although the composite moshav represents a different pattern of village and rural center organization from that embodied in the settlement of the Daroma Region, both patterns express the principles and arrangements of comprehensive regional planning. Thus, Shavur and Nishar were similar to Ometz in having been created according to these principles and arrangements. They also were similar in that they too had adequate soil and water resources and adequate provision of development capital to become viable farming settlements according to the schedule planned. Furthermore, like Ometz, they were settled by immigrants from the Atlas Mountains of Morocco; and they were affiliated to Tnuat Hamoshavim, the principal moshav federation aligned with Mapai.

The key instructor personnel working in Shavur and Nishar during the first two years of these villages, like the initial key instructors of Ometz, were middle-aged settlers of flour-

[1] Cf. p. 179.

ishing veteran villages, in this case of classic moshvei ovdim. However, a stable instructor team did not come into being until some five months after the founding of the composite moshav. Moreover, the persons filling the post of social instructor made different decisions in regard to settlers with traditional leadership claims than had Aharon in Ometz; and the persons holding such claims had different personal attributes than the gentle Ometz rabbis. The settlers of Shavur and Nishar also manifested factioanl divisions, unlike those of Ometz, practically from the inception of these villages. However, the basis of factionalism in these two villages was different, and its outcome also was different. Thus, Shavur and Nishar provide a contrast to each other as well as a contrast to Ometz. Given the attributes these three villages shared, the contrasts between them illuminate the range of additional variables which could significantly influence moshav olim development.

Shavur and Nishar, as two units of a composite moshav, are within a few minutes' walking distance of each other and of Tikva, the third village unit. Compactly laid out, each village unit has the shape of a modified "Y." Together they constitute a rough triangle, with the facilities of the center— store, eight-grade school and school kitchen, warehouse and other storage buildings—designed to serve all three units.

The settlement authorities first planned to people Tikva, Shavur, and Nishar with a culturally homogeneous population,[2] all immigrants from the Atlas Mountains. Indeed, Meir Grossman, the emissary of Tnuat Hamoshavim who "discovered" Jews in the Atlas Mountains,[3] had promised the villagers of Ait Rahhal—who, like those of Ait Adrar, had lived in four hamlets—that they would be allowed to settle together in Israel. However, fearing that the religious moshav federation would be able to take over the composite moshav, should all its units be settled in this fashion, Tnuat Hamoshavim decided to settle Tikva with families from the city of Tunis in Tunisia.

[2] Cf. pp. 199ff.
[3] Cf. pp. 300–01, 307–8.

These families were the first to arrive in the composite moshav. Brought to Tikva in January 1956, they constituted an organized group which had been recruited for land settlement while still in Tunis.[4] They were composed mostly of young families, all French-speaking and many of them at an advanced stage of assimilation to French colonial culture and middle-class status in Tunis. On their arrival in Tikva, the first question they were reported to have asked was: "Where is the school?"

Shavur was settled a few days after Tikva by a body of immigrants from Ait Rahhal, brought directly from the boat to the village. They comprised about seventy nuclear families, not all of which could be accommodated in the sixty-family village unit of the composite moshav. The overflow was located in six houses and prospective farmsteads in Nishar. These some seventy families constituted but one segment of the immigrants from Ait Rahhal brought to the new settlement district. Another segment composed of some sixty families, originally scheduled for settlement in Tikva, was instead brought to one unit of the neighboring composite moshav. Its other two units were reserved for and later settled by organized groups of immigrants from Moroccan cities.

In addition to the overflow from Shavur, two other contingents of Atlas Mountains immigrants were brought to Nishar. One contingent consisted of fourteen families, mostly from Ait Adrar, who had been in Israel since the end of 1954. The other came to comprise thirty-eight families from another region of the Atlas Mountains, from the village of Telouet, which was the seat of the Glaoui family.[5]

The contingent of fourteen families that had been in Israel since the end of 1954 had been among the Ait Adrar immigrants brought to the Tnuat Hamoshavim transit camp on arrival in Israel.[6] But instead of going to Ometz, they had

4 Cf. p. 203.
5 Cf. pp. 259–60, note 17.
6 Cf. p. 308.

chosen to join relatives [7] already settled in a moshav affiliated to the religious moshav federation. Founded in 1949, this village had originally been peopled by immigrants from Hungary, and the remaining initial settlers still constituted the majority of its population. The families from Ait Adrar had not been happy in this village. They had felt discriminated against and looked down upon by the "Ashkenazim"; they maintained that the village's secretary still held payments due them for work they had done there; and while in the moshav they had accused the same man of having sent them to do outside work in outlying places in order to have access to their women.[8] Whatever the factual basis of their discontent, they had switched their moshav federation affiliation and were resettled in Nishar.

The immigrants from Telouet began coming to Nishar around March, some weeks after their arrival in Israel. Initially they had been sent to moshvei olim in the Jerusalem Corridor founded during the phase of improvisation.[9] However, their leader and his kinsmen were transferred to Nishar under circumstances summarized below. Other families from Telouet also were transferred or brought to Nishar, until its complement of settler units was filled.

Of the families from Telouet, some had spent years in Casablanca prior to immigration. Even those who had remained in Telouet had been closer to the currents of Moroccan national life than had the immigrants from Ait Adrar and Ait Rahhal; and changes in the political climate as well

[7] I have no information about these relatives, but only repeat here the story that members of these families told me. However, I encountered in several moshvei olim founded during the phase of improvisation immigrants from Morocco who were originally from the Atlas Mountains but who had left them for the Moroccan cities and had immigrated to Israel years before the mass exodus of Atlas Mountains Jews.

[8] Cf. p. 320 for a similar accusation leveled by the Ait Adrar immigrants in Ometz against Yitzhak. Since the families from Ait Adrar in Nishar did not repeat this accusation against their former instructor to me, I did not try to probe further to see whether it had been made in good faith or merely represented a stylized pattern, pervasive enough in the Middle East, of heaping abuse and accusations on persons perceived as opponents.

[9] The long-established families in these villages, according to informants in Nishar, were originally from Yemen.

as Messianic fervor had contributed to their decision to migrate to Israel. For Jews in Telouet had handled the sale of cigarettes,[10] which was a government monopoly. Shortly after the death of El Glaoui, one of the traders was warned by an illegal nationalist band, fighting against French rule, to cease selling cigarettes. However, he continued to supply certain customers, including a boy who turned out to be associated with the guerrilla band; and he was burned alive as an example. This incident had precipitated the decision of the Telouet immigrants to leave for Israel.

This review of the background of the settlers of Nishar indicates a salient difference between them and the settlers of both Shavur and Ometz. Those in Shavur, like the Ometz settlers from Ait Adrar, constituted a body of transplanted families. Moreover, even after the immigrants from Ait Adrar were supplemented in Ometz by families not from the Atlas Mountains, clear-cut boundaries did not crystallize between those who remained in the village. The Nishar settlers, in contrast, consisted of three sharply differentiated segments. Even the old neighbors from the adjacent territories of Ait Adrar and Ait Rahhal remained separate groups in the village.

A less salient difference between the settlers of Nishar and those of the other two villages was that the majority of the Nishar settlers had previously been in moshvei olim created during the phase of improvisation. Furthermore, they had constituted a minority of new families in these villages, surrounded by settlers who had been there much longer than they and who, in several villages, were of very different background.

When Tikva and Shavur were settled, only a social instructor, agricultural instructor, and Ministry of Health nurse [11] for the mother and child clinic had been assigned to the composite moshav; and before the end of January an

[10] Jews in Telouet, according to informants, had been craftsmen, traders, and moneylenders, and they had also distilled brandy, which they sold in Marrakesh (also cf. p. 259, notes 16 and 17).
[11] Cf. p. 140.

instructress was added. Of these, the social instructor was dismissed for incompetence and negligence less than a month after his appointment; and the instructress, a young girl from Morocco, did not remain either. The nurse, despite her officially peripheral role in village affairs, played a major role in the reception of the settlers from Ait Rahhal. A girl in her twenties and a native Israeli of Moroccan descent, she not only knew Moroccan Arabic but also had the ability to take command and gain the willing collaboration of those empowered to deal with a situation but uncertain of how to go about it. She served as translator when the Atlas Mountains immigrants arrived, helped to house and settle the families, and attended to all their nursing needs until a Sick Fund nurse arrived. She also oriented the instructress who replaced the one who had left and initially accompanied her on her visits to the families.

This instructress, Miriam Godovski, was a middle-aged woman originally from Russia, and a pioneer settler of one of the first moshvei ovdim, which was located just east of the new settlement district. Miriam continued to live at home, traveling back and forth daily by bus and remaining overnight in the village center once or twice a week. During the hours she spent in the composite moshav, she worked with the immigrants no less conscientiously than Hava did in Ometz and she engaged in much the same kinds of activities with the families from the Atlas Mountains.

Before the departure of the first social instructor, Meir Grossman himself, newly returned from Morocco, was designated as social instructor of both this composite moshav and the one adjacent to it. Only one unit of the latter was settled as yet, that one peopled by immigrants from Ait Rahhal. The team of personnel at this period of the composite moshav's history can be compared with the Ometz team at an equivalent period of its history. The core of both teams shared certain attributes: the instructor and instructress were both veteran Labor-Zionists and middle-aged people, and a devoted nurse worked in collaboration with them. A young man, in this case a post-statehood immigrant from Rumania, served as agricultural instructor. However, the agricultural instructor of the composite moshav was neither simultaneously nor primarily responsible for village security, as was initially the case in Ometz.

Indeed, the sphere of military security was one in which organizational arrangements differed between the new settlement region and the new settlement district. In the former, which was one of the areas of Israel most subject to infiltration from across the frontiers, the Army was in charge of security. In the latter, which was an area relatively untroubled by armistice violations and depredations, the border police were responsible for watching the frontiers. Although military instructors were assigned to the composite moshav, they played no part in general village affairs, and their presence was even less noticeable than the daily and nightly visits of the border police patrol. Thus, military instruction and guard duty constituted relatively segregated facets of village life, as compared to their coordination with other aspects of village organization in Ometz, and this difference was correlated with the extremely peripheral role which the military instructors had vis-à-vis the other instructors.

In the sphere of health provisions also, the villages in the new settlement district articulated with the organizations implicated in Israel's rural development in a different fashion than did the villages in the new settlement region. For the Ministry of Health maintained its services separate from those of the Histadrut's Sick Fund here. Nonetheless, as a result of the personal attributes of the nurses assigned by each organization to the composite moshav, the Sick Fund's nurse rather than the nurse attached to the Ministry of Health held a marginal position in relation to the village instructors and even to the settlers from the Atlas Mountains. The Sick Fund's nurse, a young man who was a recent immigrant from Morocco, took up residence in the Sick Fund dispensary, for the time being located in Tikva at some distance from the composite moshav center. He also established a liaison with a settler girl in Tikva, despite having a wife and family in a nearby city. He considered the Atlas Mountains immigrants as primitives, and remained aloof from the instructors. Indeed, he soon developed the feeling that the latter were prejudiced against him, although successive members of the instructor group spoke favorably of his professional skill and showed no disposition to deprecate him or pass judgment on his personal life.

Military security and health were not the only areas in which the villages of the new settlement district were linked to the country's public bureaucracies differently than were the villages of the new settlement region. Their articulation with the Land Settlement Department itself differed during their first year. For the composite moshav was constituted as part of a Land Settlement Department district of a much larger region,[12] rather than in the framework of a new settlement region whose regional office administered the villages directly during their first year.[13] The new settlement district as an administrative unit of its region did not command staff resources in any way equivalent to those of the Daroma Region. For example, the director of the new settlement district was a veteran employee of the Land Settlement Department with neither the national prestige and connections nor the impressive personal endowments of the gifted young man specially chosen and trained to direct the settlement of the Daroma. In addition, the district was not known to engage the interest of Israel's Prime Minister, as was the case with the settlement of the Daroma.

Thus, the villages of the new settlement district were at a disadvantage, in comparison to those of the new settlement region, in the competition for scarce resources, specifically for personnel to fill the instructor roles. Furthermore, the Land Settlement Department district officials did not exercise the same kind of vigilance over village affairs as that shown in the Daroma by its Land Settlement Department regional authorities. Meir Grossman, Miriam Godovski, and a single agricultural instructor were for almost two months responsible for the development of all three village units of

12 Cf. pp. 228–29, 233–35.
13 Cf. pp. 304–5.

the composite moshav, which had a population of 180 families when the full settler complement was reached; and Meir had the additional responsibility of the neighboring composite moshav.

It was Meir who sought out the leader of the families from Telouet and arranged to transfer him and the remainder of the first contingent of Telouet families to Nishar. Rabbi David Peretz, then a man of thirty-eight, was originally from Telouet, where his father also had been a rabbi. Having gone to Casablanca in his teens to study, Rabbi David remained there, achieved ordination, and had become head of a religious school before he left for Israel. Withal, he retained close ties with the Jews of Telouet. Meir Grossman had known Rabbi David in Morocco and had a high regard for his abilities. Indeed, the rabbi stood out from all the other Atlas Mountains immigrants by virtue of his sophistication and smooth intelligence; and he had an ample command of spoken and written Hebrew as well as the learning and prestige associated with his status.

Meir was swamped by the plethora of his duties as instructor, and he considered Rabbi David eminently qualified for settler leadership and village responsibilities. Therefore, he attempted to make the rabbi his assistant and intermediary with the settlers of Nishar and Shavur. But whereas Rabbi David dominated the immigrants from Telouet, the other Atlas Mountains immigrants did not grant his right to secular authority.

Within Nishar, the settlers originally from Ait Adrar had undergone notable acculturation during the period they had spent in Israel. They owned livestock and household property; they had the best-furnished and most ordered homes of Shavur and Nishar and had planted kitchen gardens; the men spoke fluent if crude Hebrew, and most of them dressed in European-style clothing. Moshav veterans in comparison to the other settlers, they still smarted from the unjust treatment they felt they had received in the village they had left, and they were not prepared to be subordinate to Rabbi David.

The Shavur settlers and their overflow in Nishar had their

own claimants to village leadership. One of these was Haim Dayan, a man of the same age as Rabbi David, who had served as rabbi of his hamlet in Ait Rahhal, as had his father before him. Although, like Rabbi Avraham of Ometz, Haim Dayan was actually a shohet, a ritual slaughterer, rather than a rabbi, he served as prayer leader in the Shavur synagogue. He also had been Meir Grossman's intermediary in his contact with the other Jews of Ait Rahhal; he had worked in the Jewish Agency registration office in Casablanca and there learned to write Hebrew as well as to speak it better than anyone else in Shavur. Although he was treated as the spokesman of Shavur by representatives of the Israeli scene, his leadership claims were not accepted by other Shavur settlers without opposition, as is discussed below.

Nonetheless, the Shavur settlers were united in their opposition to the authority which Meir Grossman had given Rabbi David Peretz, and they and their old neighbors of Ait Adrar banded together in seeking to get it revoked. The two villages were agitated by crises, and the opposition to Rabbi David won.

In the meanwhile, representatives of the religious moshav federation established contact with the Atlas Mountains immigrants, and all of them united in demanding State religious Trend education. This Meir Grossman vehemently opposed, fearing that it would lead to a transfer of village federation affiliation. During a period of renewed crises the Atlas Mountains immigrants turned against all the village workers. They tried to examine nurse and instructress on their knowledge of religious law; they chased after the village workers, asking them what political party they belonged to; and when the nurse started inoculating the children, she was accused of trying to baptize them.

Meir Grossman could not prevent the settlers from exercising their legal right to vote for the school trend they desired. The Atlas Mountains immigrants chose State Religious education, whereas the settlers of Tikva continued to support State education. Thus, a second school was built in the center of the composite moshav, again vitiating in provisions for education the attempt under regional settlement to provide more economical and efficient village services than hitherto.[14]

Meir resigned from his post within about three months after he had assumed it. However, both settlers and the other village workers believed that he had been dismissed. Indeed, the Shavur settlers had signed a petition to the Land Settlement Department asking that he be removed as their instructor. During the last weeks he was in the composite moshav his prestige had so declined that a more recently appointed social instructor, formerly a petty official in the Jewish Agency and ostensibly under Meir's authority, insisted that he, not Meir, would hand the settlers their pay.

After Meir's departure, this instructor replaced him, assisted by the original agricultural instructor and another one who had been assigned to the composite moshav during Meir's tenure. However, Meir's successor held office only briefly. He shouted at the settlers, fought with the other village workers, and was unable to take hold of village affairs.

During June 1956, over five months after the founding of Tikva and Shavur, the instructor team of the composite moshav became stable. The moshav federation was able to recruit as social instructor another middle-aged pioneer settler of a veteran moshav ovdim. Ben-Harif, always addressed and referred to by last name alone, was a Third Aliya immigrant from Poland, prominent in the affairs of the federation, who brought to the job driving energy, a sharp sardonic intelligence, and a style of behavior even more authoritarian than that of Aharon in Ometz. Another social instructor, also a middle-aged veteran settler, was appointed social instructor of the adjacent composite moshav, two units of which were settled by that time. Its administration henceforth was completely independent of that of its neighbor.

At the same time that Ben-Harif took office, a third agricultural instructor was assigned to the composite moshav; and a second instructress soon was recruited. The two more

14 Cf. p. 178.

recent agricultural instructors were men in their thirties, both post-statehood immigrants; one was from Iraq and the other from Hungary.[15] The new instructress was a friend of Miriam's, a woman of the same approximate age and a member of the same veteran moshav ovdim.[16] A division of labor was then effected as follows: each of the agricultural instructors became responsible in his domain for one unit of the composite moshav; and Miriam concentrated on the Shavur families, with some attention to Tikva, whereas her friend worked in Nishar. This team's resemblances to the Ometz village team extended to the climate of fellowship they maintained and were able to create among most of the other village workers.

Nonetheless, Ben-Harif's assumption of command over the

[15] Married men, they both were settlers in nearby villages, one in a moshav olim founded during the phase of improvisation, the other in a moshav ovdim founded prior to Israel's independence. They returned home several times a week and their own farms were taken care of by their wives. More precisely, one of them, who recently had undergone an operation, rented out his farm—something of an aberration from moshav principles—and his wife took care of the chicken flock.

[16] Prior to the appointment of this instructress, the sister of the Sick Fund nurse had assisted Miriam, but was dismissed by Ben-Harif soon after he took office as the composite moshav's instructor. He felt that the girl was not qualified to serve as instructress, since she herself was a recent immigrant without any experience of moshav life. However, Miriam and the Ministry of Health nurse agreed that the girl had worked well; and they showed signs of embarrassment in speaking of her, and of Ben-Harif's decision to dismiss her. The Sick Fund nurse, on his part, cited his sister's dismissal as evidence of prejudice against immigrants from Morocco (cf. above, p. 387). He also attributed the appointment of the second instructress, Ruth Harari, to protektzia (cf. pp. 142–43), citing the recent marriage of Ruth's niece and Miriam's son as evidence of this. In fact, Ruth was the most reflective person I encountered in the instructress role, the most aware that social disorganization can accompany rapid change, and the most sensitive to the immigrants' perceptions of their new situation. Thus, she never commented on the degree of cleanliness of a household or of its members except to praise, and she never gave directives. Rather, she behaved like an experienced friend, ready to transmit skills or otherwise help the Nishar women according to their felt needs in the new environment. For example, she gave Hebrew lessons to a group of six young wives who wanted and had the time for them; she taught women who commented on Israeli dishes how to prepare them; she had almost a trained caseworker's approach to family problems. Ruth's obvious qualifications for and success in the instructress role remained lost on the Sick Fund nurse and in no way mitigated his bitterness over his sister's dismissal or his conviction that it and Ruth's appointment were manifestations of a mixture of prejudice and protektzia.

affairs of the composite moshav, like that of Aharon in Ometz, brooked no interference with his exercise of authority. Apart from occasional consultations with Miriam, he informed the other instructors and village workers of decisions not immediately relevant to their work only as it suited his mood. Indeed, gossip among the others soon had it that he made major decisions concerning village administration and finances without consulting or even always informing the Land Settlement Department district officials.

However, unlike Aharon in Ometz, he considered it his duty to initiate the settlers as rapidly as possible into moshav self-governing and administrative arrangements. Before the end of his first month as instructor he had instituted an executive committee in each village unit. Soon after, he appointed settlers to aid him in routine secretarial aspects of village administration. He also asked each village unit to choose one member of its executive committee as work supervisor, to join him and the agricultural instructors in decisions concerning work allocation.

The size of the executive committee in each village was six persons, as determined by Ben-Harif in conjunction with Miriam. Given the Nishar factions, four places on its Executive Committee were allocated to the immigrants from Telouet and two places to those from Ait Adrar. The overflow from Shavur was allowed a nonvoting observer as representative. Rabbi David Peretz was made head of the Executive

Principal Names Appearing in the Text

Village	Shavur	Nishar	Tikva	Ometz
Settler origins	Ait Rahhal (Atlas Mts.)	Telouet (Atlas Mts.) Ait Adrar (Atlas Mts.) Ait Rahhal (Atlas Mts.)	Tunis	Ait Adrar (Atlas Mts.)
Settlers with leadership claims	Haim Dayan Yitzhak Cohen Shalom Cohen (father of Yitzhak)	Rabbi David Peretz	not discussed	Rabbi Avraham Rabbi Shlomo (father of Rabbi Avraham)
Instructors	Meir Grossman Ben-Harif	Meir Grossman Ben-Harif	Meir Grossman Ben-Harif	Aharon Barzel Yitzhak
Instructresses	Miriam Godovski	Ruth Harari		Hava Barzel

Committee. However, electing a single individual from the committee to serve as work supervisor was beyond the level of consensus that could be achieved in Nishar. Its settlers refused to vote, despite Ben-Harif's repeated pressure on them to do so. In consequence, he refused to discuss with them the decisions that he and their agricultural instructor made in assigning them work.

While Ben-Harif met with the executive committees at least once a month to explain moshav organization and inform them of current issues of village development as well as to explain their duties and rights as settlers, he actually allowed the committees no more than nominal decision-making rights. For example, the Tikva Executive Committee once told a newly appointed Land Settlement Department district instructor [17] in charge of seedlings how many people to hire for the job at hand and who they were to be. All the members of this committee were gallicized young people who had attended secondary school in Tunis and had easily grasped the principles of moshav organization. Indeed, one of them had been a bookkeeper and another had clerked in a lawyer's office. The instructor accepted their instructions as binding, although the workers they assigned exceeded the number of work posts allotted by the district office. As soon as the matter came to Ben-Harif's attention, he immediately revoked the Tikva Executive Committee's decision and informed both the instructor and the settlers that no such actions could be taken without his consent.

It was from Tikva that Ben-Harif chose a secretary for the composite moshav, selecting the original organizer of its settler group, a man who was a member of the Executive Committee and relatively fluent in Hebrew. However, Ben-Harif did not choose Rabbi David Peretz of Nishar for any secretarial work. Instead, Rabbi David was given the position of assistant in the store of the composite moshav; and his appointment did not renew dissension in Nishar beyond the usual level of factional grumbling. Hostility to Rabbi David

[17] Cf. p. 234.

occasionally was expressed to members of the instructor team by some of the immigrants, including persons from Telouet,[18] but the rabbi was publicly genial to everyone in the village and complaints about him remained privately voiced.

Ben-Harif's careful handling of the Nishar factions was strained only once during his first six months as instructor. During August, the men originally from Ait Adrar staged a demonstration over work conditions, specifically over a period of unemployment in the composite moshav; this was the first time such a period had occurred since the villages were founded. When they renewed demonstrations, this time as active supporters of a work strike led by the most gallicized settlers of Tikva,[19] Ben-Harif asked the head of the Absorption Section [20] of the Land Settlement Department to visit Nishar and threaten the fourteen families with the possibility of removal from the village. This man had arranged the transfer from their previous village and already had paid visits to the composite moshav and stopped to see the families. He agreed to Ben-Harif's request, although the threat was neither meant seriously nor could it have been carried out without great difficulty.[21] But he scheduled his visit to Nishar for the evening when its synagogue was being dedicated. Since he could hardly intrude his message into the occasion, the visit was postponed. Before it could take place, the strike had

[18] Thus, one settler from Telouet had told the Nishar agricultural instructor that Rabbi David took key money from all new families entering the village and that he collected IL 2 per week from every household in Nishar. The rabbi served as translator in meetings that the instructors and land settlement authorities held with the settlers, and the agricultural instructor was also warned that the rabbi was not a reliable translator. And one old man wept to the instructress, Ruth, that he had been a religious leader (haham) in Telouet, but that in Nishar Rabbi David had "made him nothing."

[19] The strike was called in protest over work conditions attending the particular piece of work that brought the period of unemployment to an end. This work was digging the ditches in which irrigation pipe was to be laid, and the employer was the Jewish Agency itself. The settlers protested both the difficulty of the work, since the ground was very hard, and the fact that payment was made according to the amount of digging accomplished rather than by the day.

[20] Cf. p. 230.

[21] Cf. pp. 196–98.

been settled with some concessions to the settlers' demands,[22] and they had quieted down.

Ben-Harif's concern with not exacerbating settler factionalism did not extend from Nishar to Shavur. For Haim Dayan's leadership claims and their acceptance by the land settlement authorities were disputed by Yitzhak Cohen, a man of thirty. Actually, Yitzhak, who could communicate in Hebrew, spoke for his father as much as, or more than, for himself. Shalom Cohen, then over sixty, his second wife, twenty years younger, and their five young children occupied one house in Shavur. Yitzhak, his wife, and child occupied another house, and his mother spent much of her time with them, although officially listed as residing with two other younger sons who had been given a house in Nishar. This domestic situation in no way interfered with the solidarity of the Cohens.

From the same hamlet in Ait Rahhal as Haim Dayan, Shalom Cohen had been a merchant rather than a craftsman, whereas Rav Haim had practiced shoemaking. Shalom Cohen had held extensive lands in Ait Rahhal, security for loans he had made to their Berber owners; [23] he had owned a house in Demnat; and he had represented the interests of the local Jews before the Berber authorities.[24] In sum, his status in Ait Rahhal had been higher than that of Haim Dayan.

None of the aging men in the two villages stood as candidates for the executive committees. Thus, the claims of the Cohens were realized through the election of Yitzhak Cohen rather than of Shalom to the Shavur committee. However, Haim Dayan not only was elected to the committee but became its head. He also was elected work supervisor of the village, a choice strongly backed by the instructors. As head

---

[22] The first day of the new year (Rosh Hashana) had come two days after the strike was called. When work was resumed after the holiday, bulldozers were brought in to help with the digging where the ground was hardest. The immigrants from the Atlas Mountains promptly returned to work, unlike the immigrants from Tunis in Tikva. And despite the complaints about piecework, which had been voiced by most of the men of Shavur and Nishar, the work was in fact quite profitable.

[23] Cf. p. 260.

[24] Cf. p. 263.

of the committee, he was the person kept most fully informed of matters of village administration. Indeed, Ben-Harif expected him to transmit issues and decisions to the other settlers and gain their acquiescence. Dayan also was called on to represent Shavur at all public functions and in meetings with agents of the public bureaucracies. Furthermore, as work supervisor of Shavur, he joined Ben-Harif and the agricultural instructor in decisions over work assignments to the settlers. In addition, Ben-Harif appointed him to aid in routine secretarial duties.

To Yitzhak Cohen's open protests over the concentration of posts held by Haim Dayan, Ben-Harif turned a deaf ear. He maintained that Dayan was the most capable man in Shavur, the quickest learner, and a person with whom it was possible to work, whereas old Shalom Cohen was unfit for moshav life. Ben-Harif also brushed aside as trivial the evidences of resentment toward Dayan's position increasingly shown by a wider body of Shavur settlers than the Cohens and their nucleus of firm supporters. For Dayan, unlike Rabbi David Peretz in Nishar, was an excitable man who lost his temper easily. He did not hesitate to shout at the other settlers, to order them about, or even to call them such names as "donkey" in public. As prayer leader in the synagogue, he would display irritation toward members of the congregation who had lost their place in the prayer book. Moreover, the concentration of offices he held left him vulnerable to the resentment of others over conditions in the village. Thus, while he was as vociferous as anyone else in protesting the lack of work in Shavur during the two-week period of unemployment in August, he, as well as the instructors and the Jewish Agency, was mentioned in complaints by other settlers.

Getting no satisfaction from Ben-Harif, Yitzhak Cohen visited the Tnuat Hamoshavim offices in Tel Aviv in September to protest, among other things, the partiality being shown Haim Dayan. When the instructor learned of this visit he responded indulgently. He told the young man that he was pleased at this show of initiative, but that his, Ben-Harif's, judgment was trusted by the moshav movement. Yitzhak

Cohen than warned the instructors, not for the first time, that he could break up Shavur and would do so if the situation remained unchanged.

Early in October, a rumor began that the religious moshav federation was again in touch with the immigrants from Ait Rahhal. Two months earlier Ben-Harif, unlike Aharon in Ometz, had expressed a detached attitude toward the possibility that the religious moshav federation might take over the villages settled by Atlas Mountains immigrants. This was in the context of a discussion of the moshav federation's decision to bring the immigrants from Tunis to Tikva and settle the other contingent of immigrants from Ait Rahhal in the neighboring composite moshav. Ben-Harif then had deplored this arrangement as shortsighted and conducive to settler dissatisfactions in both composite moshavim. He maintained that he would try to get the two settler groups interchanged even if it should cost the Jewish Agency IL 500 per family. "So what if the Atlas Mountains immigrants go over to Poel Mizrahi?" he asked rhetorically. "The important thing is that they stay in the moshav."

But when faced, two months later, with the possibility that the settlers of Shavur again were in touch with the religious moshav federation, Ben-Harif immediately acted. He warned Haim Dayan that he, Ben-Harif, would leave the village if the rumor were true. In response, Dayan took an oath that he was not in touch with Poel Mizrahi, and he brought old Shalom Cohen to swear with him.

This evidence that old Cohen still was a person of standing among the immigrants from Ait Rahhal, and that Haim Dayan himself acknowledged this standing, did not sway Ben-Harif's judgment that old Cohen was not important to Shavur's future. And whether or not the old man's oath was truthful in October, there could be no doubt by the end of the year that the Cohens and their core of supporters had enlisted with the religious moshav federation.

Around January 1957, one year after Shavur was founded, some fifteen families, including the Cohens, openly transferred affiliation from Tnuat Hamoshavim to the moshav federation of Poel Mizrahi. At about the same time, a crisis developed in Nishar and among families who were still willing to remain in Shavur over the scheduled transfer of the first allotment of land from the Tnuat Hamoshavim holding company's management to the families' direct cultivation and responsibility.[25] Unlike the settlers of Ometz,[26] those of Shavur resisted this transfer, preferring to continue work on a daily wage basis.

I do not know to what extent this issue entered into the decision of other families in Shavur to turn to the religious moshav federation.[27] However, by the summer of 1957 all but eight families had done so and were in the process of leaving the village. The eight families who were remaining consisted of Haim Dayan and the hard core of his adherents. No settlers had departed from Nishar, except the immigrants from Ait Rahhal who had not been accommodated in Shavur and who were related to families leaving there.

Some of the people who left Shavur apparently regretted this decision within several months of making it. For in the fall of 1957 I had occasion to visit a new settlement town in the Negev and there encountered, just as I was leaving, some of the men I had known in Shavur. We had no opportunity to speak, but they ran after the car in which I was being driven away, crying, "Take us back to Shavur!"

Meanwhile, Poland had permitted the renewed immigration of some of its remaining Jews to Israel; and a contingent of families from Poland had filled the fifty-two vacant households in Shavur. On a brief visit to the composite moshav in December 1957, I heard from Miriam Godovski, still working there as instructress, of the village's accelerated development since these hard-working settlers had arrived. As for the eight families from Ait Rahhal still in Shavur, they had no representation on its Executive Committee nor any real

25 Cf. p. 180.
26 Cf. p. 376.
27 Since my period of sustained observation in the composite moshav ended during October 1956, I could not watch the decision-making process among the settlers who left Shavur.

contact with its new settlers. She expected that they soon would leave the village.

VARIABLES IN VILLAGE DEVELOPMENT:
THE EVIDENCE OF OMETZ, SHAVUR, AND NISHAR

The early histories of Shavur and Nishar contrast with that of Ometz, and the description of these histories also has differed. The history of Ometz has been presented from as holistic a perspective as I could contrive; those of Shavur and Nishar have been reviewed with the focus on variables that may illuminate the contrasting outcomes possible in three moshvei olim sharing the attributes noted. Therefore, a deterministic bias may be implicit in the selection of data presented on Shavur and Nishar. If so, such a bias does violence to one of the most common characteristics of the moshvei olim during the decade of the 1950s: the unpredictability of events in the village. Thus, during the first four months that Ometz was in existence, the stability of its settler population was far from assured; and during the first three months of Ben-Harif's tenure as social instructor of the composite moshav, Nishar seemed more threatened with potential dissolution than Shavur.

Moreover, I suggest, almost any specification of variables by means of which the moshvei olim can be characterized and compared can have very limited value for predicting the course of development of a specific village. Thus, Ometz, Nishar, and Shavur, during the period under review, shared variables that can be and have been suggested as conducive to successful moshav olim development, e.g., favorable ecological conditions, careful planning of agricultural and economic development, and a culturally homogeneous population of rural provenience.[28] In addition to these attributes,

28 These were the factors most stressed between 1955 and 1958 by Land Settlement Department officials committed to rationalization and to mitigation of the influence of Labor-Zionist ideology on land settlement policy. These factors have also been pointed out since then by some of the students of the moshvei olim. Thus, Weintraub and Lissak (1964a:102–7) note the importance of physical and material conditions in influencing village development; they also comment (in Rokach 1964c:43–44) on the faster tempo of development in villages founded during the phase of

the initial settlers of Ometz and Shavur had a basis for solidarity in their ramifying kinship ties. Moreover, the key village workers for all three settlements were hard-working and devoted middle-aged veteran settlers, and their age was associated with the right to authority in the value system of immigrants from the Atlas Mountains.

Yet the villages also differed in many ways, and the review of Shavur and Nishar has focused on some of the ways in which they were unlike Ometz and unlike each other during the period under review. For example, they differed from Ometz in the initial instability of their instructor personnel, as contrasted to the stability of the Ometz village team; in manifesting settler factionalism, which was absent in

rationalization as compared to those founded during the phase of improvisation; and they consider cultural and social homogeneity of a village's population to be "a very important condition for the success of moshavim" (Weintraub and Lissak 1964c:129). Weingrod (1966:179–80) also considers settler homogeneity more conducive than heterogeneity to village development. In an earlier chapter I noted both the stress placed by regional planning on the peopling of villages with homogeneous populations and the difficulties involved in bringing the idea of homogeneity into correspondence with the complex and variable social distinctions significant to the disparate immigrant population (cf. pp. 199–203, notes 20, 21). And while Weintraub and Lissak as well as Weingrod accept the idea that settler homogeneity contributes to village development, they use the term "homogeneity" differently; and their usages differ in turn from the way in which settlement authorities used the word during the years 1955–58.

Thus, Weintraub and Lissak clearly do not refer to ethnic groups classified on the basis of country or locality of origin, for they give as an example of a "homogeneous" type of village one peopled by immigrants from Yugoslavia (divided into two distinct subgroups, one "Ashkenzi" and the other "Sephardi"), from Rumania, and "with an admixture of other Central European, Oriental and local families" (Weintraub and Lissak: 1964c:130). In contrast, they consider heterogeneous a village settled by immigrants who were all from central Yemen, although from different localities within this region (Weintraub and Lissak: 1964c:142). In these two cases and others which they summarize, the terms "homogeneity" and "heterogeneity" clearly do not refer to consistent classes of attributes characterizing the settler populations of the villages in their sample. Instead, the authors use the terms to refer to varying constellations of factors, which seemed to have contributed to or mitigated against settler solidarity in these villages. Indeed, they explicitly make the presence or absence of such solidarity the primary basis for distinguishing a "homogeneous" village settled by immigrants of diverse provenience from a "heterogeneous" one.

Weingrod is more consistent in the referents which he gives the terms "homogeneity" and "heterogeneity," in that these terms refer to a specific difference in the social origins of the settlers of a village. How-

Ometz; and in their instructors' early creation of posts conferring authority or the appearance of authority over the other settlers on those selected to fill them, as contrasted to Aharon's policy of deferring for as long as possible the initiation of such posts.

Shavur and Nishar differed from each other in that the former was settled by transplanted members of the same preimmigration community and the latter by several groups of people of different provenience and presettlement experience. They also differed in the kind of groupings that can be termed factions: those of Nishar consisted of bounded units, each composed of a group of different provenience; those of Shavur emerged within a body of settlers from the

ever, he makes use of only a single index of differentiation: the rural or urban provenience of the settlers brought together in a village. Thus, while he limits his sample of villages to those settled primarily by immigrants from Morocco (Weingrod 1966:179,184ff.), his criteria of homogeneity and heterogeneity, i.e., common rural, urban, or mixed rural and urban background, do not take into account whether a village's settlers are of diverse or similar geographic provenience within Morocco, whether or not they shared a common preimmigration local tradition, or, among those of urban provenience, whether or not they shared other attributes, such as educational and/or class background and extent of acculturation to French colonial culture. Yet these and other attributes also could be considered relevant to the classification of a village population as homogeneous or heterogeneous.

Thus, the population of Nishar certainly could be considered less "homogeneous" than that of Shavur, but Weingrod's one-dimensional criteria would obliterate the differences between them. Similarly, the use of his criteria would obliterate the differences between the settler populations of two neighboring villages, both settled by immigrants from Kurdistan, that are discussed by Weintraub and Bernstein (1966). The latter categorize the settlers of the village which developed more successfully as more homogeneous than those of the other village. However, the village considered homogeneous by Weintraub and Bernstein was settled by immigrants who were from different localities in Kurdistan, although from the same district. Yet Weintraub and Lissak (1964c:142–43) stress the importance of origin from the same locality among immigrants of traditional background in their assignment of villages so populated to the category "homogeneous" or "heterogeneous." This is illustrated by their assignment, cited above, of the village settled by immigrants from different localities in central Yemen to the category "heterogeneous." It might be added that Weintraub and Bernstein cite the earlier publication in support of the specific points they make in their article (Weintraub and Bernstein 1966:516).

Since I do not attempt to link the course of village development to the homogeneity or heterogeneity of settler populations, I make no effort to develop criteria for the assignment of these populations to one category or the other.

same place of origin and linked by ramifying kinship ties, and the factions were not clearly bounded.

Ometz and Shavur were like each other and unlike Nishar in that both were initially settled by sixty families who were from the same place of origin and were related to each other. Moreover, both these settler bodies experienced a defection of approximately one-fourth their original number. But the timing of the defection relative to the village's founding differed, as did the composition of each settlement's population within two years after it was founded. Ometz' settlers by then consisted overwhelmingly of immigrants from the Atlas Mountains, although the village had over eighty farmsteads. In contrast, Shavur with its sixty farmsteads retained only eight families from the Atlas Mountains, and they were expected to depart soon.

Given the variables in which these three villages were paired and those in which they differed, of which the list just given could be extended, the following question may be asked: Can the contrasting outcomes in these villages, as of the period under review, be related in a systematic fashion to contrasting variables? My answer to this question is no.

I answer no for several reasons. One reason has to do with the number of features in which these villages initially differed and in which they differed increasingly as their histories unfolded. I consider these differences to be too numerous to permit their relevance to village outcome to be unambiguously dissociated from their historical context. For example, the settlers of Ometz initially were housed in temporary dwellings, whereas those of Shavur and Nishar were not.[29] Those of Ometz helped to build their permanent houses and experienced much anticipation of, preparation for, and pleasure in moving into them, all of which was absent in Shavur and Nishar. One may speculate whether the settlers of Shavur might not have developed a greater sense of commitment to the village as their home and been less preoccupied with the issues that seem associated with the village's breakup, had

29 Cf. pp. 180, 306.

they too helped to build their houses and experienced a period of anticipation over and preparation for occupying them. But one can do no more than speculate. Indeed, a period of residence in temporary housing more prolonged than that in Ometz seems to have been one of many factors that embittered some settlers of villages founded during the phase of improvisation.

Furthermore, the variables I consider most significant for village outcome, at least in the three villages now under review, are of the kind commonly known as interaction variables, i.e., aspects of village life involving people's actions in relation to other people. I consider the process of interaction over a period of time in these villages to have been too complex to be reduced to a series of comparable factors that can be examined for systematic variation in relation to the contrasting village outcomes. This line of reasoning has implications that go beyond these three villages and beyond the universe of moshvei olim. Therefore, before continuing it, I shall illustrate it through analyzing the immediate data.

My explanation of the contrasting outcomes in Ometz and Shavur begins with a feature in which their initial settler populations were similar and which may not be salient from the discussion so far. This feature was the presence, among the founding settlers of Ometz as well as those of Shavur, of several men who could assert leadership claims on traditional grounds. For in addition to Rabbi Avraham and his father, old Rav Shlomo, Ometz' first arrivals included the clever former merchant who in Ait Adrar had been an intermediary with the Berber administration.[30] He obviously was a person who still had influence among at least some of Ometz' initial settlers. However, he was also the principal leader of the group demanding affiliation with the religious moshav federation, whereas the rabbis committed themselves to remaining in Ometz and sought to convince undecided settlers not to leave the village.[31] When the former merchant saw that the majority of families were not going to transfer to

[30] Cf. p. 263, note 30.
[31] Cf. p. 317.

· 403 ·

Nshima, he too sought to change sides. But permission to remain in Ometz was denied him.[32] In Nshima he acted as leader of the families from Ait Adrar in their disputes with the immigrants from Djerba who were their fellow settlers in that village; and he later became one of Nshima's leaders.[33]

This man's departure from Ometz may explain, in conjunction with several other factors, the village's contrasting history as compared to that of Shavur. The most important of the other factors may be: (1) Aharon's delay in creating posts (including those inherent in the existence of an executive committee) giving settlers secular authority or the appearance of it over others; (2) the settlers' acquiescence in Aharon's exercise of authority; and (3) Rabbi Avraham's and his father's lack of interest in exercising secular leadership.

Moreover, these factors all contrast with elements which may be abstracted from the history of Shavur and from that of Nishar as it bears on the history of Shavur, e.g., (1) both

[32] Cf. p. 316.

[33] In his study of a village which is unequivocally the one here called Nshima, Deshen (1965:77–78) stresses the friendly relations which developed among the immigrants from the Atlas Mountains and those from Djerba within a few months after the founding of the village. He also notes that the leader of the immigrants from the Atlas Mountains, clearly the former merchant, came to be accepted as a village leader by immigrants from Djerba as well. Deshen seems to have begun intensive observations in the village in 1963 (Deshen 1965:67), and his informants' recollections of the village's early history do not consistently accord with my observations of the village during its first year. For the "situation of outright ethnic strife," which according to Deshen (1965:77) "did not last long," was manifest throughout most of that period, although friendly interaction between members of the two groups of settlers was increasingly evident during the intervals between outbreaks of overt conflict. Selective and not always accurate recollections of past events by those who had participated in them were constantly evident during my years of observation of the moshvei olim. Indeed, more than once I observed a group of informants reach agreement on past events, apparently in all sincerity; yet their statements did not accord with observations made at the time these events occurred. Instead, their recollections were consistent with a more recent state of affairs and/or with one of the partisan positions regarding an issue being disputed. Selective remembrance and the "mythicizing" of history are such common phenomena as to need no further comment. However, they rendered difficult and sometimes impossible the reliable reconstruction of events which had taken place more than a few weeks before in most of the villages I studied.

Meir Grossman's and Ben-Harif's policy of creating posts giving settlers secular authority over others; (2) the settlers' repudiation of Meir Grossman; and (3) the interest of both Rabbi David Peretz of Nishar and Haim Dayan of Shavur in exercising secular leadership. These elements, in conjunction with the presence in Shavur of both Haim Dayan and the Cohens, may be considered the crucial factors explaining the breakup of Shavur. It is not, however, the variables just specified, which contrast so neatly in Ometz and Shavur, but rather their historical connections in each village and their connections with other elements of village life that seem to explain the contrasting village outcomes.

Thus, in Ometz, Aharon's delay in delegating any of their self-governing rights to the settlers could have provoked opposition, particularly given his authoritarianism, had Rabbi Avraham been a different kind of person or had the former merchant, with his ambitions for continued leadership, remained in Ometz. This statement implies the hypothesis, which I feel is supported by the data from all three villages, that among newly arrived immigrants from the Atlas Mountains only settlers satisfying traditional leadership criteria and/or previously holding authority initially had the potential for asserting leadership claims and gaining a following in the new setting. For example, the appointment of young Moshe as aide to Yehoshua, the military instructor, was successfully opposed by the majority of the Ometz settlers, whereas they initially accepted Rabbi Avraham as holder of the same post.[34] The Ometz instructors contributed to the erosion of authority traditionally held by rabbis in Ait Adrar, and Rabbi Avraham submitted to this. But a different sort of person, or even Rabbi Avraham under different conditions, might not have been so acquiescent.[35]

[34] Cf. p. 360.

[35] Such conditions might have included the continued presence in Ometz and successful exercise of leadership by the former merchant who transferred to Nshima, for he obviously was neither liked nor trusted by Rabbi Avraham. Furthermore, I rather doubt whether the young rabbi, who had a streak of stubbornness in his makeup, would have been so acquiescent in the erosion of his diffuse traditional authority had it been attempted by

Furthermore, the Ait Adrar immigrants' acquiescence in Aharon's exercise of authority may not have been unrelated to their repudiation of another instructor, Yitzhak, Aharon's assistant. For while the immigrants had asked Aharon to be their instructor while both he and they were still in the transit camp,[36] they had much more immediate and intimate contact with Yitzhak during Ometz' first weeks. Indeed, Yitzhak's long conversations and rapport with settlers during the period of indecision over moshav federation allegiance seemed to be the crucial factor in the decision of some of the families to remain in Ometz.[37] However, the fact of this relative closeness, as well as his greater closeness to the settlers in terms of background, rendered Yitzhak more susceptible to their repudiation when his dependence on Aharon for his authority became evident.

Yitzhak's own increasing authoritarianism with the Ait Adrar immigrants, in response to the insecurities of his position, and his friendships with the new settlers of more urban provenience might have accelerated his rejection by the settlers from Ait Adrar and contributed to its virulence. However, I question whether it could have been averted, however he might have behaved, once the weakness of his position was evident. For this weakness made him the obvious target of hostilities generated by the role demands made on the settlers, particularly the decisions forced on them by the politics of Israel. By turning against Yitzhak and demanding and finally securing his removal, the immigrants could assert power without incurring the risk of reprisals. Thus, Yitzhak can be seen as a scapegoat through whose sacrifice the immigrants could submit easily to Aharon's authority.

---

less devoted instructors than the senior members of the Ometz village team. Indeed, I tend to think that the devotion and age of Aharon, Hava, and Rahel were necessary but not sufficient conditions for the young rabbi's attitude. The fact that Aharon and Hava were themselves religious, the two women's obvious respect for old Rav Shlomo, their noninterference with much of traditional belief and practice, and, as is further discussed in the text, the release of hostility against Yitzhak, Aharon's assistant, all may have contributed to the young rabbi's acquiescence.

36 Cf. p. 309.
37 Cf. p. 317.

The principal instructors of Shavur and Nishar differed from Aharon both in creating posts giving settlers authority and in choosing or backing traditional leaders to hold these posts. However, I would not ascribe the crises in the two villages to these policies as such but rather to the conjunction of factors associated with their implementation.

For it was not the immigrants from Telouet [38] who rebelled against Meir Grossman's selection of Rabbi David Peretz as his assistant and intermediary. It was the immigrants from elsewhere in the Atlas Mountains who opposed it. Rabbi David had not previously been a leader among them and some of them, those originally from Ait Adrar, had had greater experience of Israel and of moshav life than he. Moreover, when, later in Shavur's history, the Cohens warned the instructors that they could break up the village, they objected to the number of offices held by Rav Haim Dayan rather than to his post on the Executive Committee. Indeed, Rabbi David Peretz both headed Nishar's Executive Committee and had steady work in the composite moshav store without incurring open opposition during Ben-Harif's first five months as instructor.

Furthermore, I suggest that Meir Grossman's appointment of Rabbi David Peretz as his assistant, with authority over the immigrants from Ait Rahhal, was not the only basis for their repudiation of Meir himself. For Rabbi David, however threatening his full rabbinical status may have been to Haim Dayan, had traditional claims to authority that all the settlers recognized. Rabbi David also had a shrewd grasp of political tactics; and he had no trouble reasserting himself in Nishar within a few months of being deposed as Meir's assistant.

Moreover, Meir Grossman put his authority to the test in trying to influence the settlers on the school vote, unlike Aharon in Ometz, and he did so despite having already suffered an erosion of authority over the appointment and deposition of Rabbi David. Had he remained aloof from the school issue, the settlers' rejection of Meir, the man who

[38] Cf. pp. 388–89.

had brought them from the Atlas Mountains, might not have been so complete. As it was, their repudiation of him may be compared to the Ait Adrar immigrants' repudiation of Yitzhak after they were forced to vote on the school issue. An authority figure had to go if the settlers' submission to the land settlement system's demands on them was to be maintained.

Since Shavur did not begin to break up until six months after a stable instructor team had been achieved, and Nishar survived the disintegration of Shavur, I think that the initial instability of these villages' instructor personnel can be discounted as a significant factor in the outcome in Shavur. On the one hand, the settlers' conviction that they had ousted Meir Grossman served, at least according to my interpretation, to reconcile them for the time being to the demands of moshav life. On the other hand, Ben-Harif's support of the leadership claims of Haim Dayan and his disregard of those of old Shalom Cohen seem adequate to explain the disintegration of Shavur, given: (1) the presence and contending claims in the village of both Dayan and the Cohens; (2) the relations of these men with the other villagers; and (3) the plurality of posts which Ben-Harif instituted and Dayan held.

For the nature of the Shavur factionalism can be related both to the presence of the contending traditional leaders and to the nature of the ties they utilized in mobilizing their followings. Among immigrants from the Atlas Mountains, the patrilineal extended family seems to have been the largest kinship-based corporate group, i.e., the largest kin group to maintain unequivocal solidarity. A patrilineal bias was salient in many areas of life, corresponding to the patrilineal bias codified in Jewish law.[39] However, the core supporters of Haim Dayan and those of the Cohens did not seem to constitute units identifiable as patrilineages. Rather, they included matrilateral as well as patrilateral relatives of the respective men, and some of the settlers of

[39] However, the religion of the mother rather than that of the father determines whether a person is born a Jew according to rabbinical law.

Shavur were close kin of both traditional leaders. Thus, a core supporter of Dayan, married to a sister of Dayan's wife, was the son of Dayan's sister and of old Shalom Cohen's deceased brother.[40] Given the ramifying and cross-cutting kinship ties among Shavur's settlers, kinship relations did not commit a majority of the village's men to either Dayan or the Cohens. They could shift allegiances back and forth or even try to assert leadership claims for themselves and seek to mobilize their own followings.[41]

The majority of the settlers supported Haim Dayan during Ben-Harif's first months as instructor. For the village rabbi not only had the backing of the instructors but greater traditional authority than Yitzhak Cohen, although less than Yitzhak's father had possessed. But as the number of offices Dayan held increased, so did his vulnerability to increased hostility by those who were not his core supporters, and his own personality did not mitigate such hostility.

The post of work supervisor, to which the settlers themselves elected Dayan, may have been the crucial one in the crystallization of subsequent opposition to him by an increasing number of settlers. The evidence of Nishar is suggestive on this point. Its settlers' refusal to elect a work supervisor, despite Ben-Harif's pressure on them to do so, may have expressed their awareness that the tenuous *modus vivendi* they had achieved would not survive the elevation of a member of any one faction over the other settlers.

Ben-Harif, in stubbornly forwarding Dayan while deprecating the Cohens' claims, in effect pitted his own authority over the settlers, as well as that of Dayan, against the influence of the Cohens. For the instructor left the Cohens no choices beyond abdicating their claims, leaving Shavur, or seeking sources of support outside the village. Failing in the latter when Yitzhak Cohen turned unsuccessfully to

40 Clifford Geertz reports that political alliances with matrilateral rather than patrilateral kin are common in Morocco (personal communication).
41 Thus, during the high holiday period a group of settlers in Shavur decided to overturn the existing Executive Committee. They privately chose a "shadow" Executive Committee, on which not one member of the existing committee was given a place.

the moshav federation authorities, they did decide to leave. But they turned to the religious moshav federation in so doing and thereby linked the discontents within Shavur to the play of Israel's factional politics.

Whatever the respective importance of the Cohens' influence; the appeal of the religious moshav federation; opposition to Dayan, opposition to Ben-Harif and/or to the Land Settlement Department's schedule for allotting the first portion of the settlers' holdings, the combination was effective in bringing about the departure of fifty-two of the sixty families in Shavur. But I cannot accord priority to any one factor, unless possibly to Ben-Harif's early creation of the post of work supervisor and his stubbornness in supporting Dayan so unequivocally while discounting the warnings of the Cohens. It was the combination of factors in Shavur, including the personalities and decisions of the principal figures in its history, that brought about the disintegration of the village as it was originally constituted.

Shavur and Ometz were unusual in my sample of villages founded during the phase of rationalization, in that unambiguous developmental outcomes of some kind seemed to have been reached within one and a half years after their founding. Shavur was in the process of disintegration as a village settled by immigrants from the Atlas Mountains. As a settlement, it was repopulated well before the end of its second year and its development continued. But sociologically it then became a different village from the one it was when founded.

Ometz, in contrast, had become a settlement overwhelmingly peopled by immigrants from the Atlas Mountains, who had put down roots in the village and eagerly accepted their first allotment of land. Moreover, the introduction of settlers from elsewhere had not resulted, at least so far, in cleavages based on different provenience and preimmigration experience. On the contrary, the initial social distance between the immigrants from Ait Adrar and those from Moroccan villages and towns outside the Atlas Mountains had been sufficiently bridged not to have entered into the vicissitudes accompanying the initiation of settlers self-governing provisions.

However, while Aharon's policy of delaying for as long as possible the creation of posts giving settlers authority or the appearance of it may have contributed to the relative peace in Ometz, this was not the only factor to which I assign significance. The personalities of the rabbis and the absence of other people in Ometz both willing and able to assert leadership claims and mobilize a following seem to me also significant in explaining the Ometz outcome as of the end of the period under review. Moreover, the Ometz instructors' predilection to favor the young and minimize the traditional authority of Rav Avraham seems to me to have contributed to the vacuum of leadership among the settlers when Aharon finally did institute an Executive Committee. Therefore, I consider that a developmental outcome had been achieved by the end of the period under discussion only to a certain extent. On the one hand, Ometz gave every indication of having become a community, with sufficient cohesiveness among its members to enable it to withstand the vicissitudes of their continued role-socialization. On the other hand, however, these vicissitudes were just beginning in the crucial area of settler adaptation to moshav self-governing and administrative provisions.

Of the three villages, Nishar was the one in which no clear outcome had been reached by the end of the period of observation. On the one hand, its settlers had not achieved sufficient cohesiveness for the village yet to be considered a community. On the other hand, there was no likelihood of the village's imminent disintegration. Like most villages I knew, including six which had been founded years earlier during the phase of improvisation, the direction of its future development with its then current settler body was still indeterminate.

However, the fact that so many of its settlers had had previous experience with other moshvei olim and with the material conditions of those founded during the phase of improvisation suggests that these settlers would not leave

Nishar without greater provocation than that which had occasioned the departures from Shavur. This feature, in which Nishar's settlers differed from those of Ometz as well as those of Shavur, may have contributed to the stability of the village's population.

A final comparison of Shavur and Nishar involves their respective factions. Faction, as I use the term, denotes groups of people allied to each other in opposition to other groups of people, over issues in which their interests as they see them conflict. Factions may develop as the followings of competing leaders, as in the case of Shavur; but factions also may develop as opposition groups in the absence of clearly distinguishable leaders, as in the case of Nishar. I use the term leader to denote a person who advances leadership claims and is able to mobilize a following in support of them. In Nishar there was only one such person, Rabbi David Peretz, but three factions came into existence. One faction, composed of the immigrants from Telouet, was led by Rabbi David. The others, one composed of the immigrants originally from Ait Adrar and another made up of those from Ait Rahhal, simply lacked any discernible leaders. The settlers who had come to Israel from Ait Adrar consisted of a bloc of several extended families and small kin units who constituted a solidary group. The immigrants from Ait Rahhal constituted a bloc within Nishar, but their orientation to the village was minimal. Inhabiting houses which adjoined on Shavur, they consisted of six households whose primary relations were with their kinsmen in that village.

The evidence of Ometz indicates that factionalism need not develop among immigrants of diverse provenience even when such immigrants constitute blocs of kinsmen and/or clusters of solidary families. The diverse groups of settlers within Nishar, moreover, were all from the Atlas Mountains, unlike those of Ometz during most of its first year. And whatever the differences between Telouet, Ait Adrar, and Ait Rahhal, Jews from the Atlas Mountains shared a common culture to a greater extent than did those from the Atlas Mountains and those from elsewhere in Morocco. Therefore, the development of factions in Nishar may have been related less to the characteristics of its settler population than to the policies of its instructors.

For in appointing Rabbi David Peretz over the others, Meir Grossman may have crystallized into factional opposition what was initially no more than social distance and/or suspicion between the immigrants from Telouet and the others. Ben-Harif, in his turn, was not even aware initially that the settlers who had transferred from the religious moshav federation were originally from Ait Adrar and that they had had preimmigration relations with their neighbors from Ait Rahhal; and the instructor assigned little significance to this information when he was told it. It seems to me not improbable that three bounded factions crystallized in Nishar because Ben-Harif and the other village workers perceived and treated its settlers as three distinct groups.

Factionalism was endemic to the moshvei olim, although Ometz was not the only village of those I knew in which it did not occur. Indeed, it was notably absent in Tikva, despite the initiation of an Executive Committee and the creation of the posts of work supervisor and secretary. Furthermore, Tikva's first Executive Committee was overturned during the period of observation and a new one elected without any signs of factionalism and without a more than partial displacement of the previous committee's membership. In addition, Tikva did not lack several extended family and kindred units; such units simply did not constitute bounded groups within the larger settler body.

Nonetheless, the incidence of factionalism in the moshvei olim appeared far greater than the absence of it; and its occurrence has been associated with the importance of kinship ties among immigrants from the non-European countries not only by the land settlement administrators [42] but also by other students of the moshvei olim.[43] However, I consider it easier to formulate generalizations about faction-

[42] Cf. pp. 200ff., note 20.
[43] E.g., Weintraub and Lissak 1964c:135–45.

alism, settler kinship ties, and their relation to each other and/or to village development than to ensure the validity and reliability of such generalizations and of the evidence advanced to support them. For the phenomena that other students of the moshvei olim have subsumed under such terms as factions and *hamulas* or kin groups [44] are not necessarily of the same kind on the level of ethnographic specificity. Valid and reliable generalizations across a sample of villages seem to me to require: (1) clear and consistent definitions of the classes of phenomena under review; and (2) a careful analysis of concrete village data.[45]

[44] Weintraub and Lissak (1964c) and Weintraub and Bernstein (1966) both use the term "hamula," although it is used with a somewhat different meaning in each work, as is discussed in subsequent footnotes. Weingrod (1966:102,103) uses such terms as "clusters of kin" and "kin group," reserving the term "extended family" to mean two or more nuclear families linked by ties of direct descent, as is customary in anthropology. Deshen (1965:90, note 18) uses the term "extended family" to denote "all individuals tied by any kind of family relationship."

[45] Weintraub and Lissak (1964c) and Weingrod (1966:179–92) advance a number of such generalizations and consider that they are confirmed or tend to be confirmed by the data, based on a sample of villages, which they cite. However, their respective approaches lead to generalizations whose empirical referents I find unclear and which I cannot consider confirmed.

Weintraub and Lissak's generalizations concerning village development emerge in the context of a theoretical scheme involving many concepts, not all of which are defined, and relationships postulated between these concepts. Thus, the starting point of their analysis is the following statement, which is presented not as a hypothesis to be tested but, apparently, as an axiomatic proposition: "The outcome of the immigrants' confrontation with the new surroundings will, in the last analysis, depend upon (a) the extent to which his social and cultural background is similar to or different from these surroundings, and (b) the extent to which he is ready and willing to change and bridge such distance where it exists" (Weintraub and Lissak 1964a:97). Their next concern is "to classify the various groups of immigrants according to the similarity or dissimilarity of their cultural background to that of Israel" (1964a:97); and the method they adopt for doing so begins with their presentation in a series of statements of the attributes of two types of societies: the "modern-Western" type and the "traditional-Oriental" type (1964a:97). Apparently the moshav framework is to be equated with the "modern-Western" type of society. The authors do, however, note that "the two pure types do not, of course, do justice to the varied social reality; and it would be difficult to find an immigrant not endowed with a mixture of both 'Western' and 'Oriental' traits" (1964a:98). Nonetheless, these ideal types serve as the basis of their classification of immigrants into three categories—modern, transitional, and traditional—according to their "socio-cultural background" (1964c:129).

The immigrants' background, so categorized, constitutes one of the "two criteria" which the authors (1964c:129) use in constructing a further typology, one of community types to which they assign the villages in their sample. Their other criterion is the homogeneity or heterogeneity of a village's settler population, with the concepts of homogeneity and heterogeneity left undefined, as was noted above. However, the way in which they explain why a particular village population is to be considered homogeneous or heterogeneous (1964c:132–44) leaves the clear impression that homogeneity is equivalent to the existence of "a common unifying solidarity" (1964c:132) among a village's settlers.

The community types which the authors formulate on the basis of these two criteria include four main ones, namely (1) the "homogeneous modern" type, (2) the "heterogeneous modern" type, (3) the "traditional homogeneous" type, and (4) the "traditional heterogeneous" type. To these are added two more, (1) the "transitional" type and (2) the "mixed" type; and these two types are characterized as "a broad and diversified category, since they include villages with populations on different levels of the modern-traditional continuum, and various compositions of such groups" (1963a:129).

The thirteen villages of their sample are assigned to these six types, of which the "traditional homogeneous" "appears in two fundamental variations" (1963c:136) and the "transitional" and "mixed" are said to have a "range" of variations (1963c:136). More or less brief resumes are given (1964c:130–45) of seven of the thirteen villages in exemplifying the six types, including the two variations of the "homogeneous traditional" type. It might be noted that the authors state that the thirteen villages are not representative of the "immigrant moshavim" (1963a:97). Thus, their approach seems to result in the construction of six ideal types, some of them with variations, in order to discuss thirteen villages.

The question the authors seek to clarify "through the study of these types is: What are the conditions for the emergence in the new moshavim of a stable social structure, reflecting a sense of belonging to the community and a willingness to support the institutions of the village?" (1963c:129). They answer: "The general hypothesis of this study is that both modern and traditional types of villages are capable of achieving stability given certain conditions, of which homogeneity and suitable leadership are among the most important" (1964c:129–30). However, since homogeneity seems to be equivalent to settler solidarity, their general hypothesis appears to me rather tautological. For in their brief descriptions of two of the villages categorized as homogeneous (1964c:130–34,140–42)—one of them as "modern homogeneous" and the other as "traditional homogeneous"— such solidarity did not in the one case preclude, or in the other case emerge without, the departure of a considerable number (unspecified) of the settlers, i.e., this solidarity developed in the course of the villages' attainment of the populations which remained in them. Conversely, solidarity did not emerge in the villages reviewed as exemplifications of the "modern heterogeneous" and "traditional heterogeneous" types. Thus, a condition for the emergence of a stable social structure (i.e., homogeneity) appears to be largely equivalent to the outcome (i.e., a stable social structure) for which it is supposed to be a condition. For a "sense of belonging to the community and a willingness to support the institutions of the village" seem to be among the authors' criteria for both settler solidarity and a "stable social structure."

It is in reference to their "traditional homogeneous" and "traditional heterogeneous" types that Weintraub and Lissak discuss settler kinship. They preface their descriptions of villages exemplifying these types with a review of "the 'traditional' pattern of interaction . . . characterized by a very strong attachment to kinship and territorial groups, limitation of social interaction chiefly to these groups, and lack of confidence in, and capacity to work together with, people from outside the group. The basic framework of this type is the 'hamula' " (1964c:135). However, what follows is their discussion of the hamula, quoted earlier (p. 201, note 23), in which the authors make it clear that the actual social groups in the Israeli villages are not the "historical hamulas," i.e., what they also term "the Mediterranean patrilineage, territorially defined" (1964c:135) but are groups or "cliques" of families whose members are not necessarily of common patrilineal descent and common former residence. Moreover, they go on to say that the historic hamula, which they use interchangeably with the terms "neighborhood group" and "kinship group," was not an effective political unit, whereas the kind of group in the Israeli villages which they term hamula "has become the main political unit in the village" (1964c:136).

It is difficult to see how the hamula, so conceptualized, differs from any kind of cohesive social group within a village which may act politically as a bloc and whose members may have some kind of kinship link with other of the families in the group. And when Weintraub and Lissak make generalizations about "the hamula-based traditional type of moshav," such as that "its organizing principles are in the long run inimical to efficiency" (1964c:145–46), the organizing principles seem to be those of an ambiguous concept linked into a typology.

Weingrod, after a relatively detailed review of the history of one village between 1954 and 1962 (1966:44–178), in the course of which he introduces some comparative material about a neighboring village (1966:66–67, 117–20), suggests several hypotheses about village development in general, at least for villages settled primarily by immigrants from Morocco. These hypotheses are phrased in the idiom of variables, i.e., of factors whose variation is systematically associated with variability in village development (Weingrod 1966:178–93). The author introduces information on five additional villages, most of it in the form of a table labeled "Comparison of Moroccan Villages" (1966:187), and he considers his main hypotheses to be confirmed by the material presented in the table (1966: 184–89). The hypotheses which are relevant here seek to relate village factionalism variables and settler kinship variables to variability in village development. They read as follows: (1) "villages which have dominant factions led by powerful leaders will have stable village institutions, whereas villages divided among rival factions and warring leaders are unable to develop stable village-wide bodies" (1966:184); and (2) "village population stability is related to rural origins and extensive kinship ties" (1966:187).

It is my understanding that hypotheses such as these can be validly and reliably tested only insofar as (1) the variables specified have specific and unambiguous empirical referents; and (2) the hypotheses are tested by means of clearly described procedures which can be utilized by another investigator. However, Weingrod's testing of his hypotheses does not meet these specifications or even provide the reader with the data needed to clearly grasp his formulations, apart from the evidence of the two villages on which the hypotheses were based. Therefore, I cannot accept Weingrod's claim that the hypotheses are confirmed, even in only "a general way" (1966:188).

Thus, the author does not define what he means by the term "faction." The reader is left to infer whether the term denotes a cohesive group of people who act politically as a bloc, whether it refers to an alliance of people who do not constitute a cohesive group apart from being united on one or more issues in opposition to other people, whether it is the following of a leader, whatever the issues on which he chooses to make a stand, or whether it is same combination of these possibilities. If it is the latter, as the author's discussion of the two villages on which he gives data would seem to indicate (1966:102–5, 117–20), the combination should be invariable, which it appears not to be, if something about factions—e.g., whether or not they are "dominant"—is to be treated as a variable.

Moreover, the term "dominant" as the variable attribute of faction also is not defined. Used interchangeably with the word "large" in one context (1966:84), it seems to mean "majority" in another context (1966: 192). Similarly, the terms "leader," "leadership," and "symmetric" as the variable aspect of leadership also are not defined. The term "leader" in some contexts, such as that quoted below, seems to mean person with a following or constituency behind him; but in the same paragraph, the term "leader" seem to denote a person who has leadership ability but is unable to mobilize a stable following. Thus, Weingrod writes of the village with which most of his book deals and of the village which he uses as foil: "At Oren the dominant village figures were the leaders of the larger kinship groups. These men found their main support from among their kinsmen and more generally from within the faction. They were therefore guaranteed a stable base of support. At Shikma, on the other hand, the powerful leaders did not possess a guaranteed constituency. Paradoxically, neither of the two kinship-based factions had leaders who were able to assert general authority, while the two men with leadership abilities did not have the support of broadly based groups" (1966:181).

The above quotation is preceded by a paragraph reviewing data presented earlier in the study (1966:102–20) on the two factional groups in Oren, the four smaller ones in Shikma, and the *de facto* existence in Oren of a two-party system. I can find no other material in the book which is germane to Weingrod's introduction (1966:183) of the term "symmetric leadership." Other readers will have to decide whether he means by the term: (1) the fact of two parties or two factions in a village; (2) the fact of two persons with leadership ability and with sufficient kinsmen in a village to have a sure and sizable following; or (3) both. My understanding is that he means both and, in addition, that groups of kinsmen act as the core of village factions. In his descriptions of Oren and Shikma he is explicit on this final point (1966:102–4).

The empirical referent (or referents) of the term "symmetric leadership," therefore, do not seem to be independent of the referent or referents of the term "dominant faction." Nonetheless, in presenting his hypotheses and suggesting that they may be considered to be confirmed, Weingrod specifies "dominant faction"—once used interchangeably with "factional dominance" (1966:183)—and "symmetric leadership" as separate, independent variables.

Precision in concept formulation historically has been less stressed in anthropology than have been the careful collection and presentation of data. However, generalizations in anthropology have not often been phrased in the idiom of "variables" dissociated from ethnographic context. Therefore, insofar as Weingrod presents sufficient data on a village for the reader to be able to assign concrete empirical referents to the words in which he states his hypotheses, these hypotheses may be considered testable in regard to that village.

Unfortunately, I do not find such data provided for the five villages which Weingrod introduces into his study to test the hypotheses based on the two villages for which he does give data. For example, the only information which he gives about two of these five villages is presented in the

Thus, a great deal of attention has been given in anthropology to different systems of kinship organization and to the kinds of behavior associated with them. Immigrants from the Atlas Mountains seem to have lacked the kind of kinship group known as the corporate patrilineage above the minimal level of the two or three generation patrilineal extended family; and matrilateral kinship links seem to have been as important as patrilateral ones in various areas of life.[46] Correspondingly, kinship ties above the level of the patrilineal extended family did not unequivocally unite or divide settlers in Shavur into solidary blocs opposed to other blocs.

In Nishar, as contrasted to Shavur, the factions had clear boundaries, and members' kinship ties did not cut across these boundaries, at least during six months of Nishar's first year. Nonetheless, its factions were not composed of groups for whom agnatic kinship ties provided a pre-immigration and/or current basis for corporate political

---

table "Comparison of Moroccan Villages," and in a footnote to the table giving figures on the number of families or of settlers who had left the five villages (Weingrod 1966:187). And within the table, information is given in the form of the following primarily dichotomous assertions: under the heading "Origins," each of the seven villages is assigned to one of three categories: "Rural," "Mixed," or "Urban"; under the headings "Kinship based," "Dominant factions," and "Symmetric leadership," each village is assigned to one of two categories: "Yes" or "No"; under the headings "Migrate" and "Farm," each village is assigned to one of two categories: "Few" or "Many"; and under the heading "Village institutions," each village is assigned to one of two categories: "Stable" or "Unstable."

When the empirical referent of a heading (variable) is uncertain, the verbal economy of such a table hardly provides data on a village. And even when a heading (variable), such as "Migrate," seems to have an unambiguous empirical referent, the provision of even a little concrete data brings on uncertainty. Thus, according to the table, the village called Olar has settlers of rural origin, few of whom migrated; and the village called Asor had settlers of mixed origins, many of whom migrated. This might seem to support the hypothesis concerning village population stability cited above. However, according to the figures in Weingrod's footnote to the table, thirty-seven families left Olar, "most of them during the first year after their settlement," whereas forty-two settlers (not families) left Asor "in a constant exodus" (1966:187). It is not, therefore, the absolute number of persons or of families who left, assuming that a family comprises at least two persons, but the timing and flow of their departure, i.e., additional variable factors, which seems to have made for Weingrod's judgment as to whether "few" or "many" migrated.

[46] Cf. pp. 281, 408–9.

action in the village. For it was not kinship ties as such but rather intervening factors—e.g., the fact of faction formation along lines of shared provenience and presettlement experience, and of the matrilateral and affinal as well as patrilateral kinship ties that linked most of the settlers of the same provenience—which resulted in the congruence between discrete factions and discrete networks of kin.

However, immigrants from elsewhere in the Middle East may have had patrilineages of greater depth than two or three generations.[47] Among such immigrants the emergence of village factionalism might show a different relationship between factional allegiances and kinship allegiances than that existing in villages settled by immigrants with extremely shallow patrilineages. For example, bounded factions might emerge, each consisting of the local members of an agnatic descent group or an alliance of such descent groups.[48]

[47] This may have been the case among the Jews of Yemen. For Goitein (1955:7) states that the immigrants from Yemen whom he studied were "normally . . . capable of remembering the names of from five to seven direct antecedents"; and he notes that at the time of their exodus from Yemen the village population largely consisted of "six large families or clans," each consisting of ten to fifteen small or extended families with the same surname (*ibid.*). Although Goitein's terminology does not clarify the nature of the ties linking the families of a "clan," Cohen (1955) explicitly states that Jewish households in rural villages in Yemen could consist of a single patrilineal group tracing descent over three or more generations. Indeed, he notes, an entire village could consist of one such patrilineage. Moreover, the number of generations remembered by Goitein's informants contrasts significantly with the much shorter genealogical memory of immigrants from the Atlas Mountains of Morocco. Among the latter, with their shallow patrilineages, I found only a few individuals who could trace their ancestors back past the generation of their grandfathers, and these individuals were the descendents of noted rabbis. Richard Press reports similar findings (personal communication). Of the two hundred to three hundred Jews from the Atlas Mountains whom he interviewed in 1967, almost no one could remember his or her great grandfathers' names or anything else about them.

[48] Weintraub and Lissak (1964c:136–40 142–43) briefly describe two Israeli moshavim, one peopled by immigrants from Yemen and the other by immigrants from Hadramaut, in both of which factions were bounded and consisted of hamulas (cf. p. 201, note 22) or alliances of hamulas. The population of the former village remained divided for years into two factions, each made up of a hamula and each hamula consisting of people from a single locale in Yemen. The population of the latter village also had two enduring factions, each made up of an alliance of two hamulas, and all the hamulas were from the same Hadramaut town. Since the authors give no information as to whether the units they term

Without attention to ethnographic specificity, it would be easy to assume that the factions in Nishar represented the same class of phenomena as factions present in villages settled by discrete descent groups, in which the factions would consist of such descent groups or of alliances among them. However, such an assumption can lead to generalizations about factions, kinship groups, and the relation of these to village development that may be neither valid nor reliable. For example, factions composed of descent groups are likely, at least on theoretical grounds, to be more stable in duration and in membership than those which are mobilized by leaders and/or come into existence over issues.[49] Yet if factions and kinship groups are treated as undefined and undifferentiated categories, attempts to establish correlations across a sample of moshvei olim can result in the appearance of systematic variation between phenomena which may not, in fact, have been systematically compared.[50]

In none of the villages in my sample [51] did I find agnatic

---

hamula were descent groups, it is unclear in the case of the village peopled by immigrants from Yemen whether common provenience, common descent, or both contributed to the solidarity of each faction and its opposition to the other faction. The authors describe the immigrants from Hadramaut as able to maintain a "minimal over-all solidarity" despite factionalism (1964c:139), but also fail to indicate whether their hamulas were descent groups or networks of kin. However, in reviewing another village peopled by immigrants from Yemen, they describe it, after the departure of two of three hamulas, as a "one-lineage community" (1964c: 141). It may be noted that this hamula engaged in joint cultivation of orchards and field crops, and that village factionalism apparently was absent.

[49] Thus, the kinship units in two villages peopled by immigrants from Kurdistan, which Weintraub and Bernstein call hamulas in their discussion of these villages (1966), clearly are not descent groups, since they are described as consisting of relatives with "(a) close blood relations" (e.g., "father-son, sibling, uncle-nephew, cousins, grandfather-grandson"), "(b) distant blood relations . . . (e.g., third cousins), and (c) relatives by marriage" (Weintraub and Bernstein 1966:516, 516–17, note 15). Correspondingly, according to the data given on these villages, members of such hamulas in one of the two villages did not maintain solidarity in factional alignments. It may be noted that although the authors refer to the traditionalism of the hamula pattern of organization, they consider the village in which kinship units were not solidary in political action as more traditional than the villages in which they were.

[50] Cf. above, note 45.

[51] The villages I knew relatively well were those called in this study Ometz, Shavur, Nishar, Tikva, Nshima, Ba'aya, Tsarot, and an unnamed

descent groups of greater depth than two adult generations; kin groups composed of a wider range of relatives were kindreds, i.c., persons related to each other through any kind of tie, patrilateral, matrilateral, or affinal. Extended families also were cognatic as well as patrilineal. Thus, still vigorous older men headed extended families which included sons-in-law as well as sons; and vigorous younger men, asserting leadership claims, generally could count on their sisters' husbands as members of their followings—provided that the village was not settled, as were Shavur and initially Ometz, by groups of relatives among whom brothers-in-law had other, crosscutting ties. Moreover, in villages peopled by discrete and different kinds of kinship units, i.e., by nuclear families, two generation patrilineal and cognatic extended families, and/or kinship units based on any kind of relationship, factors other than kinship entered into factional alignments. I never saw members of an extended family, or sons of the same father break solidarity in factional affiliations, but other kinds of relatives might do so.[52]

---

village founded during the phase of improvisation and peopled by immigrants from India (cf. Chap. V, pp. 215–17). In addition, I carried out observations in three more villages founded during the phase of rationalization and six more founded during the phase of improvisation. All but two of these villages were settled at the time by immigrants from North Africa (Morocco, Tunisia, including Djerba, and Tripoli; one village also included a few families from Algeria). Immigrants from Kurdistan and from Kerala (India) peopled the other two villages. I also made brief visits to over a dozen other villages and heard discussions and stories about these and many more from village instructors, Land Settlement Department officials, onetime settlers of these villages, and people who still made their homes in them but were working as instructors in other villages. The sample on which I base generalizations about moshav settlers is that of the villages I knew well, with data from those I knew less well introduced only insofar as I believe the information to be reliable. My discussion of the land settlement system is drawn from my experience, which included participation in and intensive observation of the Land Settlement Department itself at the district, region, and head-office levels as well as on the level of the villages.

[52] E.g., the son of old Shalom Cohen's brother, who was a supporter of Haim Dayan (cf. pp. 408–9). Of data on this point provided by other students of the moshvei olim, Weintraub and Bernstein (1966) note that it was "distant relatives" (including affinals) who constituted the floating vote in the village settled by immigrants from Kurdistan, in which kinship ties did not make for factional solidarity. Weingrod (1966:110–11)

Thus, in all the moshvei olim in my sample, factions can be considered composed of alliances between extended families, other kinds of groups of close kin, and/or nuclear families; and membership in a kindred did not preclude crosscutting factional alignments. In consequence, the factions generally were neither bounded nor stable in membership. In some villages, furthermore, they were not stable in duration but rather formed, dissolved, and reformed in shifting patterns of alliances. Moreover, in the course of a few years or even of a few months, persons asserting leadership claims might lose much of their followings and new leaders might emerge. As far as I could tell, the relevance to village development of the presence or absence of factions or of anything about such factions varied from village to village and at different periods within the same villages, depending on the constellation of specific features with which they were associated at any time.

My data also fail to confirm generalizations that relate stability of village populations to the existence of extensive kinship ties within the population.[53] Thus, in the villages in my sample, Shavur was the only one to undergo almost total disintegration after the village's population willingly had accepted the fact of moshav life as their lot in Israel. Moreover, the factional politics of Israel could lead to the defection of a substantial settler segment from a larger body of kinsmen, as occurred not only in Ometz but among the larger body of immigrants from Ait Adrar in transit to Israel and after their arrival.[54] I also have witnessed nuclear families and small kin groups, occupying two or three households, develop cohesive and deeply satisfying ties with unrelated families and put down roots in a village, whereas large extended families departed from such villages in a bloc.

It is my impression that families who accepted a village as their home recruited kinsmen to join them. In contrast,

---

also notes a public split between two brothers-in-law in Oren, although it is not clear whether these two men otherwise belonged to Oren's two major factions.

[53] Cf. Weingrod 1966:187.
[54] Cf. pp. 307–8.

families who were initially or increasingly dissatisfied with
moshav life or with conditions in a given village tended
sooner or later to depart, whether or not they had begun
village life with kinsmen in the village. Thus, over a period
of time, which itself varied from village to village, settler
departures and replacements could lead to the attainment
of a stable village population and also could lead to a
prevalence of families with relatives in the village. However,
I know of too many cases in which people who had begun
moshav life as part of larger kinship groups departed from
villages to consider that the prevalence of such groups in
a village was directly related to the stability of its population,
across either the universe of moshvei olim or the smaller
universe of villages settled by immigrants from Morocco.[55]
In some instances such a relationship was evident; in other
cases it was clearly absent. In still other cases such a relationship came about through a process of settler turnover that
continued for a number of years and included the departure
of certain large bodies of kinsmen as well as the consolidation
of others. In each case that I know of, including those for
which ethnographically specific data are given by other
students of the moshvei olim,[56] intervening factors, including
the nature of the kinship ties themselves, enter into explanations of why some settlers left whereas others stayed, or
why some villages had less settler turnover than others.

This discussion has gone beyond the evidence of Ometz,
Shavur, and Nishar. The subject of variability in village
development brings us back to the universe of moshvei olim.
This had come into existence, as was discussed in Chapters
IV and VI, years before the exodus of Jews from the Atlas

---

[55] Weingrod's limitation of his hypothesis to such villages precludes its
examination in the light of data given by Weintraub and Lissak (1964c:
140–41, 143) on the departure of entire hamulas from two villages settled
by immigrants from Yemen. Similarly excluded is the mention by Weintraub and Bernstein (1966:520) of the departure of a bloc of immigrants
from Morocco and a hamula of immigrants from Kurdistan from the two
villages they discuss.

[56] In fact, none of the authors whose works have been referred to in the
footnotes of this chapter give much data on the families who left or on
the specific circumstances surrounding their departure.

Mountains of Morocco; and many more immigrants than they joined the moshvei olim during the period of their mass immigration and after it had come to an end.

THE UNIVERSE OF MOSHVEI OLIM

On the level of ethnographic specificity, almost any feature of moshav olim life during Israel's first decade was subject to variation across the universe of moshvei olim and within the same village over time. In Chapters IV through VI, I have tried to indicate the range of features that might vary and some of the ways in which they did vary. The comparison of Ometz, Shavur, and Nishar has indicated the extent to which villages initially similar in basic features could vary in their early development. The moshav as a village type and the goals of the settlement authorities set limits to village variability. Nonetheless, a review of settlements which came into existence with different constellations of initial features than the three which have been discussed here would present a rather different picture of the early years of a moshav olim than that offered by these three villages.

Thus, Ba'aya, a village a few kilometers from Ometz to which reference already has been made,[57] was similar to Ometz in ecological and planning features, but differed saliently in the attributes of its settlers and instructors. It initially was peopled by immigrants of diverse provenience and socio-cultural backgrounds within North Africa: nuclear and ex-tended families and small kin groups from Tangiers and Spanish Morocco, from urban Tunisia and French Morocco, and from more rural regions of French Morocco, although not from the Atlas Mountains. The majority of the immigrants of urban background were fluent and literate in one or more European languages, and some of them had assimilated European ways of behavior as known to them in country of origin.

The members of the first village team were young, and most of them were native Israelis. Only the social instructor

[57] Cf. pp. 205–6, 345–46.

was over thirty; and only he, of all the others, had known adult responsibilities in a veteran settlement—in his case a veteran moshav ovdim into which he had been born and in which he held a farmstead in his own right.

However, the social instructor spent only part of the work week in Ba'aya after its first three months; and some of the other members of the village team feuded with each other, involved the settlers in their feuds, and accorded preferential treatment, as in the assignment of appointive offices, to settlers they found personally congenial. Of the settler families, several had members who had been active in Zionist affairs prior to immigration to Israel. These individuals, who included immigrants from Tangiers, from French Morocco, and from Tunis, became leaders in the village, both members of the Executive Committee and persons with extensive followings among the body of settlers. The families the instructors favored were from Tunis and French Morocco; the extended family they turned against, which was from Tangiers, included a father, four grown sons, and a daughter and her husband. They had been the first settlers in the village, and the father was elected head of Ba'aya's first Executive Committee.

A chronicle of Ba'aya's first year would show a cast of characters caught up in factional intrigue and strife, as a young leader from Tunis and an older one from French Morocco entered into an alliance against the head of the Executive Committee. In the absence of the social instructor, the others favored the two allies; and the village rocked with crises as settlers and village team engaged in screaming public scenes and plotted the removal of one another from the village.

Given the diverse provenience of the leaders, factional disputes were discussed by the instructors and some of the settlers in the idiom of ethnic difference, i.e., as a conflict between the immigrants from Tangiers and those from Tunisia and Morocco. In fact, as was noted in Chapter V, the followings of the opposed leaders cut across the grouping of settlers according to provenience. Indeed, my observations in Ba'aya strongly suggest that the policies of the instructors not only contributed to the acrimony of factional conflict but may have brought about the crystallization of factional opposition. For the leaders themselves were not unreasonable men; and the conflicts of interest between them were several times resolved through mutually acceptable compromises effected by the social instructor during his increasingly rare sojourns in the village.

Furthermore, the drama of interaction was but one aspect of village life, for some of the settlers were serious in their attempt to become farmers and others could not accept or adapt to sustained agricultural toil. Among those who could not adapt were the sons of the leader from Tangiers. Furthermore, they were constantly affronted by the behavior of the agricultural instructors toward them, and they disdained to accept the latters' directives.

Before the end of Ba'aya's first year, the differential response of the extended families of the factional opponents to agricultural work and village life entered into the ability of these contending leaders to hold their followings. Moreover, additional contingents of settlers had been introduced into the village to replace families who had left. The latter, incidentally but not irrelevantly, included families of diverse provenience who had had no idea that the paper they had signed in transit to Israel committed them to moshav life. However, unlike Aharon in Ometz, the Ba'aya instructors did not impede their transfer from the village.

The new arrivals included a kindred originally from Cochin (Kerala) in India.[58] A few months later four brothers from

---

[58] The circumstances surrounding the arrival of this kindred in Ba'aya indicate how idiosyncratic features—apart from the ship to village policy (cf. pp. 190–95), settlers' recruitment of kinsmen to join them in a village, and the competitive politics of moshav recruitment—could influence the peopling of a village during the phase of rationalization. In this case, the Land Settlement Department regional director of the Daroma, in preparation for assuming this position, had earlier served as instructor of a village settled by immigrants from Kerala. A young man from Kerala whom he knew from his period as an instructor had joined a kibbutz. Wishing to leave it at this later time, the young man approached his friend, now the Daroma regional director, for advice and assistance in getting relocated. The regional director considered the ethnic heterogeneity of Ba'aya to be

Tangiers, who were committed to becoming farmers and had brought a tractor with them, also joined Ba'aya. In the meanwhile, the original team of village workers had been replaced. Some of the posts even had had several successive short-term occupants. Ba'aya's cast of characters no longer was the same as that which had founded the village.

By the time Ba'aya began its third year, only one of the original opposing leaders, the eldest son of an extended family from Tunis, still had standing in the village. He and his kin had taken to agricultural life. Indeed, from their first weeks in the village, they had pored over literature on farming methods. Ba'aya's founding family recently had left; the father who headed it was still vigorous in body but his spirit had been undermined by his loss of village leadership. The families originally from Cochin and the four brothers from Tangiers who had joined the village were among Ba'aya's leading families. Some thirty other households, which included many of the initial settlers from Tunis, had sufficiently accepted the demands of moshav life for the settlement authorities to turn over to them the second scheduled allotment of land. The others would continue to work as employees of the moshav federation holding company, and most of them were known to want to leave the village.

Still another village in the Daroma, Tsarot, also came into existence with a diversified body of settlers from Tangiers and Spanish and French Morocco, both urban and rural in provenience, and at different stages in the transition from traditional rural or urban mellah life to European ways. This village also had young instructors, although a turnover in instructresses brought a mature woman with training in social work into the village for several months. The settlers also included several persons asserting leadership claims and able to mobilize followings.

However, the history of Tsarot's first year took a different turn from that of Ba'aya's. For the members of the village

---

such that the introduction of the young man and his kinfolk into the village would make for a minimum of disruption in settler relations; and his judgment was borne out.

team maintained relative harmony in their relations with each other, as did the settlers. But the different settler leaders took turns in mobilizing the population in opposition to the instructors and to policies of the land settlement authorities. Tsarot, like Ba'aya, rocked with crises during its first year, but these were crises in which significant numbers of the settlers protested one or another aspect of the role demands made on them. Employment conditions, rates of pay, village taxes, the roster of the guard, availability of foodstuffs in the village store, the signing of the Land Settlement Department and moshav federation contracts, demands made by the instructors all triggered off clamorous public scenes, work strikes, demonstrations at the Land Settlement Department regional offices, attempts to beat up one instructor—the agricultural instructor, who was himself originally from French Morocco—and attempts to get him removed.

The majority of the settlers could not accept the conditions of moshav life; and those who could did not attempt to assert leadership. Instead, they remained aloof from public protestations they considered unjustified, while participating in those they felt were legitimate; and they resisted the attempts of the instructors to mobilize them as their supporters in opposition to the dissidence of the other settlers.

Settler cohesiveness was achieved before the end of Tsarot's first year, but it was not the kind of cohesiveness which promoted village development. The settlers constituted a relatively solidary congregation of interacting families, but the settlement had not begun to become a village community.

I have been in villages which had been founded two to five years earlier than Tsarot but which were still no more advanced in their development. Several of them had been partially repopulated three or more times; a few families had remained each time, while the bulk of those with whom they entered the village left it. As these were villages founded during the phase of improvisation, the settlers received their farmsteads on arrival; and the role of the agricultural instructors was to supervise them in cultivating their land according to Land Settlement Department directives. However, the yields had been low; some of the produce had been sold privately rather than through the village cooperative; [59] and settlers had departed without repaying the credit advanced to them. The Land Settlement Department had invested hundreds of thousands of pounds in each of these villages, and they had yet to show visible signs of development into viable farming communities.

As far as I could judge, idiosyncratic factors resolve the developmental stalemates in villages such as these. Thus, one such village, during its early years, was studied over a period of time; and a change in the Land Settlement Department's credit policies has been suggested as the main reason for its successful development.[60] However, this change in policy occurred in 1960, over seven years after the village had been founded and after a substantial turnover in its settler population.[61] Two years earlier, its future seems to have been indeterminate in the sense in which I use this term.[62] Moreover, the anthropologist who studied this village, in advancing the change in credit policy as the main reason for the positive outcome experienced in the development of this village, notes that the new credit policy might not have had the effect it did without the favorable market conditions which prevailed during the years 1960–61.[63] He further adds that the change in credit policies did not serve as a development catalyst in other villages.[64] Other students of the moshvei olim note equally idiosyncratic constellations of features in reviewing the differential development of the villages they discuss.[65]

[59] Cf. pp. 184–85.

[60] Cf. Weingrod 1966:167–78.

[61] Weingrod notes that nineteen families left Oren between 1955 and 1961 (1966:181). As of 1957 the village contained sixty-two family household units, of which fifty-seven were occupied (1966:62).

[62] Cf. Weingrod 1966:194; Weingrod 1959.

[63] Cf. Weingrod 1966:176.

[64] Cf. Weingrod 1966:178.

[65] Thus, Weintraub and Lissak consider that the unifying solidarity achieved in the village they cite as exemplification of their "modern heterogeneous type," despite the varied provenience and background of its settlers (cf. pp. 400, note 28, 415), can be traced back to the common experience in a communal camp of its first segment of settlers (1964c:131). In-

Given the extent of variability within the universe of moshvei olim and the interconnectedness of the particular factors that may explain the course of events in any village, I hesitate to advance general hypotheses about village development that focus on the villages themselves. Rather, I regard the universe of moshvei olim, at least on the village level, as a probability system. Within the range of moshav variability, certain combinations of factors have been propitious for village development; others have not. Those combinations that were not propitious have been continually subject to revision. Thus, the land settlement authorities could improve the material conditions of the settlements and revise village agricultural planning and their investment and development policies and schedules. Years elapsed between their decision to introduce instructors into the villages and the efforts to professionalize the instructor roles; but the effort was made and consolidated and was followed by further revisions in policy, such as the change in credit policies.[66] Settlers who

terestingly enough, part (number unspecified) of this body of settlers subsequently left the village. Without giving details, the authors also attribute the "social cohesion" of two villages settled by several hamulas from different localities in Yemen to "exceptionally capable leadership" (Weintraub and Lissak 1964c:143).

Weintraub and Bernstein (1966) contrast the friendship patterns of the settlers of the two villages peopled by immigrants from Kurdistan, suggesting that these patterns help explain the contrasting development of these villages. They furthermore note that "the leader of the younger generation—the most vocal and gifted of its members—was strategically located within the central extended family in the largest hamula" (1966: 518) of the village which they consider to be the more developed and modernized of the two, in part because of the village's friendship patterns and this young man's emergence as a village leader.

Deshen (1965) discusses how a turnover in part of the population of Yatziv (Nshima) resulted in a greater percentage than hitherto of settlers from one of two towns in Djerba, and how this contributed to a "breakdown of modernization" in the village, i.e., to the emergence of factions among the settlers from Djerba and to factional alignments, in good part along family lines and lines of common preimmigration provenience. However, it may not be irrelevant here to note again that Weintraub and Bernstein (1966) consider the village in which factional alignments crosscut kinship ties as the less modernized of the two villages they discuss.

[66] According to this change, the Land Settlement Department granted credit to each farming family individually rather than granting it to the moshav as a whole with the moshav in turn allocating credit to each family through its committees. Furthermore, the families were entitled to sell

left the villages could be replaced; young people grew to adulthood, many of them accepting the farmer role and some of them able to assert leadership claims successfully; and through various pressures or inducements the villages could be rid of settlers unable or unwilling to leave but considered inimical to village development.

As conditions in a village have changed—and these conditions include settler interaction, attitudes, and skills—the combination of factors influencing village development has also changed. Given sufficient time, sufficient investment capital, and sufficient settler and instructor turnover, a combination of factors propitious for the development of any given village into a potentially viable farming community can be expected to turn up eventually. In Ometz, the first year's combination was successful. In other villages, ten or more years have not been enough.[67] Or the settlement authorities may decide that the investment needed to bring about successful village development simply would be too great in a given instance to justify the result. I have known this decision to be made in regard to a kibbutz that had broken up. Rather than trying to reconstitute a new village, the settlement authorities turned the village site into an agricultural school.

The features explaining moshav olim development, according to this view, are ethnographically specific on the village level. Moreover, I question the possibility of validating general hypotheses about village development that refer to factors localized in the villages. For given the paucity of systematic

their crops to private merchants as well as to Tnuva, the Histadrut marketing cooperative (cf. pp. 95, 155). Weingrod, in reviewing this change (1966:167–70) gives no information as to how this reform was instituted at the policy-making levels of the Land Settlement Department. However, it constituted a truly drastic erosion of moshav ideology, for it minimized the cooperative and mutual aid provisions of the moshav as a village type (cf. Chap. III); and it also weakened the villages' ties to the Histadrut or to the analogous organizations associated with Israel's political parties.

[67] None of the villages in my sample had been in existence for ten years by 1958. However, one of the villages cited by Weintraub and Lissak (1964c:134–35) as an example of relatively unsuccessful development was founded in 1948 (Weintraub and Lissak 1964a:97), and their manuscript was completed at the end of 1961 (Ben-David 1964:11).

research on the moshvei olim during Israel's first decade, the universe of villages on which generalizations could be based is a partial one. The constellations of factors which led to the abandonment of villages by their settlers have disappeared from the record; and the early years of villages founded during Israel's first decade can be accurately reconstructed with great difficulty, if at all.[68] Neither I nor anyone else can know how many cases like Shavur complemented cases like Ometz; and I suspect that generalizations based on the sample of villages available for study also could be reduced to idiosyncratic factors if the full histories could be recovered of villages which foundered before being resettled or otherwise reconstituted.[69]

Nonetheless, village development in Israel can be ex-

[68] Thus, Weintraub and Lissak, referring to a village which almost certainly is the one here called Ometz, write that it "was for a long time in the care of a team which had spent a long time in the Atlas mountains, organized the immigration from there, and accompanied the future settlers of the village to Israel" (Weintraub and Lissak 1964b:123n). They add, apparently referring to Aharon and Hava Barzel in Ometz rather than to Meir Grossman and Shavur, "The results were extremely beneficial." Cf. also the contrast between my observations in "Nshima" during its first year and Deshen's reconstruction (p. 404, note 33).

[69] The extent to which unpredictable and idiosyncratic factors could influence the development of a particular village became evident to me only after this study was completed. During a brief visit to Israel in the summer of 1967, I found Haim Dayan still in Shavur and again its outstanding public figure. For he and his core supporters had not left the settlement after all, whereas about half the immigrants from Poland had done so between 1958 and 1963. Other immigrants from Europe who had replaced them had also left during that period, according to Dayan. Then, in 1963, he went to the Haifa port together with a representative of Tnaut Hamoshavim to meet some twenty families from the Atlas Mountains (although not from Ait Rahhal or Ait Adrar), and these families settled in Shavur. Thus, before the end of 1963, its population consisted of immigrants from Poland and immigrants from the Atlas Mountains in about equal numbers. They got along well together, said Dayan, and a marriage between members of two such groups had already taken place in a neighboring village, although not in Shavur.

Furthermore, he recounted, Shavur's settlers had voted in 1966 to abolish the cooperative provisions of the moshav form of organization. They not only sold their produce individually and as they wished, but had also abolished the moshav committees and discontinued membership in the Histadrut.

In contrast, Nishar in 1967 still had the same settler families as in 1957, and was still split into factions, one headed by Rabbi David and the other by a settler from Telouet who had spoken against him to the instructors in 1956. Ometz also had not lost any settlers, and had retained the moshav form of organization. It still had not achieved a durable executive committee.

plained in general terms and by reference to quite specific factors. An outstandingly able young official of the Land Settlement Department once set forth such factors as he saw them: "Enough immigrants, enough money and enough determination, and the villages will succeed." These same factors, of course, can be cited to explain the development of Israel's other kinds of villages, not just the moshvei olim, and the development of the new society itself. Rural community formation in Israel cannot be dissociated from the larger nation-building enterprise.

Yet a distinction may be drawn between the villages known as moshvei olim, "immigrants' settlements," during most of Israel's first post-independence decade and the other kinds of villages created in the creation of the new society. This distinction does not derive from the fact that the settlers of the moshvei olim were new immigrants, despite the term coined to categorize these villages. For practically all of Israel's villages have had immigrants as their founding settlers, at least until descendants of the immigrant generations reached the age to join in the creation of new settlements. Moreover, villages in existence since 1949 and still peopled by some of their original settlers were being termed moshvei olim well after these settlers no longer could be considered new immigrants by Israeli standards of newness to the country. Indeed, by 1957 this fact had brought the term moshav olim into disfavor among policy-makers sensitive to public relations, and use of the term began to be discouraged.

Yet whether known as moshvei olim or subsumed under the terms moshvei ovdim or the more generic moshavim, the majority of new villages created after Israel's independence differed from the pre-statehood moshvei ovdim and those settled after independence by native Israelis and immigrants in the classic pioneer tradition. The main points of difference may be summarized as follows: (1) their settlement by people who did not understand or willingly accept the values and goals of Labor-Zionist ideology; (2) the recruitment of such people as moshav settlers on a basis other than their unambiguous free choice; (3) the exercise

of governing authority over such villages by the representatives of the organizations—the moshav federations and the Land Settlement Department of the Jewish Agency—responsible for their founding and development, and the relinquishment of such authority at the discretion of policymakers in these organizations.

Yet Israel is a democracy and one of the most open of societies. Therefore, villages with these characteristics were not created by agencies of the state and were not under their immediate authority. Both the moshav federations and the Jewish Agency remained voluntary organizations after Israel's independence, and their partnership made such villages possible. The Land Settlement Department exercised administrative authority over village development and over the employment of the resources that it advanced. The moshav federations recruited the settlers, claimed to represent them, and thereby claimed pervasive authority over them. This authority, however, was no more pervasive than the claims of moshav ideology,[70] and it had been democratically delegated to the federations by villagers committed to moshav ideology and to the ideologies of the political parties to which the federations were linked. The pre-statehood partnership of voluntary organizations made possible the transformation of the consensus-based land settlement system into a system maintained by authority over those settlers who did not share the values of the system.

The recruitment of new settlers and their assignment to a village was less than voluntary from the vantage point of many immigrants, particularly those who were enrolled in the land settlement program in transit to Israel after initiation of the ship to village policy,[71] and those who lacked the background and/or information to grasp the obligations of the moshav settler role. Yet they were not constrained to remain in the villages to which they were sent or to continue to be moshav settlers. Moreover, the moshav role confers rights as well as obligations. Dissident settlers could neither

[70] Cf. p. 82.
[71] Cf. p. 192.

be deprived of the means of sustenance nor easily removed from their habitation in a village.[72]

Thus, the continued flow of immigrants and funds to Israel and to its land settlement sector and the determined efforts of the land settlement administrators were not in themselves sufficient for successful village development. The willing partnership of the settlers was also necessary. When this partnership was achieved, villages ceased to be "moshvei olim."

[72] Cf. pp. 196–98.

EPILOGUE:
NATION-BUILDING AND THE NEW SOCIETY

Communities have been considered here as "basic units of organization and transmission within a society and its culture." [1] However, in the creation of the society of Jewish Palestine and Israel, movements and organizations were at least equally basic units of organization and of the transmission of ideologies and commitments.

The development, successively, of complex organizations and of rural communities can be seen in the case of Israel as part of its inversion of the order of transformations characterizing other new states.[2] The consecutive emergence of complex organizations made possible Israel's formation as a society, including the founding of new villages and the progressive or prospective consolidation of most of them into viable communities. In contrast, established rural communities have been traditional units of organization of the societies constituted into new states; and the development of these states seems to depend on the formation and consolidation of effective complex organizations, including those which can involve villagers in new activities and new kinds of roles in relation to the larger society. Thus, the increased and diversified participation of villagers in larger-scale but more specialized systems of action than those centered in local communities has been a key aspect of rural community development in modernizing states and in disadvantaged areas of developed countries. In contrast, villages in Jewish Palestine and in Israel have been linked in a variety of ways to larger systems of action from their inception; and key aspects of their development into communities have included the creation and institutionalization of multiple and cohesive ties among the villagers themselves.

[1] Cf. p. 15. [2] Cf. pp. 3–4.

This study has focused on the class of Israeli villages termed moshvei olim during the first post-statehood decade; and the last section of Chapter IX presents my conclusions about the development of these villages. Yet, as was stated in these conclusions, the basic factors accounting for the development of these villages also apply to the other kinds of new villages created as part of the development of the new society, and to the society itself.[3] However, the other kinds of villages were created by members of movements, who made use of public resources—land and capital—which were channeled through organizations. The moshvei olim were brought into existence by organizations, and were governed by one of these public organizations—the Land Settlement Department of the Jewish Agency[4]—in partnership with movements, because the latter could not gain the voluntary adherence of new immigrants to ideologies they found, in good part, incomprehensible or irrelevant.

Thus, movements may be considered basic units of organization in the formation of new villages in Jewish Palestine, whereas organizations assumed this role after Israel's establishment as a state. This transformation in the land settlement sector corresponds to changes which took place in the post-statehood development of other sectors of the new society. In the case of land settlement, the organization in question was part of the "organizational core"[5] of a movement, the Zionist movement itself. But with Israel's independence, the quasi-governments of Jewish Palestine yielded to the state the governing authority[6] over the society and governmental organizations were brought into being. Land settlement remained within the domain of the pre-statehood voluntary organizations, and the Land Settlement Department became bureaucratized under the new conditions, as was discussed

[3] Cf. p. 433.
[4] The Land Settlement Department's authority over the villages created as moshvei olim was transitory, as has been discussed earlier (cf. pp. 222, 251, 433–34).
[5] Cf. pp. 20ff. and Etzioni 1961:53ff.
[6] On these quasi-governments, cf. pp. 70–71. Their authority was voluntarily accepted by members of the society of Jewish Palestine. The mandatory government held *de jure* governing authority.

in Chapters IV through VI. However, during and after the period under review, other spheres of action passed from the jurisdiction of the Zionist organizations and/or of organizations created by the partisan factions to that of the state.[7] Moreover, the jurisdiction of the Land Settlement Department over new settlements is temporary; villages, after their consolidation,[8] leave its administrative sphere for that of the Ministry of Agriculture.

The transformation of movements into organizations and transformations in the larger social order attempted and effected by members of movements and organizations are areas of experience shared by Israel with other new states and also with developing countries or sectors of countries which are not new states. Pre-statehood independence movements have become the governments and/or political parties of other new states; and revolutionary movements have become the governments of some long-established states. Furthermore, public bureaucracies, whether newly created organizations and/or those reconstituted from organizations created by a colonial power or an overthrown regime, have sought, together with party organizations, to bring about a new social order throughout the societies of these states.

Yet Israel may be considered distinctive among new and developing states in accomplishing its major development goals within a relatively short time after achieving statehood —approximately a decade, in the land settlement sector— while remaining a democratic country with a stable government. In Chapter I of this study, I suggested explanations of why this has been possible;[9] and Chapters II through IX may be considered documentation in support of these explanations as well as material which can be put to other use.

---

[7] Defense, education, and social security were among such spheres during Israel's first decade (cf. pp. 138–39, 169–70). In 1958 the Jewish National Fund was brought into a national land authority (cf. p. 128, note 18). In 1959 the labor exchanges, formerly in the domain of the Histadrut, were nationalized.

[8] A village is considered consolidated when the Jewish Agency has advanced 70 percent of the sum deemed necessary for the development of the village's farms (cf. pp. 182–83).

[9] Cf. pp. 3–4.

In Israel's case, the movement which gave rise to the state also gave rise to the society governed by the state. Therefore, the legitimacy of the state's claim to rule has been accepted and defended by the great majority of those subject to its sovereignty, i.e., by Jews, whatever their origins, who joined in the formation of the society. Moreover, both the World Zionist Organization and Jewish Palestine under the mandate had democratically elected parliamentary bodies. The state of Israel came into existence already possessed of a tradition of democratic government, rather than having to create one.

In the development of this tradition, the principle of parliamentary democracy and the machinery for its practice historically preceded the emergence of partisan factions and parties. For after the World Zionist Organization was created in 1897, members of the growing number of Zionist societies elected representatives to serve as delegates to the Organization's parliamentary body, the World Zionist Congress.[10] Not until the Fifth World Zionist Congress, in 1902, did organized factions begin to appear among delegates to the Congress. The spectrum of factions that became the major political parties of the Zionist system of action and of the nascent society of Jewish Palestine emerged over the next twenty-five years, as was reviewed in Chapter II. The evolution of these factions contributed the tradition of party competition within a parliamentary framework to Israel's heritage of self-government.

The development of factions, while dividing the Zionist movement internally, did not result in much schism on the level of the movement itself.[11] For "overarching attitudes of solidarity" [12] joined those committed to Zionist goals, however intense their more partisan commitments.

[10] The First World Zionist Congress was composed of Jewish notables whom Herzl and his advisers knew to be in sympathy with Zionist goals. This Congress founded the World Zionist Organization.

[11] Two schisms occurred during the history of the Zionist movement, and only one of these endured. This was the separation of the group that formed the Jewish Territorial Organization (cf. p. 37). The Revisionists broke away from the World Zionist Organization in 1935 but later rejoined it.

[12] This term is used by Almond and Verba (1963:492), and its implications are developed by Eckstein (1966:37n., 76ff.).

Also, the strength of the Zionist movement depended on its attracting the largest possible constituency of adherents and supporters. Given the diversity among Jews and the varied conditions under which they lived, the development of diverse orientations within Zionism extended the range of its appeal. For the kinds of people who might respond to one Zionist ideology were not necessarily those who could have been attracted by another. The proponents of competing ideologies and programs within the Zionist movement could enlarge their representation and influence in the movement's political system by adding to their numbers both in the Diaspora and in Palestine. But they did not necessarily compete for the same public, at least as regards the recruitment of Diaspora Jews into the Zionist movement.[13]

Some of the Zionist factions, particularly those with a Labor-Zionist ideology, came into existence as movements pressing for the development of Jewish Palestine according to the ideologies they professed. In the settlement of a largely barren land, dedicated effort by the like-minded can constitute a major resource. The pervasive ideologies of the Labor-Zionist factions, the intensity of commitment they elicited, and the ramifying organizations they developed maximized this resource; and the adherents of competing Zionist ideologies followed suit. The Zionist factions and parties [14] literally played a nation-building role in the formation of the new society.

Political parties which intensely engage their members and which develop pervasive ideologies and ramifying networks of auxiliary organizations are far from unique to Zionism. Such parties developed through much of Europe, initially as Socialist parties, following the promulgation of universal suf-

[13] After the mandatory government restricted Jewish immigration to Palestine, the Zionist parties did compete for immigration certificates for their adherents (cf. p. 71).

[14] The Zionist factions acted as parties in elections to the parliamentary bodies of the Zionist movement and of Jewish Palestine. However, some of the factions remained movements and did not formally organize as parties until Israel's independence. Factions within parties also have broken away to constitute themselves independent parties. Parties also have merged.

frage.[15] Their success in organizing the masses for political participation resulted in the adoption of some of their characteristics by parties representing more traditional interests but forced in a competitive system to seek mass support in turn.[16]

Mass parties have also been common in contemporary new states. They are generally regarded by students of these states as a means of bringing about the national integration of a country's heterogeneous population.[17] Moreover, such parties often had come into existence well before independence and had played an important role in promoting it. Thus, their authority could be regarded as more legitimate than that of the newly constituted state by segments of the population. Indeed, the party could confer legitimacy on the organs of the state, particularly in single-party polities, by working, at least nominally, through them.[18]

Therefore, mass parties in most contemporary new states have played a different role in regard to government and society than they first played in Europe. In most new states they help to develop a national identity and political community.[19] However, most of the countries in Europe were already nation-states when such parties emerged. They enlarged political participation by bringing into the electorate previously disenfranchised segments of the population; they were not agencies welding a populace into a nation.

In the case of Israel, a distinction can be made between the role parties played before independence and after. Before statehood, the parties helped to create a society and political community on the basis of an ancient national identity.[20]

15 Cf. Duverger 1959:xxviiff., 65–71.
16 Cf. Duverger 1959:xxvii.
17 Cf. Schachter 1961:299ff.; Weiner and LaPalombara 1966:413–16.
18 Cf. Schachter 1961:299; Apter 1965:213ff.
19 Cf. p. 9.
20 Although Fein (1967:48,63–66) suggests that Israel has still to achieve a national identity, he does grant (1967:57–58) that "the concept 'Jew' . . . evokes an irreducible sense of shared kinship . . . To be a Jew in the Jewish State is to be a part of history, and partner with the others." These words express my understanding of the national identity which made

Their ramifying organization then facilitated, after statehood, their recruitment of the mass of new immigrants. Membership in a political party brought such immigrants into basic groupings of the new society and into its political system. Ethnic parties had developed in Jewish Palestine,[21] but these lost rather than gained strength in the post-statehood elections. With the inclusion of new immigrants in the major parties of the country, ethnic group membership and party membership have cut across rather than reinforced each other.

Thus, in Israel as well as in other new states, mass parties can be seen as furthering national integration. However, Israel's parties, unlike those of many other new states, have not had to create a political community simultaneously. The parties enlarged their constituencies by the political mobilization of new immigrants. But a political community had been created decades before Israel's independence and to a large extent by the parties themselves, acting as basic units of the Zionist movement. Parties have existed prior to independence in other new states as well. However, the Israeli parties, unlike those in other new states, were part of a competitive political system which had become established in the society while helping to form it.

The role of parties in integrating new immigrants into both the society and its political system was particularly salient in the land settlement sector. For the villages which became or were to become communities were identified with political parties. This identification had become institutionalized as part of the classic pattern of land settlement based on pervasive ideologies. Once institutionalized, the politicization of land settlement persisted, surviving the erosion of the ideologies which had given rise to it. The kibbutz-based political parties continued to emphasize ideology after Israel's independence, but they did not engage in the mass recruitment of new immigrants. The parties which did engage in such recruit-

possible Israel's creation as a society and which legitimated the authority of the state to its inhabitants. However, Fein includes in his discussion Irael's Arabs, whereas I do not.

[21] Cf. pp. 71–72.

ment could not give precedence to ideology over other means of eliciting new immigrants' participation in national development programs. Party-linked moshav federations brought new immigrants into the land settlement sector and sought to change them while claiming to represent them. But since the settlers themselves could change their federation affiliation, they too had leverage in the practical politics of development. Party competition for their adherence sensitized them to their bargaining position.

Ideology became increasingly subordinate to practical politics throughout the new society as well as its land settlement sector from the time of Israel's independence. The exigencies of coalition government have demanded such subordination. Mapai and Mizrahi together with Hapoel Hamizrahi [22] have been coalition partners in all of Israel's governments. Indeed, the religious-secular cleavage, a basic one in the society at large, did not preclude the formation of a coalition government which included both Mapam, the antireligious Marxist party, and Poalei Agudat Israel with its theocratic orientation. Mapai also formed governing coalitions with the General Zionist Party, which represented middle-class interests.[23] The extreme pluralism characterizing Israel's politics into the 1960s did not result, as it has elsewhere, in an immobilized political system unable to bring about or absorb change.[24]

[22] Mizrahi and Hapoel Hamizrahi, which had split from it in 1922, merged for electoral purposes in 1955, forming the National Religious Party. (All four religious parties had presented a united list in Israel's first election, held in 1949.) Seligman (1964:61–63) refers to Mapai and the United Religious Party as the most pluralistic of Israel's political parties.

[23] In 1961 the Progressive Party, which had split from the General Zionist Party in 1948, merged with it to form the Liberal Party. Before the 1965 election, the Liberal Party joined forces with Herut to create a new coalition party, Gahal. Many of the former Progressives broke away to create the Independent Liberal Party. Other changes in Israel's spectrum of political parties also occurred before the 1965 elections. Mapai and Ahdut Ha'avoda entered into an alignment. Thereupon, Ben-Gurion, who had resigned as Prime Minister in 1963, and some other members of Mapai seceded from it to form a new labor party, Rafi.

With the pact between Egypt and Jordan on May 30, 1967, a unified government was created in Israel, with all of its political parties except the Communist Party participating. Mapai, Ahdut Ha'avoda, and Rafi merged early in 1968.

[24] Cf. Sartori 1966:161.

In the development of Israel's society and of its political system the land settlement sector assumed an importance disproportionate to its numerical representation in the population. However, this importance was not incommensurate with its nation-building significance during the pre-state period; and land settlement remained a key area of national development well into Israel's first post-statehood decade. The relative importance of the land settlement program then steadily diminished as its primary national goals were attained. By 1957 most of the country's arable land had been peopled and brought under cultivation. Domestically grown food was abundant, and agricultural planning was increasingly oriented to the export market. New urban centers, i.e., new development towns such as Kiriat Mizug,[25] had by then displaced the villages as a major setting for the settlement of new immigrants. The development of industry, both in such towns and throughout the country, had become a paramount national concern. No longer nascent, Israel had become a society according to the definition of society employed in this book.[26]

[25] Cf. p. 305.
[26] Cf. pp. 11–12; Levy 1952:112–113.

GLOSSARY

Agudat Israel (Federation of Israel): An ultraorthodox movement which originated in Eastern Europe in 1912 and was opposed to Zionism on religious grounds. It has been a political party in Israel from the time of independence.

Ahdut Ha'avoda (Unity of Labor): A socialist political party founded in 1954 (full name, l'Ahdut Ha'avoda-Poalei Zion). Earlier, the name Ahdut Ha'avoda had designated a post-World War I Labor-Zionist party that helped to found Mapai in 1929–30.

Aliya ("going up"): The term used to refer to Jewish immigration to Palestine and Israel.

Dunam: A unit of land approximately equal to one-fourth of an acre.

Hagana (Protection): The underground defense force of the Jewish community of Palestine during the mandate period.

Hakibbutz Hameuhad (The United Kibbutz): The federation of kibbutzim associated with Ahdut Ha'avoda.

Halutz: A pioneer.

Hamashbir Hamerkazi (also referred to in the text as Hamashbir and Mashbir, following common Israeli usage): The cooperative wholesale society of the Histadrut.

Ha'oved Hatziyoni (The Zionist Worker): A workers' organization and moshav federation associated with the Progressive Party.

Hapoel Hamizrahi (The Mizrahi Worker): A religious political party with a Socialist orientation. The largest of Israel's religious parties, it was established in 1922 when its founders broke away from Mizrahi. In 1955–56 Hapoel Hamizrahi and Mizrahi united for electoral purposes, forming the National Religious Party.

Hashomer Hatzair (The Young Watchman): A Labor-Zionist youth movement with a Marxist orientation. It functioned as an independent Zionist party, with its base in the federation of kibbutzim established by its members. In 1948 it joined in the creation of Mapam.

Herut (Freedom): A party founded in 1948 by the Irgun Zvai Leumi. It has stood for a Jewish state on both sides of the Jordan River and is anti-Socialist.

Hevrat Ovdim (Workers' Society): The holding company of the Histadrut, founded in 1923 and having an identical membership.

Histadrut (full name, Histadrut Haklalit shel Ha'ovdim Ha'ivrim b'Eretz Israel: General Federation of Jewish Workers in the Land of Israel, more generally known in English as the General Federation of Labor): A federation of trade unions, communal and cooperative settlements, service organizations, and ancillary associations, founded in 1920. (Arabs as well as Jews belong to it.)

Histadrut Ha'ovdim Haleumit (National Workers Federation): A labor federation founded in 1934 by the Revisionist movement and associated after Israel's independence with Herut. It includes agricultural settlements, a sick fund, and other services.

Hovevei Zion (Lovers of Zion): A movement founded in 1884, before the development of political Zionism. It advocated and engaged in Jewish immigration to Palestine and the creation there of Jewish agricultural settlements.

Ihud Havutzot v'Hakibbutzim (Union of Kvutzot and Kibbutzim): A federation of communal settlements, founded in 1951 by the merger of a federation of kvutzot (Hever Hakvutzot) with kibbutzim which had been affiliated with Hakibbutz Hameuhad but had left it. Ihud Hakvutzot v'Hakibbutzim is associated with Mapai.

Irgun Zvai Leumi (National Army Organization): A group within the Revisionist movement which split off and formed an underground military organization independent of the Hagana. Founded in 1936, it then had the aim of immediately establishing a Jewish state in Palestine.

Keren Hayesod (The Foundation Fund): One of the "national institutions," together with Keren Kayemet and the Jewish Agency. It was founded in 1920 to raise funds for the development of Jewish Palestine. Since 1951 it has been the financial agency of the World Zionist Organization.

Keren Kayemet (The Jewish National Fund): The oldest of the "national institutions," which include Keren Hayesod and the Jewish Agency. It was founded in 1901 to purchase land in Palestine and to hold this land in perpetuity in the name of the Jewish people. It has also engaged in land reclamation.

Kibbutz: A communal settlement. The term was first used to denote the type of communal settlement larger in size than the kvutza and characterized by the inclusion of small industries as well as agriculture in its productive activities.

Kvutza: A communal settlement.

Ma'abara: A camp in Israel for provisionally housing new immigrants.

Mapai (acronym of Mifleget Poalei Eretz Israel, Workers Party of Israel): The socialist-oriented political party founded in 1929–30 by the merger of Ahdut Ha'avoda and Hapoel Hatzair (The Young Worker), another Labor-Zionist party. Mapai immediately became the largest political party in the Histadrut, and it is Israel's majority party.

Mapam (acronym of Mifleget Hapoalim Hameuhedet b'Eretz Israel, United Workers Party): A political party in Israel with a Marxist orientation. It was formed in 1948 by Hashomer Hatzair together with Ahdut Ha'avoda and Poalei Zion Smol (Left Workers of Zion), another left-wing Labor-Zionist faction. In 1954 Ahdut Ha'avoda left Mapam and became an independent political party.

Mellah: A Jewish community or quarter in Morocco.

Mizrahi (an abbreviation of Merkaz Ruhani, Spiritual Center): A religious Zionist political party founded in Eastern Europe in 1902, and later a political party in Israel. It united with Hapoel Hamizrahi for electoral purposes in 1955–56.

Mohel: A ritual circumciser.

Moshava: An agricultural village established on privately owned land.

Moshav olim: An immigrants' settlement.

Moshav ovdim: A cooperative small-holders' settlement.

Moshav shitufi: A semicommunal settlement.

Nahal (Pioneering Fighting Youth): A special unit of the Army which engages in land settlement in frontier areas of Israel.

Poalei Agudat Israel (Workers of the Federation of Israel): An ultraorthodox movement with a Socialist orientation. It was founded in Poland in 1922, and it is a political party in Israel. Unlike its parent body, Agudat Israel, it favored statehood for Israel during the mandate period.

Shohet: A ritual slaughterer.

Solel Boneh: The construction and public works enterprise of the Histadrut.

Tnuat Hamoshavim: The first and largest of the moshav federations. It was founded in 1927 and is associated with Mapai, although its members have the freedom to vote as they wish.

Tnuva: The agricultural marketing society of the Histadrut.

BIBLIOGRAPHY

Adam, Andre
1951 La maison et le village dans quelques tribus de l'Anti-Atlas. Collection Hespéris, No. XIII, Institut des Hautes-Études Marocaines. Paris.

Akzin, Benjamin
1966 States and Nations. Garden City, N. Y., Anchor Books.

Almond, Gabriel, and Sidney Verba
1963 The Civic Culture. Princeton, Princeton University Press.

Apter, David E.
1965 The Politics of Modernization. Chicago, University of Chicago Press.

Arensberg, Conrad
1961 The Community as Object and As Sample. American Anthropologist, LXIII:241–64.

Arensberg, Conrad, and Solon T. Kimball
1940 Family and Community in Ireland. Cambridge, Harvard University Press.

Arian, D.
1956 The First Five Years of the Israel Civil Service. Scripta Hierosolymitana (Publications of the Hebrew University, III). Jerusalem, The Magnes Press.

Assaf, Ami
1953 Moshvei Ha'ovdim b'Yisrael (Moshvei Ovdim in Israel). Tel Aviv, Ayanot v'Tnuat Hamoshavim.

Baratz, Joseph
1954 A Village by the Jordan: The Story of Degania. London, The Harvill Press.

Barer, Shlomo
1952   The Magic Carpet. New York, Harper and Bros.

Barnett, H. G.
1953   Innovation: The Basis of Cultural Change. New York, McGraw-Hill Co.

Bein, Alex
1952   Return To the Soil. Jerusalem, Youth and Hechalatz Department of the Zionist Organization.

Belshaw, Cyril S.
1965   Traditional Exchange and Modern Markets. Englewood Cliffs, N. J., Prentice-Hall.

Ben-David, Joseph
1964   The Kibbutz and the Moshav. *In* Agricultural Planning and Village Community in Israel, ed. J. Ben-David. Paris, UNESCO.

Bendix, Reinhard
1964   Nation-Building and Citizenship: Studies of Our Changing Social Order. New York, John Wiley and Sons.

Ben Gurion, David
1954   Rebirth and Destiny of Israel. New York, Philosophical Library.

Bernstein, Marver H.
1957   The Politics of Israel: The First Decade of Statehood. Princeton, Princeton University Press.

Berque, Jacques
1955   Structures sociales du Haut Atlas. Paris, Presses Universitaires de France.

Black, A. G.
1953   Report To the Government of Israel on National Agricultural Plans and Programs. F.A.O. Report, No. 161. Rome, Food and Agricultural Organization of the United Nations.
1958   Reflections Upon Israel's Recent Agricultural Development and Its Relationship to the General Development.

In The Challenge of Development, A Symposium Held in Jerusalem, June 26–27, 1957. Jerusalem, Hebrew University Eliezer Kaplan School of Economics and Social Science.

Blau, Peter M., and W. Richard Scott
1962   Formal Organizations: A Comparative Approach. San Francisco, Chandler Publishing Company.

Borochov, Ber
1937   Nationalism and the Class Struggle: A Marxian Approach To the Jewish Problem, Selected Writings. New York, Poale Zion-Zeire Zion of America.

Briggs, L. C.
1960   Tribes of the Sahara. Cambridge, Harvard University Press.

Central Bureau of Statistics
1967   Statistical Abstract of Israel, No. 18.

Chaumeil, Jean
1953   Le mellah de Tehala au pays des Ammeln. Hespéris, XL: Pls. I–VIII, 227–40.

Chouraqui, Andre
1952   Les Juifs d'Afrique du Nord. Paris, Presses Universitaires de France.

Clarke, Bryan
1959   Berber Village. London, Longmans, Green and Co., Ltd.

Cohen, Rev. Dr. A.
1949   Everyman's Talmud. London, J. M. Dent and Sons, Ltd.

Cohen, Peretz
1955   Report on Moshav Tnuvoth. Israeli Institute of Applied Social Research (mimeographed).

Cole, G. D. H.
1944   A Century of Cooperation. Manchester, Cooperative Union Ltd.

Coon, Carleton S.
1951   Caravan: The Story of the Middle East. New York, Henry Holt and Co.

Crozier, Michel
1964   The Bureaucratic Phenomenon. Chicago, University of Chicago Press.

Dayan, Shmuel
1947   Moshav Ovdim: The Smallholders' Settlement in Palestine. Palestine Pioneer Library, Tel Aviv, Lion the Printer for the Zionist Organization Youth Department.

Deshen, Shlomo A.
1965   A Case of Breakdown of Modernization in an Israeli Immigrant Community. Jewish Journal of Sociology, VII:63–91.

Deutsch, Karl W., and William J. Foltz (eds.)
1963   Nation-Building. New York, Atherton Press.

Diamond, Stanley
1957a   The Kibbutz: Utopia in Crisis. Dissent 4:133–40.
1957b   A Rejoinder. Dissent 4:146–51.
1957c   Kibbutz and Shtetl: The History of an Idea. Social Problems, 5:71–99.

Drabkin-Darin, H.
1957   Housing in Israel: Economic and Sociological Aspects. Tel Aviv, Gadish Books.

Dresch, Jean
1941   Documents sur les genres de vie de montagne dans le Massif Central du Grand Atlas: Cartes. Publications de l'Institut des Hautes-Études Marocaines, XXXV. Tours.
1941   Documents sur les genres de vie de montagne dans le Massif Central du Grand Atlas: Commentaires. Publications de l'Institut des Hautes Etudes Marocaines, XXXV. Tours.

Dubnow, S. N.
1916   History of the Jews in Russia and Poland, I, trans.

I. Friedlander. Philadelphia, The Jewish Publication Society of America.

Duverger, Maurice
1959   Political Parties. Second English edition. New York, John Wiley and Sons.

Eckstein, Harry
1966   Division and Cohesion in Democracy: A Study of Norway. Princeton, Princeton University Press.

Eisenstadt, S. N.
1955   The Absorption of Immigrants. Glencoe, The Free Press.
1959   Bureaucracy, Bureaucratization, and Debureaucratization. Administrative Science Quarterly, 4:302–20.

Etzioni, Amitai
1961   A Comparative Analysis of Complex Organizations. Glencoe, The Free Press.

Fallers, Lloyd A.
1956   Bantu Bureaucracy. Cambridge, W. Heffner and Sons.

Fein, Leonard J.
1967   Politics in Israel. Boston, Little, Brown and Co.

Firth, Raymond
1954   Social Organization and Social Change. Journal of the Royal Anthropological Institute of Great Britain and Ireland, 84:1–20.

Flamand, Pierre
1950   Quelques renseignements statistiques sur la population Israelite du Sud Marocain. Hespéris, XXXVII:363–97.
1952   Un mellah en pays Berbere: Demnate. Notes and Documents X, Institut des Hautes-Études Marocaines. Paris.

Frank, M. Z. (ed.)
1955   Sound the Great Trumpet. New York, Whittier Books.

Friedmann, Georges
1967   The End of the Jewish People? Trans. from the French by Eric Mossbacher. London, Hutchinson.

Gardner, Burleigh B., and William F. Whyte
1945   The Man in the Middle: Position and Problems of the Foreman. Applied Anthropology, 4:1–28.

Geertz, Clifford
1963   The Integrative Revolution: Primordial Sentiments and Civil Politics in the New States. *In* Old Societies and New States, ed. Clifford Geertz. Glencoe, The Free Press.

Gluckman, Max
1965   Politics, Law and Ritual in Tribal Society. Oxford, Blackwell.

Goffman, Erving
1961   Asylums: Essays on the Social Situation of Mental Patients and Other Inmates. Garden City, N. Y., Anchor Books.

Goitein, D. S.
1955   Portrait of a Yemenite Weaver's Village. Jewish Social Studies, XVII:3–26.

Goodenough, Ward H.
1957   Cultural Anthropology and Linguistics. *In* Report of the 7th Annual Round Table Meeting on Linguistics and Language Study, ed. Paul L. Garvin. Monograph series on language and linguistics, No. 9, 167–73. Washington, Institute of Languages and Linguistics, Georgetown University.

Goulven, J.
1923   Notes sur les origines anciennes des Israélites du Maroc. Hespéris, I:317–36.

Gutmann, Emanuel
1963   Israel. Journal of Politics, 25:703–17.

Halperin, Haim
1963   Agrindus: Integration of Agriculture and Industries. New York, Praeger.

1957   Changing Patterns in Israel Agriculture. London, Routledge and Kegan Paul.

Halperin, Haim, and Dan Yaron
1957   Moshvei Olim: Survey of Immigrant Villages in Israel. Rehovot, Department of Agricultural Economics, The Faculty of Agriculture, The Hebrew University.

Halpern, Ben
1957   Comments on Science and Socialism. Dissent 4:140–46.
1961   The Idea of the Jewish State. Cambridge, Harvard University Press.
1962   The Role of the Military in Israel. In The Role of the Military in Underdeveloped Countries, ed. John J. Johnson. Princeton, Princeton University Press.

Hart, David Montgomery
1960   Tribal and Place Names Among the Arabo-Berbers of Northwestern Morocco: A Preliminary Statistical Analysis. Hespéris-Tamuda 1:457–511.

Hecht, Ben
1954   A Child of the Century. New York, Simon and Schuster.

Hertzberg, Arthur
1960   The Zionist Idea: A Historical Analysis and Reader. New York, Meridian Books, Inc.; and Philadelphia, The Jewish Publication Society of America.

Jewish Agency for Israel, Agricultural Settlement Department
1956   Report to the 24th Zionist Congress.

Jewish Agency for Israel, Land Settlement Department
1957   Hagdarat tafkidei ha'oved b'ezor (Definition of the Tasks of the District Workers). Jerusalem (mimeographed).

Jewish Agency for Israel, Land Settlement Department, Statistics Section
1958   R'shimot v'sikumim. Hayishuvim b'tipul hamahlaka l'hityashvut (Lists and Summaries. Villages Under the

Care of the Land Settlement Department of the Jewish Agency). Jerusalem (mimeographed).

Joffe, Natalie F.
1949   The Dynamics of Benefice Among Eastern European Jews. Social Forces 27:238–47.

Katz, Elihu, and S. N. Eisenstadt
1960   Some Sociological Observations on the Response of Israeli Organizations to New Immigrants. Administrative Science Quarterly, V:113–33.

Kaufman, Yehezkel
1949   Anti-Semitic Stereotypes in Zionism. Commentary, 7:239–45.

Kluckhohn, Clyde
1951   Values and Value-Orientations in the Theory of Action. *In* Toward a General Theory of Action, ed. Talcott Parsons and Edward A. Shils. Cambridge, Harvard University Press.

Kraines, Oscar
1961   Government and Politics in Israel. Boston, Houghton Mifflin.

Kroeber, A. L.
1948   Anthropology. New York, Harcourt, Brace and Co.

Kurland, Samuel
1947   Cooperative Palestine: The Story of Histadrut. New York, Sharon Books.

Landmann, Isaac (ed.)
1941   Universal Jewish Encyclopedia. New York, UJE.

LaPalombara, Joseph (ed.)
1963   Bureaucracy and Political Development. Princeton, Princeton University Press.

Laredo, Abraham I.
1954   Berberes y Hebreos en Marruecos: Sus origenes, seqún las Leyendas, Tradiciones y Fuentes Hebraicas Antiquas. Madrid, Institutos de Estudios Africanos.

Leach, E. R.
1954   Political Systems of Highland Burma. Cambridge, Harvard University Press.

Levi-Strauss, Claude
1953   Social Structure. *In* Anthropology Today, ed. Alfred L. Kroeber. Chicago, University of Chicago Press.

Levy, Marion J., Jr.
1952   The Structure of Society. Princeton, Princeton University Press.

Lewis, Isaac
1954   Agudism. *In* Struggle For Tomorrow, ed. B. J. Vlavianos and Feliks Gross. New York, Arts, Inc.

Lipset, Seymour Martin
1963   The First New Nation. New York, Basic Books.

March, James G., and Herbert A. Simon, with the collaboration of Harold Guetzkow
1958   Organizations. New York, John Wiley and Sons.

Mason, Alpheus T.
1946   Brandeis: A Free Man's Life. New York, Viking Press.

Matras, Judah
1965   Social Change in Israel. Chicago, Aldine.

Merton, Robert K.
1936   The Unanticipated Consequences of Purposive Social Action. American Sociological Review, I:894–904.
1957   Social Theory and Social Structure. Revised and enlarged edition. New York, The Free Press of Glencoe.

Montagne, Robert
1930a   Les Berbères et le Makhzen dans le sud du Maroc: Essai sur la transformation politique des Berbères sédentaires (groupe Chleuh). Paris, Librairie Felix Alcan.
1930b   Villages et kasbas Berbères: Tableau de la vie sociale des Berbères sédentaires dans le sud du Maroc. Paris, Librairie Felix Alcan.

Monteil, Vincent
1946   Choses et gens du Bani. Hespéris, XXXIII:385–405.
1948   Les Juifs d'Ifran. Hespéris, XXXV:151–62.

Muenzner, Gerhard
1947   Labor Enterprise in Palestine: A Handbook of Histadrut Economic Institutions. New York, Sharon Books.

Nadel, S. F.
1957   The Theory of Social Structure. Glencoe, The Free
Press.

Parsons, Talcott
1949   Essays on Sociological Theory Pure and Applied.
Glencoe, The Free Press.
1960   Structure and Process in Modern Societies. Glencoe,
The Free Press.

Parsons, Talcott, and Edward A. Shils (eds.)
1951   Some Fundamental Categories of the Theory of Action: A General Statement. *In* Toward a General Theory
of Action, ed. Parsons and Shils. Cambridge, Harvard University Press.
1951   Values, Motives, and Systems of Action. *In* Toward
a General Theory of Action, ed. Parsons and Shils. Cambridge, Harvard University Press.

Patai, Raphael
1953   Israel Between East and West. Philadelphia, Jewish
Publication Society of America.
1964   Lilith. Journal of American Folklore, 77:295–314.

Patinkin, P.
1960   The Israel Economy: The First Decade. Jerusalem,
Falk Project for Economic Research in Israel.

Pye, Lucian W.
1962   Politics, Personality, and Nation-Building: Burma's
Search for Identity. New Haven and London, Yale University Press.

Ray, Verne F. (ed.)
1959   Systems of Political Control and Bureaucracy in Human Society. Proceedings of the 1958 annual spring meeting of the American Ethnological Society. Seattle, University of Washington Press.

Redfield, Robert
1955   The Little Community: Viewpoints for the Study of a Human Whole. Chicago, University of Chicago Press.
1956   Peasant Society and Culture: An Anthropological Approach to Civilization. Chicago, University of Chicago Press.

Reining, Conrad C.
1966   The Zande Scheme: An Anthropological Case Study of Economic Development. Evanston, Northwestern University Press.

Rokach, Avshalom
1964a   Land and Water. *In* Agricultural Planning and Village Community in Israel, ed. Joseph Ben-David. Paris, UNESCO.
1964b   The Development of Agriculture in Palestine and Israel. *In* Agricultural Planning and Village Community in Israel, ed. Joseph Ben-David. Paris, UNESCO.
1964c   Agricultural Planning Since the Establishment of the State of Israel. *In* Agricultural Planning and Village Community in Israel, ed. Joseph Ben-David. Paris, UNESCO.

Rosenfeld, Eva
1951   Social Stratification in a Classless Society. American Sociological Review, XVI:766–74.
1957   Institutional Change in the Kibbutz. Social Problems, V:110–36.

Rosenthal, Celia Stopnicka
1953   Social Stratification of the Jewish Community in a Small Polish Town. American Journal of Sociology, 59:1–19.
1954   Deviation and Social Change in the Jewish Com-

munity of a Small Polish Town. American Journal of Sociology, 60:177–81.

Rubner, Alex
1960   The Economy of Israel: A Critical Account of the First Ten Years. London, Frank Cass and Co., Ltd.

Ruppin, Arthur
1936   Three Decades of Palestine. Jerusalem, Schocken.

Safran, Nadav
1963   The United States and Israel. Cambridge, Harvard University Press.

Samuel, Edwin
1956   Problems of Government in the State of Israel. Jerusalem, Rubin Mass.

Sartori, Giovanni
1966   European Political Parties: The Case of Polarized Pluralism. *In* Political Parties and Political Development, ed. Joseph LaPalombara and Myron Weiner. Princeton, Princeton University Press.

Schachter, Ruth
1961   Single-Party Systems in West Africa. The American Political Science Review, LV:294–307.

Schechtman, Joseph B.
1954   Revisionism. *In* Struggle For Tomorrow, ed. Basil J. Vlavianos and Feliks Gross, 86–99. New York, Arts, Inc.

Scherer, Emanual
1954   The Bund. *In* Struggle For Tomorrow, ed. Basil J. Vlavianos and Feliks Gross. New York, Arts, Inc.

Schwartz, Richard D.
1954   Social Factors in the Development of Legal Control: A Sociological Analysis of an Israeli Kvutza. Yale Law Journal, LXIII:471–91.
1955   Functional Alternatives to Inequality. American Sociological Review, 20:424–30.

1957 Democracy and Collectivism in the Kibbutz. Social Problems, 5:137–47.

Scott, W. Richard
1964 Theory of Organizations. *In* Handbook of Modern Sociology, ed. R. E. L. Faris. Chicago, Rand McNally.

Seligman, Lester
1964 Leadership in a New Nation. New York, Atherton Press.

Selznick, Philip
1949 TVA and the Grass Roots. Berkeley and Los Angeles, University of California Press.

Shils, Edward
1963 On the Comparative Study of the New States. *In* Old Societies and New States, ed. Clifford Geertz. Glencoe, The Free Press.

Shuval, Judith T.
1963 Immigrants on the Threshold. New York, Atherton Press.

Sicron, Moshe
1957 Immigration to Israel, 1948–1953. Jerusalem, Falk Project for Economic Research in Israel and Central Bureau of Statistics, Special Series No. 60.

Slouschz, Nahum
1927 Travels in North Africa. Philadelphia, Jewish Publication Society of America.

Spiro, Melford E.
1956 Kibbutz: Venture in Utopia. Cambridge, Harvard University Press.
1957 The Sabras and Zionism: A Study in Personality and Ideology. Social Problems, 5:100–10.
1958 Children of the Kibbutz. Cambridge, Harvard University Press.

Steinberg, I. N.
1954   Territorialism. *In* Struggle For Tomorrow, ed. B. J. Vlavianos and Feliks Gross. New York, Arts, Inc.

Steward, Julian H.
1950   Area Research, Theory and Practice. New York, SSRC (Bulletin 63).
1955   Theory of Culture Change. Urbana, University of Illinois Press.
1956   The People of Puerto Rico. Urbana, University of Illinois Press.

Talmon-Garbier, Y.
1952   Social Differentiation in Cooperative Communities. British Journal of Sociology, 3:339–57.

Talmon-Gerber, Y.
1956   Differentiation in Collective Settlements. *In* Scripta Hierosolymitana, ed. Roberto Bachi. Jerusalem, The Hebrew University.
1957   The Family in Collective Settlements. *In* Transactions of the World Congress of Sociology.
1959   Social Structure and Family Size. Human Relations, XII:121–46.
1961   Aging in Israel: A Planned Society. American Journal of Sociology, LXVII:284–95.

Tartakower, Arieh
1954   The Essence of Labor Zionism. *In* Struggle For Tomorrow, ed. B. J. Vlavianos and Feliks Gross. New York, Arts, Inc.

Voinot, L.
1948   Pèlerinages Judéo-Musulmans du Maroc. Notes and Documents, IV, Institut des Hautes-Études Marocaines. Paris.

Warner, William Lloyd, and Paul S. Lunt
1941   The Social Life of a Modern Community. London, Oxford University Press (Yankee City Series, I).

BIBLIOGRAPHY

Weber, Max
1946   From Max Weber: Essays in Sociology, trans. and ed. H. H. Gerth and C. Wright Mills. New York, Oxford University Press.
1947   The Theory of Social and Economic Organization, trans. A. M. Henderson and Talcott Parsons, ed. and with an introduction by Talcott Parsons. New York, Oxford University Press.

Weingarten, Murray
1955   Life in a Kibbutz. New York, Reconstructionist Press.

Weingrod, Alex
1959   From the Millah to the Moshav: Culture Contact and Change in a New-Immigrant Village in Israel. Unpublished Ph.D. dissertation, University of Chicago.
1966   Reluctant Pioneers: Village development in Israel. Ithaca, N. Y., Cornell University Press.

Weinryb, Bernard P.
1957   The Impact of Urbanization in Israel. The Middle East Journal, 11:23–36.

Weintraub, Dov, and Moshe Lissak
1964a   The Moshav and the Absorption of Immigrants. In Agricultural Planning and Village Community in Israel, ed. Joseph Ben-David. Paris, UNESCO.
1964b   Physical and Material Conditions in the New Moshav. In Agricultural Planning and Village Community in Israel, ed. Joseph Ben-David. Paris, UNESCO.
1964c   Social Integration and Change. In Agricultural Planning and Village Community in Israel, ed. Joseph Ben-David. Paris, UNESCO.

Weintraub, D., and F. Bernstein
1966   Social Structure and Modernization: A Comparative Study of Two Villages. American Journal of Sociology, 71, 5:509–21.

Weitz, Raanan (with the assistance of Avshalom Rokach)
1963   Agricultural and Rural Development in Israel. Re-

hovot, The National and University Institute of Agriculture, Bulletin No. 68.

Weiner, Myron, and Joseph LaPalombara
1966   The Impact of Parties on Political Development. *In* Political Parties and Political Development, ed. Joseph LaPalombara and Myron Weiner. Princeton, Princeton University Press.

Willner, Ann Ruth
1963   Management and Authority in Transitional Society. Human Organization, 22:133–41.

Willner, Dorothy
1956   Problems Involved in the Establishment of Cottage Industries in Immigrants' Cooperative Settlements. Megamot, VII:274–85.

Wolf, Eric R.
1964   Anthropology. Englewood Cliffs, Prentice-Hall, Inc.
1966   Peasants. Englewood Cliffs, Prentice-Hall, Inc.

Zborowski, Mark, and Elizabeth Herzog
1952   Life Is with People. New York, International Universities Press.

Zemach, Shlomo
1945   An Introduction to the History of Labour Settlement in Palestine. Zionist Library No. 3, Tel Aviv, Lion the Printer for the Zionist Organization Youth Department.

Zweig, Ferdinand
1959   The Israeli Worker: Achievements, Attitudes and Aspirations. New York, Herzl Press.

INDEX

Absorption Department, Jewish Agency, 71, 192, 193, 195, 228, 230, 244

Absorption Section, Land Settlement Department, Jewish Agency, 230, 231, 232, 369, 394

acculturation, immigrant, 8, 26, 219, 321–379; agencies of, 202, 242, 245; changes in attitudes toward, 245–246; contrasted with role-socialization, 165–167

administration, public, 115, 134n.–135n., 138–143, 238, 246

Agricultural Center, Histadrut, *see* Histadrut, Agricultural Center of

agricultural committee, moshav ovdim, 100, 146

agricultural instructor, 146–147, 159, 247, 248–249, 311–312, 333, 341, 370–372, 384–386, 390–391, 392, 394. *See also* instructor, village

agricultural planning, 110–111, 149–150, 170, 172–181

Agricultural Union (Mo'etza Haklait), 55, 62, 68, 77–78, 85

Agudat Israel, 35–36, 56, 60, 66, 80n., 375–376

Ahdut Ha'avoda, 74–75, 78, 79, 228, 443n.

Ait, meaning of term, 255n., 256n.

Ait Adrar * (Atlas Mts.), Jewish community of, 255n., 256n., 260–302, 306–307; agriculture in, 260, 266–267; cosmetics in, 270–271; crafts in, 266; diet in, 266–269; dress in, 269–270; emigration from, 299–302; family relations and kinship in, 265, 280–295; health and illness, beliefs and practices in, 270–275; houses in, 265; immigrants from, 306–309, 310, 312–379, 381–384, 388, 389, 392, 394, 403–404, 406, 407, 408, 410, 411, 412, 413, 422; inheritance rules in, 294; location of, 264–265; mourning observances in, 293–294; relations with Ber-

bers, 297–299, 301–302, 403; religious holidays, observance of yearly cycle in, 277–279; Sabbath observance in, 280; social control in, 276–277, 296–297; social ranking in, 295–297; subsistence in, 265–267; weddings in, 290–291; work in, 266–267

Ait Imi, 265

Ait Ouriat, 265

Ait Rahhal * (Atlas Mts.), 255n.; agriculture in, 260; crafts in, 260ff.; emigration from, 301; immigrants from, 382, 384–385, 388–392, 394–398, 400–405, 407–410, 412, 418, 432n.; Jewish hamlets of, 381

Aliya, First, 32–34, 39–43; Second, 37–41, 43, 47–48, 50, 57, 137, 227; Third, 47–48, 50, 62, 309, 311, 390; Fourth, 50–51, 86; Fifth, 51–53, 86; ideology of, 38–39, 43–44 (*see also* Labor-Zionism); illegal, *see* immigration; mass, *see* immigration; Youth, 58, 79, 146, 159, 177n, 228, 244, 312, 313, 317, 339, 348, 375. *See also* nation-building

Aliya Hadasha, 72, 85

Aliyat Hanoar, *see* Aliya, Youth

Alliance Israelite Universelle, 360

American Joint Distribution Committee, 118

Amos (agricultural instructor of Ometz), 341, 370–372

anti-Semitism, 31–32; basis of as explained by revolutionary socialism, 38; in Labor-Zionist ideology, 130–131; Russian, 32, 37–38, 74; Zionism as solution to, 34, 46

anti-Zionism, 34, 35, 37, 74, 123

Arab, abandoned villages as sites for moshvei olim, 124; attacks on Jewish villages in Palestine, 59, 69; countries and their Jewish populations, 122; invasion of Israel, 120; labor in Palestine, 34,

* Fictitious names.

· 465 ·

improvisation, 170, 321; factors in, 123; and moshvei olim, 129–130, 144–168, 384; national policies toward immigration in, 133; phase of, 148–168, 399n., 403, 411
Independent Liberal Party, 443n.
institutions, total, 81, 195. *See also* organizations, total
instructor (madrikh), accusations against by settlers, 159–161, 320; agricultural, *see* agricultural instructor; attitudes toward immigrant settlers, 160–168, 186, 309; authority of, 223–225, 242; in Ba'aya, 424–426; backgrounds of, 134, 158–167; in composite moshav, *see* composite moshav; initial role of, 129–130, 144–147, 224–225; military, *see* military instruction, Yehoshua; number of, 224; in Ometz, *see* Amos, Barzel (Aharon), Ometz, Yehoshua, Yitzhak; rationalization and bureaucratization of roles of, 172, 247–252; recruitment of, 158–159, 162; and relations with settlers, 158–168, 218, 219 (*see also* in Ba'aya, in composite moshav, in Ometz, in Tsarot); supervision of, 159, 234, 243, 247–251; transformations of role of, 225, 247, 252; in Tsarot, 427–428
instructress (madrikha), backgrounds of, 134, 158–159, 162–164, 167; in composite moshav, *see* composite moshav, Godovski, Miriam, and Harari, Ruth; initial role of, 129–130, 144–147; in Ometz, *see* Barzel, Hava; recruitment of, 158–159, 162; role defined as instructress in home economics, 247, 249–250; supervision of, 159, 167, 243, 247, 249–252
Irgun Zvai Leumi, 10n., 69, 71, 121. *See also* Herut, Revisionist Movement
Israel-Arab war, 117, 120
Israel Water Planning Authority (Tahal), 231

Jewish Agency (Sohnut), activities and funds of, 64–65, 70–71, 94, 118, 136, 147, 153, 173, 184, 213, 225–226, 237, 300–301, 307–308 (*see also* Foundation Fund, national institutions); allocation of

portfolios in, 227–228; Department of Education and Culture, 71; Department of Labor, 71; Department of Middle-Class Settlement, 71; Economic Department, 228; Executive of, 142, 227–228; jurisdiction of, 115, 222, 437; Political Department, 71; Treasury Department, 232; and villages, 153, 173, 184, 310, 331, 339, 356, 369, 370, 394n., 396, 397. *See also* Absorption Department of the Jewish Agency, Immigration Department of the Jewish Agency, Land Settlement Department of the Jewish Agency
Jewish Colonization Association (ICA), 40
Jewish Community Government, 70–71, 74, 85, 115
Jewish identity, *see* identity, Jewish
Jewish National Fund (Keren Kayemet l'Israel), 41, 43, 44, 57, 65, 72, 94, 127–128, 143, 153–154, 175, 209, 210, 221, 231, 235, 300, 310, 321, 323, 371, 438n.
Jewish State, The (Herzl), 34
Jewish Territorial Organization (ITO), 37, 439n.
Joffe, Eliezer, 43n.
Joint Guidance Center (Joint Center for Agricultural Instruction), 229, 230, 247, 249–251
Joint Planning Center, 172–173, 176–177, 229, 230, 232, 233
Jubilee Year, 41
Judaism, conversions to among Berbers, 253–254; as "great tradition" with many "parochializations," 276n.; traditional (orthodox), 29, 35, 60, 83, 276–280, 282–283, 284–285; traditions of, 30, 60, 262–296; and Zionism, 13, 29–33, 35, 36, 38–39, 50–51, 83, 301. *See also* identity

Keren Hayesod, *see* Foundation Fund
Keren Kayemet l'Israel, *see* Jewish National Fund
kfar ha'avoda, 128
kfar shitufi, 53
kibbutz (collective or communal settlement), basic features of, 41–42, 48, 54 (*see also* kvutza); commitment, intensity of among partisans of, 81–82; ideology of,